What Works in Reducing Domestic Violence?

A comprehensive guide for professionals

Edited by
Julie Taylor-Browne

Whiting & Birch Ltd

MMI

The views expressed in this publication are those of the author, not necessarily those of the Home Office (nor do they reflect government policy)

Published by Whiting & Birch Ltd,
London SE23 3HZ, England.
British Library Cataloguing in Publication Data.
A CIP catalogue record is available from
the British Library
ISBN 1 86177 036 7 (hardback)
ISBN 1 86177 037 5 (paperback)

Printed in England and the United States by Lightning Source

What Works in Reducing Domestic Violence?

A comprehensive guide for professionals

Other books of interest from Whiting & Birch

Children Living With Domestic Violence
Putting men's abuse of women on the childcare agenda
Audrey Mullender & Rebecca Morley (eds)
ISBN 1 871177 71 5 / 1 871177 72 3

The Multi-Agency Approach to Domestic Violence:
New opportunities, old challenges?
Nicola Harwin, Gill Hague & Ellen Malos (eds)
ISBN 1 86177 002 2 / 1 86177 003 0

Protecting Children: Promoting Their Rights
Norma Baldwin (ed)
ISBN 1 86177 012 X / 1 86177 013 8

Understanding Perpetrators: Protecting Children
A practitioner's guide to working effectively with child sexual abusers
Lynda Deacon & Bryan Gocke
ISBN 1 86177 022 7 / 1 86177 021 9

Casework Consultation
A practical guide to work with sex offenders and other high risk clients
Tony Morrison
ISBN 1 86177 025 1

'No-one's Listening': Mothers, fathers and child sexual abuse
Joy Trotter
ISBN 1 86177024 3

Risk Assessment:
A practitioner's guide to predicting harmful behaviour
Bryony Moore
ISBN 1 871177 84 7

The Hidden Struggle:
Statutory and voluntary sector responses to violence
against black women in the home
Amina Mama
ISBN 1 86177 005 7

Violence in the Workplace (forthcoming)
Vaughan Bowie
ISBN 1 86177 038 3 / 1 86177 039 1

Contents

Editor's preface

I am delighted to have had the opportunity of being involved with this book. I have known some of the contributors for many years and derive considerable satisfaction at seeing their work in the area of domestic violence become truly 'mainstream'. The aim of this book is to explore what works in reducing domestic violence, and it does this largely by referring to women themselves for the answers.

It is not surprising, perhaps, that the answer calls for a sophisticated response. It is not a simple matter to provide solutions that enable women at risk of domestic violence to maintain employment, childcare, safe accommodation and support networks. Yet government departments, local organisations and the voluntary sector have to develop a response that can meet women's needs, otherwise women and children will continue to feel as though they are being punished further for being victims of domestic violence.

This book is a collection of the full text of a series of reports commissioned under the Home Office Crime Reduction programme Violence against Women Initiative, devised in partnership with the Women's Unit of the Cabinet Office. The aim of these reports is to summarize what we knew about the success, or otherwise, of various initiatives and agencies in dealing with domestic violence. The book can be loosely broken down into three sections. The first deals with those primarily involved with and affected by domestic violence - women themselves, children and perpetrators. The next chapters cover the responses of, and good practice recommendations for, individual agencies, and cover the health service, the police, housing authorities, and the civil and criminal justice systems. The last four chapters set out a series of positive responses to the problems faced by agencies and women. The chapters show how outreach and advocacy can affect change, not only for an individual, but also within agencies. Multi-agency working can be effective, given the commitment of sufficient resources. The risk chapter clearly identifies priorities for rapid assistance – women who have been victimised previously, and those who have recently separated or are separating. Finally, the costs and measurement chapter gives a rationale for effective monitoring and measurement and illustrates what should be measured and by whom.

The chapters show that there have been few quantitative evaluations carried out into what counts as a successful intervention in situations of domestic violence. As a consequence, we don't know much that is certain. What we do know is that domestic violence is a crime, which usually involves repeat victimisation and we know what women have told us they want. What the chapters all have in common is the way that they contain a wealth of suggestions and indications on how to deliver this. They also contain discussions on the longer-term solutions including prevention, education, early-intervention and work with perpetrators aimed at changing the patterns of what can often be long-term offending against women.

It is clear that there has been a considerable change in the ways in that different agencies respond to domestic violence. Nevertheless, there is still much work to be done. There is too much at stake, the price paid by victims and their children is too high, and the cost to society is unacceptable. Domestic violence is still one of the most commonly committed, but least discussed crimes, and this must change for the problem to be adequately addressed. Multi-agency partnerships are clearly the way forward in identifying, publicising and monitoring strategies. Under-resourcing of these is a constant problem, yet with the enormous scope for crime prevention and reduction and the associated savings, this must be a short-sighted approach.

This book does not claim to be the definitive work on domestic violence; for example, there are gaps in knowledge about domestic violence against men and in same sex relationships. Instead, it identifies key themes that emerge throughout the chapters that may well apply to other groups of victims. These include the need for risk assessment, safety planning, empowerment, information and choice.

Can this book answer the question 'What works in reducing domestic violence?' Well, yes and no. No, in the sense that there have been few robustly evaluated studies making it difficult to prescribe a single answer or even combination of answers. Yes, in that there have been studies that do give us clear indications on how to make improvements and these are supported by feedback from women who have escaped domestic violence and from workers and activists in the field. We can say, for example, with some confidence what women want from health services, which groups of women are at greatest risk and what women want from the police service.

Key messages for reducing domestic violence include:

- Involve survivors and the refuge movement in formulating strategies and interventions.
- Focus on reducing repeat victimisation.
- Conduct rigorous risk assessment and safety planning procedures.
- Integrate child protection and family support work with domestic violence.
- Measure the costs of interventions and the costs of delaying interventions or delivering them in an inadequate, uncoordinated way.

- Use multi-agency partnerships to their full potential. The full involvement of health, education and the CPS are crucial to effective working.
- Ask women about domestic violence in health care settings – and ensure an adequate referral mechanism is already in place.
- Work with perpetrators – but liaise and support the woman partner as well.
- Ensure women and children fleeing domestic violence are given appropriate housing and offered re-settlement support.
- Monitor the recent changes in civil and criminal law, and their implementation. Ensure women and children are protected by child contact arrangements.
- Outreach and advocacy projects offer considerable potential in providing a rapid response that can influence both individuals and agencies.

There is still much we don't know, however. One of the most significant omissions is the relationship between known perpetrator rape and domestic violence. It is suspected that a large number of women who have suffered domestic violence have also been raped and sexually assaulted by their current or former partner. For many reasons, women are reluctant to disclose this fact, yet it is clear that there are many undetected serious crimes being committed for which women need medical care, and therapeutic intervention. Perpetrators also need to be detected and dealt with, and the impact on children can only be guessed at. Multi-agency domestic violence partnerships are uniquely placed to address these issues.

Current initiatives, including those funded under the Violence against Women Initiative will begin to provide at least some information on and answers to the challenges presented by domestic violence. Further opportunites for both findings and funding will be forthcoming under the Government Safer Communities and Supporting People initiatives.

The information in this book has the potential both to inform and support bids to funding bodies, and to make a real impact on reducing domestic violence.

Julie Taylor-Browne

Women survivors' views

Audrey Mullender and Gill Hague

THIS CHAPTER draws upon a literature review of the whole field of domestic violence, giving priority to those studies which have gathered first-hand accounts from survivors as to what has been most helpful in the services potentially available to them, and upon an ESRC-funded study on abused women's perspectives. Despite improvements in recent years, the unevenness of responses to survivors unfortunately continues, with women still typically speaking about feeling unsafe, including in the post-separation phase when harassment and violence continue to pose real dangers. This suggests that work in and across agencies needs to listen far more to survivors in order to build in their safety as its first priority. When individual services are considered in detail, refuges are consistently rated more positively than other agencies by survivors. 'What works' in this context appears to be a combination of concrete assistance and empowering staff attitudes, within a fundamental commitment to keeping women and children safe. In the light of this overwhelmingly positive feedback, the continued insecure funding of women's refuge, outreach and support services would appear to merit urgent attention. Amongst other agencies, few can even enumerate the work they do in relation to domestic violence or what it costs. At the inter-agency level, survivors have rarely heard about the forums in their area and it is clear that particular efforts are needed to make a reality of consulting women. These efforts could include the setting up of survivors' forums or advisory groups, and the offering of support and financial recognition to those survivors who take on the work of providing a representative voice. Overall there is a clear argument for attempting a more comprehensive, better informed and co-ordinated, more responsive and proactive approach across all relevant agencies in order to end the waste of resources on responses which may be ineffective.

Background

In a chapter on the views of women domestic violence survivors, it is important to begin by acknowledging the social movement which has been listening and responding to women survivors for a quarter of a century. The earliest responses to domestic violence were refuges, established by women for women with a strong element of self-help and self-organisation by survivors themselves (Dobash and Dobash, 1992). Safe housing, advocacy and outreach projects, helplines and women's support groups have continued to be established by women's organisations (which often themselves contain a high percentage of domestic violence survivors), despite a persistent lack of stable funding. Thus, women who have had personal experience of domestic violence have often played a key role in instigating such services, and in helping to ensure that these have been sensitive to abused women's expressed needs and wishes. Women's Aid and the refuge movement have always had strong principles and policies concerned quite directly and specifically with raising the voices of abused women and children whenever possible. Other grass-roots women's projects and campaigning groups have also consistently voiced both the injustices experienced by abused women and their children and also their aspirations. These have been usefully summarised as the need for protection, prevention and effective service provision (Zero Tolerance Trust, 1995), and were recognised long before the subject of domestic violence began tentatively to move into the mainstream.

Also beginning to be mainstream now is the routine seeking of the views of service users in relation to 'customer' satisfaction and service evaluation. Much of the response to domestic violence, however, has focused on policy development and has not necessarily been marked by involving or consulting women directly. The authors' own research (Hague et al, forthcoming) has revealed that there are some examples of sensitive methods being developed to consult, involve or devolve power to women service users. However, the majority of agencies in all sectors admit to a major shortfall between their rhetoric and their actual achievements in giving women survivors of violence real influence.

Scope of the chapter

This chapter will report briefly on general issues in regard to consultation with, and accountability to, domestic violence survivors, and will then move on to a short consideration of equality issues. This discussion is followed by an examination of survivors' views in relation to specific agencies and service providers. These include women's refuges and support and advocacy projects; social services; health provision; housing; benefits provision; the civil and criminal law and the police. The discussion continues by looking at public education campaigns and multi-agency initiatives. A brief consideration of the role of survivors who are professionals is followed by a concluding discussion of costs, possibilities for successful interventions, and recommendations.

Gender issues

The chapter will deal with women as the major users of the services concerned and as the main victims of frightening and physically dangerous domestic violence (Mirrlees-Black, 1999). It is recognised that both men and women can perpetrate violence. Women in refuges, for example, may be escaping from a woman or a man (*Violence Against Lesbians in the Home*, 1998). There have been only isolated attempts to establish services for men claiming to be the victims of women's violence and no evaluation of any such has been traced. Anecdotal evidence suggests that, while all people experiencing abuse deserve support, some men who access these services may be making counter-claims in order to conceal their own abusiveness or poor parenting (*Community Care*, 'End to battered men's refuge', 4th February 1993:2). Certainly, any such service ought arguably to run criminal and other checks to ensure that it is not inadvertently harbouring men abducting their children or failing to provide them with proper care. The risk of collusion by professionals with men's denial of partner abuse will also be potentially very high (see chapter by Mullender and Burton, this volume).

Sources consulted

This chapter builds upon literature reviews of the whole field of domestic violence undertaken by both authors in the context of earlier work (e.g. Mullender, 1996; Hague and Malos, 1998; Mullender and Humphreys, 1998) and continuously updated. These sources have been revisited with the aim of singling out first-hand accounts gathered from women who have experienced domestic violence as to what has been most and least helpful in the services potentially available to them. This has also involved consulting more 'ephemeral' material produced by women themselves (Homer et al, 1984; *Breaking Through*, 1989; *Violence Against Lesbians in the Home*, 1998; *Women and Children in Refuges*, undated). In addition, material has been used from overview information produced by the Women's Aid Federation of England through an in-depth, national consultation exercise conducted within the organisation (Harwin, 1998a) and by various local Women's Aid and other refuge groups and inter-agency domestic violence forums. Existing support groups and service user projects have also been consulted. Thus, the chapter discusses both research findings based on survivors' voices, and also consultation with survivors which service providers themselves carry out.

The chapter is further informed by the findings from a study jointly undertaken by the present authors in the ESRC Violence Research Programme, under the title, *Abused women's perspectives: responsiveness and accountability of domestic violence and inter-agency initiatives* (Award no. L133251017; Hague et al, forthcoming). This study was multi-methodological in design and included both a national mapping survey of survivor consultation and accountability within inter-agency initiatives, refuges and other agencies, and also detailed qualitative and quantitative fieldwork in selected areas, with case studies.

Inadequacy of services

Women's experience of all the public sector services has traditionally been that they are patchy and inadequate, with practitioners often assuming judgmental or woman-blaming attitudes, particularly in the past (e.g. Binney et al, 1981; Dobash et al, 1985). The Binney study, carried out in 1978, was a national study of refuges and housing provision involving interviews with 656 women, while the Dobash study of help-seeking behaviour over a period of time included analysis of 34,000 police and court records and in-depth interviews with 109 women. Many women in these and other studies have spoken of trying one agency after another in a quest for help, with delays and obstacles at every stage. The situation is often compounded for black women by institutional racism (Mama, 1996); for lesbian women by homophobia (*Violence Against Lesbians in the Home*, 1998); and for many disabled women by being trapped in the home and out of reach of publicity about services (London Borough of Hounslow, 1994).

Not surprisingly, many of the accounts researchers have gathered from women over the years have expressed dissatisfaction. This is rendered the more worrying by the message in the Dobash et al, (1985) study of help-seeking behaviour that women have often tried all the resources of self, family and friends, over long periods of time, before attempting to access external assistance. By the time they do so, the violence has often become both frequent and severe, and making contact with any outside agency may have become more dangerous in the face of prohibitions and threats from the perpetrator. To encounter a response that is neither immediate nor effective places the woman in even greater danger. If the violence continues to escalate, women typically make increasingly frequent approaches to agencies, which may be continually negated by unhelpful responses. Dobash et al (1985) made a hugely important contribution to portraying abused women, not as passive and accepting of abuse, but as 'engage[d] in an active struggle to find solutions to the violence and to seek the help of outsiders in these efforts'. This is recognised nowadays in the widespread utilisation of the term 'survivor', rather than 'victim', when discussing women who have experienced domestic violence, and in the publication of numerous self-help books, personal testimonies and academic accounts of women's help-seeking efforts (e.g. Hoff, 1990; Kirkwood, 1993).

More recent studies appear to show that women still face inadequate services. Hanmer's (1996) interviews with 30 white and 30 minority ethnic women, for example, reveal a generally uneven response, which in some cases worsened their situation. All the public sector agencies tend to suffer from internal inconsistency so that different members of staff might be helpful, indifferent or hostile. A particular gap is the inability of some to convey information about local women's organisations. The danger of post-separation violence, both to women and children, is not well recognised by agencies dealing with child care and contact issues. There is a consequent lack of urgency, little attention to safety, and failure to tackle the man's behaviour or to understand the situation from the woman's or the children's perspective. Some women end up with very negative views of the whole range of agencies involved in their and their children's lives.

Children and domestic violence

We now know that domestic violence can have varied and serious impacts on children who witness, live with, or otherwise experience it (see Mullender, this volume, for a discussion of children's issues and domestic abuse). However, children's voices are very rarely heard in relation to their views about domestic violence and about policy and practice responses. Until recently, for example, studies of domestic violence and children in the UK used mothers and professionals as their research respondents, although new work (e.g. McGee, 2000) includes consultation with children. The present authors were part of an inter-institutional team which conducted a recent study of children's views and coping strategies in relation to domestic violence, within the ESRC Children 5-16: Growing into the Twenty First Century Programme. This study has revealed that children are far from being passive victims of domestic violence. Rather, they use a wide range of coping strategies, often in an active way, to deal with the violence they experience. The research found that children would generally like to be consulted about responses, and are a rich source of good advice for other children and adults (Mullender et al, forthcoming).

While there are many new practice developments that attempt to address children's needs, few have consulted children directly. However, relevant agencies could usefully seek the views of children who have experience of domestic violence (in a sensitive and careful way) about policy and services. Scottish Women's Aid for example, published *Young People Say* (1998). Many refuges run children's workshops and hold regular, decision-making children's meetings, but few other agencies do anything comparable.

Issues for black women

Women from minority ethnic communities face extra problems when attempting to access services, additional to those experienced by all women. For example, the women informants in Mama's (1996) survey of statutory and voluntary sector responses, conducted in the late 1980s in two London boroughs, had consistently encountered unsatisfactory and discriminatory services, as well as overtly racist attitudes. In this study, which included an in-depth survey of 120 black women's experiences of both statutory and voluntary institutions, an internationally based perspective on the abuse of black women in Britain was developed, and widespread concerns about racism in service delivery were raised. Such concerns are confirmed by activist and first-hand accounts such as those published by Southall Black Sisters (1990). A more recent study in London (James-Hanman, 1995) sought the views, and ascertained the needs, of black women and children experiencing domestic violence in the London Borough of Islington. It suggests that existing provision still fails to meet language and cultural needs, leaving many black and minority ethnic women isolated and unaware of their options, and sometimes placed in additional danger, for example if interpreters are used from within their own family or community.

Where separating from an abusive husband contravenes cultural boundaries, women may have to refocus their thinking in ways that make it possible to leave; for example, by coming to regard the man and those who support him in the family structure, rather than themselves, as breaking the ties of honour (Hanmer, 1996). Hanmer further points out that women who are losing their family and community support are in particular need of both emergency and longer-term support from the relevant agencies. They have few options and need help to be delivered in such a way that it gives them the personal strength to uproot themselves and their children from every aspect of their past lives and begin again. For women who do not have British nationality, control and domination may have been exercised by the perpetrator in relation to citizenship, residence rights and required documentation. Officials dealing with all matters relating to immigration, asylum and refugee status require awareness training on domestic violence and the dangers facing women both in this country and in their countries of origin.

More recently, Rai and Thiara (1997) have provided an invaluable overview of refuge and other women's support services from the perspective of black service users and workers. Black organisations in the community are valued but other sources of help, such as counsellors and schools, are commonly experienced by women as not understanding the black experience and sometimes as institutionally racist, particularly in predominantly white areas.

Issues for disabled women

While a disabled woman may experience the same difficulties as a non-disabled woman, these may be exacerbated by her disability and she may face additional problems and discrimination. Canadian and American research (summarised by Nosek and Howland, 1998) indicates that the proportion of disabled women who have experienced abuse may be higher than amongst the general population of women. They may also face risks from staff, other service users and intruders in social and health care settings. In the home, if the partner is also a carer, the woman's dependency may trap her in the relationship and in the abuse. Her disability may also be used against her if the abuser restricts her mobility, her outings, her access to medication, and so on (London Borough of Hounslow, 1994). The abuse may continue for more protracted periods than for other women because options are fewer and harder to access. It is difficult for the woman to leave home if she is not mobile, or has had her home adapted or a complex care package arranged to allow her to remain in the community (Cross, 1999), or if accessible refuge accommodation is over-subscribed. Women with disabled children may also be stuck in abusive situations because, for example, it is particularly difficult to uproot a child from a painstakingly assembled network of social, health and educational services.

While the dynamics of abuse may be different for each disability, there are also common themes. These include higher rates of economic dependence, social isolation, and the disability being turned against the woman as a factor in the abuse so that she may feel trapped and her self-esteem may be destroyed (Nosek and Howland, 1998). There is also a comprehensive need for all agencies to re-examine the accessibility and appropriateness of services and of the ways in which these are publicised (including to women with communication impairments). Most writing on safety planning is based on an assumption that the woman can leave of her own volition. Agencies need to consider how to adapt policies for women who need help to get out of bed, for example. Many policies concerning women who set up their own households assume access to benefits and/or employment, in both of which spheres there are particular obstacles to be overcome for disabled people. A refuge disability worker interviewed in the study by Hague et al (1996b) stressed that better liaison is needed between domestic violence services and disabled people's organisations.

In general, there is insufficient documentation on domestic violence in relation to issues of equality concerning class, ethnicity, sexuality, disability and so on. The result is that the voices and views of abused women and children from minority groups of all types are inadequately represented in the literature, with consequent implications for potentially skewed and discriminatory policy development.

Women's Aid and the refuge movement

Refuge organisations provide emergency housing, support, outreach and advocacy services and have a good record of consulting service users about both provision and policy. Abused women consistently rate refuges, and outreach services provided by them, more positively than other agencies and services. The following quotes, for example, are taken from various research studies in which one or both of the present authors were involved:

> The great majority of women interviewed were extremely satisfied with the services received from refuges in all of the areas. Overall, refuges elicited by far the most satisfaction from women, as compared with other agencies (Hague et al, 1996b:73).

> Many women interviewed spoke of the importance of refuge life in terms of sharing experiences and feelings with other women, getting support from workers and building strength and self-confidence . . . 'The advantages of living with other women is that you give each other strength. You know, why it went on, you talk about all the experiences you've been through. And you find out that it wasn't you, it wasn't you. That it is the men who have the problem really' (Malos and Hague, 1993:59).

The qualitative phase of the authors' work on accountability to survivors highlights that, in the majority of cases, refuges are the only agencies that women believe can offer them safety. Conversely, mainstream agencies pay too little attention to safety, according to over half the women surveyed through a self-completion questionnaire widely circulated in Lewisham (London Borough of Lewisham's Community Safety Team, 1998). Refuge staff are generally the only professionals to whom women feel able to tell the full details of their experiences because, in most other contexts, they fear disbelief, revulsion, blame and possible consequences in terms of child protection intervention (Hague et al, forthcoming). Related issues are the respect and belief that survivors are offered by women's organisations, and the trust that this engenders (e.g. Sissons, 1999). Emergency, outreach and advocacy projects have a key role in helping survivors learn about their entitlements (Sissons, 1999), both in information passed on by workers and through the mutual support offered by other women (Kelly and Humphreys, this volume).

While there are always, of course, improvements that could be made, and the crowded conditions of many refuges continue to be rated negatively by users of the service, the generally positive tone of the feedback on refuge provision described above is confirmed by other studies. For example, Henderson (1997) found that 81% of women surveyed in Scotland had found Women's Aid services to be helpful, owing both to the actual assistance provided and the helpful attitudes of staff. Women's support groups and advice/information services are also valued highly. An independent evaluation of support groups for women survivors of domestic violence in the USA found that women attending them experienced substantial improvements in social and emotional functioning and also a reduction in violence (Tutty et al, 1993).

A wide-ranging network of Asian women's refuges now exists in the UK, both within and outside Women's Aid. In many towns and cities, there are also other specialist refuges, variously, for example, for all black women and children, for African, for African Caribbean, for Chinese, for Jewish and for other women and children from minority ethnic communities. Mama's study (1996:269-298) found some dissatisfaction among black women survivors with generalist refuges, as compared with specialist ones. However, the Women's Aid federations have attempted to address some of these problems with specific work on refuges and black women (e.g. Rai and Thiara, 1999) and through the adoption of strategies to combat racism and other forms of discrimination. It should not be claimed, of course, that these strategies are as yet completely effective, but the effort is being made. In general terms, Rai and Thiara report that black women value refuges highly, particularly in terms of saving lives.

There are also a few specialist refuges of other types, for example, for women with learning disabilities, for women who have experienced sexual assault, and for young women, all of which are generally rated highly by service users. Similarly, *Violence Against Lesbians in the Home* (1998:50), while encouraging further improvements, states of refuges: 'it is unlikely that any agency has responded more positively to Lesbians fleeing violence in the home'.

Women's Aid has a positive record in seeking survivors' views of its own services. The authors' recent questionnaire survey indicates that 90% of refuges undertake direct consultation with survivors, whereas only 40% of inter-agency forums do so (Hague et al, forthcoming). Around a third of all refuges responding consider that residents and survivors more generally have 'real power' in the running of their services, with twice as many offering some participation in decision and policy-making. Again, this is higher than for other bodies although there is some evidence from the study that it has declined in recent years. Ex-residents may serve on refuge management committees and/or become involved in public education work and in the design and delivery of training. Refuges and the Women's Aid federations have a commitment to represent the voices of abused women and children and other agencies tend to rely on them to do this.

In the light of these positive evaluations, and, in addition, of the new *Supporting People* programme, it has been strongly argued that it is a matter of national priority to consider how to:

- secure and ringfence the funding for the existing network of refuges. Refuge services represent exceptionally good value for money because costs are kept low and services are heavily subscribed. In 1992-93, the average cost per bednight for women and children in refuges in England was £11.23 (Ball, 1994).
- fund the Women's Aid National Domestic Violence Helpline. The Helpline took over 35,000 calls in the year from July 2000 to June 2001 (*Women's Aid Annual Report*, 2000/01:2); and
- develop women's advocacy, outreach and support services, within an overall long-term, strategic plan (WAFE, 1998b; Kelly and Humphreys, this volume).

Statutory services

Social services departments

Social services, both through their adult and their children's services, have a vital role to play in supporting abused women and their children (in the latter case, through both the 'children in need' and child protection provisions). Women value the practical help available from social workers (Binney et al, 1981; Pahl, 1985), and the fact that they 'know the system'. The Binney and Pahl studies found that social workers are one of the commonest sources of referral to a refuge. In a Canadian study, Home (1991-92) found that social workers did better than the police in this regard, and were generally more safety conscious, which she attributed to greater knowledge of available forms of help.

Thus, women experiencing domestic violence do seek the help and advice of social workers, despite fears (reported in most of the relevant studies, e.g. Abrahams, 1994, and again evident in the authors' own research, Hague et al, forthcoming) that they might lose their children. Surveys of refuge samples reveal that from half to three-quarters of residents have at some time sought assistance from the personal social services (Binney et al, 1981; Pahl, 1985). Amongst black women, Mama (1996) found that a third of her respondents, all of whom had housing problems resulting from domestic violence, had had contact with social services, rising to half the Asian women in the sample. In total community samples, of course, the proportions are lower, with self-reported contact with social services ranging from 6 to 17% (summarised in ESRC Violence Research Programme, 1998). Surveys of social work caseloads reveal strikingly high numbers of domestic violence survivors. Maynard (1985) found that 1 in 3 of a sample of all current social work cases in one northern town had direct references to domestic violence recorded in the file. Similarly, in a later study, at least a third of the children on the Child Protection Register in one London Borough had mothers who were being abused (London Borough of Hackney, 1993). Professional reports of this level of prevalence in their own workloads can double when social workers are given training in what to look for (Hester and Pearson, 1998).

Overall, however, the limited research evidence on survivors' views and social services indicates that a considerable shift in practice is required. All front line staff need awareness training to avoid practice which breaches confidentiality and puts women in danger (see documented examples in Ali, 1998, a small-scale, in-depth interview survey of domestic violence survivors). The avoidance of confrontation of the violence found by Dobash et al (1985) was still present in 1995 (Farmer and Owen, 1995) and practice indications are that legal powers in the amended Children Act to remove dangerous men from families in order to protect children are rarely used. There still tends to be a stereotypical assumption that the woman should leave and, if she refuses or considers it unsafe to do so, she is liable to be accused of 'failing to protect' her children, even though she has perpetrated no abuse (Humphreys, 2000). There is also a tendency to conceptualise children's needs, which are legally paramount, as if they were detachable from those of their mothers. Yet, it has been argued that good practice with abused women is often also the best approach to child protection (Kelly, 1994; Mullender and Morley, 1994). Pockets of good practice have recognised this, notably where designated staff have been appointed with expertise in domestic violence. A shift towards a family support approach could open up new avenues for positive work with non-abusing parents and for recovery work with children (see Mullender, this volume).

Health services

Women report a range of health impacts of domestic violence (see Davidson et al, this volume) which lead them into consulting health professionals who have a key role to play in meeting abused women's needs. In Mooney's (1994) survey of women in North London, seven per cent of those who had experienced violence in the last twelve months had needed an overnight stay in hospital. General practitioners (GPs) are amongst those most likely to be consulted by women experiencing domestic violence, according to women's own reports. These include 25-70% in refuge samples (see summary in British Medical Association (1998) and 14 to 22% in community samples (see summary in ESRC Violence Research Programme, 1998). Women are not only seeking help with injuries. Around half the women in Mooney's (1994) study reported mental health problems such as anxiety, depression and insomnia. Several, when interviewed, talked about suicide attempts or suicidal thoughts.

Primary care

One factor that prevents doctors from being involved in early intervention is that women say they do not always get as far as asking their advice. In one refuge sample, of 89% who had been to their general practitioner in the previous year, nearly half had been too ashamed or afraid to disclose their experiences of violence (Hopayian et al, 1983). The unsympathetic manner of some doctors and their evident lack of time constituted further obstacles for women, who were not satisfied with being prescribed anti-depressants or sleeping tablets (e.g. Dominy and Radford, 1996).

Women appreciate doctors who listen, including to the wider context of their lives beyond the purely medical, and who offer appropriate advice (Pahl, 1979; 1985). Whereas health professionals regard their role as largely confined to medical matters, women are frequently also seeking emotional support, general advice, and practical help with medical evidence for legal proceedings or housing applications (Henderson, 1997).

Crucially, women and their doctors also very often hold differing views about the asking of direct questions that could lead to a disclosure of violence. Literature reviewed by the BMA (1998) reveals that patients would tend to prefer this, with a majority saying they would use it as an opportunity to talk, whereas GPs are more accustomed to waiting for the patient to set the clinical agenda. GPs tend to go further only in suspicious circumstances such as the offering of an unconvincing explanation for an injury or the presence of an 'overprotective' partner. The BMA (1998) itself - despite reviewing the research, overseas practice, and the under-identification of domestic violence by doctors - comes down in favour of doctors considering 'what is appropriate for each patient'. Guidance in the USA (American Medical Association, 1992) is far more proactive and now favours asking routine, specific questions. The BMA (1998) considers that British patients might find this intrusive. Yet, as things stand, doctors miss many instances of violence and abuse, with life-threatening consequences.

As a result, it may be another health care professional in the primary care setting, such as a health visitor, in whom a woman chooses to confide

(Mezey et al, 1998). Since some studies have shown pregnancy and the having of children as a time of increased risk for women (Mezey, 1997), the role of health visitors and midwives may be of particular importance, with an urgent need for comprehensive training and screening protocols. There is also scope for fund-holding practices to create specific posts or to invest in counselling services more generally. A successful initiative in Leeds involved 'advice workers' provided by the Leeds Inter-agency Project, in whom Asian women who required absolute confidentiality from their family and community, and even from the doctor, were able to confide safely, with positive results for a high proportion (Leeds City Council et al, 1992). Whoever the woman does talk to, she is likely to want concrete advice and information about services available, including women's organisations, counselling, and emergency services.

Health visitors were a resource that was underused by Pahl's (1985) respondents because they were generally seen as only interested in the children. Only a minority had been experienced as taking an interest in the woman's wider situation or giving appropriate assistance. Peckover (1998), in a more recent qualitative study, found a widespread lack of awareness in the health visiting profession about domestic violence, although health visitors are undoubtedly a useful first contact point for some women and may provide much individual and group support. The Positive Lifestyles group for domestic violence survivors in Croydon is co-ordinated by health visitors, for example. Certainly, they could play a crucial role in early intervention, not least because women do not have to seek their involvement; it is automatic in relation to the birth of children. An enhanced input of training would be needed, covering both practical information and the kind of approach likely to be most helpful.

The BMA (1998) charts the potential for greater input on domestic violence in all levels of medical training, in line with progress in the USA and Canada and more isolated initiatives here. The same would be true of nursing and paramedical training. Learning should ideally take place in a multi-disciplinary context, with the refuge movement and other specialist agencies and survivors' groups involved to give the survivor's viewpoint. A Department of Health-funded national domestic violence resource pack for health care practitioners has recently been published (DoH, 2000) and professional medical associations have also produced specific domestic violence policies and protocols (see Davidson et al, this volume). There has been some survivor input into these new developments, although how much is unclear.

Mental health

Women experiencing domestic violence may be inappropriately diagnosed as psychotic, neurotic or personality disordered (Mullender, 1996). For most, however, their very real symptoms of psychological distress might be best relieved by ending the violence and mental abuse, and offering support. First-hand accounts from women make it clear that psychiatrists and other mental health professionals can have enormous influence over whether survivors regard themselves, and are regarded by others, as having lost their sanity or whether they regain health and strength and go on to a new life (*Breaking Through*, 1989).

Particular care needs to be exercised where an abusive partner attempts to convince the woman and others around her, including medical staff, that she is mentally unwell. It is potentially possible for the County Court to displace a husband or cohabitee as 'nearest relative' under s.29 of the Mental Health Act if he is a known abuser. As in other service settings, all the professionals in community mental health teams need domestic violence training.

Hospital services

Abused women also access services in accident and emergency departments, obstetric settings (Bewley et al, 1997), and in all other health and hospital contexts, including ear, nose and throat and dental services following punches to the jaw and head. The abuse may not be an immediately obvious cause of the injuries presented, for example where a man might have been driving recklessly to frighten the woman and has caused a road accident.

All health care staff need appropriate training. Full history taking, looking for a pattern not a single incident, sensitive but direct questioning in an interview conducted away from the partner, and knowing about other sources of help are all important. Posters and leaflets, as in all service settings, help women to know that they can raise issues of abuse and will be taken seriously if they do so. Good practice is now beginning to be developed in the UK, for example in Glasgow (SNAP, 1997).

Housing

According to survivors' testimonies and to research evidence, one of the principal needs of women and children escaping violence in the home is for access to safe and secure temporary and permanent housing options - in other words, for somewhere safe to go. While temporary housing may be provided by the refuge movement, or through the homelessness legislation, access to permanent housing is a more problematic issue. Women and children who are homeless due to domestic violence make extensive use of local authority and housing association provision, and their treatment by their local housing department is of key importance in this respect. As with social and health services, women survivors questioned in housing consultation exercises and wider-scale research projects with housing-related content (e.g. Malos and Hague, 1993; Henderson, 1997), consistently highlighted the need for:

- a sympathetic, believing approach;
- a non-judgmental service;
- removal of obstacles to service (e.g. the requirement of certain forms of 'proof' or insistence that legal remedies to remove the perpetrator be substituted for rehousing the woman);
- an ending of unreasonable delays in being accepted as homeless and in being rehoused;
- the safety of women and children to be the priority;
- confidentiality;
- effective services delivered promptly;
- both emergency and permanent housing to be available, secure, and of a reasonable standard in an area the survivor considers safe.

In a 1993 study (Malos and Hague, 1993), 80 women who had experienced domestic violence were interviewed twice, over a period of time, in several local authority areas. The women interviewed, all of whom were in the process of seeking rehousing through their local authority, repeatedly spoke of the need for a believing, sensitive approach to the issue and felt strongly that intrusive interviewing by homelessness officers should be avoided. They called for the provision of specialist, or at least specially trained, officers and the option of being interviewed by a woman or by someone of a similar ethnic background, if desired, with adequate translation and interpreting services in place. They wished to see this coupled with ensuring that delays were not extended or access impeded by obstructive housing policies, such as pressure to seek legal remedies rather than rehousing. There was support for the adoption of specific domestic violence policies or good practice guidelines by housing authorities and associations, and for the provision of specialist training for housing staff. Other studies have confirmed this need for policies and practice to underpin the need for improved attitudes: 'they treated me like a bit of trash' (Henderson, 1997:108).

Of course, none of this will help unless there is also adequate practical provision. Women in the Malos and Hague (1993) study made it clear that their priority was the provision of secure emergency housing provision, followed by access to permanent housing which was safe and of a decent standard. Some women were very happy with the accommodation they actually received, while others found the quality and location of their offers problematic. This is a common theme in such research: 'they gave me a tip in a rough area' (woman's account in Henderson, 1997:108). In the Malos and Hague study, black women were often particularly anxious about the area to which they were rehoused owing to the existence of known racist environments and, for some women, complex extended family networks. Housing staff needed to be sensitive to these issues without resorting to stereotypes since some women need to flee tight-knit communities while others wish to stay within them. Black women may also be reluctant to involve the police, thus making it more difficult for them to 'prove' abuse, and may encounter negative attitudes from some staff, as well as facing particular residence and tenancy issues (Mama, 1996). For disabled women, there may be particular problems in being reluctant to leave specially adapted housing or in facing long delays before such accommodation can be allocated elsewhere. Being forced to move more than once to flee post-separation violence naturally compounds the difficulties.

Thus, there is a need for housing and homelessness staff and housing associations to develop further knowledge and expertise concerning domestic violence and its impact upon victims. Examples of ways in which this may be relevant include recognition that domestic violence can result in noise, damage and debts (WAFE, 1998b) which, if pursued at face value, may threaten the woman's own tenancy or chance of being rehoused. Homelessness staff, in particular, need to understand:

- the needs of single and childless women;
- the possible dangers for women in being forced to have recourse to civil law remedies or to reoccupy the family home; and,
- the fact that women's 'local connections' may be in areas where they are least safe.

Changes in housing legislation in recent years have in some ways diminished rather than increased the rights of women fleeing domestic violence, particularly due to the removal of the right to permanent housing for the statutorily homeless under the 1996 Housing Act. The impact of this contraction of housing rights has, to some extent, been ameliorated by subsequent regulations, and there have also been some improvements in definitions of domestic violence used and in responses to tenants who are perpetrators. Overall, though, there remain many problems in practice. WAFE (1998b) lists difficulties caused by the imposition of exclusions in allocation policies, the lack of housing eligibility for women returning from violent relationships overseas, and the fact that the Code of Guidance on homelessness is not mandatory. In addition, there is an overarching need for a national approach to fast-tracking homeless referrals, making emergency transfers, facilitating mobility, and planning emergency and temporary accommodation and advice in conjunction with local women's organisations and survivors. Women-only space in temporary accommodation for women with and without children would be useful (James-Hanman, 1995) and is appreciated by users where it exists. Women in bed and breakfast provision say that they often feel very unsafe from their abusers, with sexual and racial harassment from other residents and unsuitable facilities for children frequently posing additional dangers (James-Hanman, 1994). The Homes Bill, due to be reintroduced into Parliament, is expected to deal with some of the above recommendations for improvements, but will still leave much to local policy and practice.

Good practice examples include the believing approach adopted by a variety of local housing authorities and the information guide produced by the Shelter Housing Aid and Research Project (1998) for use by service users and professionals in Leicestershire. It is also most encouraging that increasing numbers of both housing authorities and housing associations have adopted good practice guidelines in relation to domestic violence.

Housing can be a crucial determinant of what happens to abused women, not least because many women apparently decide against taking action owing to concerns over what would happen to their abuser in term of potential lack of housing (although no research was traced on women's views on this issue). Domestic violence was the most common reason for homelessness cited by 30 to 39-year old women without statutory rights to housing in a recently published qualitative study (Anwen, 1999). Amongst these women were some who had lost children into care and others who had been in care themselves. Thus, for a woman who is already battling with multiple problems, finding herself with a violent partner can be the factor that defeats her best efforts to make a life for herself and her children, leading in some cases to social exclusion and/or to heavy costs upon the state.

Benefits provision

Benefits provision has been less researched and has generally featured less in the literature than other services yet is accessed by large numbers of survivors. It is important to remember that, in countries where unwaged women do not have access to financial support on separating from a violent partner, women are frequently forced to remain in life-threatening situations (e.g. author's interview with a refuge worker in Greece). In the UK, the social security system makes a major contribution to assisting women and children to rebuild their lives. Yet it is rarely visible in inter-agency working (Hague et al, 1996b) and Henderson (1997) reports, from a Scottish overview of services for women experiencing domestic violence, that most Benefit Agency offices do not recognise they might have any particular input to make.

Women's own priority (Henderson, 1997) is to receive the practical, financial help that they are seeking, with obvious criticisms relating to problems or delays in this being fulfilled. However, other serious issues highlighted by Henderson's respondents include:

- failures of confidentiality (e.g. an address divulged);
- incorrect advice;
- a lack of understanding of the urgent and dangerous situation faced by women fleeing domestic violence; and
- unhelpful staff attitudes which can be demeaning and unethical (e.g. expecting intimate details to be discussed in front of children).

From surveys with refuge residents, WAFE (1998b) further reports that local practice and budgetary commitments can vary, so that there may be obstacles to accessing or receiving emergency payments. In general, there have been substantial cutbacks in social security benefits in the last fourteen years which have adversely affected abused women and their children (Hague and Malos, 1998). Women also need facilities for children in waiting areas, and publicity aimed at telling those who may have been kept dependent on their abusers that they can claim benefits in their own right.

There is an argument for giving official recognition to the fact that, where a woman flees domestic violence and leaves behind all her possessions and sometimes all family and community links, she has no resources from which to repay a loan. In addition, she may well be too traumatised to work, may have left home without many of the normal proofs of identity (and may not be able to return safely to collect them), and may in some cases be forced to seek recourse to public funds in circumstances where this would normally be proscribed, for example on immigration grounds (WAFE, 1998b). All of these issues could usefully be considered for special treatment in policy review. The latter was indeed recognised in the Women's Unit document, *Living without Fear* (Cabinet Office, 1999), in the same way that the Child Support Act recognises the particular circumstances of a woman for whom it would be dangerous to name her child's father. In the USA, for example, there are exemptions and waivers in some cases to the work requirement for abused women applying for welfare (Thelen, 1996).

Overall, evidence from Women's Aid, other refuge providers and from women service users indicates that the social security system requires policy development, comprehensive domestic violence awareness training for front line staff, and, ideally, some level of link with local inter-agency initiatives.

Using the law

From 12 to 22% of community samples of women experiencing domestic violence consult solicitors (summary in ESRC Violence Research Programme, 1998). Until its recent overhaul, the civil law was typically a grave disappointment and left many women unsafe (Barron, 1990). Now, new reforms introduced by the Family Law Act 1996 need to be monitored and evaluated, including ascertaining survivors' views in order to judge their impact. Fears expressed by women's organisations that certain changes could act against victims, for example that they may be pressured into mediation and other joint meetings with their abusers (WAFE, 1998b), need detailed investigation. Research on preliminary information meetings prior to seeking a divorce (Walker, 1999) indicates that by no means all women can attend these events safely and that the staff dealing with them require careful training on domestic violence issues. Women's refuges are suggested as suitable venues for such meetings for their own residents, whilst some women need to be made exempt from attending at all because their abusers leave them no safe opportunity to do so. Importantly, the Government is currently reviewing such aspects of the new divorce legislation, and children and family reporters within the new Children and Family Court Advisory and Support System (CAFCASS) service, who also act as advisers to the Family Court, already have recommendations in place within their *National Standards* advising against joint meetings in cases of domestic violence.

There is a clear need to consider the civil law in conjunction with criminal justice approaches to domestic violence (see below) in order to ensure that the two - as the major planks in the framework of protection for victims - are fully integrated and complementary. For example, evidence of criminal proceedings could be uniformly accepted as proof of violence in divorce proceedings, while family law could be brought into line with the harassment legislation by enforcing injunctions with criminal sanctions for any breach (WAFE, 1998b). This latter proposal could create a useful route for referring more perpetrators through to programmes aimed at ending their offending (see Mullender and Burton, this volume). Arguably, a national register of injunctions could assist in the transfer of relevant information between agencies (WAFE, 1998b), although there would need to be extreme caution exercised in relation to confidentiality and safety for victims.

Gaps in current civil legislation and associated processes include the lack of comprehensive access to Legal Aid for those experiencing domestic violence, and the unequal protection offered to unmarried as against married and to same sex as against heterosexual partners. Research and scholarship overseas would suggest that third party injunctions (Humphreys and Kaye, 1997) would be well worth pursuing here, through the implementation of s.60 of the Family Law Act 1996. This might increase the numbers of women who could be protected under the law since many are reluctant to take action themselves for fear of repercussions.

Policing domestic violence

The police, as the most important emergency service in this context, have a vital and central role to play in meeting the needs of abused women and their children. They frequently top the list of agencies contacted by domestic violence survivors for help (ESRC Violence Research Programme, 1998) and the major improvements in policing policy over the last decade have been broadly supported by women who have experienced domestic violence and by their advocacy organisations, such as the refuge movement. For example, 90% of women respondents in Kelly's (1999) study of the experimental *Domestic Violence Matters* project, formerly located in North London and discussed in the chapter by Hanmer and Griffiths in this volume, agreed that domestic violence must always be treated as a crime. This should not be taken to mean, however, that survivors are as yet at all satisfied with the individual responses they receive from the criminal justice system.

In many localities, women continue to report little change in criminal justice responses. This is an analysis which has been backed up by Home Office studies of domestic violence policing, (Grace, 1995; Plotnikoff and Woolfson, 1998), which found only patchy improvements across the country, though considerable in some areas. Despite the definite improvements in police policy and practice (particularly with reference to the work of police domestic violence units [DVUs]) that have been reported by domestic violence survivors in the last few years, the authors' research on accountability to women revealed that women continue to feel remarkably unsafe in the post-separation phase (Hague et al, forthcoming). Survivors also report that police attitudes outside of the DVUs often contrast markedly with those within them. This has implications for increased efforts to re-educate the wider and longer-serving police service that times have changed. A predominantly male workforce also needs to be particularly aware of evidence from survivors' experience that those in public life tend to believe their male partners in preference to them. Again, this has training implications and practical messages in relation to interviewing the partners separately, and privately, at any scene where domestic violence is alleged to have taken place. This is a matter that is recognised by many of those local police services that have explicit domestic violence policies and practice guidelines in place. The fact that survivors speak about a continuing process of intimidation and abuse in the post-separation phase means that the recognition in the Protection from Harassment Act 1997 of a 'course of conduct' is particularly welcome.

Greater use of this legislation, combined with the other suggestions contained in this section, could potentially assist many women.

Overall, survivors want prompt and effective police action that makes sense within their own experiences. While most women favour a strong criminal justice response, and while women's organisations consistently call for a pro-arrest stance (WAFE, 1998b), not all victims are happy about their partner being arrested (Bourlet, 1990). This may be partly because they may depend on him or love him, and because, if they and/or their partner are black, they are likely to be reluctant to involve the police and the courts in their lives (Mama, 1996). Very frequently, though, the hesitation springs from fear of reprisals and repercussions from the perpetrator (Kelly, 1999) because women simply do not feel safe. The key points emerging from data on abused women's views in Kelly's 1999 study in London, supported and expanded by Henderson's (1997) research in Scotland and related work nationwide, are that:

- women want respectful treatment by, and assertive action from, the police but they do not always receive either or both;
- survivors think domestic violence should be responded to as a crime, but need support and protection in order for this to be a viable option;
- it is crucially important that police officers interview the woman and her abuser separately, in private, in such a way that she is able to give her account in safety;
- a proportion of police officers persist in communicating that domestic violence is trivial and/or that they do not believe that women will pursue prosecution;
- there are major problems in translating arrest into effective action against perpetrators; where prosecutions do occur, the sentences passed are perceived by victims as failing to place sanctions on men's behaviour;
- it would also help if the police, when called to an incident, routinely knew of other sources of support, including how to access emergency accommodation.

Recent developments have included:

- the rather contentious and uneven spread of perpetrators' programmes (see Mullender and Burton, this volume);
- extensions of community alarm and mobile phone schemes to women most at risk of repeat victimisation (e.g. London Borough of Lewisham, undated); and
- some innovatory work in the criminal justice system, for example the three-year pilot *Domestic Violence Matters* project in Islington, North London, noted earlier.

An evaluation of this last project (Kelly, 1999), together with an evaluation of one perpetrator's programme and a parallel service for women in London (Burton et al, 1998), suggests that women experiencing domestic violence often favour a proactive, interventionist response in which agencies take responsibility for making an offer of support, provided this is done safely, rather than waiting for the woman to come forward. The advantages of the proactive response in the view of survivors are that:

- someone other than the woman takes responsibility for naming the violence;
- the first contact can be one in which belief is established very quickly;
- women can be invited into a support network at a much earlier point than may otherwise happpen;
- even where support is not taken up, the possibility of it has been registered, and future access might be made easier as a result (Burton et al., 1998).

Other major improvements which have been called for (notably in WAFE, 1998b, on the basis of an accumulation of research through refuges and with refuge residents) include:

- making domestic violence a notifiable offence in terms of its seriousness and a top priority for policing;
- improving evidence collection so that prosecutions need not rely on victim statements alone;
- paying greater attention to the safety of women and children when deciding whether to release alleged perpetrators on bail;
- introducing specialist prosecutors within the Crown Prosecution Service with training and experience of domestic violence;
- reviewing charging standards to prevent routine downgrading and to evaluate differences in attitudes and awareness between an increasingly aware police service and the Crown Prosecution Service (still much criticised for failing to deal with violence against women appropriately) in order to achieve a more integrated response;
- moving to a rebuttable presumption that victims of domestic violence are 'vulnerable or intimidated witnesses';
- providing independent victim advocacy and support services;
- greatly improving facilities for victims and their children in court settings, with an emphasis on their safety;
- imposing stronger sanctions on perpetrators both on conviction and on any breach of a court order, for example, failure to comply with a condition to attend a perpetrators' programme;
- keeping victims informed about the release of perpetrators from custody and paying due attention to their safety;
- creating new offences to deal with those who harass or intimidate

residents of women's refuges and who, for financial gain, track down those who are fleeing domestic violence;

- requiring that domestic violence be included in community crime audits; and
- reviewing the homicide law in terms of gender anomalies within the use of certain defences (e.g. provocation).

Overall, survivors of domestic violence state that they need a comprehensive, prompt and effective response from the entire criminal justice system which is delivered in a sensitive way and in which support for the woman who has been abused is a consistent feature. It is likely that more specialised but better integrated services will provide the way forward; for example, the new 'domestic violence court' in Leeds (White, 1999). The widespread provision, often through the activist shelter (refuge) movement, of victims' advocates in the USA to advocate on behalf of abused women and children has been noticeably absent in the UK context. Although limited to date to one experimental study, evaluation of the benefits American advocates have provided (in terms of reduced violence, improved quality of life and social support, and easier access to resources) has been positive (Sullivan and Bybee, 1999) and would be a useful adjunct to other improvements in the criminal justice system here. In this context, the outcome of the current replications of the Duluth model of a co-ordinated community response being carried out in the UK (as discussed in various chapters of this volume) are eagerly awaited. This work is currently most developed in the London Borough of Hammersmith and Fulham.

Partner support services

The likely expansion of perpetrators' programmes (see Mullender and Burton, this volume) raises issues about the kind of support for women that should be developed alongside them. As noted above, there are real advantages in offering a proactive service to women whose partners are going through a group. This is also an essential aspect of safety in that women need to know what they can realistically expect and to be warned if their partner misses sessions or ceases to attend. Furthermore, women's feedback has been shown to be the key ingredient in evaluating men's programmes (see Mullender and Burton, this volume). This constitutes the most accurate way of gauging whether or not the man is still violent or abusive and whether the quality of life has improved for his family.

All of this points in the direction of having partner support services in-built as an integral part of work with perpetrators and, indeed, this is the policy of Respect (2000). It will be important that any such development is closely linked to existing national networks of women's organisations if mixed messages and duplication of effort are to be avoided. Crucially, the first contact for many survivors with proactive helping services needs to be handled sensitively and appropriately, on the basis of long-standing relevant experience (Healey and Smith, 1998). Logically, then, the Women's Aid federations and other refuge providers in the UK need to be invited to play a central role in developing plans to meet the interests of female survivors, in conjunction with any national expansion of perpetrators' programmes, since they are the agencies that emerge with the best track record from research (see above). As the major children's charities, including child protection agencies, move into domestic violence work in areas well outside their traditional domain, for example, there must be a concern that survivors' commonly reported fear of having their children removed will make those experiencing domestic violence less rather than more likely to use such a project, so that again, joint work with the refuge movement and women's support projects will be vital to successful outcomes.

Public education campaigns

Survivors have been asked for their views on public education campaigns and the impact of these on help seeking has also been gauged. A number of the campaigns have been externally evaluated, particularly in Scotland, with evidence of increased take-up of emergency services provided by women's organisations as a result. In Edinburgh, 79% of the public commented favourably about the Zero Tolerance campaign (Kitzinger and Hunt, 1993; see also Cosgrove, 1996).

At the national level in England, the Home Office funded a multi-media campaign in 1994 with the slogan 'Don't Stand For It'. Although welcome, the campaign has been criticised by women's organisations for targeting victims rather than perpetrators (to take the initiative for change by reporting incidents), and for representing far less in terms of financial outlay than has been spent, for example, in Australia, Canada and even Papua New Guinea (Morley, undated).

A media campaign funded by the Scottish Office in the second half of 1994 was independently evaluated (Scottish Office Central Research Unit, 1995). Survivors consulted by the researchers felt it offered recognition and support but that particular care was needed in the choice of words and images if women were to identify with the campaign. Worryingly, one woman had evidence that the screenings could actually prompt an attack; her partner had been angry and had seen the advertisement as signifying women being defiant and fighting back. Victims also found that the imagery recalled memories of their own abuse. Giving out a freephone number that led, not to a helpline, but only to the sending of an information pack was regarded as of no help in an emergency and as dangerous if the pack were to be delivered to an address shared with the abuser. These responses emphasise the importance of involving domestic violence survivors in designing training and public education materials, such as posters and leaflets, so as to avoid conveying unintended messages. Encouragingly, figures for the year in which the campaign took place showed an abnormally large, 47% increase in referrals to the 14 Scottish local Women's Aid groups surveyed, though Scottish Women's Aid has argued that this was not accompanied by any increase in governmental funding of comprehensive services for women and children escaping violence and so placed great strain on their already stretched services. There is also the argument that, as in the 'Don't Stand for It' example, one of the aims of the campaign was to encourage women to have the confidence to report abuse - thus placing the onus on them rather than on perpetrators to take action. The campaign was not effective in encouraging perpetrators to change their behaviour, according to self-reports, and, although the men questioned were aware of the media publicity as part of a growing climate of disapproval, they reported that it had not led to their receiving direct adverse comment from others. A further conclusion of the independent evaluation was that, though aware of the campaign, the public was still left not knowing how to respond to domestic violence, for example when to call the police or other agencies, and that a further campaign would be needed to educate people on these issues.

Overall, the qualitative stage of the authors' own research suggests that survivors are aware of a far higher level of publicity about domestic violence these days in the media and in public places such as libraries and doctors' surgeries. However, they often set this against the negative attitudes they continue to encounter from some staff in all of the relevant agencies and the fact that, in their own lives, they still do not feel safe. Nor do they have confidence in the ability of any agency, other than a refuge, to ensure their safety. This constitutes the strongest of arguments for listening to the voices of survivors and taking a lead from them about the fundamental priorities in this field of work.

Consulting survivors

With the exception of women's refuge, support and advocacy services, it appears from anecdotal evidence and from the authors' research that few agencies consult systematically with domestic violence survivors about service provision and policy development (Hague et al, forthcoming). Nevertheless, a variety of current policy initiatives contain consultation requirements that can be used creatively to seek service users' views. These include Community

Care Plans, Children's Services Plans, Crime and Disorder and Community Safety Partnerships and Strategies, Best Value regimes, and so on. (For further discussion, see also below; and Hague, this volume.)

Multi-agency initiatives

The only national study to date in the UK of multi-agency initiatives as a response to domestic violence (see Hague, this volume) found that domestic violence forums and other inter-agency responses could sometimes take a creative approach to tackling domestic violence but that women experiencing violence were rarely involved. Only 5 out of 70 women survivors of domestic violence who were interviewed had heard of the multi-agency initiative in their area on any level, even where it was particularly active locally, and only two were involved in any way (Hague et al, 1996b:70). A very few good practice initiatives were reported by forums themselves. Survivors were often distressed to find that so much domestic violence work had been done in their local area without their knowledge, for example:

> How do they know what to do if they don't ask women in the situation? It doesn't make sense, does it? It's stupid if they go and set up things without women knowing about it and without asking women what they need, doesn't make sense to me. (Woman interviewee)

A perhaps surprising research finding was that hardly any of the women interviewed who were living in refuges which were actively participating in the local domestic violence forum reported that they knew about the forum in any of the study areas. This confirms the point that, while the presence of a refuge group will usually ensure that abused women's views are represented, this should not be assumed by agencies to meet direct user consultation criteria without a strategic and practical approach to opening up appropriate channels.

Some of the ideas which women survivors themselves suggested to the research team (by no means a comprehensive list) included:

- listening to women;
- questionnaires on the effectiveness of forums and services;
- snappy slogans and campaigns;
- more publicity and public awareness campaigns;
- more involvement of abused women in worker training sessions and in domestic violence training overall;
- more participation of abused women in new services established by forums;
- the setting up of a local domestic violence ombudsperson post in the community;

- a principled avoiding of the exploitation or 'using' of women participants;
- adequate compensation for time spent on consultation and other forms of participation, plus expenses;
- using refuges as a 'conduit' for passing information between survivors and multi-agency initiatives.

There is no single way forward in improving women's representation and, clearly, many different views are held. The specific means adopted will depend on local circumstances, but overall guidelines and good practice strategies have been shown to be needed (Hague et al, 1996b; Hague and Malos, 1996). Findings from the present authors' research indicate that, while 80% of forums subscribe to concepts of empowerment and service user involvement, few have ideas on how to go about it in terms of structures or working practices (Hague et al, forthcoming). The study addressed possible ways forward by gathering case studies and interviewing survivors and professionals in more depth. Suggestions and best practice examples included:

- survivor forums or advisory groups. These can advise and monitor the work of the forum or of agencies. There are equality issues to be addressed in terms of who is accountable to whom and for what. A further important issue is the provision of support, training, preparation, expenses and facilities (e.g. accessible venues, childcare) and payment or some other form of compensation for the work done;
- the principled (as opposed to ad hoc) use of Women's Aid and other refuge groups to represent the voices of women service users and to relay information between survivor groups and forums. This needs to be done as a strategic and agreed part of refuge work in a regular and systematised way, not informally or unofficially. Difficulties include the overwork and lack of time for such activities faced by refuge groups, and the fact that women residents or ex-residents may not be in a life position where they feel able to make such contributions, owing to the personal crises which they may be facing;
- the use of existing consultative mechanisms, e.g. Crime and Disorder Audits, Community Care Plans, Supporting People initiatives, and so on, in order to collect and respond to abused women's and children's views;
- regular focus groups of abused women, supported and funded, which examine the work of the local domestic violence forum;
- other consultation mechanisms of various types between forums/ agencies and survivors. For example, forum chairs or co-ordinators may attend meetings with women's support groups; special one-off consultation meetings can be held, and so on;

- questionnaires, exit questionnaires after service use, user surveys and other evaluative mechanisms;
- informal consultation and involvement;
- the principled involvement of women from different minority ethnic communities who have experienced domestic violence;
- the principled involvement of other equality groups including lesbians, disabled women and women of different ages;
- strategies for consulting children who have lived with domestic violence, if possible in confidence and with safeguards in place to to ensure an ethical, sensitive approach.

All these suggestions, and others that may emerge subsequently, would apply equally to forums and to individual agencies. They should be read in conjunction with the general lessons derived from listening to women, as reviewed in this chapter.

Professionals who are survivors

A footnote to all the above discussions is that many domestic violence survivors participate, as employees of agencies or on inter-agency forums, in domestic violence work as professionals. A complex range of factors affects whether or not individuals in this situation disclose their own personal experiences. Certainly, although they are present (on forums, for example) to represent their agency and not to be the voice of survivors or survivors' groups, their personal involvement in the issue is likely to add to the depth and richness of understanding and awareness. It is important that national policy should acknowledge and foster this profound, but unseen, contribution, and that employing agencies should not distrust or penalise staff who do disclose past abuse.

Costs

In a pioneering, multi-methodological study, Stanko et al (1998) estimated the costs to key public services dealing with domestic violence in a single London Borough as in excess of £5 million in 1996 and possibly as high as £7.5 million if the full range of relevant services were to be included. It was further estimated that the cost of 'providing advice, support and assistance for those facing domestic violence in Greater London' (p.7) was £278 million a year.

Nor are these estimates comprehensive. They do not include criminal justice system involvement with perpetrators nor the wider costs to the economy in terms of social security expenditure or working time lost. In Mooney's (1994) North London prevalence study, 19% of those who had experienced violence in the preceding year had had to take time off work. The costs to family and friends approached by victims for help, who may themselves be victimised or made ill by the stress, are likewise not included.

An interesting issue arising from the methodology of the Stanko et al study is that very few agencies were able to cost their own service provision to domestic violence survivors or even to estimate the number dealt with in any stated period. Not only is domestic violence frequently a hidden problem but, even when victims do ask for help, agencies other than specialist women's projects are typically bad at naming and recording it. Social services departments, for example, have been criticised for masking domestic violence behind vague terms such as 'marital problems' and for failing to collect relevant statistics at the point of referral (Mullender, 1996). Alongside some tangible improvements and changes in attitudes in recent years, this chapter has catalogued failures by doctors to ask the right questions, by police to record crimes committed in the home, by the CPS to prosecute perpetrators, and so on. All of these practices keep domestic violence submerged in often ineffectual, yet still expensive, non-responses to women's increasingly desperate attempts to make themselves and their children safe. Stanko et al (1998:8) sum this up by reporting domestic violence as often a 'background feature' of the lives of troubled children, homeless women, and so on. Only when painstaking scholarship reveals the details does it become possible to begin quantifying both the levels of demand and the cost of agency responses.

The one major exception to the above is Women's Aid, both because it can usually give an immediate account of the number of women and children experiencing domestic violence who have been helped in any one year and also because its work on domestic violence is positively evaluated by its service users.

The starting point for costing services in all other agencies is to monitor the proportion of new referrals and existing caseloads which involves domestic violence, broken down by ethnicity and other factors relevant to quality standards (James-Hanman, 1995). Once this begins to raise awareness, a key factor in cost effectiveness might be inter-agency integration both at policy level and between front line staff. A policy framework, established with the assistance of appropriate inter-agency bodies and forums and accompanied by policies and good practice guidelines within each participating agency, is essential in avoiding duplication, gaps in services and 'reinventing the wheel' (Hague, Malos and Dear, 1996b; Humphreys et al, 2001). Within this, agencies will need to decide whether it is most efficient to employ or designate specialist staff or to spread appropriate responses more thinly. In-house experts can certainly improve the service to survivors, but their presence does not obviate the need to offer comprehensive training to all front line staff. Such training is needed not only because these staff will be required to make appropriate referrals but also because domestic violence will remain present in workloads right across social services, housing, health, criminal justice, and so on - often in hidden forms such as mental ill-health, nuisance to neighbours, road traffic accidents, and the like.

Agencies which want to attempt an early costing of their current involvement in domestic violence-related work can apply the Stanko et al (1998) prevalence formula and its associated cost estimates. It should be noted, however, that this provides only a sense of what is currently being spent, not of what it would cost to provide a service which would meet either the needs or the aspirations of survivors once the actual problem of domestic violence began to be comprehensively charted. In other words, a hidden problem frequently attracts inappropriate responses which may be more costly than effective help, because they miss the point, or less expensive (in purely monetary terms) because they choose to ignore it. There is a whole fresh area of research to be carried out on comparing the costs of effective and ineffective responses and survivors' views of these responses. A related possibility would be the conducting of a cost-efficiency evaluation which compared needs-led responses suggested by survivors with resource-led ones.

One important point to note, however, is that 'success' in this context in the criminal justice system would be measured by an increase, not a decrease, in the crime statistics - the opposite of what is normally sought in crime prevention. This is because the present crime statistics do not constitute a baseline from which to measure any future reduction in incidence that might be achieved (see Mullender and Burton, this volume). Unlike the victims of car theft or burglary, around 40-45% of women have never told anyone about the violence they are experiencing (McGibbon et al, 1989; Mooney, 1994); they also wait an average of 2.5 years before seeking help (Dominy and Radford, 1996). If more women start to feel able to report incidents to the police, and to do so earlier and more frequently in the expectation that something effective will be done, and if this leads to a higher rate of arrests, prosecutions and convictions, then this will be a measure of real progress but it will have major cost implications. Any savings which may result from improved deterrence or reform of perpetrators, which are in any case by no means guaranteed (see Mullender and Burton, this volume), will take some years to become apparent.

Investment in this context will need, then, to be based on the ethical argument (Gondolf, 1997) that it is the expressed wish of survivors and of entire communities that action be taken against domestic violence, as part of a 'Best Value' rather than a cost-cutting approach. It is, after all, exceedingly poor value to go on pouring money into a problem we are not even properly naming, let alone tackling. Cost effectiveness arguments can easily be sustained, in fact, by adding together all existing public expenditure on domestic violence-related work, as Stanko et al (1998a) have done for one local government area. This issue (like many others that revolve around inequalities - health inequalities and social exclusion being other examples) requires a 'joined-up' policy approach. Costing the involvement of any one agency or sector creates a false impression since 'doing nothing' may at first glance look cheaper. However, it is the cost to the society and the nation as a whole which must be balanced, both in sheer economics and in terms of the human suffering involved (which public opinion has clearly begun to show will no longer be tolerated).

If early intervention can be shown to work, then it may be cheaper at one level, because the impact of the violence will be less severe in any individual case, but more expensive at another because so many more cases will fall into the net. Early intervention is likely to be the only way forward, however, because domestic violence becomes intractable once the pattern is established. Relevant policies would include:

- referring a man to a perpetrators' programme when he first breaches an injunction rather than waiting for him to work his way up the criminal justice tariff;
- picking up on victims' requests for help the first time they confide in a doctor, social worker or housing official; and
- taking a proactive approach through policing and health visiting when these professionals first see what is going on in the home.

These are all examples of ways in which action might begin to be taken sooner.

Recommendations

Survivors' views of services and improvements needed

Though by no means a comprehensive list, what has consistently emerged from the expression of survivors' views in research, service evaluation and self-generated materials is the need for:

- women and children's safety as the paramount consideration;
- a sympathetic and believing approach;
- an early response (recognising that, by the time an agency learns of the abuse, it is likely to be well established);
- a proactive approach - asking pertinent questions in confidence, making it clear that help is available, not waiting for an abused woman to have

to take the dangerous step of disclosing before she even knows what reception she will get;
- prompt, effective, co-ordinated action;
- respect and sensitivity;
- an anti-racist, anti-oppressive approach appropriate to the needs of diverse communities;
- a non-judgmental attitude, including where a woman has left and returned on earlier occasions;
- a thorough understanding of confidentiality, within a potentially life-and-death context;
- resources for support groups and for involvement in inter-agency forums;
- a national funding strategy for funding refuges and advocacy services;
- sensitive mechanisms for user accountability;
- domestic violence training for all gatekeepers and front line staff;

How survivors' views can be represented

It is not possible to offer either a comprehensive or a prescriptive list of ways to involve abused women more actively. Different approaches work in different local circumstances but the following general suggestions emerge from work reviewed above:

- general written guidelines on how to involve survivors are helpful;
- sometimes, informal methods may be better than bureaucratic ones provided that they are still accorded weight and are part of agreed decision-making with an agreed and effective way to influence policy;
- the refuge movement and the women's voluntary sector more generally need to have a key voice, but structured, agreed methods are also needed for them to be able to consult women and to act as a conduit for information exchange and decision-making;
- survivors' forums/survivors' advisory groups can monitor and advise agencies although this is a complicated issue and good practice is only just commencing;
- women's support groups constitute an essential underpinning for all other work;
- support and training are needed to enable survivors to be involved and consulted;
- payment for time spent in such activities, together with childcare costs and other expenses, translation and interpretation fees, and accessible venues are all part of making survivors' participation real;
- isolated survivor involvement (for example, where one survivor attends an inter-agency forum of professionals) does not work well;

- focus groups, consultation meetings and so on can be routinely introduced with beneficial effects;
- existing legislation and policies that demand user consultation, such as Best Value regimes and community safety audits, can provide a useful framework where used sensitively and in a way which is more than cosmetic;
- performance indicators can be developed to include consultation with survivors.

Conclusion

The single most important performance measure for any agency or practitioner to apply in working with domestic violence is: 'Will my intervention leave this woman and her children in greater safety or in greater danger?' The issue of giving survivors a voice, both individually and collectively, revolves around the fact that they usually apply safety as their overarching criterion and that they are likely to be able to make judgements about it more knowledgeably and skilfully than professionals alone. They also ask the searching questions about system failures - why the victim was not adequately protected, why the perpetrator was not held accountable, why effective services were not provided - that help domestic violence forums and other inter-agency responses to become more than talking shops and assist individual agencies to make radical improvements in their services. Survivors report continuing gaps in provision that leave them vulnerable and unsafe. It is surely the case that lives may be saved by listening to them.

Meeting the needs of children

Audrey Mullender

This chapter is based on a literature review and research findings both from a recent study in the ESRC Children 5-16 Programme in and from a mapping project of all relevant intervention with children in the UK, funded by the Joseph Rowntree Foundation. Children who live with domestic violence typically know it is going on and are now considered likely to be affected themselves by the fear, distress and disruption to their lives, even when they are not directly abused. Many men who abuse women do also threaten and abuse children, however, with up to two-thirds of the cases on Child Protection Registers demonstrating this overlap. Contact visits and handover meetings with abusive fathers raise particular concerns for the safety both of women and children. Children are not passive victims. They have varying degrees of personal resilience and a wide variety of coping strategies to draw upon. In a sensitive research environment they can talk about their perceptions and experiences of domestic violence and their views could usefully inform a more coherent inter-agency approach. At present, too much spending is locked into an investigative approach which offers no protection to women, leaves many children at risk, and draws resources away from family support and direct work with children. The only comprehensive attention to the needs of children is in refuges, where childwork provision is chronically under-resourced. There is every argument for mainstreaming the service responses that can help mothers keep children safe, challenge perpetrators to be non-violent partners and parents, work with children to overcome negative experiences, and influence the next generation to regard violence as wrong and themselves as able to work towards ending it.

Introduction and background

The impact on children of living with domestic violence

The majority of children are aware if their mother is being abused, often more so than their parents realise (NCH Action for Children, 1994), seeing or hearing much of what takes place because they are present or nearby (Hughes, 1992).

Children who live with domestic violence are now considered likely to be affected themselves, even when they are not directly abused. One Canadian study found 2.5 times the rate of behavioural and psychological problems in children who had lived with domestic violence as against other children (Wolfe et al, 1986). The precise way in which an individual child will react depends on factors that include age, personality and family circumstances. Infants are only able to indicate their distress through their health or development, while older children and young people may display a wide variety of problems in their emotional, psychological or social functioning, and/or their behaviour or adjustment at home or at school. It is important not to forget that children also have varying degrees of personal resilience and protective factors in their lives, and that many recover from earlier adverse effects once they feel safe (Wolfe et al, 1986). Others, though, may display longer-term impacts on self-esteem, social adjustment or mood (summary in Edleson, 1999a), though the notion of intergenerational transmission remains highly controversial (Morley and Mullender, 1994a and Walby, this volume).

The context and circumstances engendered by the violence may also have an impact on children. Their lives may be disrupted by being forced to leave home, sometimes repeatedly, with the consequent impact on schooling, friendships and contact with wider family networks (Mullender et al, forthcoming). Children's needs may be unavoidably neglected because their mother is rendered unable to attend to them or because the perpetrator deliberately prevents her from doing so (Wolfe et al, 1986). Black and other minority ethnic children, including Asian children (Imam, 1994) and Gypsy and Traveller children (Van Cleemput et al, undated), may be forced to leave a supportive and protective local community and may face discriminatory attitudes from agencies from which they and their mothers seek help (Mama, 1996). They may also be at risk of being abducted overseas by the perpetrator (Saunders, H., 1998).

Domestic violence and child abuse

Many men who abuse women also abuse children, with estimates of the overlap for physical abuse in the range of 30 to 60 per cent (Edleson,

1999b). A UK-based study found that at least a third of children on the Child Protection Register in one London Borough had mothers who were known to be being abused (London Borough of Hackney, 1993). This degree of overlap may double when research expertise is involved in looking for it (Farmer and Owen, 1995; Hester and Pearson, 1998). There is also evidence to suggest a substantial overlap between child sexual abuse and domestic violence; in just under half the cases studied by Goddard and Hiller (1993) in Australia, for example. Risks to unborn children are well established, with violence frequently commencing or escalating during pregnancy (Mezey, 1997; see chapter by Walby and Myhill for a discussion of the statistics). Stanko et al (1998) found 2 per cent of women respondents in a general practice waiting-room survey reporting a miscarriage that they considered attributable to domestic violence.

It is thought that the combination of direct and indirect abuse may be particularly harmful for children (Edleson, 1999a) and also most dangerous. Enquiries into the deaths of children (O'Hara, 1994) and into child protection practice (Farmer and Owen, 1995) suggest that violence towards women may coincide with their children being at the greatest risk. Both sources, together with a wider literature on the failure to engage men in child care work (Milner, 1993), indicate that child protection professionals lack skills in confronting male perpetrators in these situations.

Other direct dangers to children include threats from perpetrators to hurt or kill them in order to coerce the adult victim to meet his demands, or being forced to participate in abusing her (Pence and Paymar, 1990). Abused women may punish their children more harshly than normal in order to forestall a worse beating from an abusive man, or may lash out when 'at the end of their tether' (Mullender et al, forthcoming). Children can be at risk of accidental injury if they get in the way of an attack upon their mother or try to protect or help her (Dobash and Dobash, 1984).

There is official acknowledgement in the revised *Working Together* (Department of Health et al, 1999) of the link between domestic violence and child abuse that was not present in the Children Act 1989. A consequent emphasis on effective inter-agency co-operation across these two fields of work, including between domestic violence forums and Area Child Protection Committees, has already begun to happen in practice in some parts of the country.

Child contact

Women and children have died or been seriously injured and children have been abducted as a result of contact visits (Hester et al, 1997; Saunders, H., 1998). In a 1997 survey of 54 Women's Aid refuges conducted by the Women's Aid Federation of England (WAFE) (reported in Saunders, H.,

1998), two-thirds reported cases of women being abused during handover and almost a third knew of children being physically or sexually abused during contact visits. In a sample of 53 women in England (Hester and Radford, 1996), all but three had been assaulted in the context of contact.

This has led to criticism of the judicial system. In the WAFE survey mentioned above, 14% of the refuges surveyed had experienced incidents where the contact order revealed the address of the refuge, thus endangering all the residents. In the Hester and Radford study which compared a Danish and English sample, two-fifths of the English sample of women (n=53) said their children had previously been abused, yet contact had been granted, with little provision for the safety of the children. In 1997/98, in only three per cent of County Court cases was contact refused; solicitors may advise against even attempting to oppose it because of courts' presumption that it is in the best interests of the child (Saunders, H., 1998). Mothers who have failed to comply with a contact order, even when in fear of their own or their children's safety, have been found to be in contempt of court. Yet contact takes place during one of the most dangerous phases in the pattern of domestic violence. A third of women killed by male partners have already separated (Edwards, 1989a) and the danger may intensify during attempts to end the relationship (Wilson and Daly, 1992).

The shortcomings in current policy and practice

In many ways, policy and practice regarding children leave much to be desired. The imbalance between child protection and family support (Department of Health, 1995) is as much in evidence here as in other areas of childcare practice. One outcome of this is that the forms of intervention which are being routinely offered in some parts of Canada, the US and Australia to assist children in overcoming their experiences are being only patchily developed in the UK. These have been established almost entirely through the isolated efforts of an interested voluntary sector, as demonstrated by the emerging findings of a UK mapping project (see below). There are no routine protocols or assessments to ascertain whether children using child welfare, child protection or child health services are living with domestic violence. The Children Act 1989 does not mention domestic violence and proceedings involving children have not traditionally recognised it as an issue, thus leaving many women and children in danger, including through contact visits. At the more general level, opportunities to teach children and young people that violence is wrong and what to do about it are only now beginning to be taken up, again in an entirely *ad hoc* way.

At a time when social scientists are beginning to listen to children as never before (e.g. through the recent Economic and Social Research Council

'Children 5-16 Programme'; see Hallett and Prout, forthcoming, for some of the key studies), domestic violence researchers are finding that children are able to talk about their perceptions and experiences. This is providing the study is designed sensitively and appropriately (McGee, 2000; Mullender et al, forthcoming). The views of children who have lived with domestic violence could inform a more coherent inter-agency approach, responsive to the wishes and fears of children and young people and informed by their perspectives and understandings.

Structure and sources of this chapter

The chapter will focus on possible responses within three broad categories:

- primary prevention (working to prevent domestic abuse from happening at all), e.g. work in schools and youth settings to educate children and young people about domestic violence;
- secondary prevention (stopping it short as soon as any agency learns it is happening and preventing its recurrence), e.g. intervention by statutory and voluntary agencies in situations of domestic violence in ways that have relevance for children;
- tertiary prevention (reducing the harm to those who have already experienced it), e.g. direct work with children and young people, chiefly in groups but also through counselling and other one-to-one work.

Recommendations will be offered on constructive ways forward.

The chief sources of relevant information have been a literature review (updating those already published in Mullender and Morley, 1994; and Mullender and Humphreys, 1998) and the gathering of policy and practice examples from the UK and overseas. It also draws on the findings from a mapping project of all relevant intervention with children in the UK, funded by the Joseph Rowntree Foundation and conducted at the Universities of Warwick and Bristol (Humphreys et al, 2000), and to some extent on an ESRC-funded study 'Children's Needs, Coping Strategies and Understandings of Women Abuse (ESCR Award ref no. L129251037).

Primary prevention

There is fascinating scope for primary prevention with children and young people through work in schools and youth settings to prevent young men from commencing a pattern of domestic violence and to help young women learn that it need not be tolerated in relationships.

Education

There is considerable potential for work in schools on domestic violence, and on non-violence more generally, which is only just beginning to be tapped. Education can raise levels of awareness about domestic violence and help children and young people both to seek and offer help appropriately. It is one of the very few contexts in which genuine primary prevention can be undertaken, helping young people to respect themselves and one another sufficiently to develop non-abusive relationships.

The need for such work has already been amply demonstrated by studies showing that negative attitudes develop early. A survey of 2,039 young people aged 14 to 21 in Scotland and the North West of England revealed that almost half the young men surveyed and a third of the young women thought there could be circumstances in which it would be acceptable for a man to hit a female partner (Burton and Kitzinger, 1998). One in five young men also considered it acceptable for a man to force his wife to have sex. One in eight considered 'nagging' a justification for violence, e.g. 'Some women just need a slap to the jaw and put into the bedroom to calm down' (p.1). The vast majority of the young men and a small majority of the young women thought women were 'often' or 'sometimes' to blame for domestic violence.

In a recently completed ESRC-funded project (Mullender et al, forthcoming) in the Children 5-16 Programme, age-related questionnaires on what they knew and thought about domestic violence were completed by 1,395 children in primary and secondary schools in three areas of England. This also revealed a gendered and worrying pattern. At all ages, boys were less clear than girls as to who was at fault and more likely to excuse the perpetrator. Boys' attitudes began to diverge markedly from girls at 13-14 years of age and continued to move apart thereafter. Only 56% of 15-16 year old boys as against 78% of girls of this age saw the father as being more responsible for his own violence than the mother in a particular scenario described in the questionnaire. Over three-quarters of 11-12 year old boys thought that women got hit if they made men angry, with more boys than girls at all ages believing that some women deserve to be hit.

Young people do want to learn more about domestic violence. Focus group members in the Burton and Kitzinger (1998) research valued the opportunity to discuss the issues during the research process and welcomed the idea of a campaign aimed at young people based around participative discussion and the expression of opinions, not just being told that violence was wrong. Peer and media pressure, parent and teacher attitudes were all seen by them as potentially part of the problem and thus part of what would need to be considered. In the Mullender et al (forthcoming) study, the vast majority of secondary children and just over half at primary age wanted lessons on domestic violence in school covering both why it happens and what they could do about it. In McGee's (2000) qualitative study for the NSPCC of children who had lived with violence, children said that they particularly wanted an opportunity to talk with other children about their experiences of living with domestic violence. They also wanted their friends and teachers to understand when they did so, which lends further support to the development of work in schools.

Children and young people do see themselves as potential social actors in situations of violence. Asked to suggest in the Mullender et al (forthcoming) research what a young character in a specific situation should do about violence at home, three quarters of all children thought the child concerned should do something practical, most often calling the police or telling someone. This, in addition to preferred learning styles (see above), is a reason why teaching on the subject should take a participative approach, including involving children and young people in developing their own learning materials.

Educational and background materials are already available. Islington's *STOP* pack, sub-titled *Schools Take On Preventing Domestic Violence* (London Borough of Islington, 1995), is perhaps the best known. Its effectiveness in changing attitudes and increasing awareness has not been evaluated. *Guidance for Schools*, produced in Leeds (Leeds Education and Leeds Inter-Agency Project, not dated), is aimed at educators who wish to begin thinking about the issues. Work extensively developed in Ontario, Canada, links gendered thinking about domestic violence into broader learning about mutual respect, including between adults and children, and peer-based conflict resolution skills (Hague et al, 2001). In the UK, a comprehensive focus on bullying could potentially be integrated with a wider anti-violence curriculum, (including anti-racism), provided that the substantive gendered content on domestic/sexual violence does not become lost within this. Canadian approaches have also shown that a whole school, whole community approach can be particularly fruitful. This should involve parents, local media, community arts groups, school governors in a range of events and in developing relevant teaching materials for every subject on the curriculum. This has been found to be more successful than confining learning to a single slot within the curriculum (Mullender, 1994b). Training and preparation for staff must, of course, precede any work with pupils. It is also important to have active links in place with education, social services and local women's refuge and outreach organisations. This is because the work may well lead to disclosures from children currently living with both direct and indirect abuse and to a heightened awareness of problems affecting both parents and staff members. All work within the school curriculum needs to be based on the recognition both that domestic violence is widespread and that it is a crime and no longer socially tolerated.

Youth Services

As was illustrated above in respect of schools, there is a great deal that can be done to raise young people's awareness of domestic violence so that they can become a resource to one another in the present and think about non-violent relationships in the future. Fife offers a rare example in the UK of extensive work with young people on domestic violence. There, a youth strategy gained local authority funding under the auspices of the UN Declaration on the Rights of the Child which, under Article 12, accords children and young people the right to be heard on issues which affect them.

In Fife, those who mounted it considered the youth strategy one of the most successful aspects of the wider Zero Tolerance campaign (Reid-Howie Associates, 1996). The strategy's use of peer education theatre (a play developed in further education toured schools and community centres) has been evaluated by the campaign co-ordinator. Two thousand young people saw the play, with just under one in ten of these (172) opting to complete an evaluation sheet. The vast majority of respondents (99.4%) had found the play interesting; detailed comments showed that young people felt they had gained new information in a way that had utilised drama and humour to convey a serious message. Most (91.8%) felt the content was relevant to young people in their region, for example because violence could happen to anyone. Importantly (and in contrast with public feedback on the Scottish Office campaign aimed at adults; see Mullender and Hague, this volume), most of these young respondents said they had learned to know what to do and where to seek help if they found themselves in a similar situation to that portrayed. The majority (88%) felt that school was the best place to explore the issues, other suggestions included special projects or a conference. Of those completing the evaluation forms, 95% wanted to see Zero Tolerance as part of the school curriculum.

A clear majority (84.3%) had found the youth information pack distributed in conjunction with the play useful, notably in listing sources of help such as Women's Aid and conveying knowledge about young people's rights. Crossing over into public education work more generally, 67.4% of respondents had seen Zero Tolerance posters or information in the area, mainly in school and on buses (and widely beyond that but with no particular pattern). Using take-up as another measure of effectiveness, the theatre production, the youth conference and promotional rock concert were all heavily subscribed and, between them, reached thousands of young people. Evaluation forms distributed at the youth conference once again drew a 95% view that Zero Tolerance should form part of the school curriculum.

Other areas of the country are increasingly involving young people in Zero Tolerance initiatives, including a recent 'Respect' campaign in Scotland.

Secondary prevention

Secondary prevention in this context refers to stopping the domestic violence as soon as any agency learns that it is happening and preventing its repeat against the same or another victim. This category currently covers the bulk of current services, both in the public and voluntary sectors, and includes:

- all emergency and outreach provision for women and children;
- health and welfare services for victims and survivors; and
- criminal and civil justice responses to perpetrators.

Clearly, there is a need for effective multi-agency work in co-ordinating these responses, particularly where they impact on children. Some domestic violence forums have established children's sub-committees of interested professionals to offer advice and spearhead positive developments.

All agencies that work with domestic violence will find children living in households where there is domestic violence occurring and all have a legal or moral responsibility to help make the situation safe for those who are being abused, whether directly and/or indirectly. Contemporary 'wisdom' tends to be based on the assumption that the adult victim of severe and persistent violence, usually the woman, should leave and that, where there are children, it is her responsibility to protect them as well. The complex and interrelated reasons that keep women in a relationship with a violent man include child-related issues. For example, the perpetrator is often the man with whom the woman has borne, or raised, children. In a family centre survey carried out by NCH Action for Children (1994), women did not want to leave the family home (58%) or to upset the children by uprooting them (54%). For disabled children with a complicated network of educational and care services, such a move can be particularly disruptive. Since the advent of increased local autonomy of schools it has become harder for all children known to have problems to obtain places in new schools (Mullender et al, 1998), and women may be especially resistant to disrupting their children's education. Services need to work with an understanding that most women strive to give the best to their children, whatever is happening to themselves. In the end, it is quite often the realisation that living with violence is having a detrimental effect on the children, or that one or more children is being directly threatened or abused, that prompts women to leave (NCH Action for Children, 1994).

Child protection

Secondary prevention of the harm to children of living with domestic violence is often linked with a child protection role for the relevant agencies. The 'message from research' (Department of Health, 1995) that much investigative work does not lead to intervention, let alone to helping families, is particularly apposite here in that it can mean that women and children are left in danger (Farmer and Owen, 1995).

A great deal of domestic violence awareness-raising training has gone on amongst child protection professionals in recent years, for example on the overlaps between domestic violence and child abuse, noted above, and the impact on children of living with domestic violence. The channelling of this awareness into pre-existing child protection frameworks, however, has sometimes meant that, particularly in the public sector, domestic violence has constituted a new reason for policing families by imposing a blanket category of 'emotional abuse'. This may lead to an automatic child protection referral where children are found to be living with domestic violence (see Parkinson and Humphreys, 1998) and not a new platform for offering help. Unfocused thinking about 'dangerous families' or 'marital violence' fails to hold abusive men responsible for their own actions so is not only unhelpful but may actually increase the danger to abused women and children. Too often, case conferences (Humphreys, 1997) and the failure by involved professionals to challenge the behaviour of the male perpetrator who is presenting the danger (Farmer and Owen, 1995) mean that the woman is left to be the buffer against his violence without support or help. She may then be blamed and controlled because she is not considered to be protecting her children from him at the same time as being forced, by the inadequacy of service interventions, to continue living in fear. This view is further supported by findings from a project on accountability to women (see Mullender and Hague, this volume) which show that women interviewed in depth continue to talk about not being safe, despite being involved with a range of services. It would be more fruitful to classify children living with domestic violence as 'children in need' under s.17 of the Children Act 1989 and thus to open up access, both for the child concerned and for the non-abusing parent, to family support services. One refuge childworker, for example, has negotiated a route for direct referrals to the local family centre, instead of women having to trigger child protection concerns before they and their children can receive any attention from a hard-pressed social services department. A proportion of Children's Services Plans does now mention domestic violence, though by no means all and often in no great depth.

The addition to the Children Act 1989 (by Schedule 7 of the Family Law Act 1996) of exclusion orders under certain circumstances in emergency protection and interim care proceedings does offer one specific way of removing the danger that perpetrators present which may help in some situations. Unfortunately, it would appear that this opportunity is not currently being fully exploited, even in those situations where it can apply, with only isolated instances of its use to date (see Edwards on civil remedies, this volume). This could usefully be monitored in a more systematic way.

On a more positive note, there is evidence that the involvement of domestic violence experts in training and in decision-making can lead to more positive outcomes (e.g. Hester and Pearson, 1998). This is particularly the case where a holistic assessment is made of needs, and risks, and of protective factors that exist or can be introduced into the situation. Also, police services are increasingly recognising that they need to check on the safety of any children present when called to an incident of domestic violence. Some make an automatic referral to social services though, owing to a scarcity of resources, this sometimes leads to an unhelpful blanket response such as a routine letter to the home which could potentially place the woman and/or the children in greater danger. One important area for future attention could be cross-referencing between child abuse and domestic violence records by the police so that those officers are always aware of the potentially overlapping dangers (Browne and Hamilton, forthcoming).

Very little of the relevant child protection work has been evaluated, although there are studies which identify key gaps in practice and ways of filling these (Humphreys, 1997; Hester and Pearson, 1998). Studies of court welfare work (Hester et al, 1997) are also relevant for the light they throw on post-separation violence and the patchiness of professional recognition that cases should be screened for a history of violence before attempting joint meetings. On the basis of national monitoring of problems encountered by women escaping violence and their children, WAFE (1998b) has called for good practice guidelines to be drawn up for all court proceedings under the Children Act. These would be for use in all cases as it would not always be known when domestic violence has occurred. Particular points at issue include the need to ensure that:

- the safety of the parent who is to care for the child and that person's ability to lead a normal life are not endangered by any court order;
- seek and find orders under s.33 of the Family Law Act 1986 are not used in cases of domestic violence;

- guidance and training on domestic violence are provided for social workers; and
- separate representation and separate attendance are facilitated at meetings and case conferences, with a differentiation between the abusing and non-abusing parent in relevant professional practice.

Practice in court welfare and mediation has also been shown by Hester et al (1997) to be patchy, with a failure to screen all cases to ascertain whether a history of domestic violence might make joint meetings dangerous. WAFE (1998b) has called for the Children Act 1989 to be amended to include, where there is evidence of a history of violence, a rebuttable presumption of no contact until it can be shown to be safe for all parties. The law has already been amended in Australia, New Zealand and Northern Ireland. In the USA, a model statute of the National Council of Juvenile and Family Court Judges (1994, cited in Saunders, D., 1998) states that visitation (contact) should be subject to safety provisions for the child and the adult victim. These might include:

- use of a visitation centre;
- supervised handover;
- no overnight stays; and/or
- the requirement that the perpetrator successfully complete a treatment programme. (This might be a useful channel into such programmes; see Mullender and Burton, this volume.)

In England and Wales, the approach has been not to change the law, but to issue guidance (Advisory Board on Family Law, Children Act Sub-Committee, 2001), and to allow case law to establish precedent. A judgement by the Court of Appeal in four contact cases (*Re L, Re V, Re M* and *Re H*) was delivered in June 2000. It means that, in future, the conduct of both parties towards each other and towards the children, the effect on the children and residential parent, and the motivation of the parent seeking contact should all be considered in contact applications featuring allegations of domestic violence. This represents a belated judicial recognition of the impact on children of exposure to domestic violence in their household. There is no presumption against contact, but, in all these four cases, the resumption of direct contact was refused. In Northern Ireland, however, the law has been amended to include, in all cases where there is evidence of a history of violence, a rebuttable presumption of no contact until it can be shown to be safe for all parties. A comparative study to monitor and evaluate the impart of legislative change in the Province, as against guidance and case law in England and Wales, would be of particular interest.

Family support

Couple and family work with the perpetrator present, including mediation, is now widely considered inappropriate in situations of continuing abuse or intimidation (Mullender, 1996). Instead, each parent/partner should be worked with separately where violence is a factor. Systemic theories on 'dysfunctional' (or dangerous, or violent) families are having to be replaced by an understanding of the abuse of power and control and of the need for perpetrators alone to take responsibility for this, while women have quite separate practical and emotional support needs.

'Family work' also needs to be reconfigured, and to be thought of in terms of the need for more support services for women and children who are living with domestic violence, or where women are now heading families alone as a result of abuse. Family support and children's services are needed which can empower women and children to survive and recover from abuse, and to assist non-abusing parents to continue parenting in safety. Black and minority ethnic families need services that engage with them appropriately and accessibly, respecting the diversity and strengths of black family life and providing safe and supportive environments for children (Butt and Box, 1998). The health, welfare and educational needs of disabled children and of children with disabled carers must be met in ways that also ensure that they are safe.

Independent services for abused women and children

For women experiencing domestic violence, often the greatest fear about seeking help is that their children will be removed (NCH Action for Children, 1994). This inevitably means that many will be reluctant to approach social services or other child protection agencies. Women who are in touch with social services have complained of a lack of support (McGee, 2000).

For these reasons, it is important that local authorities provide adequate funding for independent refuge projects, particularly for the work they do with children. Children's workers in refuges are seriously under-resourced; an NCVCCO (National Council for Voluntary Child Care Organisations) evaluation (Ball, 1990) called for local government to fund one children's worker for every six adult beds available in women's refuges yet many refuges still rely on voluntary help or, at best, unstable and inadequate funding (Hague et al, 1996). These practitioners are in direct touch with a large number of children who have lived with domestic violence. In 1996/97, refuges affiliated to the Women's Aid Federation of England admitted approximately 32,000 children (and approaching 23,000 women). This is a vital national resource in meeting the needs of a highly vulnerable group.

Refuge projects also provide outreach and often advocacy services (see Kelly and Humphreys, this volume), not only for women and children while they are in the refuge, but also for many still living with the violence or who are trying to rebuild their lives elsewhere. Other voluntary organisations, particularly the major children's charities, are beginning to run valuable support services on a more localised basis (Humphreys et al, 2000) which have both a secondary and tertiary prevention function (see below). There is an urgent need for greater national recognition of such work and for it to be offered on a more comprehensive basis within an overall family support framework.

Work on parenting

Work with perpetrators

The contemporary recognition is that domestic violence is a crime and that the most effective response to it is arrest, prosecution and conviction of the perpetrator, followed by a programme of re-education (see Mullender and Burton, this volume). This can be linked to an expectation that perpetrators should learn to take their responsibilities seriously, in learning not only to be non-violent but also to act as effective parents. Mathews (1995) outlines a programme in use in the USA which aims to increase fathers' understanding of their children and of the effect of their own violent behaviour upon them, while also confronting the violence and developing new parenting skills. The spread of such groups has involved men being court-ordered to attend, either after or in parallel with a perpetrators' programme, often because they have used inappropriate force in punishing their children. Referrals may also come from child protection agencies for men to attend on a voluntary basis. Amongst the issues tackled are unrealistic expectations of children based on lack of knowledge of child development and effective discipline as against the exercise of control through punishment. Mathews describes men learning cognitive behavioural change skills to use with their children's undesirable behaviours which parallel the approach used with the men themselves in perpetrators' groups. The groups build on the men's feelings for their children and for family life in a way that Williams (1994b) has noted can be a particular motivator for black perpetrators. Mathews does not refer to any evaluation of the groupwork model in question although it grew out of more general parenting education which has been extensively studied. In the UK, the Probation Service perpetrators' group in Birmingham has recently introduced material offered by the Children's Society workers who run children's groups locally (see below). This is a valuable development, although care needs to be taken not to dilute both forms of re-education if attempting to cover them in the same group.

In the USA, in agencies where pro-arrest policies have inadvertently led to more women finding themselves in the court system after defending themselves against their abusers, some women have also found themselves mandated to attend parenting groups related to domestic violence. Observation by the author of one such group, and discussion with practitioners, revealed that they had very different content and process from groups for male perpetrators. Men tended to require coercion to attend, they resisted accepting the impact of their violence on their children, and were often ignorant of basic child development. Women attended willingly, they had often stayed in the violence for the sake of the children, and accepted more than their fair share of responsibility for their children's well-being. Their ex-partners had also subjected many to repeated court proceedings involving the children, often in a way that appeared intended to open up new opportunities to continue exerting control and intimidation.

Work with the non-abusing parent

In Canada, there are examples of groups that involve mothers and their children together and of separate, parallel groups that share the last couple of sessions. Bilinkoff (1995) offers a detailed account of work undertaken in the USA with mothers who have become the lone heads of households after separating from violent partners. Programmes concentrate on developing confidence and relevant skills in their new role, and positive family patterns. Topics covered include:

- restructuring the family with mother in charge;
- setting non-violent boundaries for children's behaviour;
- safe ways of talking together about what have been family secrets;
- disclosing other secrets (e.g. direct child abuse);
- comparing memories of traumatic events (of which children may know more than their parents think, yet may have an incomplete knowledge or understanding); and
- establishing a more open pattern of communication for the future.

They also cover finding non-violent alternatives in the extended family, taking a family-wide stand against violence, and seeing themselves as survivors across two or more generations with strengths that give them a choice of creating a non-violent future together. Mothers of children in children-only groups (see below) have sometimes said they would have welcomed more information about the group (Marshall et al, 1995) so it is useful that ways of involving mothers more fully continue to be explored.

Other services

Education

Living with domestic violence can affect children's education and ability to learn in numerous ways. Fear and distress may manifest themselves in psychological and behavioural problems. Some children may try to reduce the tension or to protect their mothers by staying home (which might explain absences from school) or, equally, might be reluctant to go home because they think their presence causes conflict. It is important to remember, too, that not every child will be affected educationally. For some, school may be the only safe or enjoyable place in an otherwise problematic life, while others may perform to very high standards imposed by controlling and punitive fathers.

There are a range of ways in which education authorities and individual schools can offer practical assistance to women and children, including those forced to leave situations of domestic violence. Prompt acceptance into a new school and help with obtaining the required school uniform are concrete examples, while a designated refuge liaison officer in the local education authority can undertake wider-scale awareness-raising and advocacy work. Most fundamentally, it is important not to stigmatise or judge children because of their home circumstances (McGee, 2000) and to ensure that key staff can work sensitively with the relevant information about particular pupils, while working within strict observance of confidentiality.

Health

Health professionals who need raised awareness about domestic violence and its effects on women and children include:

- GPs and health visitors;
- school nurses;
- obstetricians, gynaecologists and midwives; and
- health promotion staff.

However, it is also important to recognise that injuries and adverse effects on physical or mental health may be presented in any health care setting. All relevant multi-agency forums need effective and co-ordinated health representation when looking at child protection, child welfare and family support. The Department of Health (1996) has advised, for example, that there is a health service role in assisting local authorities to identify children in need, a category which has been argued to include children living with domestic violence (Mullender and Morley, 1994).

Social exclusion

Some young people leave home and live on the streets in preference to remaining in a situation of domestic violence (Taylor-Browne, forthcoming) or where both they and their mothers are being abused. Others find their schooling disrupted by the impact of the abuse on their physical or emotional well-being or by constant moves; this may lead to truancy, school exclusion or lack of educational achievement. Those involved in dealing with any of these problems require an awareness of domestic violence, as well as of direct child abuse (James-Hanman, 1998).

Tertiary prevention

Tertiary prevention consists in reducing the harm to those who have lived with domestic violence by helping them to overcome and make sense of their experiences. Direct work with children can include groupwork, counselling and other one-to-one work. (See Humphreys et al, 2000, for examples.)

There is still an acute shortage in the UK of direct services for children who have lived with abuse. Those who try to refer children for help are frequently confronted with either a lack of services in particular areas or long waiting lists. The main national expertise is centred in refuges amongst Women's Aid childworkers. Were family support services to come more to the fore, they would provide a community-based framework within which such work could be undertaken more comprehensively than is currently the case.

Childwork in refuges

Childworkers in refuges provide advocacy and support for children, as well as organising workshops, children's meetings and other events that build on children's own perceptions and understandings. A study of childwork in refuges completed by the author and others (Hague et al, 1996; Mullender et al, 1998) evaluated it positively.

The study found many refuge childworkers to be offering what they called 'one-to-one work', that is, structured time with individual children when they can talk about whatever is on their mind. Although both children and their mothers largely welcomed this opportunity, a few had concerns that children should not be seen as 'disturbed' just because they had lived with domestic violence. Perhaps a distinction needs to be drawn between acknowledging children's needs, on the one hand, and pathologising them, on the other. Childworkers stressed that they were not qualified counsellors and would help a mother seek specialist help elsewhere for any child who appeared particularly disturbed. On the other hand, refuge workers have always been trusted by women and children with disclosures of child abuse, including child sexual abuse, pre-dating the recognition by other agencies of child protection issues and today's more powerful medical and legal discourses. Refuges continue to be a safe place where children may find themselves able to talk about their abuse for the first time. One refuge worker (Mullender et al, 1998) was being approached so often for advice by local social workers, that she eventually worked with them, and with the local branch of a national children's charity, to establish a specialist resource solely for sexual abuse survivors (Hague et al, 1996). More typically, however, childwork in refuges is not respected by the courts or by other professionals, and childworkers themselves underestimate what they are offering to children; hence these services remain under-resourced with many refuges still forced to depend on part-time and volunteer help (see section on 'Costs' below).

Groupwork

In terms of intervention to help children move on from their experiences, most work internationally has been in the form of groupwork (Mullender, 1994a), this being furthest advanced in Canada (Hague et al, 2000) and the USA and with some interesting projects also developing in the UK and Australia.

The key issues for children in groups include:

- discovering that they are not the only one to have had such experiences;
- learning that domestic violence is wrong and not their fault;
- recognising and coping with the feelings involved;
- talking to others about what has often been a family secret; and
- discussing how to seek help safely.

Some content on direct child abuse is also included. Without groups, there can be a tendency for parents and professionals to assume that children are unaffected because they do not talk about the violence; in fact, they have often been keeping their feelings bottled up and know far more about the violence than their parents may have realised (Mullender et al, forthcoming).

In London, Ontario, every child who needs it can be referred to a group, and there is over a decade's experience of this work (Hague et al, 2001). A rolling programme of groups for 4 to 16 year olds in 1996 admitted 185 children into 25 groups. There is a single access point through a full-time groupworker/co-ordinator, used by all the child welfare and child protection agencies in the city. These agencies contribute a proportion of staff time to co-running the groups. Evaluation of the work has been positive and, as well as obtaining good feedback from both children and their mothers or other carers (92% of children and 87% of carers surveyed rated the groups positively), has shown effective outcomes. The groups can change children's hitherto mistaken views about their responsibility for the violence, as well as their understanding of how to protect themselves and how to seek help safely (Marshall et al, 1995; Loosley et al, 1997). Children also demonstrate learning about non-violent conflict resolution, and about abuse and non-violence more generally.

Similar groups in the USA have also been evaluated. Again, both children who have attended and their mothers have given positive feedback. Groups emerge as able to effect change in participating children in relation to self-esteem, attitudes towards violence and who is responsible for it, and learning safety skills (summaries in Mullender, 1994a; Peled and Edleson, 1992). In addition, agency co-operation can improve when such groups are jointly planned, which may assist in developing a generally more integrated community response. A qualitative study (Peled and Edleson, 1992) showed that children's groups are also effective in breaking down what have been family secrets and hence in helping children to break out of their own isolation and tendency towards self-blame. In addition, group participants learnt some specific techniques for self-protection, were helped to express their feelings, and 'experienced the group as a safe, fun, and self-affirming environment' (p.340). There were individual differences according to the child's personality, family circumstances, and personal and family history of abuse. These indicate a need for careful attention to be paid to group composition and to the messages conveyed by workers since the likelihood is high, for example, that directly abused children will be present in any group.

Children's Counselling Services

An alternative to groupwork is to offer children an individual opportunity to talk about their experiences and come to terms with them, arriving at a better understanding of who was to blame and what might happen in the future. This may be a better option where a child is currently too distressed or disturbed to settle into a group, or where continuing danger and the likelihood of further unplanned moves make a commitment to group attendance unrealistic. Some agencies in the USA and Canada have found that children can be helped by individual work to graduate to groups, and that others gain most from participating in both in parallel.

All practitioners who offer individual help to children, such as child psychologists, child psychiatrists and residential social workers, need to know the impact that living with domestic violence can have and the issues to which it gives rise. At present, such expertise is rarely available to children. Other practitioners work in specialist settings with children and young people who are misusing drugs, committing offences or not attending school. They will encounter youngsters whose problems have been sparked off by living with violence at home but they typically have no routine procedure in place to ask about this.

Beyond Women's Aid, there is little in the way of a specialist response to individual children who have lived with domestic violence. One children's counselling service is run by Warwickshire Domestic Violence Support Services, and is currently planning an evaluation.

Ways forward

What children living with domestic violence need are services that:

- help their mothers and themselves to be safe and to regain their confidence and control of their lives;
- confront and tackle the behaviour of men who abuse women and children;
- minimise the disruption caused by having to flee from domestic violence; and
- undertake direct work designed to help children understand and recover from the impact of what they have experienced.

A framework of co-ordinated and measurable responses by all relevant agencies to cover primary, secondary and tertiary prevention would effectively integrate child protection services and family support services, as opposed to the current situation, where the former predominate.

Inter-agency working is vital. It is now well recognised that child abuse, maternal ill-health and domestic violence frequently coincide (Stanley and Penhale, 1999), yet current responses do not result in women being helped to be well or safe, with consequent adverse effects for children. In both the UK (Mullender and Morley, 1994) and the USA (Schechter and Edleson, 1994) there have been calls for child care and domestic violence services to work more effectively together. Evidence from a family support mapping survey indicates, however, that progress in this direction to date in the UK is patchy and confined largely to the voluntary sector (Humphreys et al, 2000). Specifically child-focused inter-agency groupings which may be able to move things forward include Area Child Protection Committees (ACPCs), groupings of organisations which come together to draw up Children's Services Plans, and children's sub-committees of domestic violence forums. These bodies could give detailed attention to the ways in which the social and health services, education, housing, all civil and criminal justice agencies, and relevant women's and children's voluntary sector agencies could work more effectively together to meet the needs of women and children and tackle the behaviour of their abusers. In some areas, for example, the ACPC has taken the lead on strategic planning and guidance for children's issues in relation to domestic violence (e.g. Cleveland ACPC, 1995), with multi-disciplinary conferences and training events. Its role is different from that of a local domestic violence forum but needs to be integrated with the work of any such body.

Children's Services Plans can be used to estimate current levels of need, to note relevant aspects of existing services and to outline future plans. These may include comprehensive assessment guidelines, collaboration between agencies to establish new services for children and their parents, and the allocation of designated staff to develop domestic violence policy and practice.

Services for children living with domestic violence will only improve if staff in all relevant agencies receive training to raise awareness and develop more appropriate responses. Training materials already exist (Hester et al, 1998a and 1998b) and need monitoring and evaluating in use. They are likely to work best where there are policy statements and good practice guidance already in place providing staff with an agreed philosophy on domestic violence, rooted in equalities issues more generally (Humphreys et al, 2001). It is important to involve Women's Aid and other relevant women's organisations in training events, whether as trainers or as participants, because of their specialist and long-standing experience in working with women and children living with domestic violence. Training should extend beyond raising awareness and building confidence into considering appropriate responses by staff involved at particular stages of the process, including:

- offering information and advice;
- assessing needs and risks;
- supporting the woman in seeking help elsewhere; and
- meeting women's and children's needs more effectively within existing legislative and policy contexts.

Costs

Neither what has been described in this chapter as primary, nor that referred to as tertiary prevention as yet exists in anything but isolated projects in the UK. There has been no British work on estimating the costs of providing such intervention on a comprehensive basis, though relevant information would be available from parts of the USA and Canada. In London, Ontario, a blanket approach to providing children's groups (tertiary prevention) is sustained with just one co-ordinating post and additional groupworker time seconded from the participating child protection, child welfare and child mental health agencies. This might well be a model that agencies could consider in the UK, perhaps through a domestic violence forum or the local Area Child Protection Committee. Although groupwork expertise has been allowed to decline in British social work, sufficient expertise does remain to offer appropriate training and consultancy. This would add to start-up costs but would not necessarily represent a recurrent expenditure once enough practitioners had gained the necessary experience to induct others into the work.

Performance indicators for the work are available in the American and Canadian evaluations (see above). A simple 'before and after' measurement of children's attitudes on key measures (such as who is responsible for the violence), levels of self-esteem, and so on, could provide useful information as to whether groups were worthwhile. Follow-ups over time could also be considered, although any recurrence of danger in the child's life would be likely to contaminate the findings. Outcome measures for primary prevention work in schools could also be based on 'before and after' attitudes. Whether these translated into adult behaviour could only be measured through sophisticated longitudinal studies and would have little chance of holding other factors constant or making any confident pronouncements about 'cause and effect'. Nevertheless, the evidence from research on teenage attitudes gives cause for grave concern and would certainly appear to justify expenditure in this area.

As far as secondary prevention is concerned, agencies are already spending a very great deal of money, largely on 'picking up the pieces' after domestic violence has taken place. It has been estimated that £7.5 million a year is spent on domestic violence-related services in just one local authority area (Stanko et al, 1998), yet with no evidence that this level of expenditure avoids the problems or gaps in service highlighted in this chapter.

Considerable information is available (Ball, 1990; Hague et al, 1996) about the cost of providing childwork services in refuges. Not all refuges that would like to are able to provide childworkers and those that do are dependent on insecure, temporary funding on which considerable fund-raising effort has had to be expended. The charity, BBC Children in Need, has contributed a sum to funding this work only slightly lower than that contributed by local government, for example. Annual funding for children's work ranges from £240 to £44,500 per local Women's Aid or equivalent group, not counting holiday playschemes. Many refuges manage with voluntary or part-time workers, with provision ranging from 2 to 159 hours per week (the latter with several paid workers in place). Many also lack the play space and resources they consider they need to underpin their services to children, particularly in second stage housing (Hague et al, 1996). Yet the work that many refuges achieve has been positively evaluated, including through women and children's own feedback (Hague et al, 1996), and could very easily be built on should a national strategy for funding the work be agreed. When Women's Aid childworkers are sufficiently well funded, they make a contribution to developing the expertise of other services, for example through collaborating on educational inputs and materials in schools, helping to run children's groups and contributing to the continuing professional development of other professionals. Thus there is 'added value' right across primary, secondary and tertiary prevention in having a strong childwork resource available in the women's voluntary sector, over and above the fact that it is the prime service assisting children who leave home with their mothers in emergency circumstances.

Overall, resourcing for children living with domestic violence needs to be considered as part of an intended altered balance between family support services and child protection investigations (Department of Health, 1995). The need to re-channel resources on a scale able to provide comprehensive direct work to children in need as a result of domestic violence and to their non-abusing parents can only be discussed in this macro-level context. It will also be necessary to consider how local government expenditure can ensure that Community Safety, Community Care and Children's Services Plans are integrated to incorporate properly thought-out policies on the abuse of women and children which enable them to live in safety and to regain self-esteem and control over their own lives.

Conclusion

There has been a great deal of attention in the UK over the last decade to the issue of children living with domestic violence. Arguably, this has led to more policing of families but to little real support for those experiencing the abuse, directly and indirectly. There are isolated pockets of work aimed at helping children who have lived with violence to recover from their experiences and at teaching the next generation to grow up with attitudes less tolerant of violence against women. Effective models of work have been developed under all these headings, both here and overseas, with the main British expertise lying with childworkers in Women's Aid and in some projects run by the major children's charities. Their wider-scale implementation would require a major diversion of resources into family support, work in schools and direct work with children. However, this would fit well with some other national priorities such as the rethinking of child protection work away from a chiefly investigative approach and the work already being conducted on anti-bullying strategies in schools.

The final argument may be a moral one as to whether we are content to know so much about the adverse impact on children of living with domestic violence yet to do so little about it in any constructive sense. Alternatively, as has happened in Fife, children and young people themselves may argue their right under Article 12 of the UN Convention on the Rights of the Child to be heard on this issue. The rights of children and young people under all variants of national legislation within the UK to be protected from harm should give them an absolute expectation of agency intervention in respect of domestic violence.

Dealing with perpetrators

Audrey Mullender and Sheila Burton

The chief sources for this chapter were an international literature review, drawing particularly on material from the UK, the USA and Australia, and a mapping of perpetrators' programmes in the UK. There has been a convergence of thinking in recent years that the most appropriate model for working with perpetrators in groups is a broadly cognitive behavioural approach combined with challenging negative gender attitudes. The emphasis is on offenders accepting responsibility for their own violence. The work remains contentious because ineffective interventions could leave victims in greater danger, divert perpetrators from more severe criminal justice sanctions, and lose many participants through non-completion. Compliance has been dramatically improved in one American project by rigorously applied court reviews at the beginning, middle and end of the process. In the UK, Respect (2000) provides minimum standards and good practice guidelines, including an emphasis on the safety of partners and children. This is a notoriously difficult area of practice in which to gauge effectiveness for a wide range of methodological reasons. The more sophisticated evaluations now emphasise partner reports on repeat violence and quality of life as the most reliable measure. Findings from the USA suggest modest success in reducing overt violence, with the most dangerous time being the first six months after the group and a worryingly hard core of men continuing regularly to inflict serious injuries. British research is more limited, both in size and number of studies conducted. Overall, since effectiveness cannot yet be proven, it may be necessary to decide whether to proceed with perpetrators' programmes on moral or other grounds. Certainly, cost need not be an obstacle according to American work which suggests that programmes are relatively inexpensive when compared with other disposals, other kinds of groups and, of course, the continued cost of doing nothing. At the same time, useful messages could be sent to perpetrators through the wider work of the probation and police services and through altering public attitudes, particularly amongst teenage boys.

Introduction

In recent years, there has been a decisive shift in public policy towards recognising domestic violence as a crime, as serious as any other form of assault. As a consequence, ways must now be found through the criminal justice system to hold the perpetrators of the violence accountable for their actions. The major question arising from this is whether anything effective can be done to make perpetrators change their unacceptable behaviours and attitudes.

There is a certain urgency about answering this question. If the criminal justice system aims to arrest and prosecute more domestic abusers, then constructive sentencing options will be needed to deal with them. It is also to be hoped that demands upon the system will be further raised by women's increased willingness to pursue incidents through the courts once they see more effective action being taken, and particularly if they believe this is likely to stop the violence. Meanwhile, public education campaigns and changing public attitudes will raise expectations of what can be achieved.

Government backing has been given both to probation service and voluntary sector work with perpetrators. The former has been spearheaded by 'Pathfinder' projects which will be evaluated against standardised American results. The challenge is to demonstrate that such programmes constitute an effective way of tackling the problem. Yet intervention with perpetrators is not uncontroversial. In New South Wales, for example, the development of perpetrators' programmes was largely prevented for a period by opposition based on lack of evidence of their success and a drive to prioritise funding for services for women and children (Newman, 1996).

Fundamental issues for policy makers in this country include:

- how not to avoid or dilute the normal legal consequences of criminal behaviour;
- the effectiveness of programmes;
- whether the degree of effectiveness demonstrated justifies the cost;
- lack of clarity about how to improve programmes;
- problems in conducting comprehensive, long-term evaluations of new programmes; and
- the dangers inherent in overstating effectiveness claims, notably in offering false hope to partners and ex-partners who may make plans on this basis.

Before considering what light research may be able to cast on these matters, this part of the review will explore more detailed service delivery questions. These include:

- the search for a model of intervention that challenges rather than

colludes with perpetrators' denial and minimisation of their violence;
- the need to agree underpinning principles of best practice;
- the selection, training and support of programme facilitators;
- high attrition rates between referral and programme completion;
- the position of court-mandated as against voluntary attendance at programmes;
- other aspects of integration with the criminal justice system;
- accountability to survivors for their safety; and
- diversity amongst the perpetrator population as it relates both to the appropriateness and the effectiveness of programmes.

This review focuses primarily on provision for men because they come before the courts in statistically far greater numbers than do female perpetrators and are also the subject of existing programme development.

Sources of information

An international literature review was undertaken, drawing particularly on material from the UK, the USA and Australia. It built on earlier work by the present authors (Mullender, 1996; Burton et al, 1998). The most important overseas sources were a report for the US Department of Justice (Healey and Smith, 1998), and the report from the National Campaign Against Violence and Crime Unit (1998) of the Australian Attorney-General's Department. We also drew on the websites of two key university-based research centres in the USA (the Minnesota Higher Education Centre Against Violence and Abuse at www/mincava.umn.edu/arts/asp and the Mid-Atlantic Addiction Training Institute at www.iup.edu/maati/publications). Canadian and British material on preventive work with young people, previously gathered by one of the authors (see Mullender, 1994; Mullender and Humphreys with Saunders, H., 1998) was also considered.

In order to obtain a current impression of relevant work in the UK, a mapping of perpetrators' programmes has been drawn on (Humphreys et al, 2000). This was conducted by the authors in 1999 as part of a wider study funded by the Joseph Rowntree Foundation (JRF), 'Mapping Good Practice in Working with Families where there is Domestic Violence'. The relevant phase of the JRF study aimed to: 'undertake the mapping of service provision of projects that challenge perpetrators of abuse'. It was undertaken by questionnaire survey of the National Practitioners' Network (which has since developed into Respect: the National Association for Domestic Violence Perpetrator Programmes & Associated Support Services), all local probation services in England, Wales, Northern Ireland and the Channel Islands, and relevant sections of social work departments (SWDs) in

Scotland. Twenty-six responses were obtained: six from the voluntary sector, fourteen from probation services, and six from Scottish SWDs. There is no way of knowing what proportion this represents of services actually running projects for perpetrators of domestic violence since a non-response may or may not equate with a lack of involvement in this area of work. In addition, there may be some services that do not fall into any of the categories circulated (though probation services were asked to pass on the questionnaire to voluntary organisations where relevant). However it compares favourably with the number then known to the National Practitioners' Network to be operating (see below) and listed in earlier surveys (Scourfield, 1994; Mullender, 1996).

Perpetrator treatment programmes in the UK

In the UK, the agencies most likely to establish projects to work with domestic violence perpetrators are voluntary bodies and the probation service. The May 1999 update of the Network Directory lists 27 groups, of which 14 are primarily run within the criminal justice system and a further two have extensive overlaps between the two sectors. This is not a high number when set against the size of the UK population which is approaching three times the size of that in Australia yet, there, a national audit located 39 organisations running 55 programmes for around 1,600 men a year. In other ways, however, the situation described is similar to here, with fairly recent development of provision - currently expanding, poorly resourced and inadequately evaluated. In addition, there are moves to develop minimum standards, and debates as to whether there should be government funding and increased provision for court-mandated as opposed to voluntary participants (National Campaign Against Violence and Crime Unit, 1998). In the USA, where the work has a longer history, by 1990 there were already 500 programmes, as well as another 100 in Canada (Thorne-Finch, 1992).

Initially in the UK, the majority of programmes were run within the voluntary sector. A refocusing is to be expected now that domestic violence is increasingly being treated as a crime, and was predicted: 'new growth may well switch to probation now that there is Association of Chief Officers of Probation (ACOP) and Home Office backing for such work' (Mullender, 1996: 224). Despite this movement towards the mainstream (at least in resourcing terms), the effectiveness of the intervention and of the linkage with the wider criminal justice system (for example in imposing sanctions for non-compliance) remain in question. A further question has been raised as to whether a degree of diversity of provision is healthier. Respect in the UK has argued that the creativity and diversity of the voluntary sector should be preserved, as well as its role in working with men who are not convicted perpetrators but who are nevertheless part of the major social problem of domestic violence. There is a fear that too much standardisation may stifle innovation and continued development (see also Healey and Smith, 1998). On the other hand, however, it could help provide a baseline for the evaluation necessary to demonstrate the effective outcomes that Respect also seeks.

Models of intervention

The move towards accepting domestic violence as a crime and perpetrators as responsible for their criminal behaviour has been mirrored in thinking about the most appropriate models for the work. As the National Practitioners' Network (1994: 2) has put it: 'The focus of intervention should be on men as perpetrators and not as victims' (see also Respect, 2000). This means that, whatever other problems an abusive man may have, it is not considered appropriate to allow him to shift the focus of the groupwork. This may include trying to blame his partner or their relationship, his family of origin or childhood experiences, his mental health or substance misuse, or any other factor which might be used to rationalise or excuse his violence. Groupworkers in perpetrators' groups work hard to avoid colluding with such diversion of focus (Morran and Wilson, 1997). In so doing, they follow national advice: 'men's violence is defined as learned and intentional behaviour rather than as the consequence of individual pathology, stress, alcohol abuse or a "dysfunctional" relationship' (Respect, 2000: 1). This leads to a behavioural rather than a psychotherapeutic approach. (See Mullender, 1996, for a fuller exposition.)

Alcohol misuse

In line with this retention of focus on the offending behaviour, the published manual from the CHANGE programme (Morran and Wilson, 1997) deals with substance misuse on the basis that alcohol does not 'cause' violence. Instead, abusing drugs or alcohol is one of the choices men make in failing to control their own behaviour. This approach was commonly found in the authors' national survey of current perpetrators' programmes, most of which would accept men with alcohol or drug problems, within limits. However, they would view this as needing to be worked on in parallel to the perpetrators' work and understood as not explaining the violence.

There is also research backing for this view. Though a national random sample survey in the USA did show more heavy drinkers being violent to their partners (Kaufman et al, 1987), 80 per cent of heavy and 'binge' drinkers did not hit their wives at all during the year of the survey. Thus most incidents took place with the abuser sober, from which the researchers concluded that alcohol was neither a necessary nor a sufficient cause of woman abuse; instead, cultural approval of violence appeared to be heavily implicated for these men. Nor would drinking explain why there is target choice in hitting a partner. It is more likely that drink is, for some men, an intervening variable: they may drink to give themselves 'dutch courage' or permission to be violent, or to provide an excuse to call on after the event. They can deny any memory of the attack or say they lost control and did not really mean it; some partners believe them and hope they will change if they stop drinking. However, men are actually disinhibiting inhibitors they have already decided to disobey (see self-reports in Ptacek, 1988).

Recent American research has looked at the extent of alcohol use amongst domestic violence perpetrators. Half of Gondolf's (1996) total sample reported being heavy drinkers and slightly more than this (56% on one measure and 64% on another) had clinical levels of alcohol misuse. On the other hand, nearly a third of the total sample seldom or never used alcohol. Once again, these data do not support assumptions of cause and effect. Continuing to drink heavily during follow-up after a perpetrators' programme may be predictive of further abuse (Gondolf, 1995). However, this provides another argument for responding to both of the problematic behaviours in the man's life, not for combining the two in the same intervention.

Not anger management

Early confusion between work with domestic violence perpetrators and anger management is now less common than previously. It is hard to argue that domestic abusers are simply unable to manage their anger. They choose their targets and the circumstances of their attacks (Wood and Middleman, 1990), and, in Hearn's research (1998), perpetrators spoke of clear intentions to cause specific amounts of hurt and damage. The concept of anger management can feed into perpetrators' denial and minimisation of their behaviour; 'a problem with my anger' does not sound criminal, unacceptable, or commensurate with the physical and emotional damage inflicted. Nor does it require a re-examination of attitudes; hence it may be less effective in ending violence (see 'Gender attitudes', below). Men may learn anger management techniques that they later use to interrupt and control discussion with their partners by announcing that they need 'time out', and courts may see the approach as an attractive 'quick fix' solution. (See Mullender, 1996, or Healey and Smith, 1998, for further discussion.) This is not to say that perpetrators' programmes do not appropriately work on recognising how anger masks other emotions that need dealing with if abusers are to control and change their behaviour.

A similar critique can be made of assumptions about perpetrators as having 'skills deficits' since many possess the social skills to cope perfectly well in the rest of their life.

Not couples work

Similarly, work with couples and families (except where preceded by work with the man and a closely monitored, violence-free period) is now typically understood as contra-indicated. This is because it makes assumptions about shared blame and may place the woman in greater danger. A woman is unable to participate openly and honestly if her abuser has threatened her with repercussions (Mullender, 1996; Respect, 2000). Work with couples-based groups has also been suggested to be both less effective and to fail to tap the population of men that come through the courts (Tolman and Bennett, 1990, cited in Gondolf, 1997).

Social learning/cognitive-behavioural work

As a result of these developing understandings, there is now some degree of uniformity between programmes. In the USA, a research overview in 1995 (Tolman and Edleson, 1995) reported that most groups were based on a cognitive-behavioural or other social learning approach. Here, violence is viewed as a learned behaviour that can consequently be unlearned. This is done by engaging some level of the men's understanding about the thought patterns that have been involved in their attitudes towards women. The intervention explores the rewards and punishments to which they have responded, and which can now be engaged in working towards changing their own unacceptable behaviour.

This fits well with a criminal justice response (Healey and Smith, 1998), first, because it requires perpetrators to accept responsibility for their past actions and future choices. Secondly, its phased approach lends itself to a condition of regular attendance at a group. Thirdly, the close monitoring of perpetrators' behaviour over a period of time and liaison with partners to validate accounts of behaviour (whilst also offering them safeguards) are closely compatible with criminal justice goals.

Gender attitude change

The additional element included in many groups, over and above the cognitive behavioural content, is the belief system that convinces male perpetrators they have a right to control women in intimate relationships. Unless this is also tackled in groups, there is a danger that men will switch from physical to emotional abuse and threats, and that women and children will continue to live in fear. This introduces the need for a gender analysis into groupwork content and typically leads to a combined model. For example, the profeminist Domestic Abuse Intervention Project in Duluth, Minnesota (Pence and Paymar, 1990) has been influential in introducing both gendered and social learning groupwork content into Britain. In the national survey conducted by the present authors, all but one of the detailed responses (i.e. those providing perpetrators' services) referred to the Duluth project as a major influence. The next most frequently mentioned influence was cognitive behavioural work.

Nine respondents had gleaned their detailed knowledge of the relevant approach from the CHANGE manual (Morran and Wilson, 1997), itself based on Duluth. The most common self-description by projects was 'educational'.

Recent evidence has emerged that altering gender attitudes may positively affect the success rates of perpetrators' groups. This comes from research with a four-site, longitudinal sample comparing different groupwork models (Gondolf, 1998d) which asked participants how they avoided further violent incidents. At the 15-month follow-up, more of the men - though still a minority - in the two longest programmes (five and a half and nine months, respectively, as opposed to three months in duration) had learnt to talk things through. Importantly, this was statistically linked with the third of women who reported 'a great extent' of change in their partners, half of whom attributed this to participation in the programme. The women who reported 'some extent' or 'a great extent' of change were less likely to have been re-assaulted and more likely to be still with their partners and, again, there was a link, though a weaker one, with the two longer programmes. It may have been the length of time in the group that helped men learn to discuss their violence rather than the groupwork approach since one of the shortest of the four groups set out to be more discussion-based and one of the longest was more didactic in model. However, the latter resulted in more men using discussion to avoid violence than the former.

Workers in the programmes studied by Gondolf considered behavioural techniques easier to teach, particularly to men with more limited cognitive or social abilities, and most men did learn behavioural techniques of interrupting a potentially violent incident. However, there is a risk that men who are accustomed to controlling women and to abusing their power in a relationship may use 'time out' and other interruption techniques still to impose their will on the outcome of an incident. Burton et al (1998), from a UK-based evaluative study, furnish some examples of this (together with evidence that men often failed to move on to more sophisticated techniques), as do Healey and Smith (1998) in an overview of high profile American projects.

The men in Gondolf's (1998d) study were more likely to show attitude change if they had learnt to avoid violence through discussion or respect for women and their point of view. He concludes 'The programs in our study appear to succeed in teaching avoidance techniques, but less so at furthering attitudinal change. The attitudinal change is associated with less abuse, and may be a desirable goal' (Gondolf, 1998d, pages unnumbered). Gondolf (1997: 85) sums up the resultant combined model as 'a gender-based, cognitive-behavioural modality'. He suggests that other programmes should undertake more work on gender beliefs in order to combat social reinforcement of negative attitudes towards women, noting that this might require longer and more discussion-based group programmes, linked with community outreach and public education efforts, also directed at attitude change.

Groupwork

One crucial corollary of the Gondolf findings about attitudinal change is that the essence of groupwork skills needs to be valued and retained. It may well be groupwork process that obtains the best results and not a simple instructional format. This is supported by Dobash et al (2000), based on what men said had had most effect on them in two programmes studied in Scotland, which revealed that not only specific aspects of the content but also the discussions in the group had been influential. The researchers comment (p.ix):

> Group work it seems is very important in providing a context in which violence can be discussed with others who have had similar experiences and with group leaders who focus clearly on the offending behaviour and provide new ways of seeing and understanding violence.

The skill of the practitioner lies in challenging directly and in facilitating challenging discussion, including after behavioural techniques have been practised, so as to draw men into confronting one another's denial, minimisation and projection (blaming others) and the other problematic attitudes that maintain abusive conduct. The ability to do this cannot be learnt from a manual; it requires adequate training and professional experience both in the groupworker and in the person supervising their work, as well as an approach to resourcing which does not expect the same results in a curtailed period of intervention. Where line managers lack the necessary expertise, it may be advisable to provide appropriate consultancy so that both groupwork skills and specialist knowledge about domestic violence can be reinforced in workers.

One way of thinking about what is being aimed for is as an equation: Behaviour + attitudes = conduct. It is the whole pattern of conduct that is unacceptable in perpetrators and which should be of interest to the courts and policy makers, not simply a set of isolated behaviours. Certain behaviours could be extinguished whilst still leaving women to live with threats and fear.

Non-completion rates

Literature in all the countries reviewed shows a problem in getting men through an entire programme. As well as being dangerous for women and frustrating for practitioners, this leads to attrition in evaluation samples that makes results harder to judge. In Australia, non-completion rates can exceed 50%, with additional high drop-out rates prior to programme attendance (National Campaign Against Violence and Crime Unit, 1998). Gondolf (1997; 1998b) cites rates of over a third 'no shows' (failure to report to the group) in one programme in the USA, and, in an overview of American research, 40-60% of men dropping out and overall completion rates as low as 10% of initial referrals. In the UK, according to the authors' survey, completion rates are said to range from 30 to 90% of those starting a group.

The evaluation of the Violence Prevention Programme in London (Burton et al, 1998) reveals the attrition rates at each stage of the process. An initial assessment refused places to 12% of referred men for reasons including drug, alcohol or mental health problems or lack of acceptance of responsibility or of a need to change. There was a very large 'no show' group and almost a third of those who started a group attended fewer than six sessions. The 'no show' and drop-out rate added up to a 57% failure to complete after acceptance onto the programme. Most of these had been voluntary attenders. Only 31 men out of the 351 in the project's 'log' went on to the second stage group. No factors were identified in the research which could differentiate or predict 'no shows', drop-outs or completers, although the project workers report that self-referred men are more likely to progress into the follow-up group and to complete both stages of the programme. They also report improved completion rates since the study was conducted. They further point out that, even where men do not attend their first assessment session, their partners are typically contacted by the associated women's service so that some benefit does derive from the referral.

These figures are especially worrying, however, when one considers that women may be more likely to return to a man who has at least sought help, even if he has dropped out of the group or failed to respond to it. Consequently, it would seem important to find some remedy for low completion rates.

There are several approaches that could be tried. In Pittsburgh, in the context of a diversion scheme, a 'court review' leads to the issue of an arrest warrant if the perpetrator does not appear at the programme intake interview, or if there is no evidence of compliance at 30 days or of programme completion at 60 days (Gondolf, 1998b). Findings suggest that this dramatically increases compliance. The 'no show' rate dropped from 36% to 6% between 1994 and 1997. The immediacy and consistency of the court's response may explain why this short programme appeared to have rates of re-arrest prevention comparable to longer post-conviction programmes. In the UK, the Burton et al (1998) study found that a much higher percentage of court-mandated perpetrators (70% as against 43%) than of other men completed the first stage of the group. In this study, however, it was also the case that probation officers sometimes failed to apply sanctions against those who ceased to attend. The critical success factors emerged as getting the man to the group and then holding him there for more than five sessions. These might therefore be the key 'court review' points if such a model were to be adopted here with court-mandated men. Burton et al (1998) also list more positive ways to get men started in a programme, including through pre-entry groups, one-to-one support from an established attender, and early arrival at the programme venue by new participants before their first meeting. One is, of course, struck by the fact that men who inflict so much harm on others should be described as 'feeling squeamish and scared' about attending a group (Burton et al, 1998:26), but violence is perhaps symptomatic of weakness rather than strength.

The issue of alternative sanctions to the somewhat self-defeating exclusion of a man from a group if he reabuses has been reviewed by Mullender (1996). Various alternatives traced, mainly in the American literature, include insisting on the man starting the group programme again, having the man agree to place money and a signed confession at his partner's disposal for future use, and collecting donations for the local refuge. The most interesting trend is towards ensuring that the man's partner, and/or women more generally, should benefit from the sanction imposed on the man (Myers, 1993). This accords with the emphasis in the programme itself on his not being allowed to escape a challenge to accept full responsibility for his actions and for his partner's safety. No evaluation of the application of these sanctions has been traced.

All workers involved in referring to any kind of men's programme need to be keenly aware of the issue of low completion rates - particularly in warning men's partners not to expect too much and to keep in place a safety plan for themselves and their children. 'For some women, returning to their partners may be a safe decision; however, treatment groups for batterers will surely fail most victims' expectations' (Edleson and Syers, 1991: 242).

Mandatory versus voluntary attendance

Connected with the move towards programmes being run in the statutory sector is a move towards participation being 'mandated' by the courts. Self referral to a group offers no guarantees of attendance or completion and is harder to monitor. Mandated participation offers the benefits of 'integrated service delivery, monitoring of a perpetrator's activities and whereabouts, consistently applied penalties for non-attendance, and increasing penalties for continued breaches' (National Campaign Against Violence and Crime Unit, 1998:17). Mandating should therefore be able to tackle issues of 'no show', drop-out and non-compliance with conditions, including poor attendance, and consequently improve the ability to monitor change and to prioritise survivors' safety. There may also be gains in effectiveness. Involvement with the courts at intake was one of only two variables in the study by Edleson and Syers (1991) which were predictive of lower rates of violence at follow-up, the other being an absence of prior mental health treatment.

Given that group facilitators have to be confrontative with participants from the beginning, there is little opportunity to engage trust or motivation through relationship building. Men's belief in the need to change, let alone the possibility of it, may be slow to kindle. Consequently, there is little positive incentive to attend initially and a negative incentive in the form of sanctions may be a necessity for many. All of this assumes accurate record-keeping by programmes and close links with the courts and wider criminal justice system, as well as with partner support services so that women can be informed when perpetrators fail to attend.

There is a further question as to whether court-mandated men should be integrated into the same groups as voluntary attenders. In the UK generally, the authors' survey showed a typical mix of voluntary and mandated attenders, with the proportion of the latter in probation-run groups ranging from 5 to 100%. More recently, the Probation Service has tended to move to working only with men sent by the courts. Burton et al (1998) found that the group facilitators in the project they studied spoke of better results when there was a mix of voluntary and mandated men in the group. Those working with victims also wanted there to be provision for men not subject to court action. These authors further point out that so-called 'voluntary' attenders are often under a 'community mandate' to attend, in the form of an ultimatum from their partner or from an agency threatening some form of sanction.

Principles of best practice

Duration

Respect (2000) bases its good practice recommendation for group duration on the experience of long-established programmes in the USA, requiring at least 75 hours over 30 weeks in 'groupwork-linked contact, on the specific issue of men addressing their violent behaviour' (p.7). It clearly states that 'Programmes of less than this duration are potentially harmful' (p.8). In the authors' national questionnaire survey, groups listed by respondents ranged from 20 hours over 10 weeks to 120 hours over 48 weeks, the latter also incorporating 12 hours of one-to-one work. The shortest of these clearly does not meet the recommended standard.

Facilitators

The Respect (2000) minimum standards state that:

- all groups must have a minimum of two facilitators;

- they should be one man and one woman or two women and one man; and
- workers should be allowed to make their own judgement as to how many men they can comfortably and safely work with, not be put under managerial pressure on this point.

The authors' national survey revealed groups setting a ceiling of eight to twelve members (though several do not set a maximum), and actually working with an average attendance from as low as four to as high as 15.

The benefits of a male/female worker pairing are seen as being the opportunity to demonstrate equality, mutual respect and joint conflict resolution and to bring different viewpoints to bear (including empathy with female partners). Several groups will not run without a woman co-facilitator present, presumably because of the risk of collusion between group members and male practitioners. Equally, a skilled male facilitator is able to challenge collusion between members.

The ethnicity of workers might also usefully be thought about (though it is rarely mentioned), particularly where there is going to be a sizeable number of minority ethnic men in perpetrators' groups. This would be in line with the call from Respect (2000) for practitioners to be trained in equalities issues. There is now a sizeable American literature on ethnically sensitive groupwork with perpetrators (e.g. Williams, 1994a; 1999).

Training

RESPECT (2000) also places emphasis on adequate training for the method of intervention selected and in domestic violence awareness and child protection issues. It recommends a minimum of five days of training specifically on programme delivery and related issues. The national survey already referred to found a varied picture. Facilitators virtually all had some basic awareness training on domestic violence, though sometimes this was as little as a one-day course. A majority, but by no means all, had had training specifically in working with perpetrators and this had typically lasted longer. Not all had had child protection training or any work on the safety issues affecting women and children when perpetrators are challenged to change their behaviour.

Accountability to women: Issues of women and children's safety

The danger involved in the lack of guaranteed success is a very strong reason for never setting up a men's project in isolation. Programmes need to be linked with other services which are designed to meet the support and safety needs of women and children. There also need to be clear communication channels whereby women can alert the programme co-ordinators if the man's involvement in the group is having any adverse effect on his treatment of her and which they, in turn, can use to warn her if they believe her to be in danger. Ideally, the programme would also be offering the female partner a realistic view of how the programme works and its lack of guarantees of success. It should also take the initiative to check with her periodically about her safety, reinforcing the view that the violence is the man's responsibility, not hers, and finding ways, with her consent, to build her views into its evaluation of its success.

There is a real sense in which the programme accepts responsibility for the woman's safety. There is evidence that women base decisions whether to leave or stay with the perpetrator on the fact of his entering a programme. This means that they must never, at any time, be given false hope or be left in ignorance of what the group involves or of their partner's progression through it. The National Practitioners' Network (1994:2) stated the principle that 'The safety of women and children must be at the forefront' of this work and this has been endorsed as good practice by central government (Cabinet Office, 1999:38). Even crime prevention was explicitly seen by the Network as a secondary consideration: 'Every intervention and decision made in this work must be chosen with increasing women's safety as the *primary criteria*' (National Practitioners' Network, 1994:1). Clearly, there would be little point in establishing a national network of groups if these made women and children less, rather than more, safe.

Ways in which it is possible to take responsibility for ensuring partners' safety include:

- informing the woman when her partner or ex-partner starts a programme;
- raising her awareness of realistic levels of change to expect and, conversely, never giving her false hope;
- keeping her informed of his progress of attendance through the group, particularly if he drops out or is asked to leave before completion;
- giving her information about the perpetrators' programme and about ways in which the man may use it against her to reinterpret her behaviour or to control her;
- offering her confidential contact at any point;
- telling her about other agencies and crisis services open to her;
- taking a believing approach towards her;
- respecting her confidentiality;
- not guaranteeing complete confidentiality to the perpetrator or to anyone else if this would place the woman at risk;
- avoiding competing for funding with services for domestic violence survivors;

- seeking dialogue with women's groups working with survivors of violence about the approach and content of the perpetrators' programme; and
- demonstrating an active commitment to wider social change to end gender oppression.

All 19 of the respondents in the authors' UK-wide survey who were currently running perpetrators' services reported that men's rights to confidentiality were limited so that women could be given information appropriate to their safety needs. This is generally one of the conditions of participation that men sign on being admitted to a group. The supervising probation officer, where appropriate, is also kept abreast of the man's progress in the group and of any disclosures of repeat violence or other concerns. All 19 respondents also said that contact with women was routine and that they had direct links to support services for women. Worryingly, however, seven had no child protection policies, four had not consulted women's organisations when establishing their programme, and three did not keep partners informed if men failed to attend the group. Clearly there needs to be more consistent practice in this area.

More will be said about parallel work with women and children below, and in the chapter on survivors (see Mullender and Hague, this volume).

Diversity

Both the Australian and American literature (reviewed respectively in National Campaign Against Violence and Crime Unit, 1998, and in Healey and Smith, 1998) now deals at length with particular groups of men who may require specific provision or be least able to participate effectively in existing groups. These include:

- men in isolated rural areas who are poorly provided with groups;
- those who are screened out of programmes on mental health or substance misuse grounds or because of a learning difficulty;
- imprisoned men;
- those whose spoken English is not adequate to participate fully (there is practitioner evidence that written tasks in the group can be adapted around drawing or having items read aloud but, clearly, comprehension of both instructional and discussion-based material is essential); and
- members of minority ethnic groups.

Williams (1994a) writes about making groups 'culturally competent' and there is practitioner evidence that cultural norms can be used to positive effect in specialist minority ethnic groups where men are freer to talk seriously about family and community values without fear of racial stereotyping and abuse. (See Healey and Smith, 1998, for a full discussion of this issue.) In addition, gay men are another group who may require separate programmes as they would be likely to encounter extremes of heterosexism and homophobia in mainstream perpetrators' groups where they would automatically be 'outed' by being required to name their partner. In addition, same-sex partner abuse (Island and Letellier, 1991; Renzetti, 1992) has to be understood in a particular social context and is not necessarily compatible with all the assumptions about relationship dynamics conveyed in perpetrators' groups. In addition, there is evidence from the USA that those perpetrators who come through the criminal justice system tend to be from the lower educational and occupational strata of society (Johnson and Kanzler, 1990). This suggests that other socioeconomic groups are not being reached and this may be an issue to be addressed both in programme design and in related criminal justice considerations.

A different argument relating to diversity has been the attempt to improve programme effectiveness by subdividing perpetrators into 'types' who might respond to different designs of programme (see, for example, Gondolf, 1997; Healey and Smith, 1998). This is sometimes referred to in the literature as the avoidance of a 'one size fits all' uniformity. The categorisation has been variously suggested as needing to be based on psychological factors/personality types, risk assessment/behavioural indicators, or history of substance misuse. No research findings with clear policy or practice implications have so far emerged from this work, which has been interesting in theory but inconclusive in practice. Gondolf (1998a), for example, found that, at the 15-month follow-up in his multi-site survey, different personality types did not relate to outcome, nor to programme model, and nor did behavioural characteristics or situational factors.

One particular issue is that there are sometimes worrying attempts within this categorisation approach to single out some men as more dangerous or 'anti-social' than others. Since the typical pattern of domestic violence is an escalating one, including after the relationship ends, what a perpetrator has done so far may say very little about what he is capable of doing in the future. On the other hand, it could be worth considering specialist provision for men who have been, or would be likely to be, excluded from mainstream groups owing to the extremes of their attitudes or additional problems. The practitioners who might work with such men should look to the USA for exemplars (see Healey and Smith, 1998) since the men involved would not have the normal range of awareness or motivation through which to generate a dynamic of change in the group.

Effectiveness

To date, there has been insufficient and insufficiently rigorous monitoring of perpetrators' programmes in all countries in which they have begun to develop. At the same time, much of the practice-based literature makes over-stated, impressionistic claims for success. Where evaluation studies *have* been carried out, they have largely been tailored to individual programmes and have not been replicable. Nor has it been possible to combine the results to form a bigger picture since varying definitions of success have been applied, together with different evaluative methods over a range of timeframes.

Making progress in this area will not be easy since this is a notoriously difficult area of practice to evaluate in terms of effectiveness. Eisikovits and Edleson (1989) reviewed a literature of more than 50 publications on perpetrators' groups and concluded that, although sophistication was increasing, there were still severe methodological shortcomings. The problems, which they and others have cited, include the issues of:

- the mix of techniques used in groups, making it hard to isolate those which work, if any (Eisikovits and Edleson, 1989);
- the source of the study too often being the same person who ran the programme, giving no guarantee of objectivity (Chen et al, 1989; Eisikovits and Edleson, 1989).
- the source of the data. Since it is well established that female partners report more incidents of abuse than their abusers (Edleson and Brygger, 1986; Poynter, 1989), it is essential to go beyond male self-report (Eisikovits and Edleson, 1989). The woman should be asked what has happened since her partner started or stopped attending the programme;
- defining violence. There is evidence that, whereas physical abuse may decline or stop, threats of abuse may continue or even escalate so that the woman still lives in fear (Edleson and Grusznski, 1989; Eisikovits and Edleson, 1989; Edleson, 1990). Yet several studies have used a measure of conflict which incorporates only physical violence (Poynter, 1989);
- the lack of control groups in many studies (Chen et al, 1989; Tolman and Edleson, 1989);
- their frequent vagueness over key information such as the source of follow-up reports (Edleson, 1990);
- the risk that a positive effect may have resulted from some other factor, such as the threat of a return to court, the partner having left, or other sources of support, rather than the programme of intervention itself (Eisikovits and Edleson, 1989);
- low response rates, low recruitment, and high drop-out from

programmes (Chen et al, 1989) which mean that those whose response is measured may not be typical, together with the fact that those sentenced to attend may not resemble those who do so voluntarily;
- the difficulty of measuring the rate of abuse where the partners are no longer together (Edleson and Grusznski, 1989), together with the difficulty that studies may not distinguish the intact from the separated couples, who also may separate and reunite more than once;
- the fact that contact with a programme itself sensitises both partners to the issue of abuse and may make them more likely to report it at follow-up (Edleson and Grusznski, 1989);
- the fact that evaluation studies have mainly been underfunded and hence small and not necessarily systematic (Edleson, 1990);
- the need for far longer periods of follow-up before we know whether positive effects really are maintained over time (Poynter, 1989).

Defining success

There is also a problem in establishing a criterion of success. Should this be: less violence, no violence, no longer subjecting the partner to a life of fear, or changing the man's attitudes towards women more generally?

Tolman and Edleson (1995) point out that it would be problematic to establish anything other than a complete cessation of violence as the criterion of success since reduced violence would still leave the woman in danger. They further point out that, in attempting to measure cessation, the source of that measurement is critical. The three main sources commonly used are:

- *Perpetrator self-report*. This consistently emerges from research as unreliable: Gondolf, (1996) found that only about 40% of men acknowledged recent assaults and less than a fifth admitted having used severe tactics in the last three months, even though they had been required to attend a programme. Self-report particularly understates the more serious forms of violence and its frequency (Dobash et al, 2000).
- *Partner reports*. As mentioned above, these routinely include more incidents of abuse than do those of perpetrators (Edleson and Brygger, 1986; Poynter, 1989). The differences between male and female reporting in the research conducted in Scotland by Dobash et al (2000) were polarised in this predictable way; three-quarters of women reported persistent pushing, grabbing and slapping as against only one-fifth of men. More women reported injuries and at a greater frequency, while men tended to judge both violence and injuries as less serious. The reliability and validity of women's reports have been

tested (Gondolf, 1998e), with minimal inconsistencies revealed between their accounts over time or between answers to related interview questions, together with evidence of accurate reporting when checked against arrest and hospital records. This makes partner reports the single most important measure available.

- *Official data.* The measures usually used are further reports to the police, recorded crimes, rearrest, repeat prosecution or reconviction. There is attrition at each of these stages, and even reports to the police constitute an under-representation of incidence. This is because women by no means always call the police to incidents of violence (estimates vary from 2 to 27% - see Mullender, 1996). As Tolman and Edleson (1995) remark, the absence of crime is not the same as the absence of abuse. Dobash et al (2000) clearly demonstrated the unreliability of the use of reconviction figures (which suffer the worst attrition). The researchers found that convicted men both on programmes and in a control group subject to other disposals had low reconviction rates after a one-year follow-up and that, on this measure, the programme men were only slightly more successful than those with other disposals (7% as against 10%). However, self and partner reports by questionnaire revealed 33% and 75% failure rates respectively; dramatically different from reconviction figures.

Best evaluative practice is now regarded as being based on a combination of all these sources of reports of abuse (Tolman and Edleson, 1995). Over and above this, women's reports on 'quality of life' are a useful adjunct since they can incorporate the non-criminal or non-reported aspects of an abusive pattern of power and control in the relationship that is the incubator of both violence and fear.

There are further reasons for exercising particular care in reading claims for success rates. Firstly, these may be given as a percentage of widely differing baselines: those being referred to a programme, those commencing it, or those continuing to attend through to completion, for example. Tolman and Edleson (1995) give an example of a large-scale follow-up in which a two-thirds success rate could justifiably be claimed (non-violence being sustained by two-thirds of those programme completers who could be traced at follow-up), but where this represented only 20% of initial contacts with the agency. Secondly, without experimental studies (with randomised controls), we cannot know whether the same proportion of men might have achieved this result without assistance. This caution is borne out by a study (Feld and Straus, 1989) which did find cessation of violence in the general population without formal intervention.

There is some evidence that practitioners running programmes are able to predict outcomes with almost 80% accuracy (Gondolf, 1995). This does not mean that their risk assessments could safely be used to make predictions in individual cases and certainly not to reassure women that they would be likely to be safe. They might have other uses, however, such as evaluating progress with the man at midway review and in planning further work he might undertake voluntarily after the completion of a programme (Gondolf, 1995; see also an example from practice in Burton et al, 1998). They might also assist in judging men's degree of participation in and benefit from the programme, for example to feed into any subsequent sentencing or intervention decisions, such as whether to allow a man onto a programme for a second time or move to immediate imprisonment. Other factors worth building into assessments emerge from Gondolf's (1995) research as being whether the man is still drinking heavily and whether or not he has separated from his partner.

Findings from American research

A typical finding from the most rigorously conducted studies is that programmes have a modest effect in reducing repeat offending (see review in Healey and Smith, 1998). Taking studies overall, with less regard to methodology, though most do report successes in reducing overt violence – in the region of 53% to 85% according to a review by Edleson and Tolman (1992) – it must be remembered that the evidence for this is far from firm. Even if the violence has stopped, the women concerned may not be living a life free from fear. A more sobering finding, for example, comes from the Domestic Abuse Project in Minnesota. Although two-thirds of completers were reported non-violent at an 18-month follow-up, most persisted with controlling or threatening behaviour (Edleson and Syers, 1991).

The longest evaluative project in the literature is probably that by Edward Gondolf in which a 53% combined success rate has been found across four types of programme. Court-mandated perpetrators in four cities have been followed up at 12, 15 and 30 months and the study is planned to continue to 48 months (Gondolf, 1998c). This study is also impressive in size. At 15 months, there were 840 male perpetrators in the research sample, 82 per cent of them being court mandated. At 21-24 months and again at 30 months, telephone interviews were conducted with 580 court-mandated men (and with 66% of original and 71% of new partners).

Nearly half the men (47%; both completers and non-completers) used violence at some point during the 30 months. It should be remembered that this percentage is calculated only on those who commenced the programme, not on those who may initially have been referred to it - their inclusion might considerably have worsened this picture. Looked at in more detail, the results are of some concern. Partners reported 77% of men verbally abusive, with threats from 53%, injuries inflicted by 27%, and 7% of the women having sought medical care in the 30 months since contact. Only

21% of men were reported by their partners to have been neither verbally nor physically abusive. The most dangerous time was the first six months (nearly half of those who would re-assault had first done so by then, and a third within the first three months). The vast majority of those who were not violent at 15 months was still violence-free at 30 months. However, 23 per cent of the men were repeatedly violent throughout the follow-up and they also inflicted the majority of the worst injuries. Any system of 'court review' might usefully be built around these findings. The type of programme did not seem to affect re-assault rates, other forms of abuse, or how safe the woman felt.

Statistically associated with likelihood of re-assault were:

- completing less than three months of a programme;
- being frequently drunk, or having antisocial tendencies; and
- evidence of severe psychological problems (major depression, thought disorder, paranoia or borderline personality).

There was apparently no link with ethnicity, marital status, separation/contact with the partner, prior arrests, current alcohol use, or other personality factors. It is important to note that research of this kind cannot establish a direction of influence, even if one exists. Thus a man might reoffend because he is drinking heavily, or drink heavily because he cannot stop reoffending; he might continue being violent because he has left the programme before it has had time to be effective, or leave because he chooses to continue being violent. It is also possible that two problems, such as heavy drinking and continued violence, are both caused, not by each other but by a third factor such as a particular personality type or something in the man's social situation.

By the 30-month follow-up, 60 per cent of the initial partners were no longer living with the perpetrator and a quarter of the total sample had no contact. This latter fact certainly represents a kind of crime prevention that may have been assisted by the existence of the group. Of course, the men may have gone on to be abusive in new relationships - at least a quarter of the 24% who had no contact with their original partners at 30 months had new partners by that time. In terms of quality of life, 69% of the women questioned felt 'better off', 84% considered it 'very unlikely' that their partners would hit them and 83% felt 'very safe' at 30 months. Only 12% felt 'worse off'. These are important, and more hopeful, findings.

For those who seek to know what kind of programme works best, Gondolf's frustrating conclusion was that outcomes from all four programmes were similar. This may be because, to some extent, the similarities between the interventions were greater than their differences. All were linked to the courts, all used cognitive behavioural techniques, all were gender-based in the analysis offered of partner violence, and all were integrated with partner services (Gondolf 1998a and 1998c). However, they did range from a three-month to a nine-month intervention and one intervened pre-trial as opposed to three post conviction. Gondolf suggests that the speed of the pre-trial response may have compensated for the shortness of that programme, at only three months. An alternative explanation could hypothetically be that a similar proportion of men would have changed without any intervention.

There is one notable exception to the reports of success in a worrying study from the USA by Harrell (1991, cited in Tolman and Edleson, 1995, and Healey and Smith, 1998). This found that participants in three perpetrators' programmes who completed mandatory attendance at short-term groups had success rates no better than others who were found guilty but subjected to other disposals. Partner reports and criminal data were used to ascertain reoffending, with other measures of controlling behaviour and attitudes, risk factors and victim safety also used. The men going through groups actually had worse results on one measure, that of physical aggression. These groups, at only 12 sessions of 1-1.5 hours per session, fell below the nationally recommended minimum standard in the UK (Respect, 1994) so may have been less effective than programmes in other studies. However, the figure that stands out in the findings is the low re-assault rate by the men who did not attend a group. No reason for this finding can be given, except that the men had all been through a court.

Overall, the literature from America offers contradictory findings, a continuing lack of studies that build in all the elements necessary to conduct research that is able relatively confidently to make 'cause and effect' claims, and, amidst the claims that are made for success, still quite worrying levels of repeat assaults. It does, however, suggest that cognitive behavioural techniques with gender attitude change are a useful way forward, that men who stop their violence for six months have a good chance of sustaining this pattern and that an encouraging proportion of partners feels safer. This may amount to sufficient reason to pursue groupwork programmes as a useful intervention.

British research

Britain has had, to date, two high profile external evaluations conducted of particular programmes (Dobash et al, 2000; Burton et al, 1998).

The evaluation of the CHANGE programme and of Lothian Domestic Violence Probation Project by Dobash et al (2000) in Scotland found 67% success in avoiding further violence for a year after the programmes, as measured by partner report, as against only 25% success for men subject to other disposals. Most of the re-assaults in both categories occurred in the first three months: 30% of men in groups and 62% of others. There was only one further programme failure in the next nine months who had not already been violent since the programme ended. Violence had not been replaced in programme participants by other controlling behaviours, which had also significantly reduced. Although female respondents' own quality of life was only slightly better, most reported a consistent improvement in the men's overall behaviour and attitudes and in their relationship together. This was compared with a more typical deterioration amongst men in this study receiving other disposals. Both the men and women concerned considered the improvements to be a result of the programme and most men were very positive both about the group and about their own hopes for the future.

Because the sample inevitably declined over time, the suggested 67% success rate represents only 40.2% of those who responded initially. While still considerably better than for the comparison group, the performance of the programme group probably falls within the range typically reported by reviewers of the American research. The numbers in this study were really quite low by the end, with just 28 female partners of the programme group at the 12-month point being asked about their (ex) partners' current behaviour. Cause and effect claims would be safer with larger numbers than this.

The evaluation of the Violence Prevention Programme (Burton et al, 1998), part of the Domestic Violence Intervention Project in London, also suffered from low numbers by the end (although workers report that completion rates have since improved). Only 31 men out of 351 went on to the second stage group. Numbers of court-mandated men were too low to analyse. The number of cases in which both men and women could be tracked and interviewed following substantial programme participation was just six. Of those who completed stage one, however, 91% did report a change in their understanding of domestic violence, which typically included recognition of their own responsibility for it and/or of its impact on others. More concretely, some women used their partners' participation on the programme as an opportunity to separate safely; in some cases the men's programme encouraged the man to leave and there were also situations in which separation motivated the man to use the programme to change sufficiently for a safe reconciliation.

Many programmes are building in their own evaluations using the above and/or other measures. The Cheshire programme (Skyner and Waters, 1999), for example, has employed an external evaluation that added testing of attitudinal and behavioural changes. This recorded statistically significant changes in the men's attitudes towards the offence and in their acceptance of responsibility. However, not only were numbers small, with only 21 completers, but these were self-reports from a user group notoriously given to minimisation and denial. Also, 'before and after' testing does not allow for a follow-up period during which gains could decline. Psychological testing must be of limited usefulness in domestic violence perpetrators' work, therefore, when compared with partner report.

In the authors' UK survey, only two respondent programmes had not had any evaluation carried out and one of these was in the process of developing it. Rather more had had external evaluations than had relied solely on internal measures. Several were able to point to changes that had been instituted as a result, including one instance of increased contact with partners, one of more work on the safety of children, and a range of alterations to programme content or the evaluation process. Worryingly, three programmes appeared not to be drawing on partner reports as a measure of men's level of change, if any, whereas only one did not ask the men for a self-report.

Future evaluations

Length of follow-up

Evaluations that have a follow-up period of anything less than a year will not be taken seriously by the expert community. Gondolf (1997:86) describes six months as 'short-term' in the American context; the National Campaign Against Violence and Crime Unit (1998) cites twelve months as a recommended minimum for Australia.

Longer is almost certainly better. Since the longest period traced in the literature is only 2.5 years to date (Gondolf, 1998c), it is hard to say at what interval continuing to collect the data ceases to be useful. There is some evidence (Dobash et al, 2000; Gondolf, 1998b) that most men fail in the early stages but that there will continue to be some further lapses over time. It would be interesting to know whether and when these become so low as to cease to affect the statistics materially or whether most perpetrators eventually lapse if tracked for long enough. Certainly, given that any widescale initiative in England and Wales would be being undertaken here for the first time, it would seem wise to err on the side of caution and to build in the longest possible follow-up period.

Gondolf (1997) further suggests periodic contact every two to three months in order both to retain respondents in the sample and to ensure clarity of recall. It would be ironic, of course, if evaluators kept in touch with programme participants while service delivery personnel did not. There is a practice-based argument for offering 'aftercare' and relapse prevention work to programme completers (Healey and Smith, 1998). Perhaps this could be the incentive for men to remain in the follow-up sample.

Outcome measures

Data must be triangulated at least to include self-report, partner report, and some form of official data. Subsequent convictions are one of the least accurate measures (Dobash et al, 2000). Police call-outs would be a far higher number but still a serious understatement. Other sources of data could be added (e.g. probation records, medical records) (Gondolf, 1997) but are unlikely to add much to women's reports.

The questions asked must go beyond the discrete incidents of violence that are the normal fare of criminal justice. They should be informed by what is known about the pattern of domestic violence and go into broader issues of subtler forms of abuse/controlling behaviour and sexual abusiveness (Tolman and Edleson, 1995). In methodological terms, this implies including qualitative elements alongside the gathering of quantitative data against standardised baselines (National Campaign Against Violence and Crime Unit, 1998), in line with current thinking about multi-methodological approaches to research (Bryman, 1988; Brannen, 1992).

Response rates

To combat poor response rates through an extended follow-up period, Gondolf (1997: 87) recommends 'elaborate tracking plans', with contact numbers on record for neighbours, relatives and friends in order to avoid losing track of men over the follow-up period. Given that follow-up information from women is the single most important source of data but that many women may be trying to leave dangerous men over this period, there needs to be very careful thought given as to how similar information could safely be held about partners. Certainly, it would have to be stored in conditions of utmost confidentiality, with a clear statement about who could access it and under what circumstances. Advice from Women's Aid nationally would be invaluable on such a matter since they are the agency with the longest-standing expertise on women's safety following domestic violence. Effective tracking of both men and women might also be improved by taking care to engage them carefully at the beginning of the evaluation process and possibly by offering incentives to remain in touch (National Campaign Against Violence and Crime Unit, 1998).

Control groups

Unlike in medicine, where a placebo may safely be given, there are problems in criminal justice research in having a pure control group with no sanction applied where a man is known to have offended. The only randomised control trial traced in the literature (Palmer et al, 1992), did not succeed in gaining sufficient partner reports to analyse, which makes it probably highly unreliable.

The alternatives are either randomly to allocate to different disposals or to use a control group already sentenced differently by the courts (e.g. Dobash et al, 2000). It would seem unlikely that British judges or magistrates would agree to random allocation to a range of disposals since this would remove their sentencing discretion. It might also potentially prejudice women's safety. Those commissioning evaluations will need to be aware, however, that not all approaches will pass muster with the purists (Sherman, 1992) and that they risk a degree of bias in the sample; there could, for example, be sentencer bias, though a comparative baseline can be sought through *post hoc* matching (Dobash et al, 2000).

Weaknesses in effectiveness research

Evaluation designs need to allow for the potential effect of intervening variables and of the programme and evaluation designs themselves. For example, partner support might alter the woman's response to the man and hence have an impact on him which is separate from the effect of his programme participation. When results are reported and interpreted, it is particularly important that such influences are allowed for and that cause and effect claims are not overstated. Even where a direct link appears to have been demonstrated, it is impossible to say for certain in which direction it is operating, or whether it might in fact be a reflection of some other, unexplained aspect of the situation.

Non-completion rates

Results should not be reported based solely on programme completers (Gondolf, 1997). Percentages of men who are violence-free after stated periods should be additionally cited as percentages of those accepted onto the programme, and arguably also of those initially referred to it.

Wider issues

Of crucial importance is the warning by the most experienced researchers in this field that no evaluation of perpetrators' programmes, however sophisticated, is likely to be able to produce conclusive evidence as to whether or not they work (Tolman and Edleson, 1995; Gondolf, 1997). Gondolf's (1997) suggestion is that, as has happened in biomedical ethics, final decisions about interventions of choice might be based on ethical standards derived from a broader value base (e.g. where an intervention is so important that it has to be tried, even though the evaluation evidence is inconclusive). This is not a vague proposal; such an approach to holding men accountable could, he states, be actively developed and tested through the procedures and programming of groups. The agreed standards of Respect (2000) would seem to offer a very useful first step towards this. Tolman and Edleson (1995) add that the uncertainty which continues to surround perpetrators' programmes means it is important not to direct all our efforts or resources into this work; wider preventative efforts, and particularly emergency and follow-up services for women and children, require renewed commitment also.

Costs

No UK information was traced in the mainstream literature on the costs of perpetrators' programmes. Individual programmes may well have their own data but it could be useful to import an approach akin to that in use in health economics to study this whole area. Future costings would need to bear in mind the existence of widely agreed best practice standards, including the principle stated by the National Practitioners' Network (1994) that unit costs should be calculated to include at least the minimum standard of work with the man's (ex) partner, we also know something about the enormous cost of allowing domestic violence to continue uninterrupted, which has been gauged in one London borough alone as standing as high as £7.5 million per year (Stanko et al, 1998).

Some relevant material is available from the USA. Snow Jones (1999) compared the costs of four contrasting domestic violence perpetrators' programmes. The analysis revealed that the estimated cost per individual session of attendance was lower than that for group sessions in mental health or substance misuse contexts. The lowest cost *per session* was at the site with the longest, most comprehensive programme, though it kept staffing costs down by using sessional staff rather than permanent, full-time staff to run the groups.

The lowest costs for *overall attendance* are obviously achieved by the shortest programmes although this must be set against effectiveness data in order to arrive at cost-effectiveness measures (not offered in the literature traced) as opposed to simple cost. These total costs are, like sessional costs, lower than in programmes on substance misuse. They ranged from $265 to $864 per overall programme attendance.

The work by Snow Jones, though derived from an entirely different social welfare and justice context to our own, might provide at least a set of measures and component costs which could be applied in the UK. Costs can be calculated per session, per completed programme, and/or per programme participant including all non-completers. They can be further broken down by funding source if relevant.

In the American context, even court-mandated programme participants were paying from a fifth to the whole of the cost of their own attendance in the form of fees, partially recouped in some cases from the men's insurance cover. In the UK survey undertaken by the authors, two voluntary projects were charging fees to self-referred men, on a sliding scale according to income and outgoings, and did find that this could help to enhance motivation and completion. Charging has since become common in the voluntary sector, frequently as a one-off payment in advance. Ironically, men on court orders cannot be charged a fee, as this would amount to a fine. Charges would be contra-indicated in the mainstream if they risked lowering completion rates still further. Conversely, practice evidence from America (Healey and Smith, 1998) suggests that they may cause some men to take the programme more seriously and even to avoid reoffending so as not to incur further such expense. Care needs to be taken that any sliding scale of charges goes low enough to ensure that unwaged and low paid men, or those with high dependency costs, are not obliged to decline a programme as a sentencing option through inability to pay. Arguably, charges could also go high enough as to represent a real penalty to affluent men. One additional concern is that there is anecdotal evidence from refuge contexts that abused women are not infrequently forced to pay their partners' fines and the same might become true of programme fees (although the survey did not reveal this happening).

There are other costs to the man, as part of his punishment, beyond financial considerations, and benefits, too, to him and his family. He has to give up time to attend the group and have his behaviour and whereabouts over the previous week questioned and monitored. In addition, he is required to disclose his unacceptable behaviour in front of a collection of frequently unsympathetic and highly challenging strangers, is expected to work hard in the group and on 'homework' tasks in between, and may feel as if he is back in school. On the positive side, Burton et al (1998) list a number of gains which stage one completers were able to cite in their own, their partners and their children's lives; 72%, for example, listed greater security for the children and 59% cited learning alternatives to violence.

Cost-effectiveness always has to be measured against alternatives. If perpetrator programmes work, they might potentially prevent very heavy costs to the criminal justice system in the form of numerous further call-outs, arrests, prosecutions, court hearings and any sentences imposed on the men (including imprisonment in some cases). There are also potentially large savings to health (including mental health) and social care agencies in terms of services for victims (Stanko et al, 1998). There are immeasurable future costs too where children who live with violence do not fulfil their educational potential or where women are lost to the community as active citizens, workers and mothers, through being injured or killed. It is also important to remember that domestic violence has a long-term pattern; it typically goes on over many years, thus multiplying all the costs manifold. Dobash et al (2000) point out that an effective response, whatever the outlay, might bring a halt to this expenditure over time and thus eventually save money.

Any new provision with realistic sanctions would incur costs in relation to rearrest and resentencing for those men who failed to comply, in addition to the cost of providing and evaluating the programmes themselves.

One further point of relevance is that what programmes offer in terms of value for money goes beyond apparently interrupting or ending violence in some individuals, at relatively low cost. Being sentenced to attend a group does have a cost to the man and is less costly to society than many other sanctions. In addition, it may give the woman a chance to leave, it monitors her partner's behaviour and gives her at least a weekly respite plus contact with partner support services, including someone to take her seriously and believe what she is saying. Therefore it could be worth running groups as a form of punishment with spin-off benefits, even if they are not proven to be rehabilitative. Furthermore, perpetrator groups offer other services of value. The best are directly associated with proactive work with the men's partner and they operate in an inter-agency context, feeding into child protection case conferences, contact proceedings, probation enforcement of court orders, and so on.

There are some particular problems to note concerning cost-effectiveness calculations in relation to domestic violence. First, this is one field in which rising criminal justice costs will be a sign of success. So under-reported are the crimes associated with domestic violence, that there will be spiralling expenditure if women start to report them in anything approaching true numbers (see Mullender, 1996, on incidence and prevalence). Cost effectiveness analyses might usefully attempt to calculate the cost to society of one single 'untreated' perpetrator pursuing a career of domestic violence through a lifetime, taking into account the impact on women and children in potential serial relationships and the involvement of a wide range of agencies.

Inter-agency working

Perpetrators' programmes need to be well integrated into the criminal justice system and also into wider inter-agency networks involving women's organisations, child welfare and child protection agencies and public education work. Gondolf (1997), in an overview of progress in perpetrators' programmes to date and of remaining unresolved issues, states that there is evidence that links with the courts, with advocacy and services for women, and with wider work on public attitudes and assumptions, may all have an impact on programme success. Some of the best developed work with perpetrators in the USA, for example in Minneapolis and Duluth, Minnesota, forms one part of a co-ordinated response to men, women and children which is widely regarded as setting a model of best practice.

Inter-agency forums (see Hague, this volume) can play a key role in:

- making agencies more aware of one another's practice;
- sharing good practice;
- drawing up good practice guidelines;
- offering joint training;
- creating channels for referrals to perpetrators' programmes;
- increasing the accountability of these programmes; and
- linking the work into a comprehensive approach to primary, secondary and tertiary prevention. They may also establish new services to fill gaps in provision.

Links with criminal justice

Syers and Edleson (1992) found that court-mandated attendance at a programme that followed police calling at the home and arresting the man was more effective in ending repeat violence than other combinations of criminal justice actions. In England and Wales, this means probation (and any voluntary sector groups taking mandated men) being a clear part of a concerted effort by the entire criminal justice system, including the police, Crown Prosecution Service (CPS) and the courts, to achieve arrest, prosecution and appropriate sentencing for domestic violence perpetrators. It also involves sending clear messages to men throughout this process, and after, that their behaviour will not be tolerated and will incur appropriate sanctions. This implies:

- pro-arrest policies;
- tackling 'no criming' tendencies by the police;
- effective prosecution without downgrading of charges by the CPS;
- consistent sentencing from a magistracy and a judiciary appropriately trained in domestic violence awareness; and
- mandatory attendance at a programme as an element of sentencing, with appropriate sanctions for non-attendance.

Repeat offences, together with breaches of sentencing and of protective orders, must incur strict penalties that are made known to perpetrators at the time of conviction. Since domestic violence almost always involves a pattern of repeat offences, it is important that courts take persistence as well as seriousness into account when sentencing.

Action should be taken by the police, CPS, courts and probation service to minimise non-completion rates by referring men through to programmes as quickly as possible and by actively pursuing non-compliance with realistic sanctions. Programmes themselves can also implement measures to assist men in engaging with the programme at the beginning and in the early stages. This could be thought of as a 'carrot and stick' approach. This is particularly important because most failures (re-assaults) occur early. Dobash et al (2000) found that the majority happened in the first three months after the commencement of programme participation; this was even more pronounced amongst men on the perpetrators' programmes than amongst those with other disposals. American findings have also pointed to the importance of the earliest stage of group attendance (see above).

Co-ordination, speed of response, monitoring of compliance, rigorous enforcement of penalties, sharing of information, links with substance misuse and mental health provision, and co-ordination with services for women and children are also all of relevance. There is a strong case for implementing advocacy schemes on the American model (see Healey and Smith, 1998), so that women have someone to support them while their partners' cases go through the courts. Such schemes may be very useful, also, in maintaining a careful statistical overview of the nature and progression of such cases.

Links with women's organisations

The necessity of working with female partners and ex-partners in order to keep their safety and their reports of re-assault rates to the forefront of definitions of success requires a close link with providers of emergency and follow-up services for women. Women's organisations first identified and responded to the issue of domestic violence, offer the best safeguard against collusion and dilution, and receive the most positive feedback from women themselves (see Mullender and Hague; and Kelly and Humphreys, this volume). It is crucially important not to bypass the major women's organisations in building any new efforts for change.

Inter-agency working is also highly relevant in so far as women are the key source of valid and reliable data on reoffending and on the effectiveness of change efforts. Services to protect and support women are channels for evaluation as well, of course, as key elements in prioritising women and children's safety. They can comment, too, on the practical and ethical standards which programmes should meet.

Links with child welfare and child protection agencies

Another chapter (Mullender, this volume) outlines the evidence of a clear link between domestic violence, direct child abuse and the harmful effects on children of living with domestic violence. There need to be good links between the relevant agencies, established in ways that do not deter women or children from seeking help. Practitioners in men's programmes need child protection training, and can assist services working with women and children through effective referral, assessment and reporting. Social Services Departments, in turn, are important referral sources for perpetrators' programmes, and may enter into service level agreements to obtain multiple places for dangerous men.

Widening the net: Working with other perpetrators

There are also other opportunities for the civil and criminal justice systems to 'send messages' to perpetrators that their behaviour is unacceptable and to intervene where appropriate. The probation service, for example, finds itself dealing with many men who talk about the abuse they have perpetrated against current and former partners, in situations where this is not the index offence (Mullender, 1996). In the authors' UK survey, only a minority of probation respondents reported that their colleagues were routinely directed to ask questions about domestic violence. In such circumstances, wider work on offending behaviour, attitudes of zero tolerance towards the abuse of women and children, and probation involvement in inter-agency forums can all be important.

There is a further reason why all probation officers and their managers should receive training on domestic violence. Except in Scotland, the perpetrator's supervising officer is unlikely to be a facilitator of the programme he attends. This means that the officer concerned (and his or her supervisor) needs an understanding of the aims and content of the programme in order to reinforce, not undermine, the process of re-education and change it seeks to pursue (Healey and Smith, 1998). Well trained and supported probation staff would be better able to boost men's attendance at and engagement in a programme, underscore the messages conveyed, and promote accountability to and the safety of partners. Where this does not happen, there can be a tendency to hand over all responsibility for responding to the man's abusive behaviour to the programme (Burton et al, 1998), while the supervising officer deals with other issues. Since this officer is the person who may have to 'breach' the perpetrator for non-compliance, a 'hands off' approach of this kind is likely to be detrimental to programme effectiveness, particularly if the offender senses that he is unlikely to face sanctions for non-attendance. Finally, all probation officers could offer aftercare support to programme completers with whom they retain contact for other reasons and could undertake relapse prevention work with them (Healey and Smith, 1998).

Given the high numbers of younger offenders dealt with by probation officers, they may well have opportunities to reach domestic abusers early in their offending career. Not to say or do anything at this point, when the abuser talks about his domestic violence crimes, may will be interpreted by him as tolerance and collusion. Thought needs to be given to the appropriate action to be taken by probation officers when being told of such offences, particularly when these have not previously been prosecuted.

Preventive work

An interesting insight into the views of young people aged 8 to 16, some of whom will become the perpetrators and some others of whom the survivors of the next generation, is available from an ESRC-funded study, 'Children's Needs, Coping Strategies and Understandings of Woman Abuse' (ESRC Award ref. no. L129251037), recently completed, which involved both the current authors together with colleagues at the Universities of Bristol, Durham and North London (Mullender et al, forthcoming).

A key finding from a questionnaire survey administered to well over a thousand children in primary and secondary schools, as part of this research, is the scope for awareness-raising work in class. This needs to start in primary school and to target boys for the most intensive work, including throughout secondary school. At all ages, boys emerge as having a less clear understanding than girls as to who is at fault in situations of domestic violence and as being more likely to excuse the perpetrator. Of particular concern is the strong suggestion from the data that boys become less rather than more clear as they get older that men should take responsibility for their own violence. Boys' attitudes begin to diverge markedly from girls' at 13-14 years of age and they continue to move apart thereafter. Furthermore, over three-quarters of 11-12 year old boys think that women get hit if they make men angry, with more boys than girls at all ages believing that some women deserve to be hit. By the age of 15, girls are far more likely than boys to recognise that it is hard for a woman to leave the violence and that pregnant women also experience violence. The vast majority of secondary children and just over half at primary age wants lessons on domestic violence in school. They want to learn what to do about it and how to stop it, as well as to understand why it happens.

There clearly needs to be an early start in raising levels of awareness. The most developed models for such work exist in Canada (Mullender, 1994) and there are also some useful projects in Britain, with training materials/educational packs now available. Islington's *STOP* pack (London Borough of Islington, 1995), is in widescale use, for example, as is *Guidance for Schools*, produced in Leeds (Leeds Education and Leeds Inter-Agency Project, not dated). Training and preparation for teachers must, of course, precede any such effort and it is also important to have the education authority, school governing bodies, and staff groups involved before work begins with pupils and their parents. Links also need to be in place with social services, Women's Aid and ChildLine.

Conclusion

Despite some remaining areas of contention in policy and practice, a considerable body of practice wisdom and of research-generated knowledge has been accumulated since the first perpetrators' programmes began in the USA in the late 1970s. It is now essential to work to nationally agreed practice principles. Perpetrators' programmes are a field of intervention in which it is possible to do harm as well as good. The first allegiance of practitioners should not to be to the men in the groups they are running but to those whose safety is put at immediate risk by those men and to the expectations of the wider public that offenders be held accountable for their actions. There has to be an external benchmark which ensures that safety and expectations of accountability remain to the fore whilst, at the same time, constantly incorporating new knowledge into the minimum standards and good practice guidelines against which groups operate.

One aspect of these standards has to be effective evaluation. It is crucial to learn more about whether violent men can change as a result of intervention because, even if a couple separates, there may be reconciliations and abusers are also often violent in serial relationships. Certainly, no new programmes should be established without in-built evaluation, preferably externally conducted and working to the principles outlined above of prioritising partner report and long-term follow up, while being aware of the effect of attrition rates.

Overall it should always be remembered that programmes will be working with only a tiny minority of abusers, even if the proposed national coverage of groups is established through the probation service. They will recruit men solely, or largely, who have been reported, arrested, charged, prosecuted, who have pleaded or been found guilty, and then sentenced high enough up the tariff to attend the group. Clearly, there are many more perpetrators at each of these stages with whom no work of this kind is being done so we will continue to know little about the potential for change of the generality of abusers. Furthermore, far fewer men 'make it' through to the point of follow-up evaluation than fail to complete. This amounts to one whole area in which programmes can as yet be said to be far from successful whatever the best efforts of the practitioners. This is not to be taken as an argument against programmes, however, and there are possible remedies, both 'sticks' and 'carrots', which might be applied. The role of the courts in applying effective sanctions is likely to be crucial in probation-run groups.

Unresolved issues (Gondolf 1998a) include sanctions for non-completion and reoffending and early and intensive intervention designed to tackle those who reoffend early and persistently. There is a need for additional services to deal with the factors that may be somehow associated with re-offending (though not necessarily causally), including treatment for alcohol misuse and for various mental health problems. There may also be a need for 'aftercare' and relapse prevention work with programme completers.

Work with perpetrators will only ever be one part of the domestic violence picture and of secondary importance to meeting the needs of women and children for emergency services, outreach and aftercare. It should not take a disproportionate amount of public funding. However, there is modest cause to believe that it can work with some men and that the groupwork skills of practitioners are an extremely valuable asset to a society aiming to confront collusion with the denial and minimisation of violence.

What role can the health services play?

Leslie L Davidson, Valerie King, Jo Garcia, Sally Marchant

Domestic violence is a frequent cause of injury and emotional trauma to women and accounts for a substantial proportion of health service use. The health services can serve as a nearly universal and possibly neutral point of contact for women looking for assistance. Recognition by the health services of the importance of domestic violence has increased substantially in the UK over the past decade and the Department of Health, the Chief Medical Officer and several professional organisations including the BMA, the RCOG and the RCM have published advice about professional practice.

Research evidence makes it clear that women expect health professionals to include domestic violence as a health care issue. Women expect to be asked about it, and to be offered support and appropriate referral and advice. There is ample evidence as well that health professionals find discussing domestic violence with women challenging and often do not feel appropriately prepared for the interaction. Very few health professionals have received training and very little of the training has been evaluated.

There are few studies addressing the impact on later outcomes of intervening in domestic violence by identifying, assessing and supporting women through the health sector. The studies that exist primarily investigate the best way to ask women about whether they are experiencing domestic violence. The health services need to investigate the impact of the new policies on the well-being of women experiencing domestic violence. Studies need to look at both benefit and potential harm. This will require establishing what outcomes to measure and developing appropriate experimental interventions. In the meantime, the Health Service must respond to the expressed needs of women. The current recommendations that exist include:

- *The responsibility of all health professionals to be aware of the importance of domestic violence.*
- *The development of local strategies and guidelines for the identification and support of women victims, including multi-agency working.*
- *The provision of information in clinics about sources of help for victims.*
- *That routine questions about violence be included in asking about social*

problems and that obstetricians and gynaecologists should ask all women about violence.
- *That all women are seen on their own at least once during their antenatal care.*
- *That routine questioning must be accompanied by training for professionals and provisions for referral.*
- *That an interpreter should be provided if needed who should not be a partner, friend or family member.*

Introduction

This chapter reviews and summarises research about effective health based interventions to decrease both health and other consequences of domestic violence to women. We have restricted our discussion to women and their unborn children, although it is clear that men and children of both genders can be victims as well. In particular, there is a vast literature on children witnessing domestic violence as well as children as victims of the same violence. It is important to recognise the links between violence against women and other types of family violence and these issues are addressed in Chapters 2 and 11.

Although definitions of domestic violence can vary, for the purpose of this review we adopted a broad working definition, currently being used by the Home Office. Domestic violence is defined as violence between current or former partners in an intimate relationship, wherever and whenever the violence occurs. The violence may include physical, sexual, emotional/psychological or financial abuse. This includes violence by men to women and, by women to men and within same sex relationships but does not include other violence in a domestic setting such as child or elder abuse or between siblings or flat sharers.

The first section of this chapter reviews what is known about the prevalence of domestic violence and the relative importance of domestic violence as a proportion of the violence experienced by men and by women. It goes on to consider the magnitude of its health and economic consequences. We will also discuss the opportunities for, and possible limitations of, health service based domestic violence interventions as well as the barriers to providing appropriate care. The next section is a systematic review of the effectiveness of interventions based in the health sector. The findings of the review will be discussed in terms of key questions that the health service must address in implementing interventions designed to address domestic violence.

Although this comprehensive review of the literature has revealed some innovative interventions, there are many areas of health services where domestic violence is not well studied. The vast majority of published research on domestic violence is North American, though there have been a small number of researchers in the UK and other countries who have been involved in this topic for many years.

There are recent signs of a wider interest in this country in the health impact of domestic violence and in attempts to address women's needs in the context of health care. However, systematic attempts to identify and help women experiencing domestic violence are still few and far between in the health services in the UK. Therefore, we will conclude the chapter by indicating the areas where changes in practice are clearly indicated and with recommendations for research programmes that should narrow the gaps in critical knowledge.

Methods used

We searched the UK and international English language literature through March of 2000 for published and unpublished reports of the evaluation of screening, identification and assessment and treatment interventions for domestic violence in health care settings regardless of the gender involved in the intervention. We also searched for interventions in health care once a woman had been identified as being the victim of abuse in any other agency or setting. We also searched websites related to violence and consulted with members of the UK Domestic Violence and Health Research Forum for knowledge of work not yet published.

We found only a small number of evaluations of good scientific quality and these are described in the text. The criteria for inclusion in the review were the following: experimental interventions with controls and/or pre-post measures of the outcomes in question. Interventions could include an increase or change in knowledge and attitudes as well as an increase in identification, assessment or intervention or an increase in key outcomes. We have noted the methodological limitations of the evaluations that we have used.

Domestic violence and health care

Health service goals

The goals of the health care system with regard to domestic violence primarily include the identification and the assessment and treatment of the physical and psychological illness resulting from domestic violence and the referral of women to appropriate services. This includes interventions designed to ameliorate or eliminate its effects or to limit future exposure to violence for the victim. These health service goals focus on harm minimisation and are thus distinct from the explicit crime reduction emphasis of the criminal justice system. Health related literature on the aetiology, epidemiological associations and prevention of violence is broad. It is not our aim in this chapter to thoroughly review that literature though we have made use of some of the relevant studies to provide a sufficient background to comprehend the appropriateness of interventions.

Published good practice recommendations

There has been a growing interest in domestic violence and health on the part of professional and government bodies.

A joint letter giving guidance on domestic violence from the Director of the Health Services and the Chief Inspector of Social Services was circulated to all Chief Executives of Health Authorities and of NHS Trusts, Regional Nurse Directors and Directors of Social Services in November 1997. The impetus for this letter was a change in civil law under Part IV of the Family Law Act which came into operation on 1st October 1996. In addition, the circulation of the joint letter from NHS and Social Service executives underpinned the advice to initiate multi-agency work in this area. It particularly targeted primary care, accident and emergency and gynaecology and obstetric services.

As part of the guidance, an appendix was attached giving specific information about increasing awareness of domestic violence by clinicians. It suggested asking initial questions about overall social and emotional well being (e.g. Is everything all right at home?) and following these up with a series of direct questions about potentially abusive scenarios which might be physical and/or emotional in nature. Detailed advice was also provided about making a record of information divulged during such an interview, the autonomy of the person to refuse this and the legal implications of action taken on behalf of an individual at risk. This letter was followed up by a reminder and second copy of the letter and by an article in a newsletter sent to all doctors by the Chief Medical Officer of England (CMO's Update 19, London, August 1998).

The Royal College of Obstetricians and Gynaecologists, the Royal College of Midwives, The Royal College of General Practice, and the British Medical Association produced recommendations for practice regarding domestic violence in 1997 and 1998. The Community Practitioner and Health Visitor Association followed in 1999, and the Royal College of Nursing in 2000 (CPHVA, 1999; RCN, 2000). While these guidelines do not put forward exactly the same recommendations, (reflecting that the health sector has not yet developed a comprehensive and integrated approach), they all support the emphasis on multi-disciplinary involvement, education and training. These aim to raise awareness both amongst victims of domestic violence about the potential services available to them as well as to change the attitudes and practice of the health professionals who have contact with them.

The main recommendations of the professional organisations centre on improving the identification of women experiencing domestic violence. For example, they all:

- cite the need for better information and training about domestic violence;
- support the need for a non-judgmental and supportive approach;
- recommend the development of local policies and guidelines;
- recommend asking questions about incidents that might be due to domestic violence rather than the leaving the victim with the responsibility of bringing it up and stipulate the need for a safe and private clinical environment;
- suggest the use of brief initial questions followed up by more detailed enquiry;
- cite the need for health professionals to have information on the resources and local initiatives available for women needing referral; and
- include the need for further research to develop appropriate screening tools, strategies to raise awareness and the need for specific training of the professional involved.

The primary difference between the recommendations centres on when to ask and which women to ask about their experience of violence. All recommended asking women about incidents which might be due to domestic violence rather than leaving women with the responsibility of bringing up the issue. The BMA does not take a position on whether to screen women or not. The RCM recommends asking about violence where the midwife suspects the occurrence of domestic violence whereas the RCOG publication recommends asking routine questions about violence to all women who come into contact with the health services through obstetrics, gynaecology, general practice or maternity care, a position supported broadly by the RCN guidelines.

The focus of the position paper by the Royal College of Midwives (1997) is on the accountability of the midwife alone though they emphasise the need for a multi-disciplinary approach. The RCM paper states minimum standards required by midwives when taking responsibility for women in their care who may be victims or potential victims of violence. This includes documentation and referral and issues around child protection.

The RCOG book, *Violence and Women* (1997), as suggested by its title, takes a broader look at violence and the lives of women. It adopts a multi-disciplinary approach within health, reviewing much of the research evidence to develop their recommendations.

The British Medical Association report, *Domestic Violence, a health care issue?* (BMA, 1998) advocates a multi-agency approach and makes recommendations that apply far beyond the health sector. In addition, the BMA broadens the responsibility in the health sector for implementing strategies related to the awareness and management of domestic violence by stating that all Health Authorities should be required to introduce domestic violence into health improvement programmes by consulting and collaboration within a multi-agency setting. With the exception of the CPHVA, few of the guidelines explore the issues of the overlap between domestic violence and child abuse.

The last triennial Confidential Enquiries into Maternal Deaths 1994-1996 (Dept of Health, 1998) has highlighted violence as a cause of maternal death and made a series of recommendations, broadly based on those of the RCOG, the RCM and the BMA. It supported:

- The responsibility of all health professionals to be aware of the importance of domestic violence.
- The development of local strategies and guidelines for the identification and support of women victims including multi-agency working.
- The provision of information about sources of help for victims in clinics.
- That routine questions about violence be included when taking a social history in midwifery, obstetric and gynaecological practice.
- That all women are seen on their own at least once during their antenatal care.
- That routine questioning must be accompanied by training for professionals, provision of referral working together with local groups.
- That interpreters should be provided if needed and should not be a partner, friend or family member.
- That all women are seen on their own at least once during their antenatal care.

These recommendations were accompanied by a Health Service Circular

(HSC 1998/999) issued by the Medical Director of the NHS and the Chief Nursing Officer to all health authorities and trusts and relevant professionals. The circular stated that 'all the recommendations should be implemented as part of local care and audit plans'.

The Department of Health published a resource manual of good practice to help health professionals in a range of settings and for use in the development of local multi-agency protocols (Department of Health, 2000). The resource manual builds on and consolidates the separate guidelines which have been issued by the various Royal Colleges in recent years.

Extent of the problem

Chapter 11 on risk assessment identifies the incidence and prevalence of domestic violence suffered by women, and the fact that they are twice as likely as men to suffer injury during an attack. A recent Scottish study identified 235 victims of violence seen in an emergency department, of whom 46 (20%) were women (20%) and 189 (80%) men. Of the women, 19 (41%) were victims of domestic violence, compared to only two or 1% of the men (Wright and Kasiya, 1997). Domestic violence is an important problem for the health service to tackle in women, but, while recognising that men are also victims of domestic violence, it would be inappropriate to make it a priority in men. The high estimates of domestic violence make it one of the most prevalent health related conditions suffered by women with one study of women in London reporting a 27% lifetime experience and 8% in the previous year (Mooney, 1993).

Health impact of domestic violence

The specific health consequences of domestic violence are numerous. They can range from psychological effects to physical injury and death. There are serious limitations to the information documented about the extent, severity or long term consequences of the injury sustained by women due to domestic violence. This is in large part due to the nature of the routinely collected data in the health sector in regard to injury. Injury and death are recorded as intentional or not, but the relationship between the victim and the assailant is not routinely recorded. Accident and Emergency sources may record the short-term health service consequence: discharge to home, follow-up, admission or death, but not the outcome - disability or complete recovery. The legal data available record the relationship and the presence of injury or use of a weapon but not detail about the impact of injury itself. In order to fully understand the impact of domestic violence on those experiencing it or on the health services, it will be necessary to develop better outcome measures that involve the impact and long term consequences of injury. To develop evaluations of interventions, similarly, better measurement of outcomes will be imperative (Davidson, 1996).

A Swedish emergency department study found that trauma was the cause of the visit in about one third of women presenting with domestic violence as an underlying cause. The trauma most commonly involved bruises, abrasions and fractures. The injuries were primarily caused by punching, kicking and being knocked down (Brismar et al, 1987). A US study of accident and emergency visits of 9,057 women aged 19-65 found that 280 were battered in an incident that day, representing 3.1% of all visits and 11.2% of visits for an injury. The location of the injuries frequently involved the head, face, neck, thorax and abdomen in contrast to non-battered women who presented with injuries who were more likely to be injured in the extremities. The authors developed a model of 12 injury types which, taking any one as a criterion, identified 81% of women battered that day. The authors concluded that injury type was insufficient as an identifier of domestic violence and recommended universal screening in all injured women (Muelleman et al, 1996).

Victims of abuse are much more likely to suffer poor health, chronic pain, depression, suicide attempts, and problems in pregnancy compared to women who do not experience abuse (Plichta, 1992). Although there is controversy regarding whether pregnant women actually experience more abuse than their non-pregnant counterparts, domestic violence in pregnancy may predispose women to poor perinatal outcomes. Domestic violence in pregnancy has been associated with fetal distress and fetal death (Dye et al, 1995), late entry to antenatal care (McFarlane et al, 1996; Taggart & Mattson, 1996) low birth weight (McFarlane et al, 1996; Bullock & McFarlane, 1989), preterm labour and chorioamnionitis (Berenson et al, 1994).

Women who are abused are at particularly high risk for psychological problems: a Swedish accident and emergency study found that battered women were far more likely to have had a history of using mental health services than non-battered women (Brismar et al, 1987). Over half the battered women reported depressive symptoms in a recent US national survey by the Commonwealth Fund (Collins et al, 1999). The same survey also noted that these women had more physical health problems and higher levels of disability. A relationship between abuse and gastrointestinal illness and poor outcomes was found in a review by Drossman et al, in 1995. In addition, women living in violent situations may fail to, or be prevented from, taking up preventive health services and other approaches to healthy living. For example, the Commonwealth Fund survey found that women who had experienced violence were twice as likely to smoke compared with women who had not experienced violence (32% vs 16%). Living in an abusive situation can mean that these women may not use acute and chronic health intervention services at all or in a timely manner. In the US over twice as many women with histories of abuse faced problems with access to care. It is not clear whether poor use of care arises from financial difficulties or restrictions on free movement or both. While the UK lacks most of the financial barriers to health care access that are present in the US there may still be access problems stemming from other correlates of abuse. Furthermore, only 29% of US women reported that they discussed their abuse with a health care professional compared to more than double that proportion who said they had confided in a friend or relative. When women did discuss abuse with a doctor only 44% were referred to support services and less than a quarter were referred to the police (Collins et al, 1999).

Children: Although beyond the scope of this chapter, there is a substantial literature which links domestic violence and child abuse within families and which in addition notes the intergenerational transfer of violent behaviour to children (McKay, 1994; Hall and Lynch, 1998). Women who have a history of being abused in childhood are more likely to experience domestic violence as adults (Collins et al, 1999; Coid et al, 2001). Families in which abuse occurs are more likely to have children under the age of 5. These children are also exposed to higher levels of factors highly correlated with developmental delay than are children in non-violent households (Fantuzzo et al, 1997).

Costs of domestic violence within the health sector

There is little information on the costs of domestic violence in England and Wales. A study in Hackney estimated the health sector costs for injury care and for psychological care as a consequence of domestic violence as £590,000 in 1996 (Stanko et al, 1998). This study excluded the costs of medication and of hospitalisation. The Scottish Needs Assessment Programme report on domestic violence (SNAP, 1997) estimated the additional health service resources attributable to domestic violence using different assumptions. They did not apply costs to these but the increased resource use was substantial.

Women who are victims of domestic violence have greater health service utilisation than other women, even though there is evidence that their health needs are often not adequately met. A Swedish study found that a group of battered women had approximately three-fold greater numbers of hospital admissions for both traumatic and non-traumatic indications over the period of 1983-4 compared to matched community controls (Bergman et al, 1992). Similarly, an Australian study found that abused pregnant women had higher rates of admission to hospital during pregnancy (Webster et al, 1996) thereby causing substantive additional costs.

Measured in 1991 US dollars, a survey of US mental health professionals reported that the annual costs of counselling and mental health treatment received by victims of assault (including domestic violence) and of all rape was $885.5 million and $863 million respectively. Their survey also estimated that only 4% of assault victims obtain mental health care and that those who do often receive inadequate amounts of care. Thus, the actual cost of domestic violence to the mental health service might be substantially greater than these figures were utilisation to be more appropriately linked to need (Cohen and Miller, 1998).

Koss et al (1991) studied the increased outpatient health service utilisation in a US case control approach to study the impact of a past history of criminal victimisation, including domestic violence on the use of outpatient services by working women between 19 and 69. This study does not differentiate between domestic and other violence so the results are not specific. The study also eliminated psychotherapy, dental services and care in pregnancy. They found increased service use with increasing past exposure to violence in the year studied which was costed, using outpatient charges as $161 for a never victimised person compared to $401 for someone with a history of multiple exposure. They concluded that the cost of long term increased health service utilisation must be studied as well as the immediate health care costs of violence.

Another report that does not differentiate domestic from other violence reviews the estimated costs of violence against women in British Columbia in Canada by costing charges in different sectors. An estimated $7 million was spent on drug and alcohol treatment for women experiencing violence regardless of the sector in which it was spent. Though this report includes mental health costs reported as 'partial' at $18 million annually, they did not make estimates of the costs of emergency medical care, relying instead on two unpublished reports of costs in the health sector for all of Canada. The first estimated $12.7 million for emergency costs (Greaves et al, 1995, as quoted in Kerr and Mclean, 1996). The second made lower estimates for emergency costs - $7.6 million for emergency costs and $1.6 million for dental repair work, but also gave an estimate of additional medical costs of $255 million. (Day et al, as quoted in Kerr and Mclean, 1996).

A US report commented on the wide range of estimates of the costs of domestic violence. It concluded that this was largely due to the varying prevalence of violence used in the analyses and the absence of a comprehensive economic model that included both direct and indirect costs (Friedman et al, 1997). They found estimates of $1,633 per person per year (1992) for accident and emergency room visits (excluding mental health visits) and some estimates of the costs of hospitalisation. They were unable to find any nationally representative data on costs for many other outpatient costs, including training costs for health professionals (Hartmann et al, 1997).

Points of contact with the health service

Health services may have a role in the primary prevention of domestic violence, but are more likely to be involved in the identification, assessment and treatment of women who experience domestic violence. Although health effects are but one aspect of the impact of domestic violence, contact with health services may offer the only possible contact point with professionals who could recognise and intervene in the situation. Health settings and workers are generally accepted as a neutral point of contact and are used by virtually all women in Britain. Furthermore, women are also likely to use health services in their roles as carers for children and older people. Health services may be particularly important for women whose contacts with the outside world are restricted by a violent partner. Women experiencing domestic violence represent a high proportion of those seen in accident and emergency units, primary care, maternity services, psychological and psychiatric services along with many other possible health care arenas. For example, particularly high rates of domestic violence have been found among attenders of gynaecological clinics (Schei and Bakkesteig, 1989). Orthopaedic and plastic surgery service providers may also encounter domestic violence victims in both acute and chronic health care settings.

Challenges, barriers, and constraints

Women's views

Chapter 1, on women survivors, discusses the views of women victims of domestic violence about their needs and help from a range of sources. Women's views of health care interventions about domestic violence have, until recently, received little attention from health researchers or practitioners in this field. In the past, information has tended to come from general studies of women in refuges or population samples that included assessment of women's views of the various agencies likely to be involved. This has changed recently, and a number of studies have been published where both abused and non-abused women in health care settings were asked directly about their health care in relation to domestic violence. This has included being asked about or explicitly screened for domestic violence (eg. Hayden et al, 1997; Rodriguez, 1996; Caralis and Musialowski, 1997; Stenson et al, 2001; Richardson et al, 2001). In general, women have confirmed that they do not mind being asked and that direct questions are more useful than indirect approaches. Confidentiality for the woman, however, is of primary importance. A relationship of trust is necessary for disclosure and appears to be facilitated by continuity of care (Covington et al, 1997). One useful study explored the views of abused women about desirable and unwelcome aspects of doctor behaviour and also asked how often the women had encountered each aspect (Hamberger, 1998). In a recent review of the North American qualitative literature (Sleutel, 1998) women's reports of contacts with health professionals were often negative because of caregivers' tendency to ignore the signs of abuse, or to be unsupportive if they did acknowledge what was happening. If asked, women in the studies covered by Sleutel's review recommended that health professionals ask women about abuse, listen to women and refer them to other sources of help. Women's support for routine screening was high (75%) in the one study that asked about it directly (Caralis and Musialowski, 1997).

Henderson (1997) reports the results of a government sponsored study of domestic violence in Scotland. The views of women experiencing domestic violence were sought by postal questionnaire (sent to a volunteer sample) and by interviews with women contacted through Women's Aid. Similar issues emerged from both sources of information. Women often sought help from GPs and health visitors. They wanted time to talk and to be taken seriously. They were unhappy with the tendency of some GPs to prescribe medication in response to their visit. Their satisfaction with GPs and health visitors was linked to the professional's attitude and response, rather than to any practical action taken on the woman's behalf. Some women mentioned that they would like more time to discuss domestic violence during a consultation and would like the caregiver to take the initiative in asking if they had a suspicion that violence was involved.

Health care workers

Health care workers may explore the possibility of domestic violence with their patients less frequently than recommended for a range of reasons (see a recent review by Watts, 1998; Rodriguez et al, 1999). Health professionals in both UK and US have rarely received education or training in the area of DV (Easteal and Easteal, 1992; Abbot and Williamson, 1999). Health care workers vary in the degree to which they believe that domestic violence is a health issue. Overall, however, doctors, nurses and health visitors feel that the health services should identify women experiencing domestic violence, although fewer feel that they should be involved in interventions to reduce or eliminate DV. Fewer dentists felt that they had a role (Ferris and Tudiver, 1992; Tilden et al, 1994). Health providers often feel that they have nothing to offer these women or may not know what to do once a victim is identified (Short et al, 1997; Hepburn and McCartney, 1997; Marchant et al, 2001). Some may be concerned that the discovery of domestic violence may result in a lot of work for them (Sugg and Inui, 1992). There may also be fears about danger to themselves from violent partners.

A negative bias toward women experiencing domestic violence that could affect professional interactions has sometimes been reported by women. In addition, health care workers who interact with multiple members of a family, in addition to the woman who is being abused, may feel that their care for the others is in some way compromised or complicated. Discovery of domestic violence in a family with children also raises the issue of whether there is child abuse occurring. A thoughtful review in this area can be found in Warshaw (1994).

Confronting domestic violence more explicitly and widely in the health services may also be assumed to have effects on health care workers and the service itself. Health care workers may have experienced domestic violence themselves, either directly or as a close friend or family member.

An area not addressed frequently in practice recommendations or in the research literature is standards and approaches to documentation. Careful documentation of clinical findings can be of enormous assistance to other care providers for the woman and for her children. Documentation of injuries is also important to police and the criminal justice system, although attention needs to be paid to issues of confidentiality (Chalk and King, 1998).

Health care systems

Health care systems rarely have a comprehensive approach to the identification and treatment of women and their children experiencing domestic violence (Cohen, 1997). The chapter on inter-agency work and domestic violence in this book (chapter 10) refers to the relative absence of the health sector in many of the UK forums. Opportunities for speaking to the woman without her partner or other person in the examination room may be limited in certain health care settings, and may be particularly difficult for non-English speaking women who may need a family member with them if no interpreter is available.

This creates a particular conflict in UK maternity care, for example, where there has been an effort to involve partners in all aspects of care (Mezey and Bewley, 1997). A fear that the health care professional will report the battering can also limit disclosure from the woman. The woman may rightly question who will see her 'confidential' information and the uses to which it will be put. In practice, inter-agency collaboration among health services, social services, and the criminal justice system may be necessary for dealing effectively with the woman's complex set of needs.

Health care systems may not be best organised to best meet the needs of victims of domestic violence. The services necessary to explore the problem and support the victim may not be available when needed. This is particularly true of emergency departments where many visits may be made out of hours (Birnbaum et al, 1996). One study attempted to increase identification and assessment of women experiencing domestic violence by reviewing A&E notes for risk factors and then later telephoning women to screen for domestic violence. They failed to reach the vast majority of the women seen in the emergency department and only identified a small number of cases not already identified making it an inappropriate approach to increasing recognition (Sixsmith, 1997).

There is little research evidence documenting either success or failure to integrate across women's and children's services to address family violence. Child Protection, Messages from Research, (DoH, 1995) documented the failure of most child protection processes to provide enough support services for the child or any support services to the mother of the child. Though promoting refocusing resources away from merely documenting abuse to provide more family support, it does not comprehensively consider the role of family violence that also involves the mother as a victim. None of the 41 projects funded with £700,000 in 1996 to address the refocusing strategy addressed domestic violence, though several provided parent or general family support (DoH press release, 26 September 1996).

Effectiveness of health service interventions

There have been no comprehensive reviews of the effectiveness of interventions in the health sector for domestic violence though Violence against Women (Bewley et al, 1997) reviews much of the published literature up to 1997. A recent review of effective interventions in family violence was recently published from the US National Research Council and the Institute of Medicine (Violence in Families, 1998 at www.nap.edu, and Chalk and King, 1998). Some of their central findings were echoed by our review and others went beyond the scope of this review but are of central importance. First, they concluded that findings from small-scale studies are often adopted without sufficient proof or replication. They note that identification and treatment possibilities predominate over preventive strategies. They highlight the lack of co-ordination of services for prevention or treatment and note the ensuing difficulties of evaluation that go along with that fragmentation. Finally they comment that the need for services may extend over a much longer time frame than previously estimated. The review conducted in this report did not include primary prevention interventions within the health services. It did not find multi-agency interventions nor did it find many long term outcomes included in the interventions evaluated. These remain as challenges for the future.

The Findings

Identification and screening

We identified a number of studies dealing with some aspect of screening that met our inclusion criteria. All of these studies are in US health care settings, raising an initial question of direct applicability to health service settings in the UK.

Most organisations who have made recommendations for screening have suggested a universal approach. We are aware of several studies investigating approaches to identifying women experiencing violence that document the inadequacy of opportunistic or case finding approaches in accurately identifying victims of domestic violence. It appears that care providers do not ask and may also not document asking about abuse. Compared to when abuse is systematically identified (using defined protocols, instruments, or patient interview), routine nurse or physician practices miss identifying a substantial proportion of abused women. It is not, however, known whether case finding is adequate to identify situations in which a woman has substantial risk of death or serious injury or where other interventions might be most appropriately applied. A variety of instruments have been tested, identifying a substantial proportion of women experiencing violence. Simply putting a system in place without ongoing support and training cannot bring long term changes. The following describes the most important of these studies.

Screening for domestic violence in health care settings

Hamburger et al, 1992

Sample and Design: 394 women in a US community-based family practice clinic.
Findings: Nearly 23% of women interviewed reported being physically assaulted by their partners within the previous year with an injury rate of over 13%. Lifetime prevalence was nearly 40%. Fewer than 2% of women overall reported having had their physician ask about physical abuse during their last office visit.

The authors concluded that rates of victimisation in primary care patients are high and rates of physician enquiry about domestic violence are low. They call for development and evaluation of improved methods of detecting and treating abused women. Case finding via routine care systems does not identify the majority of abused women who present for care.

McFarlane et al, 1991

Sample and Design: Compared the use of a self-completed intake questionnaire that included abuse assessment questions to the same questions administered in a face-to-face nurse interview at a Planned Parenthood clinic. A group of 477 women used the questionnaire and another group of 300 women attending the same clinic received the interview.
Findings: Identification rates for all four categories of abuse were significantly higher using the nursing interview. The reported proportion of positive answers to each category of question is as follows: 1) Physical Abuse; 7.3% vs. 29.3%, 2) Abuse in Pregnancy; 1.5% vs. 8.3%, 3) Forced Sexual Activity; 1.3% vs. 14.7%, 4) Fear of Partner; 2.1% vs. 22.7%.

Covington et al, 1997

Sample and Design: Pregnant adolescents within a state health department prenatal care clinic. A historical control group of 129 had routine care that included questions about domestic violence as part of the normal intake process. The study cohort of 117 received routine care plus a systematic screening protocol involving questioning about domestic violence in each trimester of pregnancy. Violence from any perpetrator was recorded.

Findings: The systematic protocol was better at identifying violence at the first assessment (not statistically significant), and more than twice as good at identification over all assessments (statistically significant). The systematic protocol also consistently documented the perpetrator (partner 68%, parent 14%, sibling 9%, friend/other known person 9%) compared to little such documentation in the routine care process. Multiple systematic assessments during pregnancy improved detection.

Norton et al, 1995

Sample and Design: A low-risk obstetrical population in Rhode Island was used to compare the use of a routine social service assessment that asked about abuse to the 5 question Abuse Assessment Screen (AAS). The routine group formed a historical control cohort of 191 and the AAS group of 143 was prospectively screened.

Findings: The authors report that the AAS was superior at detecting any history of violence within the past year, violence within the last year, and violence during pregnancy.

McLeer and Anwar, 1989; McLeer et al, 1989

Sample and Design: A retrospective cohort of 470 female trauma victims seen in an urban Pennsylvania emergency department during 1985 were studied. This emergency department had implemented a specific staff training system and screening protocol in 1977.

Findings: They compared the identification rate found on chart review for these women to a 1976 pre-implementation baseline rate of 5.6% and a 1977 post-implementation rate of 30%. Over the time from 1977 to 1985 several key staff had moved on and both the training and screening protocol had lapsed. They found the proportion of women trauma victims identified as suffering domestic violence in 1985 was 7.7%. The authors conclude that ongoing training and use of a screening protocol is needed to maintain adequate identification of trauma victims who are subject to domestic violence.

Waller et al, 1996

Sample and Design: A two stage screening approach was tested in a US A&E Dept where first nurse triage noted the presence or absence of any sign that might

indicate violence without asking the woman verbally and, if present, stage two was a nurse assessment. Of 595 women over the study period, 19% were screened at both stage one and stage two.
Findings: This method missed one half the women later identified as experiencing domestic violence. It reinforces other research evidence that trying to use indicators of violence or risk of violence misses significant groups of women and that women must be asked about violence.

Feldhaus et al, 1997

Sample and Design: 3 approaches to screening women were tested in 322 women in two US A&E departments: a brief 3 question instrument, the Index of Spouse Abuse and the Conflict Tactics Scale (the latter two longer than the first).
Findings: Prevalence rates ranged from 24-30%. These screens identified between 64 and 71% of women experiencing violence and there were minor differences between them.

Furbee et al, 1998

Sample and Design: This US pilot study tested an innovative approach to screening in health care settings: a tape recorded questionnaire against a face to face interview with a doctor in 175 women. Confidentiality for the woman was maintained by using headphones and a coded form which did not contain anything identifying the actual question being answered.
Findings: The proportion of positive responses by each method was not significantly different. This study was too small to detect less than a 20% difference in identification between the two methods, but authors concluded that it might be a possible way of overcoming provider barriers in asking women while protecting patient confidentiality.

Risk Assessment

Several authors have suggested that when a woman is found to be subject to domestic violence that a 'danger assessment' should be conducted prior to her discharge from the health care system (Campbell, 1986; Langford, 1996; Ambuel et al, 1996; McFarlane et al, 1992). This is similar in concept to completing an assessment of risk of suicide with a depressed patient and is designed to help the woman assess her risk of serious injury or death in the immediate future. We did not identify any studies that assessed the effectiveness of danger assessment instruments at preventing homicide or injury. This type of longitudinal research is difficult to undertake and the use of the instrument is perhaps best described as a treatment intervention rather than a screening intervention. At least one researcher has suggested that the very act of assessing the lethality of her situation may move her to take protective action (Campbell, 1986). One fruitful way of evaluating danger assessment would be from the woman's perspective. Did she find the exercise useful? Did it prompt her to any actions that she would not otherwise have taken?

In summary, much of research on screening interventions is limited by small sample size, retrospective study design, non-contemporaneous control groups and institution or locale specific conduct. Comparison across studies is hampered not only by questions of comparability of populations but also because few studies use the same study instruments to assess domestic violence. All of the research studies we identified took place in the US and may be of limited applicability to the UK. We identified no randomised controlled trials in this area although screening would be an appropriate intervention to test in a randomised controlled trial.

However, with these caveats we feel that several provisional generalisations can be made. It appears that routine, primarily physician-based care or the use of patient demographics and sentinel medical conditions are inadequate methods of screening for domestic violence. At least two studies suggest that face-to-face assessment is superior to self-administered screening. Systematic protocols using brief questionnaires may be adequate in clinical practice to detect the majority of domestic violence victims, but have low sensitivity compared with research instruments. However, given that the time that screening takes in clinical practice is an identified barrier to implementation of any screening, these short forms may be the only feasible method of screening. Their use should be specifically evaluated in the UK setting (Violence Research Programme Home Page 1999, see also Bewley et al, 1997, Discussion pages 179-188). Repetitive screening in pregnancy improves detection of domestic violence with a systematic protocol. Finally, the work of McLeer and colleagues suggest that if ongoing training and use of a protocol does not happen, the screening programme will fall into disuse.

When should screening or assessment take place?

A paper by Acierno and colleagues considered the multiple points at which case identification of domestic violence can fail. While their model of required steps in case identification is written from a health service perspective, it could be applied to other assessment situations outside of health care as well (Acierno et al, 1997). These steps include:

- The victim must perceive and label the event she has experienced as an assault and must furthermore encode it in her memory.
- The clinician must inquire about the assault using language for the event similar to the patient's and this inquiry must cue the victim's memory of the event.
- The victim must be willing and able to disclose that assault has occurred and must feel safe in doing so.

- Finally, the clinician must define the reported event as assault in order to identify successfully a case of domestic violence.

Thus, in this process there are a number of separate points at which failure of case identification can occur.

Steps to take after identification

There are very few practical descriptions and far fewer audits or evaluations of what actually happens in health care settings after the identification of domestic violence. This area includes the evaluation of the impact of protocols and good practice guidelines as well as specific interventions. Once a woman has been identified within the health service as experiencing, or being at risk of, domestic violence we need to establish what steps will be taken by health professionals to help her. In preparing this chapter we listed some needs that we thought could be addressed and that would guide the search for studies in these areas (Richardson and Feder, 1997; British Medical Association, 1998):

- access to appropriate health care - immediate and longer term;
- opportunity for discussion or advice;
- confidentiality;
- help with planning for safety and support; and
- appropriate referral to other agencies.

The review searched for evaluations in all these areas and found very few. One was outside health care, and so did not meet the criteria, but it had some health outcomes and other interesting features and was included because it was the only randomised controlled trial we had found.

Support and advocacy

It is a study by Sullivan and colleagues (Sullivan et al. 1992) of an intensive advocacy intervention for women leaving a domestic violence shelter in a Midwest USA city. Initially 146 women were approached; four were excluded because they dropped out within three weeks of the start and one was murdered a week after leaving, so 141 were followed up. They were randomly assigned to either a control group who had the research interviews (at entry to the study, 10 weeks, 6 months, 12 months, 18 months, and 2 years) but no extra help, and an intervention group who were seen by advocates regularly over a ten week period. The advocates were undergraduate women who were given training about domestic violence and how to use community resources. Women in the intervention group saw their advocate for an average of 6.9 hours a week face to face and had 2.5 hours of phone contact, making this a substantial intervention. The advocates in this study were volunteers, working in as part of a university project; a scheme of this type would be costly if put into practice using paid advocates. The outcomes were use of sources of help, emotional well-being, experience of physical and emotional violence and involvement with the assailant. The intervention had some impact up to the time of this report, which does not cover the full period of follow-up. Initial findings were that:

- Women in the intervention group were somewhat more likely to access the sources of help that they wanted and reported a better quality of life and better social support.
- Women needed a great deal of support in the period after leaving the shelter.
- By the end of the 10 week intervention there were no differences in the percentage who had contact with their assailant, or who had had further abuse over that period.
- It was interesting to note that women who remained in contact with their abuser were more likely to suffer violence (70%) compared to those who had avoided contact (29%) regardless of whether they were in the intervention or control group (Sullivan et al, 1995, 1999).

Another study took place in public antenatal clinics in an unspecified location in the US (McFarlane et al, 1997). Women who reported that their male partner in the year prior to the screening assessment had physically or sexually assaulted them were offered three sessions of advice and counselling during pregnancy. The sessions aimed to help women plan for safety and focused on community resources. Women in the intervention group (n=132) were followed up at six and twelve months after the birth. A control group was also recruited (n=67) from among women who were attending the hospital and had had a baby in the last two months. They were offered a wallet card with useful addresses and were also followed up at six and twelve months. The design does not allow any assessment of the effectiveness of the intervention, but there were a few interesting findings. The intervention included an assessment of safety behaviour - like hiding money, removing weapons and so on. The authors found that all of the safety behaviours were used more as the pregnancy went on, with often a substantial increase after the first intervention session. This suggests that the sessions may be useful, though there was no comparison group. They found that women suffering more severe violence were more likely to use sources of help, and they also found substantial differences between ethnic groups in the use of police and other community sources of help; Hispanic women were less likely to use them than White and African American women.

A small study evaluating advocacy provision within an emergency department used no controls but a pre and post assessment of change found no change in protection orders or in subsequent injury rates though the design of the study was insufficient to estimate any change appropriately. They found an increase in the use of shelters and of counselling services after the introduction of the advocacy programme (Muelleman and Feighny, 1999). This study and the previous one, though not methodologically rigorous enough to change practice provides support for planning and implementing a larger randomised controlled trial of the provision of advocacy services within accident and emergency departments or antenatal clinics.

Evaluation of protocols

A recent New Zealand study used a quasi-experimental approach to evaluate the impact of an emergency department protocol backed up with the training of 89% of staff. The study compared a total of 8,051 medical records for rates of identification, case confirmation, case documentation and interventions offered to those in another emergency department without a protocol. In comparing records before and after the intervention, they found differences in the confirmation and documentation of cases and in the number of interventions offered but no differences in the rate of identification (Fanslow et al, 1998 - outcomes and Spinola, 1998 - process). A US study compared the introduction of an abuse assessment protocol linked to the introduction of a routine printed form documenting the results of screening for abuse. The study compared the proportion identified and assessed in two large prenatal clinics to the results in a similar clinic without any protocol or designated form (all three served primarily Hispanic patients). They reviewed a random sample of medical records over a 15 month time period before and after the intervention. Outcomes included identification and assessment of domestic violence as outlined in the protocol. They found an increase in identification from 0.8% to 7% and an increase in assessment from 0 to 88% of cases in the protocol clinics and no change in the control clinic at three months with modest decline found at the 12 month audit. They also found better documentation in the records (Wist and McFarlane, 1999). Neither of these two studies randomly allocated the intervention, but with pre and post measures, both provide support for the effects of introducing protocols.

Because of the very different patterns of services in the UK, the relevance of these studies needs to be tested. We need to have descriptions, for women in UK contexts, of pathways of care including referral within and outside the health service. Are there guidelines being developed and used and evaluated? We need proposals for interventions and methodologically sound evaluations. Follow-up must be long enough to judge the most important impacts on the woman and any children she may have. It should be possible to design and evaluate an intervention strategy based on a woman's individual needs and preferences.

Legislative approaches

One study investigated the impact of a law requiring mandatory reporting of domestic violence to the police. This law was enacted as California Assembly Bill 1652, 1994 amending the California Penal Codes to require health care workers to report patients with injuries inflicted as a result of assault or abusive conduct. Using a Poisson regression analysis, this study found no increase in the percentage of biweekly dispatches of police to medical facilities for the investigation of domestic violence using dispatches for the two years before and after the law was enacted. Though they found an increasing trend in the number of total calls to the police for domestic violence, there was no concomitant increase in the percentage of calls from a medical facility in the year following the legislation (Sachs, 1998).

Working with other agencies

The importance of working with agencies outside the health service is emphasised by several authors in the book edited by Susan Bewley and colleagues (Bewley et al, 1987), and in the recent BMA publication (British Medical Association, 1998). This must be a key challenge for health services, and the current British approach of multi-agency forums (see for example SNAP, 1997) may present some difficulties for health service staff (British Medical Association, 1998). A survey of maternity units undertaken by the National Perinatal Epidemiology Unit reveals information about the involvement of maternity unit staff with other agencies and forums (Marchant et al, 2001). So far we have found no studies about links between health and other services other than that summarised by Hague in Chapter 10. Nor did we find any evaluations of attempts to improve such links.

Training

We found three studies that evaluated educational interventions for staff, sometimes linked with changes in record keeping.

Olson and colleagues (1996) wanted to increase the rate of identification of domestic violence in a US emergency department. They added a routine question to the forms used in the notes used and also ran a seminar for staff. They carried out a review of notes before and after the change in the forms and the seminar. There was a small difference between the rate of domestic violence in the control month and the two months where the chart had an extra question on it. However, without knowing how variable the monthly figures usually are it is hard to know whether the change in the notes led to an increase in detection.

Roberts and her colleagues (1997a, b) carried out a study in an Australian emergency department. After an initial study to look at how well domestic violence was recorded in the notes when compared with an interview, they carried out an educational intervention for all staff, and then repeated the validation study. The methods used for the two validation studies are very poorly described. A survey of staff was also carried out to look at views on domestic violence, but response rates were very low. The impact of the intervention is difficult to assess, partly because of the before-and-after design, and because the paper does not describe clearly what was done.

Harwell et al (1998) conducted a pre-post assessment without controls of a multi-disciplinary staff training programme at 4 community health centres in the US. The outcomes used were knowledge, self-perceived comfort in screening for DV, change in rates of screening, assessment and referral (derived from medical record review at baseline and at follow-up) assessed 6 months after the training. Their three month follow-up of provider experiences had a 35% response rate and therefore cannot be interpreted. Their 6 months outcome measures depended on a review of pre and post intervention medical records. Screening went from 5 to 25% and safety assessment from 5 to 17%, referral from 2-4%. Though a change was implemented, the effect was incomplete if they were aiming for universal screening. The training involved a total of 3-6 hours and had pre-set goals and structure. It included a follow-up session geared to provider specified difficulties.

A more intensive approach has been taken in primary care in Seattle in the US where all staff in two randomly selected large primary care clinics (114 health care providers serving 44,237 people) were trained in two 4 hour sessions. The educational outcomes at 9 months have been published (Thompson, 1998) but the impact on practice is not yet available.

The final study was rather different and involved medical students at two universities in California (Short et al, 1997). In one University, a new curriculum was introduced to address domestic violence. The paper describes how it was planned and put into practice and also reports on the assessment of the curriculum by outside reviewers. The views of students in both universities were assessed before the curriculum was introduced and after. The views of students appeared to shift more at the intervention than the control University in relation to their ability to identify and refer appropriately, and their intentions about dealing with domestic violence when they encountered it in practice. There is a useful methodological discussion, and reflection on the process of setting up the new curriculum.

Educational interventions for health professionals and health service staff need to be designed to address local circumstances, and to be based on research that has explored women's views about the service and staff attitudes and needs. Evaluations of training programmes should be methodologically robust. The training provided needs to be robust, designed with sound educational principles based on appropriate theory and structured to address practice needs.

Cost effectiveness

As our discussion of health care-based domestic violence interventions shows, there is little information on the effectiveness of such interventions. The cost-effectiveness of an intervention cannot be determined without research on its effectiveness. No experimental study that we identified collected cost data with which to make a determination of either the cost or cost-effectiveness of the intervention. The Scottish Needs Assessment Programme report on domestic violence (SNAP, 1997) sets out a list of the information that would be needed to address cost effectiveness:

- basic epidemiological data about the prevalence of domestic violence;
- detection costs;
- costs of training and education;
- health care use and treatment costs;
- possible averted costs as a result of better management;
- possible increased costs as a result of increased detection;
- costs to women themselves;
- appropriate summary outcome measures by which to assess effectiveness;
- changes in health related quality of life; and
- information about the timing of costs and benefits so that programmes with different cost benefit profiles can be compared (SNAP, 1997).

Future evaluations of interventions in health care must include economic evaluations from the start which are appropriately designed and implemented, following the guidelines outlined by the British Medical Journal Economic Evaluation Working Party (Drummond et al, 1996).

Evaluation should take place of new approaches and structures for ensuring that women who are identified within the health service get the help they need. Key weaknesses demonstrated in reviewing the literature include the lack of co-ordination of services. Of paramount importance would be interventions to ensure collaboration across women's and children's services to address family violence and the well studied correlation between child abuse and domestic violence. Possible approaches to evaluate could include:

- designated staff within a hospital who can be called on to provide support for women;
- confidential information systems which could be linked to referral agencies with the woman's permission;
- mechanisms for ensuring knowledge and availability of resources inside and outside the health sector;
- restructuring hours for social service staffing of A&E.

We have not found any evaluations of structures and policies of this kind. In particular, the failure to find experimental approaches to linking child protection and domestic violence work is disturbing.

Conclusions and recommendations

The impact of domestic violence on women's health is enormous. The health of women is directly affected due to injury; beyond that, the mental and physical health of women and children are affected by fear and anxiety and because of the likely impact of violence on the use of drugs and alcohol and lack of access to preventive services. In addition, there is limited evidence that unborn babies may also be damaged by violence. We have cited evidence that abused women have higher rates of long term ill health and an increased use of health services compared to non-victimised women. Figures for prevalence vary a great deal because of different definitions (for example whether or not psychological abuse is included) and different ways of identifying those at risk. There may also be geographically and culturally based variations. The cost implications for the health service are also subject to a great deal of uncertainty, but even the lower estimates indicate huge costs of the direct and indirect effects of violence.

Health services encounter women suffering abuse when they come for immediate care, or consult about some of the other health impacts. In addition, in this country, all but a handful of childbearing women make contact with maternity and primary care services, and this can provide the opportunity to ask directly about domestic violence. Although there is disagreement over whether women are more at risk of domestic violence during pregnancy, the effects of violence can certainly differ if abuse occurs during pregnancy (Gazmararian et al, 1996).

A number of professional bodies in the Health Sector have recommended universal screening in the form of asking all women coming into contact with the service (the RCOG, the BMA, the RCM, and draft recommendations from the RCGP). Screening for domestic violence may be a component of any health sector intervention since identification of battered women, whether it is by case finding or more universal-type screening is a pre-requisite to offering any other type of intervention to them. Screening may also be seen as an intervention itself as it may influence the course of abuse for the woman screened. Heightened awareness, either on the part of the woman or her caregiver, could influence her subsequent interactions with the health care system and with other agencies.

However, universal screening programmes may be justified, but in settings of limited time and personnel, may also lead to omitting other important interventions. Should screening be undertaken when effective interventions may not exist? Health care interventions may do harm as well as good and may indeed do more harm than good: this possibility has rarely been discussed in the literature about domestic violence. Do we know enough about the risks of health care based interventions for victims of domestic violence (Bewley et al, 1997). Women appear to be at the highest risk of being murdered by their abusers at the time of leaving the abusive partner or ending the relationship. If health care workers, with the best of intentions, encourage the woman to leave the situation in which she is abused without adequate safeguards might they also put her at increased risk for being killed in the process? Will the identification of violence without adequate plans to provide help and support for women, and contact with appropriate agencies, be helpful to women or demoralising?

As with other interventions, screening may have positive and negative consequences. Negative effects might include stigmatisation, direct or indirect endangerment of either the woman or her caregiver and lost opportunity costs within the health service. The question of whether to screen all women coming into contact with the health service or a subset of them (for instance, all pregnant women), is a complex one. In general, any type of screening test or procedure should be offered only if there is an effective intervention available, if early detection influences outcome or when knowledge of the condition would otherwise be able to affect the woman herself and/or the care she receives.

A large multi-disciplinary study to assess the prevalence and characteristics of domestic violence in pregnancy and the postpartum period and its health impact was completed in 2000 at Guy's and St. Thomas' Hospital in London. The study evaluates specific screening instruments and the effects of screening on both midwives and users of the service. The results, which should begin to be available in 2001, should be an immense contribution to UK research and practice (Violence Research Programme Home Page, 17 September, 1999).

The failure to identify women suffering from domestic violence simply because there are not yet 'effective' interventions which clearly change outcome is also not acceptable. It is clear from the analysis of studies documenting women's views and experiences that women expect the health services to be involved in identifying and supporting women experiencing domestic violence. It is clear from the studies reviewed that there are serious deficiencies in the knowledge of health service providers and attitudes that inappropriately blame the victims of the violence. There is evidence that training and education can improve this situation. Training and education of health care workers has a positive impact on identification and possibly on assessment and referral of women. However, surveys have demonstrated that many health professionals have had little training in the area and often feel unable to help women experiencing domestic violence. In addition, there is limited support from research that advocacy programmes within health care settings may have an impact on increasing women's use of services designed to assist women experiencing violence. Research needs to be designed more rigorously and implemented using randomised controlled trials where possible and controlled trials using a quasi-experimental approach where randomisation is not possible.

There is much that can be done currently which is supported by the research findings. Developments in future practice can be implemented hand in hand with appropriately designed and executed experimental studies. For instance, the RCOG support for routine questioning about violence during pregnancy can be carried forward by carrying out a well designed randomised controlled trial which studies the outcomes in the women and their children, taking account of both positive and potential negative effects. There needs to be serious discussion of what outcomes to measure. Simply measuring injury is not enough and whether the woman stays in the relationship may not be appropriate. Outcomes need to include the quality of life of the women and the children.

There is no need to stand still and simply wait for more definitive knowledge. Much can be done now, both in research and in practice.

Recommendations for research

- It is important to develop better health outcome measures for the impact of injury. We also need to identify and refine a wide range of health and other outcomes for the evaluation of interventions to reduce the impact of domestic violence.
- The views of women and staff about routine questions on domestic violence are currently being studied in more than one health setting. This research will be important for planning evaluations of different approaches to identification. It may be necessary to extend that work to different parts of the UK, and in particular to look at the views of women from minority ethnic groups.
- Local studies are needed of the process of care and referral that follow from identification.
- Further qualitative work on the experience of women victims identified through the health services. This should be carried out prospectively, and should, if possible, include longer follow-up to give women a chance to reflect on the effects of screening and subsequent help. It can also be carried out alongside a trial of screening.
- A randomised controlled trial of screening pregnant women for domestic violence should be carried out, measuring both the possibilities for benefit as well as harm.
- Experimental studies of guidelines for care and other health based interventions are essential as well. Some of these can be designed as randomised controlled trials but some, particularly those involving women's choices, which cannot be randomised, will need to be evaluated by other methods.
- All evaluation will need to look beyond outcomes that are wholly within the health sector. In addition, outcome measures that assess the

quality of life of the women over the longer term need to be incorporated into the evaluations proposed.

- There is currently no research to guide decisions relative to costs or cost-effectiveness of interventions. Effective intervention strategies are likely to be expensive. However, it is also likely that UK women who are victims of abuse make extensive use of the health service. Any research on health service based interventions should include economic evaluation following the guidelines published in the *British Medical Journal* (Drummond et al, 1996). Given that this is an area that requires multi-disciplinary approaches, economic evaluation should also cover different sectors of health and social care.

Recommendations for practice

- Ensure health sector membership at a senior level in the local inter-agency DV forum.
- Review provision for confidentiality in notes.
- Provide private settings for discussion.
- Ensure time for the woman to talk alone with health care workers.
- Provide links to child protection teams.
- Consider provision of services on nights and weekends when women experiencing DV might need it most.

Key recommendations from women for individual care-givers include:

- listening to women;
- providing enough time and privacy;
- asking directly about abuse;
- responding with sympathy and understanding;
- making clear their rejection of domestic violence;
- not blaming women or making a joke of the situation;
- taking care about confidentiality and safety;
- being well informed about abuse in general and local resources;
- referring women appropriately;
- not relying on medication as the only response; and,
- not being critical if a woman does not resolve the situation quickly.

Effective policing

Jalna Hanmer and Sue Griffiths

This chapter examines recent studies on policing domestic violence. Three studies are examined in-depth, Merseyside, West Yorkshire (Killingbeck) and Islington, London and their foci, findings and issues raised are compared. The chapter then explores a number of unevaluated policing projects which demonstrate the range of interventions applied in different police forces. The discussion on policing strategies includes multi-agency approaches to domestic violence and individual strategies such as the pro-arrest movement that began in the US. Here the debate concerning arrest as a cause of further violence is explored. Finally the chapter identifies 11 areas of good practice that are central to the assessment of effectiveness in policing domestic violence. The chapter concludes that whilst cost-benefit and cost-effective analyses of policing domestic violence are in their infancy, such analyses need to be considered in relation to achieving gains in prevention, protection and provision.

Introduction

During the 1970s and 1980s research began on women's experiences of violence from men known to them. The first study of police records, in Scotland, found that 25% of all assaults were domestically located crime by men against women partners (Dobash and Dobash, 1979). Interviews with women in Scotland (Dobash and Dobash, 1979), in England (Hanmer and Saunders, 1984) and in Northern Ireland (McWilliams and McKiernan, 1993) included women's reports of police responses to calls for assistance and the reasons why women were reluctant to report partner assault. The problems experienced by women in obtaining police assistance consistently called into question minimal or non-intervention strategies and identified the attitudes and beliefs of officers that impeded positive responses to women. The pivotal role of women in setting a new agenda for research and action, in particular Women's Aid in England, Northern Ireland, Scotland and Wales, cannot be over-estimated. The Parliamentary Select Committee on violence in marriage (1975) supported fundamental changes and the funding of research on agency responses, including those of policing (Faragher, 1985). Later in the 1980s, there were several studies specifically on the policing of domestic violence in England (Edwards, 1989a; Hanmer and Saunders, 1987), while other influential studies included police views on domestic violence (Smith and Gray, 1983).

Support for change gathered pace and in 1990 the Home Office for England and Wales (Home Office, 1990) and the Scottish Office (1990) recommended a more proactive response to domestic violence incidents through arrest, thorough investigation and recording. Improved understanding of and response to those experiencing domestic violence also were recommended. Five years later almost all forces in England and Wales had introduced policies on domestic violence, but deficiencies in their implementation were widespread (Grace, 1995). The Home Office Inter-Agency Circular of 1995, encouraged statutory and voluntary agencies, including the police, to work together in order to respond effectively to domestic violence. Organisational and managerial issues in policing domestic violence were examined next (Plotnikoff and Woolfson, 1998). This report drew attention to policies, the role of the domestic violence officer, organisational structures, training, information management and monitoring and the need for further improvements. Witness intimidation has been identified as a major issue in obtaining successful prosecutions (Phillips and Brown, 1987). The Home Office addressed vulnerable and intimidated witnesses in domestically located and other crimes of violence in its report *Speaking Up for Justice* (1998).

Similar developments took place in Scotland beginning with the Scottish Office circular 3/90 (Scottish Office, 1990) and followed by a report on the police response to domestic violence in 1997 (Scottish Office, 1997). Research included studies on:

- service provision for women (Henderson, 1998; MVA Consultancy, 1995);
- proactive policing (Amey, Hale and Uglow, 1996);
- the effectiveness of programmes for violent men (Dobash et al, 2000);
- victims' experiences (MacLeod et al, 1996);
- witness intimidation and protection (Fyfe and McKay, 1999); and,
- a media campaign on domestic violence (MacAskill and Eadie, 1995).

In Northern Ireland a Regional Domestic Violence Forum was established in 1995 to pursue Government objectives including the policing of domestic violence (Northern Ireland Office, 1995).

Knowledge of the cost-effectiveness and/or cost-benefits of domestic violence policing initiatives are rudimentary, although important aspects of assessing police efficiency and value for money (HMIC, 1998a). As domestically located crimes of violence are likely to be repeated, policing costs and efficiency are particularly relevant (Hanmer, Griffiths and Jerwood, 1999)

The term 'repeat victimisation' comes from criminology and first appeared in the 1970s (Farrell and Pease, 1993). Repeat victimisation as an approach to crime reduction first took place in the UK in 1986 with a burglary project in Kirkholt (Pease, 1998). In 1996 repeat victimisation was designated a key performance indicator for policing in England and Wales and a police officers' guide to addressing repeat victimisation was published in 1998 (Bridgeman and Hobbs, 1998). The idea of repeat victimisation emerged from a growing recognition that a few people were being subjected to an inordinate proportion of crime. Using data from the 1992 British Crime Survey Farrell and Pease (1993) demonstrated that 4% of the respondents suffered 44% of the offences reported. Pease (1998) went on to explore the possibility that repeat victimisation rates vary between crime types. Using British Crime Survey data for the years 1982 to 1992, he found that 2% of those victimised by property crime (excluding car crime) suffered 41% of reported crimes. This figure was worse when personal crime (primarily violent crime) was examined: 1% suffered 59% of personal crime.

As a strategy repeat victimisation has been applied to a number of crime types. These include racial crime in East London (Sampson and Phillips, 1992, 1995); burglary and car crime in Kirkholt and Huddersfield (Forrester, Chatterton and Pease, 1988; Anderson, Chenery and Pease, 1995); and domestic violence in Merseyside and Killingbeck (Lloyd, Farrell and Pease, 1994; Hanmer, Griffiths and Jerwood, 1999). Tackling repeat victimisation has been premised on the routine activity theory of crime (Cohen and Felson, 1979). Here, crime is conceptualised as comprising three elements: victim suitability, lack of capable guardianship (forms of deterrence or protection), and a motivated offender. Removal of one or all of these elements is theorised as the means of reducing the likelihood of repeat victimisation.

During the 1990s there were three evaluated domestic violence projects in England, two of which drew on repeat victimisation; Merseyside and West Yorkshire (Killingbeck Division). The third evaluated study in Islington, London was a loose replication of the London, Ontario approach whereby support from non-police agencies is provided to women immediately following police attendances. These raise issues of the police role in policing domestic violence. International initiatives particularly influential in the UK are the US studies on the effectiveness of arrest for misdemeanour offences and the different models of intervention implemented in Duluth, Minnesota, and in Ontario, Canada. These raise issues of the efficacy of arrest, and multi-agency and inter-agency responses. The tension between empowering women victimised by violence from their male partners and criminal justice interventions also remain a central concern.

These three evaluations began, or have the potential for, cost-benefit and/or cost effective analyses. Also, these policing strategies have general relevance as they have been, or are currently being, adopted in other force areas. For these reasons, they are described in some detail and used as examples. While varying in significant ways, they share the common aim of developing more effective responses to domestic violence and its repetition. The Merseyside study paid the greatest attention to the measurement of cost-benefit and cost-effectiveness (Farrell et al, 1993).

As almost all reports to the police of domestic violence are from or on behalf of women, policing initiatives are primarily directed at violence to women by men, estimated at 90% of domestic violence police attendances. A relatively small proportion of men are injured either by their female partner or by male relatives or other men, often as a result of their abusive behaviour to their female partner. Policing responses to same sex and female to male domestic crimes are yet to be evaluated. Repeat victimisation of women by men can lead to adverse consequences for both women and men, but primarily for women. There is growing recognition of the effects of domestic violence on children who witness and may become directly involved (Morley and Mullender, 1994a & b), although there are no evaluated studies of how policing affects these outcomes.

Methods

A literature review of contemporary research, practice and theory was undertaken in order to locate evaluated projects with cost-benefit and/or cost effective analyses, or their potential, and on-going work that may be relevant for evaluation. The review included studies of current policing practice with recommendations for improvements, and the experiences of domestic violence victimisation. Traditional sources of university libraries and electronic bibliographic search engines were used for journals and ISBN publications and contact by telephone with organisations able to provide information on current unevaluated projects. Additional searches of governmental websites for the UK were undertaken focusing on the Home Office equivalents for Scotland and Ireland. A similar search method was used with justice departments in Australia, Canada, New Zealand, North America, and Scandinavia.

In this review of policing domestic violence, the criteria for inclusion as an evaluated project example were cost-benefit and effective analyses, or their possibility, terms of reference, indices to measure the programme's effectiveness, bench-marks to measure programme performance, monitoring and logging procedures, findings. These criteria were also applied to international evaluated programmes for their similarities and differences. Projects that were monitored, but not subject to rigorous analysis, were identified as unevaluated.

The review included an examination of reports on police managerial and organisational structures and their influence on domestic violence initiatives. Understanding the protocols of policing and the processes whereby policies become (or fail to become) practice is necessary when evaluating initiatives as these can increase or reduce the effectiveness of programmes.

Evaluated studies in the UK

Merseyside (First Evaluation)

Focus

The research focused on women who experienced repeated domestic violence and were allocated pendant alarms (Lloyd et al, 1994) and an analysis of the cost-benefit of this crime prevention initiative (Farrell et al, 1993). The objectives of this project were to:

- introduce quick response pendant alarms for women identified by the crime prevention officer and the domestic violence prevention worker;
- set up a domestic violence database on police attendance;
- improve the transfer of injunction details from courts to the police;
- offer support and information to those experiencing domestic violence; and
- heighten awareness of domestic violence amongst officers.

A computer software programme to record domestic attendances, modelled on that of the West Yorkshire Police, was set up although no checks were made on the thoroughness of police coding of domestic attendance. Satisfaction was expressed with the identification of at least some of the 'turbulent' households, as these were eligible to receive the pendant alarms. Findings are reported in Farrell et al, (1993) and Lloyd et al, (1994).

Findings

Over a 25 month period, 62% of calls required a repeat attendance. Lack of a bench-mark precluded evaluation of the effectiveness in terms of an increase or reduction in repeat victimisation. The study did establish the time intervals between repeat attendances. Within five weeks 35% of households required a repeat attendance, and after a second attendance,

45% required a third. The police and other agencies made 35 referrals for alarms. A total of 37 alarms were installed and qualitative information obtained from women indicates that the installation of an alarm was very positively received.

Costs

Merseyside provided data on cost-benefit and cost-effectiveness. The costs included the appointment of a domestic violence prevention worker and telephone equipment and operating costs. The benefits included the creation of:

- an early warning database in which attendance to domestic calls were recorded;
- an aide-memoire for police officers on domestic violence;
- information cards for women; and
- closer co-operation between the police and courts through the development of a formal, systematic and reliable means of daily transfer by fax from the court to the police of information of injunction details.

This latter process assisted both officers and the courts in the provision of an improved service.

The total capital outlay of the project was £136,000 over two years with additional recurrent costs of £450 per month. This included equipment costs of the alarm base station and computer, cellular technology, alarms, phone costs, employment of one worker, running costs of the Centre Against Partner Assault in a local community centre, salaries and computing costs of researchers. In terms of non-police costs, the effectiveness of this temporary intervention required assistance from local authority housing in order to arrange re-housing for at least some of the women. These costs were not calculated.

Benefits

The basis for calculating financial benefits is said to be to develop a crimes prevented model. Five types of preventive effects were considered:

- direct incapacitation;
- indirect incapacitation;
- special deterrence;
- general deterrence; and,
- 'domino prevention', that is, the allocation of alarms triggering good practice from police and other agencies.

Positive results of alarm installation for the police is a 'feel good factor'; for courts, enforceable injunctions; and reduction of fear of crime. The alarms needed are relatively few in number with multiple beneficiaries as their loan is short term. This is described as a 'drip-feed' approach to denote the relative constancy of effort over time that comes with a strategy of preventing repeated victimisation. As this resource achieves continued use over time, it will achieve high cost-efficiency.

Benefits are claimed for other agencies; refuges, social services, housing, health, GP facilities, mental health, and in improved attitudes by children to the police, but these are not analysed. Qualitative evidence confirmed that pendant alarms increased the physical and psychological safety of women and children thereby improving personal functioning and their mutual relationship.

Finally, repeated use of successful initiatives reduces costs as the initial investment, a one-off, can be recouped through replication.

Issues raised by the Merseyside project

The evaluation of this project began the analysis of cost-benefit and cost-effectiveness in relation to new initiatives in policing domestic violence. The authors raise a number of questions that could not be answered by their limited research design. Does relying on one intervention, alarm technology, reduce police attendance? Could the provision of alarms increase separation as a means of achieving safety for women and the displacement of men to other women where their violence continues? Could a scale of social values be developed that includes non-pecuniary considerations, such as morality and public attitude, similar to the quality of life measures used in health care? Could a scale of social values be converted into a social-cost of crime scale based on severity that would generate proxy values for the relative costs of different crimes? They recommend a scale for crime prevention work in general. This could include detection, displacement, improved police-public relations, police feel-good factor, and fear of crime. Prevention of repeat victimisation is a further dimension.

Merseyside (Second Evaluation)

The second Merseyside evaluation is of a police divisional domestic violence unit during 12 months of 1991-1992 (Farrell and and Buckley, 1999). The evaluation explores the usefulness of repeat victimisation as a performance indicator for policing. The crime prevention work of the domestic violence unit is described as largely indirect. They conclude that although it is possible that the unit had a positive impact on some of the 'less entrenched' cases of repeat calls, it is unlikely to have done so on frequently repeated, chronic cases. Developing more direct crime prevention as a measure of police performance through attention to chronic cases on repeat calls, and further evaluation of domestic violence units are recommended.

Issues raised by the second Merseyside evaluation

This study raises the issue of how to measure the number of crimes prevented. Attention is drawn to the baseline data required for comparative purposes; that is, repeat attendance by police officers to domestic incidents. How is the work of domestic violence officers in relation to crime prevention to be categorised and assessed? How does the organisation of domestic violence into separate units contribute to crime prevention?

Killingbeck, West Yorkshire

Focus

The focus of the West Yorkshire project was to reduce repeat victimisation through a three-tiered programme of incremental interventions. It required an equal focus on the victimised woman and the offending man in order to set up an interactive crime prevention approach that both protected the victim and de-motivated the offender. The programme required all officers to implement the force policy on domestic violence; that is, to proceed proactively and to ensure the safety of those experiencing domestic violence, along with closer inter-agency involvement with organisations supporting the victimised and/or responding to offenders. The only new tasks relate to the work of the domestic violence officer and, in a limited way, the community constables and patrol officers. The model overcame the major shortcomings involved in restricting the responsibility for domestic violence to one or two officers within a division or station by incorporating the work of all officers in the model. The project is discussed in Hanmer et al, (1999).

Intervention Model

A three-tiered graded response for domestic violence police attendances consisted of measures of increasing intensity; Level 1 measures were introduced after the first police attendance, Level 2 after the second and Level 3 after the third or more. The model is based on the understanding that decreasing victim suitability and de-motivating offenders require the application of progressive measures of intervention to constrain the offender's future actions. As the offender is known, providing capable guardianship is achieved by a focus on interventions applied directly to women and men. These reinforce the victims' confidence to call upon the police and reaffirms the message to offenders that domestic violence is treated seriously and strategies are or will be used to ensure women's future safety.

The project calculated repetitions in relation to police attendance to perpetrators in the previous twelve months. With repeat attendances the level of intervention moves from Levels 1 to 2 to 3. However, in assessing the initial level of intervention the full police record of domestic violence is reviewed, and entry at higher levels could be required. While policing interventions varied by type of offence, i.e. common law or criminal, there were four primary interventions:

- letters that varied by level, by offence type and whether to victim or offender and, depending upon attendance level;
- police watch;
- cocoon watch; and,
- additional attendance by officers.

Findings

The main achievements were both programmatic and organisational. The three-tiered programme both reduced repeat attendance and increased the time intervals between attendance by responding more appropriately to men who required firm action from the police and to women who required their assistance. The time intervals between repeat attendances were established for each level of intervention. They demonstrated that time intervals decrease in length with repeat attendances, but for all levels the lengths of time without a repeat attendance are much longer than those of the Merseyside sample. The median survival time, i.e. the time in which 50% of all men at each intervention level required a repeat attendance, was over a year at Level 1, 270 days at Level 2 and 150 days at Level 3.

Improvements were made in the standard and consistency of police responses. Women and their supporters were encouraged to ask for police support through interventions at each level and the numbers doing so increased over the year of the project. Chronic repeat offenders were identified, individually assessed and over the year their numbers were reduced. Important developments in the statistical analysis of domestic violence repeat victimisation were the identification of factors reducing or increasing offenders and the proportion likely to re-offend in the future. Closer working relationships were established with other criminal justice agencies and with some social and welfare agencies.

Cost-benefit/cost-effectiveness

While repeat victimisation projects can be organised in many ways, the task was to establish a resource limited operational model. The aim was to devise and evaluate a project where almost all the resources required could be achieved solely by the reallocation of existing staff and their duties to reflect a change in priorities or to meet priorities more effectively.

The new resources were: one additional domestic violence officer, (the other was already in post), a half-time clerk, the shared use of a police car by the domestic violence officers, printing of letters for men and women, aide-memoire cards for officers, and business cards with agency addresses for women. All officers in the division were offered a two-hour training session on domestic violence awareness and the new model of intervention and follow-up training was given to the community constables to improve performance. Training enabled the project to be implemented and, along with consistent monitoring of data recorded by officers and managerial support, standards and consistency of service delivery improved. The research costs were the time taken for project group meetings attended by 3 to 5 officers monthly and research staff costs.

While the specific costs have not been calculated, this could be done both overall and for each level of intervention. The benefits in reduced repeat victimisation and the increase in time intervals between attendance could be calculated using the pre-project data as the baseline. During the year the total number of attendances remained constant with an increasing reporting rate at Level 1, the level requiring the least expenditure.

While less easy to measure financially, reductions in costs to other agencies and the social benefits to women and children of more effective police interventions could be explored.

Issues raised by the West Yorkshire study

The West Yorkshire study developed some of the issues raised in the two earlier Merseyside studies by differentiating between levels of intervention and assessing their impact on repeat offending, constructing baseline data for comparative purposes, and developing new statistical approaches that measure the de-motivation of offenders as well as crime reduction. But the West Yorkshire study also raised questions. Do post-arrest outcomes influence repeat victimisation to the same, lesser or greater extent than arrest alone? Amongst the multiple interventions which are most/least effective? Could the three-tier model be applied to other violent crime types or extended to non-police agencies? Further areas of work suggested by the West Yorkshire study include the development of policing strategies specifically for chronic offenders, construction of victim satisfaction indicators for future evaluations, further examination of policing when couples are living together or separate.

Islington, London

Focus

This project attempted to replicate a Canadian model of responding to domestic violence. In London, Ontario agencies providing services to women joined forces with the criminal justice system to improve the effectiveness of the criminal justice system's response to wife assault (Jaffee et al, 1984; 1986). Women are offered crisis intervention and referrals to other agencies and the project provides a link between law enforcement agencies and social services. When police attend in London, Ontario, women are provided with information on community support services and the response to offenders is to arrest whenever possible. The Islington project is reported in Kelly (1999).

Intervention model

In this civilian model of intervention the police refer those who experience domestic violence for follow-up action. The response to perpetrators is the responsibility of the police who are expected to arrest and charge as these are seen as the most effective actions to be taken. The Islington project aimed to make contact with women within 24 hours of police being called to offer short-term support, advocacy and, in some instances, longer-term contact. Amongst the aims of the project were to:

- increase the likelihood of prosecutions being followed through and of referrals to other agencies being taken up;
- establish the principle that domestic violence is a crime through encouraging and enhancing law enforcement; and,
- improve inter-agency co-ordination, promote consistent practice within the borough, and highlight gaps in service provision.

Findings

Implementing and maintaining this project was difficult. During the third year in particular, the number of referrals from police officers declined substantially. A number of issues were in dispute, in particular the role of civilians in policing domestic violence. These focused on the relationship between civilians offering a direct service to those experiencing domestic violence and police officers responding to emergency calls for assistance, domestic violence officers and senior management. Over time problems intensified with patrol officers and managers and remained unresolved. However, with domestic violence officers some progress was made.

The work of the emergency services is based on prompt and appropriate responses, but the activities required could not be agreed between the project and the police. In part this relates to the finding that 'neither the force nor divisional policy on law enforcement was being consistently enforced' (Kelly, 1999:43).

Women said they wanted respectful treatment and assertive, unequivocal action from the police. Project users thought domestic violence should be responded to as a crime, but the researchers conclude that they need support and protection for this to be a viable option. Assertive action includes the removal and arrest of the perpetrator, or stopping the abuse and/or warning the perpetrator. In contrast, Jane Mooney's research, based more generally on women in the community, found that women wanted the violence to stop and the man to change (1994). This suggests that to achieve these more general aims women want the police to respond in specific ways that correspond to the expectations women have about policing.

The evaluation found that following up calls for police assistance within 24 hours was effective with the service users at the time. Early intervention by the project enabled women to talk through their feeling, review available options and gain confidence in taking action to ensure their own safety. This corresponds with the success recorded by other professional groups, such as social work, with crisis intervention and other immediate response techniques.

The project interventions also increased confidence in the police amongst service users. Where women were enabled to pursue prosecution conviction was likely, most commonly when the perpetrator pleaded guilty.

The Islington project examined police processes and distinguished between problems in (Kelly 1999:45, 48-49, 50) and problems for policing. Problems for policing that adversely affect women experiencing domestic violence are:

- assumptions of prosecutors that women will withdraw;
- courts and prosecutors failing to provide victim witnesses with the protection necessary to enable them to give evidence; and
- police knowledge of pressure and coercion to withdraw on the woman not being reflected in magistrates' decisions regarding bail applications and by not taking breaches of bail seriously.

Cost-benefit and effectiveness analysis

This project had six civilian workers, a co-ordinator, four support workers, and an administrator. The police contributed office space, some office supplies and an unmarked car. While data were not logged with a view of carrying out cost-benefit and effectiveness analysis, some relevant data were collected. The cost-effective outcomes of savings in police time, reduced repeat calls, appropriate referrals to other agencies, are not sufficiently substantiated to be financially measured.

Issues raised by the Islington project

This project raises questions about agencies effectively working together. It raises questions about the extent to which non-police approaches and groups can impact on policing practices. Importantly, the project demonstrates the limited effectiveness of programmes where police officers fail to support the initiative and police management structures fail to challenge this lack of support. This in turn suggests that further work on police structures and management is needed if strategic policing is to be implemented effectively (Plotnikoff and Woolfson 1998). Further questions include: What are the boundaries between the role of police officers attending domestic violence incidents and social and welfare follow-up support? Does an organisational split between victim and perpetrator as the focus for agency interventions mean that a less effective approach results? How can inter-agency work increase the agency input with criminal justice agencies (probation, Crown Prosecution Service, magistrates, solicitors etc.)?

Comparison of evaluated projects

These three evaluated projects provide conceptual variations on the police role in domestic violence. These conceptual differences have greater relevance than variations in actions taken as all three projects provided direct support for victims and facilitated contacts with other agencies. It is the meanings and organisational forms attached to these actions that distinguish understandings of the police role. Primary aims varied;. Islington and Merseyside focused on support for those victimised, while West Yorkshire focused on reducing men's violence.

The women assisted in the two Merseyside and Islington projects were likely to have been at Level 3 in the West Yorkshire project. In Islington the police role was seen as the pursuit of crime while external agencies provided support for victims. In contrast, the Merseyside project distinguished between internal policing roles for the pursuit of crime and support. The domestic violence officer's role was to offer direct support to victimised women and to undertake preventative work, while other officers pursued perpetrators. The West Yorkshire project understood the police role to reduce men's violence through an integrated approach by officers to the pursuit of crime and the support of victims.

Domestic violence officers assumed responsibility for the implementation of measures in the Merseyside and West Yorkshire projects. This was a task shared between the civilian project and domestic violence officers at Islington. Programmes were managed through customary police infrastructure in Merseyside and the West Yorkshire projects and through an inter-agency committee at Islington. Measures were implemented after the initial police attendance to a call for assistance in all projects.

Merseyside drew attention to the need for a control group while the Islington project attempted a comparative assessment, but the incompleteness and dissimilarity of data made this statistically non-viable. West Yorkshire measured the effectiveness of interventions by level and via a control group.

Unevaluated projects

There are potentially many unevaluated projects given the growth of domestic violence policing and partnership initiatives in the UK. New policing partnership initiatives may include monitoring and reports, but have yet to be fully evaluated. They may have different agency partners and different aims.

For example, the joint Fife Constabulary and Fife Council Social Work Services Domestic Violence Unit project begun in 1996 has progressively extended inter-agency work, the recording of domestic violence attendance, and is implementing all the recommendations of the Scottish Office report (1997).

Partnerships may focus on particular groups of women and include domestic and other forms of violence, such as the proposed project in Hackney for women in prostitution or the Essex project on how Asian women perceived access to support (Currell and Gill, 1998).

Newcastle Domestic Violence Forum has joint protocols between probation, women's aid, police and the criminal justice system. Each agency has a service level agreement in relation to the needs of the other agencies; for example, prompt communication with the police regarding court set bail conditions. Canterbury has a similar project.

Sunderland police, other agencies and Sunderland Health Authority are developing training for various health professionals in order to raise the profile of violence against women that begins in pregnancy.

The police are involved in various domestic violence projects initiated by other agencies, for example, the inter-agency strategy on domestic violence of the Department of Public Health, Glasgow.

There are several current loose replications of the Domestic Abuse Intervention Project in Duluth, an inter-agency model of response to both those experiencing domestic violence and perpetrators, in progress or in planning; for example, in Fulham Hammersmith and Gloucester. The aim is to integrate and co-ordinate community response to domestic violence. These involve practical, policy, procedural and service measures in order to improve safety for those who are victimised, increase offenders' accountability for their actions, enhance evidence gathering, deliver more effective prosecution and sentencing of abusers and strengthen the message that domestic violence is not tolerated.

The West Yorkshire repeat victimisation model is beginning to spread to forces outside West Yorkshire. As well as replication, there are likely to be variations in the introduction, interventions, recording practices, and management.

Restorative justice projects are beginning to be discussed with other agencies, for example in Basingstoke, Hampshire. Modelled on a Canadian project, and centred on family group conferences, the strategy is to transfer developments in child protection and youth justice to domestic violence. The Hampshire project is seen as a community safety strategy in response to the Crime and Disorder Act. This approach is fundamentally different in that it interprets violence against women as a 'family' problem.

Some forces are developing investigative and evidence gathering techniques as an alternative to, or corroboration of, women's statements that may have beneficial effects on charging, decisions to prosecute and successful prosecutions. This has included the use of instant cameras to document injuries and/or criminal damage observed by responding officers.

Cleveland is developing evidence diaries kept by women and safety plans for women experiencing domestic violence.

Crime and disorder partnerships also provide multi-agency responses to domestic violence. The implications of crime and disorder partnerships for multi-agency domestic violence work and the agencies involved, such as the inclusion of the voluntary sector and historically less involved statutory agencies of education and health, are some of the issues.

By developing cost-benefit and cost-effectiveness frameworks these and other projects could be considered for further evaluation.

Partnership approaches to policing domestic violence

This section discusses some of the key elements in policing domestic violence effectively. It goes on to identify some of the current debates in practice and the remaining gaps in knowledge.

Partnership approaches

Repeated violence in the home often requires assistance from a number of agencies offering services, in particular housing and income support as well as policing as women who require the most assistance usually have dependent children. Multi-agency projects involve different agency types. For example, the first Merseyside project focused on housing, Islington on the social welfare sector, and West Yorkshire on the criminal justice system more than social welfare agencies.

Inter-agency forums or groups are seen as a way to improve liaison and good relationships between the police and other agencies and to develop joint initiatives (Home Office, 1995; Victim Support, 1992; Sorsby and Shapland, 1995; Grace, 1995). The Scottish Report Office report (Scottish Office, 1997) calls attention to the importance of referrals to other public services and voluntary agencies that can provide assistance. These responses are particularly important as only a proportion of women report to the police. Inter-agency involvement by the police was seen by non-police agencies as beneficial; it improved understanding between agencies and developed greater consistency in dealing with domestic violence (Grace, 1995; Hague this volume).

The thematic inspection report of policing refers to partnerships rather than multi-agency or inter-agency working. The report makes the point that partnerships do not automatically prevent crime (HMIC, 1998b). Good practice in effective partnerships include a range of partnerships at different levels which must be coherent throughout the force area with close monitoring and evaluated outcomes of individual partnerships. A lack of co-ordination and direction are identified as key factors undermining effectiveness. These deficiencies can stem from a number of aspects of programme design such as ill-defined aims and objectives, inadequate managerial level of support, lack of monitoring and evaluation criteria.

The US Duluth, Minnesota, model is an integrated partnership approach involving all agencies responding to domestic violence, including the police (Pence, 1983; 1988; Shepard and Pence, 1999). True replications cannot be carried out in the UK as local government responsibilities vary considerably between the two countries, rather it is a question of taking on board the concepts that inform it. The basic principle is that the burden of confronting abusers and restricting their behaviour rests with the community. To achieve this requires co-operation between services and interventions that are responsive to the totality of harm rather than single incident or punishment focused. Protection must take priority with intervention principles based on accountability to those experiencing domestic violence (Morley and Mullender, 1992).

Levinson (1989) describes a few societies where their male partners rarely abused women, nor did women abuse. Violence was not valued within these communities and it was this social context that provided support for those victimised by violence and discouraged violence. In the Western world policing is located within societies that are deeply ambivalent about the uses of violence with opinion often veering between the extremes of holding either the victimised or the criminal justice system responsible when unacceptable levels of violence are brought to public attention. Partnership approaches can be seen as attempts to engage both with the needs of those who experience violence for multiple services and to engage the larger community in ending these abuses.

The Debate on Pro-Arrest Strategies

As well as practical policing initiatives, there are conceptual issues to resolve. In moving from minimal or non-intervention in domestic violence to more proactive strategies, policing practice in the UK shared important commonalties with that of other Western countries, but the approaches to change depended upon political and social contexts.

The shift towards arrest as the most appropriate response to domestically located violence in the US was initially fuelled by the demands from women actively supporting abused women and from successful civil law litigation for monetary damages in cases of serious injury resulting from a lack of proactive policing. Commitment to law enforcement, i.e. arrest and prosecution by the criminal justice system, continues to be the demand of legal and social welfare advocates of women. Given this social context the Minneapolis experiment (Sherman and Berk, 1984; Stark, 1993) had a major influence on legislation and police operations, not impeded by criticisms of the methodology, interpretation of results, and dissimilar findings from other studies.

In the UK the demand for change in policing domestic violence was, and is, a policy issue to be pursued primarily through individual police forces and local government with Government guidance.

Arrest and repeat victimisation

Issues raised by the US studies on arrest for misdemeanour offences of particular relevance to UK policing at the present time are:

- the relationship between arrest and repeat victimisation;
- attendance versus arrest as the focus for interventions;
- police intervention with either the perpetrator or those victimised or both; and
- selecting one element in a sequence of actions associated with arrest versus all elements (release, charging, court, outcomes).

Arrest: The cause of further violence or the identification of violent men?

The original study in Minneapolis led to six, not strictly comparable, replication studies in various US cities (Milwaukee, Omaha, Charlotte, Metro-Dade (Miami), Atlanta, Colorado Springs), and arrest continues to dominate criminological work on domestic violence in the US. These studies raise questions about the relationship between the core tasks of policing; that is, crime prevention, order maintenance and pursuing crime, as well as research methodology. While Sherman acknowledges that the interpretation of his findings that arrest causes violence remains problematic, he suggests that 'the weaker the suspect's social bonds, the more likely it appears to be that arrest will backfire by causing increased violence'. Weaker social bond factors were identified as non-marriage and lack of employment.

In the West Yorkshire study, arrest became one of the variables to examine in relation to the entry level of men into the programme of interventions and their subsequent repeat attendance. Arrested men were 51% more likely to require a repeat attendance than those who were not. This result corresponds with the direction taken by US studies, but approaches based on progressive interventions permit a different analysis of arrest and repeat offending.

The statistical results in the West Yorkshire study show no significant variation between arrest and entry level. Variation occurs after arrest when release without charge was greatest for men at Level 1 and progressively reduced as men moved from Levels 1 to 2 to 3. Increased police charges after arrest suggest that men who progress to higher levels of intervention are prepared to behave more violently and that their offences increase in severity.

Data on the precise variables claimed by Sherman to be associated with 'weaker social bonds' were not available to the West Yorkshire study, but whether couples were living together or separately at the time of attendance were. While the percentage of women continuing to live with perpetrators decreased as entry levels increased, police attendance to women and men living together or separately was not significantly different for Levels 1, 2, and 3, nor was the length of survival time between attendance. The significant variation was in policing, as arrests with criminal charges were more likely to occur when women lived separately from men, and arrest resulting in breach of the peace (a US misdemeanour offence), when living together.

In the West Yorkshire study, arrest did not significantly reduce repeat victimisation; this was associated with early and progressive police interventions. Repeat attendance and arrest is understood as a statistical correlation, not a causal relationship. The causal factor is the ability and willingness of men to use violence towards their female partners. Arrest is a factor in identifying future chronic offenders as well as a response to common law offences and criminal assault. Arrest is a means of identifying men who are more violent and is useful in assessing the risk of future calls for assistance. Understanding the full potential of arrest as a policing strategy and integrating this into police work are major issues.

Improving policing

The following critiques and recommendations identify good practice issues and are relevant to the assessment of effectiveness in policing domestic violence from cost-benefit and cost-effectiveness positions by future projects.

Uneven service delivery

A major complaint of agencies and women seeking police assistance is the unevenness of police response. This can vary from the excellent to the abysmal depending primarily upon the response of officers who initially attend the incident. The studies of police forces in England and Wales by Grace (1995), Plotnikoff and Woolfson (1998) and of police forces in Scotland by the Scottish Office (1997) identify problems impeding systematic service delivery and thereby good practice.

Under-reporting

An inability to deliver domestic violence good practice systematically is a major reason women do not report domestic attacks to the police. Estimates of under-reporting of domestic violence vary. The British Crime Surveys found that reporting of domestic violence increased from 20% in 1981 to 30% in 1995 (Mirrlees-Black et al, 1996). A 70% non-reporting rate is similar to that in Scotland where 89% of men and 68% of women said they had never informed the police about any incident of force used against them (Scottish Office, 1997). This is a prevalence statistic and unreported incidence will be greater. Thus when women or others call for assistance it is very unlikely that this will be the first assault. Increasing the reporting of incidents and the number of women reporting are measures of the effectiveness of police action.

Victim satisfaction

Victim satisfaction with police actions is crucial to the likelihood of re-contacting the police if necessary. The Scottish Office noted the importance of the quality of police intervention at the first report of violence, its perceived effect on the offender's behaviour, and in securing the safety of those victimised (1997). As with earlier studies, Grace found that women consistently wanted their situations, needs and wishes treated seriously by the police (1995). She recommended follow-up visits to those victimised by domestic violence as an element of good practice. The Scottish Office report recommends guidelines for the identification of those victimised by domestic violence who require follow-up attention (Scottish Office, 1997).

Domestic violence and child abuse

Domestic violence and child abuse often occur in the same families (Morley and Mullender 1994b). Officers attending domestic calls should be aware that more than one member of the family may be experiencing violence and abuse even though the call is for a single child or the woman. Recognising the link between domestic violence and child protection is relevant for all officers (Scottish Office 1997).

Police discretion

A major unresolved issue for policing is how to combine 'victim sensitive' approaches with proactive strategies and the exercise of police discretion. Mandatory arrest policies in the US were a response to dissatisfaction and while support for this approach continues, mandatory arrest has led to harmful effects (Zorza, 1995). These include a higher proportion of arrest and more serious offence charges for women, disparities in the arrest of minority men (both more and less) in comparison with the white majority, and harm to children with the arrest and prosecution of their victimised mothers.

An alternative developed in Manitoba, Canada is to re-locate discretion in the court with the aim of empowering women victimised by domestic violence. The police are required to charge if a complaint is made. This has resulted in an increase in probation orders and court mandated treatment programmes for men, along with the development of 'testimony bargaining' where the victim witness influences the court outcome in return for testifying. This replaces plea bargaining between the accused, his lawyers and the crown where charges are reduced in exchange for an admission of guilt. Court specialisation in Manitoba with its new strategies is said to permit vigorous prosecution with 'victim sensitivity'. In this approach women influence, if not determine, the initial charge and court outcomes. (Ursel, 1997)

In the Scottish Office Circular (1990) and Report (1997) a pro-arrest policy is described as a pro-charge policy. While arrest can secure the immediate safety of those victimised and other vulnerable family members, charging sends both the offender and the victimised a clear message that 'an independent person believes the actions of the accused were criminal' (1997:3). Good practice also requires establishing why the victim witness may not want to proceed, taking action to overcome fear of reprisals, and pursuing prosecution without the victim witness statement (1997). This view contrasts with that of Manitoba, Canada where 'victim sensitivity' is defined as following the wishes of the woman even when the ultimate result of this form of 'victim sensitivity' and understanding of empowerment for women leads to repeat victimisation and her homicide (Ursel, 1997).

Another approach is to develop organisational structures, systems and procedural guidelines to encourage consistent interventions that meet policy objectives. Discretion is an integral part of policing. In best practice, responses are tailored to individual circumstances within broad frameworks of policy and good practice guidelines. Discretion can be modified and differing expressions of discretion can have major impacts on project success. For example, in the West Yorkshire project police discretion was reduced as no further action was eliminated as a possible response. Further intervention occurred automatically once an attendance was designated as a domestic incident. In Merseyside and Islington police discretion determined whether a referral was made to the projects. How police discretion is incorporated into projects is an aspect of their design.

Differing definitions of domestic violence and repeat victimisation

Encouraging consistent intervention begins with the definition of domestic violence and repeat victimisation. Forces have differed in their definition of domestic violence thus impeding comparison of force statistics (Plotnikoff and Woolfson, 1998; Scottish Office, 1997). The Scottish Office in recommending that forces develop a standard definition of domestic violence, included physical, sexual and emotional abuse in the context of a close relationship between adults (1997). The 1999 Home Office definition limits domestic violence to sexual partners, current or past, and a range of behaviours, i.e. physical, sexual, emotional/psychological, and financial. The Best Value Performance Indicator (BVPI 153), in 2000 extends the definition to family members, including intimate partners over the age of 18 years.

Plotnikoff and Woolfson noted wide variation in the interpretation of the term repeat victimisation (1998). Repeat victimisation can be defined in relation to the household, the victim, offender and stages in the policing process. Repeat victimisation cannot be defined by prevalence or incidence as the police do not have information on the current or historic numbers who experience domestic violence or the number of assaults. Police data begin with calls for assistance.

Domestic Violence Officers and Units

The need to respond appropriately to those victimised by violence has and continues to drive policing changes. In 1995 just over one-half of forces in England and Wales had specialist units with some responsibility for domestic violence while only five had dedicated domestic violence units. Organisational variation continues between forces and even within forces some divisions have domestic violence officers or units, while others have no specialist provision (Plotnikoff and Woolfson, 1998). The Scottish Office report (1997) recommends that all forces should have full or part-time specialist domestic violence officers.

Domestic violence officers were found to have little impact on general police responses to domestic violence and found it difficult to cope with the volume of work generated by their success in responding to women victimised by domestic violence (Grace, 1995). Plotnikoff and Woolfson found no standard model for domestic violence officers (1998). Their work covered a wide spectrum of activities, ranging from a focus on those experiencing domestic violence to training delivery within their own force. They recommend research to evaluate different models of the domestic violence officer's role, in particular the use of domestic violence officers in investigative roles and the contribution of civilian support personnel.

But the underlying problem is identified as less to do with structure than with the status of domestic violence within forces. 'No single structure emerged as more or less problematic than any of the others' (Plotnikoff and Woolfson 1998:41).

Managing domestic violence work

A new research area for securing consistency in policing domestic violence is police management. There are a number of issues. Grace identified a tension between policy and its implementation where awareness of how domestic violence should be policed was not always put into practice at officer level (1995). Managers were more confident about operational officers' knowledge and training on Home Office Circular (60/1990) than was borne out in the findings (Grace, 1995).

This analysis was continued by Plotnikoff and Woolfson, (1998). In many forces where responsibility for domestic violence officers was devolved to divisions, force headquarters retained little or no managerial oversight for the force response or responsibility for inconsistencies in response by divisions. Management processes for domestic violence work were unclear with a lack of managerial commitment and undefined lines of accountability. The lack of direction from headquarters marginalises domestic violence. Its management confirms the low status of policing domestic violence.

There is a tension between devolution and centralisation in the management and performance of policing. While forces are devolving responsibilities to their divisional structures, which partly explains the internal variation in organisational responses to domestic violence, the 1998 thematic review implies greater centralisation (HMIC, 1998b). 'There is a need for a consistent, integrated and cohesive approach to crime with all the strategies and policies aligned to produce a reduction in crime.' (p.17). The report identifies unequivocal leadership, robust accountability and good management support as essential for effective and sustainable crime reduction.

Training

Training is basic to knowledge of policy, good practice and new initiatives. Despite the prominence of domestic violence in policy, most forces did not have a coherent training strategy to ensure effective implementation (Plotnikoff and Woolfson, 1998). A minority of officers had no knowledge of Circular 60/1990, while even more had not received new guidelines or initial or refresher training. The burden of training often fell on domestic violence officers, in addition to their other duties.

The Scottish Office report (1997) recommends a review of the content and extent of in-force training on domestic violence. Training should include awareness and procedural elements, and should involve Women's Aid in delivery and new provision to first line managers.

For multi-agency work, Grace identifies joint training with other agencies as the best way to develop a common approach and understanding (1995).

Information management

Inadequate and inconsistent recording practices across forces make it difficult to know the extent to which reported incidents result in arrest, charge or conviction (Grace, 1995; Scottish Office, 1997; Plotnikoff and Woolfson, 1998). Few forces used domestic violence statistics to monitor standards or had a systemic approach to monitoring which would have allowed them to examine how effectively all the police functions involved in force operations worked together.

Mechanisms for identifying domestic violence were unreliable (Plotnikoff and Woolfson, 1998). Responding officers could not rely on control rooms for information on previous incidents at the address. Information in manual records, such as injunctions, was seldom communicated to responding officers. Local domestic violence records contained more details than command and control systems. Domestic violence officers spent excessive time seeking information on incidents that should have been routinely provided. Few forces integrated information on child protection and domestic violence. Ready access to child protection register information was not available to officers responding to domestic violence. Domestic violence officers were sometimes left to make own judgements in contacting social workers about children in households reporting domestic violence. The Scottish Office report (1997) made similar points and recommended improvements in information sharing, new systems and their contents.

Repeat victimisation studies require a high degree of accuracy to have confidence in repeat patterns. To use repeat victimisation as a performance indicator also requires greater accuracy in recording domestic attendance. For example, the officers in the West Yorkshire division project area believed they made around 1,000 home visits a year as this was the number they were recording, but with thorough checking it was found to be over 2,000. This corrected figure permitted accurate identification of the proportion of domestic violence as violent crime; this was one-third of the divisional total, and other statistics dependent on police attendance as the base figure.

Overcoming the low status of domestic violence as police work

The low status of domestic violence as police work, a constant refrain in critiques of policing domestic violence, was confirmed by Grace (1995) and Plotnikoff and Woolfson (1998) as the basic problem. To raise its status, Plotnikoff and Woolfson recommended a schedule of statistics be developed to facilitate performance monitoring at the national level and that Her Majesty's Inspectorate of Constabulary assess the quality of forces arrangements for domestic violence. They also recommended that forces and divisions within forces should audit their data collection and referral mechanisms to ensure that the statistics produced accurately reflect the work being undertaken. This would establish the amount of police resources being used and required for this work. The newly established Best Value Performance Indicators in 1999 require police forces to report to the Home Office the percentage of domestic violence incidents, where there is a power of arrest, that result in arrest and the number of repeat attendances.

Conclusion and recommendations

In summary, during the 1970s and early 1980s the focus of research was on the recognition of domestic violence as a serious crime that required proactive policing. In the late 1980s, policing policies acknowledged the seriousness of domestic violence and in the late 1990s, attention turned to operational and managerial aspects of its policing. Multi-agency and inter-agency approaches began to be adopted in the late 1980s and these, too, became confirmed policy. During the 1990s there were three fully evaluated domestic violence projects on policing initiatives used as examples in this chapter. Unevaluated policing initiatives on domestic violence draw primarily on approaches developed as a result of policy initiatives in the UK and on US and Canadian projects. Evaluated research and critiques of the effectiveness of policing show gaps in knowledge. Assessing the effectiveness of domestic violence interventions in relation to costs and benefits provide the framework for new evaluations with guidance on cost-benefit and effectiveness indices from the Home Office (Dhiri and Brand, 1999; Stockdale et al, 1999).

Our conclusions are that cost-benefit and cost-effectiveness need to be considered in relation to achieving gains in prevention, protection and provision. New projects should address current policing issues by evaluating the organisation and management of the policing of domestic violence as well as the outcomes for those experiencing and committing domestic violence along with other agency responses where relevant. While there are few fully evaluated domestic violence projects and the building into research designs of cost-benefit and effective measures are at a preliminary stage, new projects can build on past research and establish new initiatives. Measurable benefits will be needed to justify the costs and to establish best value.

Good practice issues to be considered in developing new cost effective approaches to domestic violence are improved reporting and increased satisfaction with policing on the part of those experiencing domestic violence, improvements in police organisation, training and management, including information management, audits and statistical reporting, and effective partnership approaches. Policies and guidance on policing domestic violence remain to be fully implemented. We regard uneven service delivery as the major outcome of ineffective domestic violence policing and its management. This is at least partly responsible for under-reporting and dissatisfaction with the policing of domestic violence by those who require policing services, including agencies responding to victimised women.

There are two major approaches to policing domestic violence in the UK. These can be combined or developed separately, but for operational policing each depends upon the other. The first focuses on the organisation, management, and delivery of policing domestic violence. The second is a partnership approach in which the police are one of several or many participating agencies. While the police alone cannot solve the many problems created for individuals by domestic violence, contributing effectively to partnership approaches requires good policing services. The recommendations bring together the outcomes of previously evaluated policing projects, critical reviews of the policing of domestic violence and policy recommendations for future policing strategies in order to respond to gaps in knowledge.

The repeat victimisation approach, with its cost-effective resource implications, has been shown to measure effectiveness in policing domestic violence. This approach:

- concentrates resources on a high crime area;
- focuses on those at greatest risk of repeat victimisation;
- fuses the historically separate roles of victim support and crime prevention;
- targets offenders;
- identifies chronic offenders;
- improves information gathering for investigative purposes;
- promotes consistency in service delivery;
- increases reporting of domestic violence; and,
- develops early intervention strategies.

Partnership models too, can be cost-effective, and offer many of the same benefits. In addition this approach:

- identifies agencies needed by those experiencing domestic violence;
- increases knowledge of the work of other agencies;
- reduces the number of agencies approached in the search for appropriate assistance;
- improves information gathering and sharing; and
- encourages co-ordinated and systematic responses.

Recommendations

- Cost-effective and cost-benefit projects could include secondary analysis of the fully evaluated projects in order to establish benchmarks against which to develop and measure future programmes. While the data sets vary in their completeness and comparability, some financial comparison between their approaches to policing domestic violence could be undertaken. This would require an analysis of direct and indirect costs and conceptual developments in relation to social costs and benefits and their financial worth. Alternative bases for scaling social costs would need to be developed.

- New projects could arise out of the questions and issues raised by the three previously evaluated projects in Merseyside, West Yorkshire, and Islington.
- The full implication of policing responses to couples staying together or separating in stopping or encouraging violence has not been explored. Men who are not present at the time of police attendance are less likely to be followed up which has cost effective implications. Policing initiatives which reduce this differential response to perpetrators should be developed by following up and charging men who are absent from the house when the police arrive (Buzawa et al, 1999). Displacement, the movement of men from woman to woman, can be monitored through a man's domestic violence history. This was a very small, but very important, problem in the West Yorkshire project as these perpetrators included extremely violent men.
- Cost-effectiveness could be explored through investigative and alternative evidence gathering techniques that supplement or are alternatives to women's statements. These could be evaluated for their effects on charging, decisions to prosecute, prosecution outcomes and repeat victimisation.
- Achieving cost-effective policing of domestic violence requires a reduction in repeat victimisation. Analysing offending profiles, developing risk assessment and specific strategies with chronic offenders could be undertaken. This could include a comparative study of variations in prior police interventions with domestic homicide and serious assault.
- The relationship between repeat victimisation and the outcomes of arrest, with and without charging, and with or without court appearance, would offer valuable insight into the cost-effectiveness of arrest.
- The three-tier intervention model developed for the West Yorkshire project could be replicated or extended, by adding factors such as: other types of violent inter-personal crime, for example, racial and homophobic attacks; the relationship between repeat victimisation of women and abuse of children in the home; domestic attacks on men. Alternatively the interventions at each level could be altered in order to explore their individual and collective effectiveness in the policing process.
- Cost-effective policing of domestic violence could be assisted by more effective intervention by other agencies. Extending the concept of a three-tier intervention model to other statutory agencies may assist in the reduction of repeat attendance by police officers.
- Partnership involving different agencies and with differing levels of integration could be evaluated for their service delivery effectiveness to

those experiencing domestic violence and to policing cost-effectiveness.

- The impact on first-time reporting, victim satisfaction and repeat victimisation on dedicated police organisational forms for domestic violence should be evaluated. This should include varying officer responsibilities, the development of victim satisfaction indicators and cost-effectiveness.
- Cost-benefit and effectiveness would be furthered if successful projects wrote explicit detailed manuals for other forces to assist with replication. These should be step-by-step guides covering all aspects: rationale, how new initiatives were introduced, their organisation, training required, management structure and responsibilities, information management and communication, effective problem solving.

Accommodation provision

Debra Levison and Nicola Harwin

There has been relatively little written about the housing needs of those experiencing domestic violence, although it is known that between 16-18% of households accepted as homeless have lost their accommodation through violent relationship breakdown. These figures are likely to be an underestimate. Leaving home because of domestic violence is a major step for women. It causes disruption to childcare and schooling arrangements as well as social and support networks. In addition, it may place a woman in increased danger. Research points to the need for housing bodies to take a sensitive, consistent and believing approach to women seeking assistance and advice.

This chapter discusses the duties of local authorities towards women suffering domestic violence and sets out the criteria for rehousing women under the homelessness legislation. It discusses the problems women face in temporary accommodation and their need for support during resettlement. To ensure the consistent application of guidance on rehousing the report recommends increased training and monitoring of the implementation of guidelines on dealing with domestic violence.

Introduction

Relatively little has been written specifically about housing and domestic violence and the amount of research and publicly available good practice material in this area has, until recently, been fairly limited. The studies that have been undertaken and published tend to have been very localised and small scale and, until recently, there has been no thorough overview of accommodation provision for households experiencing domestic violence in England, let alone something which has considered the situation from an international perspective. However, national research undertaken for the Department of Transport, Local Government and the Regions (DTLR), in conjunction with the Women's Unit (WU) and the Department of Health (DoH), and due to be published this year, will provide a wealth of information about accommodation and support for households experiencing domestic violence.

Many local authority housing departments and voluntary agencies are implementing excellent policies and procedures for dealing with households experiencing domestic violence who need accommodation or require additional support or other services in their current accommodation. However, a detailed analysis of individual housing authorities and organisations is beyond the scope of this review, which is based largely on published and publicly available material.

This report is based on a review of available literature. This has been obtained mainly through extensive searches of library databases and the Internet, trawls of bibliographies and talking to experts in the field.

The need for housing

Housing is of vital importance when considering the safety of people experiencing domestic violence. Housing responses to domestic violence do not necessarily involve the provision of alternative accommodation. For most people experiencing domestic violence, leaving their home is seen very much as a last resort. There are various civil and legal remedies available to people who want to keep the perpetrator away or remove the perpetrator from the home and the surrounding area. In addition, in some areas, there is a range of safety and security measures available to make homes less vulnerable to attack and to increase personal safety. Such measures can clearly contribute to crime reduction and are relatively cheap to provide, compared with the costs of providing temporary accommodation and rehousing.

However, where the risk of violence is perceived to be acute (and possibly other remedies have been tried but have failed), victims may see no alternative but to move from their current home in order to escape further attacks. This is a major step for most people; losing a home will usually involve the loss of much more, particularly when the move is to a new area and especially where there are children. In practice, it is generally the victim rather than the perpetrator who leaves - primarily because the violent partner has no incentive to do so. For people who leave a violent situation, safety is the primary concern and it is particularly important for housing providers to recognise this when determining the types of accommodation that they will make available for this group. In addition, people fleeing violence are likely to be extremely vulnerable and, again, this needs to be recognised by housing providers so that services are delivered in a sensitive and sympathetic way. Being dealt with in a rude or abrupt manner, being disbelieved or being placed in accommodation that is inappropriate may result in a victim returning to a violent situation.

Box 1: Housing options for people escaping domestic violence

- remaining in the family home without the violent partner

- leaving the family home on a temporary basis and subsequently either:
    - returning to the family home and to the violent partner, or
    - returning to the family home but without the violent partner;
    - leaving the family home permanently and seeking rehousing elsewhere, for example:
        - from a local authority or registered social landlord (RSL) (through the local authority housing register or RSL direct waiting list)
        - in the private rented sector
        - with friends or family (although in practice such arrangements are rarely sustainable in the long term)
        - buying a property.

Box 2: Factors that may affect people's housing-related decisions

- access to information and knowledge of what their options may be;
- the nature, severity and duration of the violence they have experienced - and the likelihood of it continuing into the future;
- whether any of their children have experienced violence within the family and, whether they have or not, whether this is likely to happen (again) in the future;
- whether or not they are able or willing to leave the family home;
- whether they believe that it is possible to permanently exclude a violent partner from the family home;
- perceptions of what else is available to them, if they leave the family home;
- whether or not they have children;
- if they have children, the ages and sexes of the children;
- options for and the effectiveness of other actions being taken under the civil and criminal law (e.g. Part IV of the Family Law Act 1996 and the Children Act 1989);
- their ability to access state resources and the effectiveness of responses when they seek help;
- their access to personal financial resources;
- the degree of support they require; and
- whether they have any special needs over and above the experience of domestic violence.

Background

Although both men and women commit acts of domestic violence on partners, women are twice as likely as men to be injured and are also more likely to suffer repeated attacks. A high proportion of women experiencing domestic violence has children. In Hackney, for example, 64% of women in a recent study had at least one child. It can therefore be said that a 'typical' household experiencing domestic violence comprises a woman and one or more children, (Mirrlees-Black, 1999; Stanko et al, 1998), although violence can occur in all types of close relationships (both heterosexual and gay and lesbian) and affects women both with and without children. Domestic violence can also occur between family members other than partners. It would therefore be wrong for housing providers and social landlords to frame their policies on the assumption that violence is confined to women with children, although they are in the majority.

In practice, people escaping domestic violence may pursue a number of different options over time. For example, a woman may leave a violent partner temporarily on a number of occasions before finally moving for good – around a fifth of women leaving refuges in England return to the abuser at least once (WAFE, 1998a). Alternatively, she may make the decision to remain in the family home, try but ultimately fail to exclude a violent partner over a prolonged period and eventually have little choice but to move elsewhere.

The role of local authorities

In England, local authority housing departments' involvement in domestic violence can come about in a number of ways, and people experiencing domestic violence may approach their housing department through a variety of access routes. In many areas, the local authority will be the only way to access not just council housing but also, through the nomination process, registered social landlord (RSL) accommodation.

As table 1 shows, in 2000/01, 17% (17,950) of the 114,350 households accepted as homeless in England gave violent relationship breakdown as the *main* reason for the loss of their last settled home. During the same period, this was the main reason for homelessness for 19% (826) of the 4,352 homeless acceptances in Wales. In Scotland, during 1998/99 (the latest year for which figure are available), of the 18,600 households accepted as homeless, 20% (3,800) had lost their accommodation because of a violent dispute with a spouse or cohabitee.

Table 1
Violent relationship breakdown as reason for loss of last settled home 2000/01

	Accepted as homeless due to:- Violent relationship breakdown		Other reason		Total	
	number	%	number	%	number	%
England	17,950	16.0	96,400	84.0	114,350	100.0
Wales	826	19.0	3,526	81.0	4,352	100.0
Scotland[1]	3,800	20.4	14,800	79.6	18,600	100.0
Great Britain	22,576	16.4	114,726	83.6	137,302	100.0

1. Figures for Scotland refer to 1998/99.
Sources: England: DTLR P1E returns. Wales: National Assembly for Wales. Scotland: Scottish Executive, Housing Statistics Branch, Homelessness Database.

Box 3: How people experiencing domestic violence access local authority housing departments

- by applying for housing through the homelessness legislation;
- by applying for housing via the housing register;
- as an existing council tenant, applying for a transfer to another social rented property;
- as an existing council tenant with a domestic violence clause in the tenancy agreement - the local authority can serve the perpetrator with a notice to quit (NTQ) and issue the remaining tenant with a new tenancy;
- as an existing council tenant, requesting the local authority to use Part IV of the Family Law Act 1996 to transfer the tenancy to her name; or
- as an existing council tenant, requesting additional safety and security for their current home.

Reliability of data

It is possible that domestic violence would also have been present for many other households accepted as homeless but not recorded in the official figures as the main cause of homelessness. Official figures for England are derived from the P1E return, which asks local authorities to provide aggregate information on homelessness and is submitted to the DTLR each quarter. Amongst other things, the form asks local authorities to provide the 'reason for the loss of last settled home' for households they have accepted as homeless during the quarter and 'violent relationship breakdown' is one of the categories available. Where domestic violence has been given to the housing officer by the applicant as the main reason for their homelessness, they will be categorised under the 'violent relationship breakdown' heading. However, where domestic violence is but one of a number of reasons for the loss of their home, their case may be categorised under a different heading (for example, rent or mortgage arrears).

Another possible reason that can be given for the loss of last settled home on the P1E form is 'relatives/friends no longer able or willing to provide accommodation'. People who have left a violent partner and have been living with friends or family for a substantial period of time may well be placed into this category, rather than 'violent relationship breakdown'. Finally, in some cases people experiencing domestic violence will not mention this when they make their homelessness application. There may be some scope for improved monitoring in this area.

Official figures will also not include those people who apply as homeless but have their application turned down by the local authority. This situation is discussed in more detail in section 3.

Unfortunately, no figures exist on either the number of people being allocated a property through the housing register or the number who obtain a transfer within the social rented sector on grounds of domestic violence. This is partly a reflection of the vastly differing policies and practices adopted by local authorities and registered social landlords, for example in terms of the level of priority given to households experiencing domestic violence. It is also because of the lack of consistency in the way that different local authorities collect, collate and monitor their figures (even where their policies and practices are similar). In some authorities, information is collected on domestic violence on a case by case basis but, for reasons of confidentiality, it is not input onto computer and as a result aggregate figures cannot be derived. There is undoubtedly scope for the comprehensive and consistent collection, collation and production of figures on domestic violence for both new tenants and transfers.

In terms of lettings by RSLs, during 2000/01, just under 2% of permanent general needs lettings were to households whose main reason for housing was domestic violence. This amounted to just over 2,800 households (NHF/Housing Corporation, 2001). The figures are far higher for *supported* RSL housing - which is mainly short term; in 2000/01, just over 8,000 households experiencing domestic violence moved into this type of accommodation (most of which would have been refuges). Unlike local authorities, RSLs complete a pro forma for every letting they make (as part of the CORE (continuous recording) system), giving a range of information about the household and the property, including details about domestic violence. This information is then aggregated and published on a regular basis.

The homelessness legislation and domestic violence

Local authorities in England have specific legal duties towards homeless people and those threatened with homelessness under Part VII of the 1996 Housing Act. In addition, local authorities should have regard to a code of guidance that accompanies the Act.

This section starts by summarising the aspects of the legislation and guidance that either specifically refer or are relevant to households experiencing domestic violence. It goes on to look at the operation of the legislation and guidance in practice.

Summary of the legislation and code of guidance

In order to accept an applicant as homeless, a local authority must be satisfied that the applicant:

- is eligible for assistance;
- is homeless or threatened with homelessness;
- is in priority need; and
- is not intentionally homeless.

The authority also has the discretion to determine whether the applicant has a local connection, but this does not affect whether a duty is owed.

When someone is eligible for assistance, unintentionally homeless and in priority need, the local authority must arrange accommodation for a minimum period of two years, unless it is satisfied that there is other suitable accommodation available for occupation in the local authority area.

In many areas, women fleeing domestic violence who are accepted as homeless will spend a period of time in temporary accommodation. However, where there is a plentiful supply of permanent housing, it is possible that some women in this position may be rehoused immediately (as long as they have the necessary priority under the local authority's allocation scheme). Such speedy rehousing may not, however, always be appropriate. For some women, a short period in supported temporary accommodation (such as refuges), where they can receive advice and support and have time to consider their options, may actually be beneficial.

However, Women's Aid (1999) has argued that more than six months in temporary accommodation can prove detrimental to the family and to the children. This is because of:

- the need for self-contained accommodation;
- the need for greater privacy;

- the need for greater independence and control (and the need for people that have dealt with their immediate crisis to 'move on' and re-establish themselves);
- the need for settled, long term accommodation (for example, because of children's schooling and in order to develop social networks);
- where physical conditions are poor, the basic need for accommodation of a reasonable standard; and
- the negative effects of living with others in a 'crisis'.

Eligibility for assistance

Certain persons from abroad are ineligible for assistance under the Act. Broadly speaking the same groups are ineligible for Social Security benefits. These include:

- people whose leave to enter or remain in the UK has been granted on the basis that they will not have recourse to public funds;
- people who have entered the country illegally or overstayed their leave.

Women experiencing domestic violence who are ineligible for assistance from local authorities may seek help from refuges or RSLs. However, for most refuges Housing Benefit is a major source of their funding and it is extremely difficult for them to provide accommodation free of charge. For RSLs too, the extent to which they can house applicants who do not have the means to pay their rent and service charges is likely to be very limited.

Homeless or threatened with homelessness

According to the Act, a person is homeless if there is no accommodation anywhere that it is reasonable for them to occupy or there is accommodation but it would not be reasonable to continue to occupy it. In relation to domestic violence, the code of guidance states that

> (1) It is not reasonable for a person to continue to occupy accommodation if it is probable that this will lead to domestic violence against him, or against:-
> (a) a person who normally resides with him as a member of his family, or
> (b) any other person who might reasonably be expected to reside with him.
> For this purpose, 'domestic violence' in relation to a person means violence from a person with whom he is associated, or threats of violence from such a person which are likely to be carried out.
>
> (2) In determining whether it would be, or would have been, reasonable for a person to continue to occupy accommodation, regard may be had to the general circumstances prevailing in relation to housing in the district of

> the local housing authority to whom he has applied for accommodation or for assistance in obtaining accommodation ... '
> (paras 13.7 and 13.9, p55)

A person is threatened with homelessness if it is likely that s/he will become homeless within 28 days.

Making enquiries

The code emphasises that 'it is not for the applicant to 'prove' his/her case' and gives guidance to local authority on how to deal with applicants claiming to be fleeing domestic violence:

> in cases involving violence or the threat of violence, the applicants may be in considerable distress. Wherever possible an officer of the same sex as the applicant should conduct the interview, preferably someone trained specifically in dealing with circumstances of this kind. If the applicant reports violence or the threat of violence, the authority should not normally seek proof directly from the alleged perpetrator, since doing so may delay the assessment and may generate further violence. (para 11.4, p89)

Homeless in a refuge

Women living in refuges are sometimes placed on the housing register, but not accepted as homeless. However, case law has shown that a woman remains homeless while she is in a refuge (*R v Ealing LBC ex parte Sidhu (1982)*). Moreover the code of guidance states that

> securing accommodation in a refuge may not count as a discharge of their (the local authority's) duty (to secure accommodation for two years). Authorities should not delay in securing other accommodation for an applicant placed in a women's refuge in the hope that she might return to her partner. It is also important to ensure that places in refuges continue to be available for others in need. If the refuge terminates a licence to occupy because the household no longer need to be in the refuge, the authority have a duty to secure alternative accommodation straight away. (para 21.28, p89)

Priority need

According to the Act, a household is in priority need if:

- it has dependent children;
- it contains a pregnant woman;
- it contains a person who is vulnerable as a result of old age, mental illness or handicap, physical disability or some other special reason; or
- it is homeless or threatened with homelessness as a result of emergency (fire, flood or some other disaster).

In relation to domestic violence and vulnerability, the code of guidance states that:

> Authorities should consider whether men and women without children are vulnerable as a result of having suffered violence or abuse from persons with whom they are associated, or whether they are at risk of further violence or abuse if they return to those persons. (para 14.17, p60)

and that:

> Housing authorities should be ready to take action where household members are at risk from violence or abuse. Where young people under 18 are involved because of a breakdown in the relationship with their parents, or where there is a risk of abuse, the housing authority should alert the social services authority to the case. (para 9.39, p38)

Intentional homelessness

The Act states that

> A person becomes homeless intentionally if s/he deliberately does or fails to do anything and as a result s/he ceases to occupy accommodation which was available for her/his occupation and which it would have been reasonable for her/him to continue to occupy. (s.191, p115)

Homelessness is also intentional when someone colludes in the loss of accommodation in order to become entitled to assistance, or fails to take up accommodation when assisted to do so under s.197 of the Housing Act 1996.

The DTLR's guide to relationship breakdown for social landlords (London Research Centre (LRC), 1999) sets out the three main issues that should be considered when investigating intentionality for people applying as homeless following relationship breakdown. These are as follows:

- whether it is reasonable to remain in the accommodation;
- whether someone who has legal rights in a property (or the possibility of establishing such rights) should be expected to exercise them; and
- the consequences of losing a home as a result of debts which have resulted from the breakdown of the relationship.

In terms of legal rights, the code of guidance states that

> Injunctions ordering persons not to molest, or enter the home of, the applicant will not necessarily deter people and the applicant should not necessarily be asked to return to his/her home in this instance. Authorities may inform applicants of the option to take out an injunction, but should make it clear

> that there is no obligation to do so if s/he feels it would be ineffective. (para 13.10, p55)

Shelter has recommended that the code be changed to spell out explicitly that injunctive powers are usually only short term remedies and may not be available at all in cases of threatened violence (Birch, 1999). Case law has also made it clear that injunctions are not to be used by local authorities as a way of remedying housing need.

The code also provides local authorities with guidance on the issue of debt, suggesting that:

> someone who loses or is forced to sell their home because of rent or mortgage arrears caused by family breakdown should not normally be considered to have made a deliberate act or omission. Nor should they be considered intentionally homeless if they sell or give up possession in advance of a court order, if it is clear that they would have had no defence against the proceedings. (DETR, 1999, p56)

Local connection

Local authorities have a duty to arrange accommodation for applicants who qualify under the homelessness legislation and have a local connection (e.g. because of family, employment or residence) with their area. Where there is no local connection, a local authority can refer an applicant to an authority with which there is a connection. However, the Act makes special provision for households experiencing or at risk of domestic violence, stating that a person may not be referred to a district where s/he will run the risk of domestic violence.

New code of guidance

At the time of writing, a revised code is being drawn up (following consultation). The draft code that was issued for consultation contained some amendments and additions relating specifically to domestic violence. In particular, the draft code provides a fuller definition of domestic violence, as follows:

> ... any form of physical, sexual or emotional abuse between people in a close relationship. Authorities should be aware that domestic violence can take a number of forms such as physical assault, sexual abuse, rape, threats and intimidation. (para 11.17, p6)

It also states that:

> ... it is not good practice for authorities to expect evidence of violence. (para 11.19, p7)

The revised guidance on injunctions is also much clearer, acknowledging that they are 'usually temporary', 'cannot always be renewed' and are 'ill advised in some circumstances'.

Extension of the priority needs categories

The Government is now consulting on a draft order which would extend the priority needs categories. Among the groups specified in the order is 'a person who is vulnerable as a result of ceasing to occupy accommodation by reason of violence from another or threats of violence from another person which is likely to be carried out'. Accompanying the draft order are amendments to the Code of Guidance and also draft good practice guidance, which sets out the considerations to be taken into account when determining whether or an applicant should be considered 'vulnerable'. This draft guidance states that in cases of domestic violence, local authorities should not seek proof of violence or contact the perpetrators. It also recognises that the effects of domestic violence can be cumulative, and that incidents occurring over time may erode a victim's self confidence and contribute to making him or her vulnerable.

Furthermore, the draft guidance states that 'it would be wrong to reach any conclusions about the severity of violence or abuse suffered and the impact on the applicant based only on the immediate circumstances in which they are left'. (Source: DTLR Draft Supplementary Guidance to DTLR, Homelessness (Priority Need for Accommodation) (England) Order 2001, p.2.)

The homelessness legislation in practice

Most of the studies looking at local authorities' policies and practices were undertaken before the improvements to the legislation and code of guidance were made. For example, a study looking at local authority responses to women and children escaping domestic violence was undertaken in the early 1990s by the Women's Aid Federation England and the University of Bristol (Malos and Hague, 1993:69).

One of the main findings was the wide variation 'observed between the (four) local authorities in the study in their policies and practice regarding women and children homeless due to domestic violence and in their use of discretion.' and the 'uneven application of the homelessness legislation both between authorities and also between individual officers within authorities.... [with] ... inconsistencies, large variations in both policy and practice and departures from the code of guidance ... widely reported ...'. (page i of summary)

The authors of this study found that local authority responses to women and children fleeing violence could be grouped into three following broad categories:

- generous interpretation of the legislation, often using formally agreed domestic violence policy and practice guidance as a means to greater clarity and consistency of policy and improved service delivery;
- interpretations which broadly follow the code of guidance although this is sometimes selective and not always consistent throughout an authority's practice; or
- rigorous interpretations of the law, often termed 'a policy of minimal legal compliance', in which statutory duties are defined as narrowly as possible.

(page ii of summary)

In particular, it was found that rigorous interpretations of the law were most likely to affect women without children, those without a local connection, owner-occupiers and those who had experienced violence from outside the home or non-physical violence.

Other practices which the study defined as unacceptable included:

- adversarial interviewing techniques;
- pressurising women to use legal remedies;
- referring women back to their 'home' authority, where there was a risk of violence; and
- demanding detailed proof of violence.

The study underlined the need for the development of good practice by local authority housing departments and registered social landlords. In particular, attention was drawn to the adoption of domestic violence policy and practice guidelines and also to the need for appropriate training. In addition, it made various recommendations for improvements in local authority policy and practice and changes to government policy. Furthermore, a 1996 study on the effectiveness of the code found that 2% of local authorities said that they always insisted that applicants experiencing domestic violence pursued legal remedies as a condition of accepting them as homeless, and another 26% said they usually did. (Birch, 1999)

Since these studies were carried out, there have been substantial revisions both to the homelessness legislation and to the accompanying code of guidance with more to be made shortly. These address many of the issues raised. Progress has also been made within some local authorities and other agencies, relating to the implementation of the homelessness legislation and the approach to dealing with households experiencing domestic violence more generally.

There is little information on local authority policy and practice in this area, following the implementation of the 1996 Housing Act and the revised code of guidance. What there is tends to be based on very small or localised studies. For example, two small-scale surveys of women who had experienced or were experiencing domestic violence have been undertaken in an inner London borough (London Borough of Lewisham Community Safety Team/Lewisham Domestic Violence Forum, 1998). These both suggest that some problems still exist. In the 1999 study, women were asked about their views and experiences of using a variety of services, including housing, in relation to domestic violence. Some women reported that their treatment by housing officers had been 'rude and unsympathetic, ... neglectful and ignorant'. One, from an ethnic minority, said that officers had failed to find her an interpreter and that she had had to tell her story again and again to various different people. Having to provide evidence of violence was also raised as an issue, with one woman commenting that '... it has been very hard, going to the homeless unit and having to give proof of the domestic violence before they would look at my case'. In the 1998 study, nearly a third of the women who had approached the homeless persons' unit had found the service to be poor and a further third had found it unacceptable. Given the lack of information on other areas, it is difficult to know whether or not the situation in this borough is replicated elsewhere.

Women's Aid and Shelter have argued that some local authorities are still rejecting applicants fleeing domestic violence because they have no local connection or because they have not taken out an injunction against their violent partner. They also believe that some local authorities are routinely not considering domestic violence as a ground for vulnerability when determining 'priority need' for women without children. The above organisations believe that there is therefore evidence that some local authorities may be failing to follow the homelessness legislation or have due regard to the code of guidance. (WAFE, 1999)

Many of the issues outlined above have been examined as part of the large scale national DTLR/DH/WU study referred to above.

Good practice in the delivery of the homelessness service

An increasing number of local authorities have produced policy and procedure guides on domestic violence for staff. Overleaf are some examples of good practice for staff contained in recent guides.

Training of housing staff, in both policies and procedures and also issues around awareness, is also provided by some agencies delivering housing services. It is important for such training to be part of a rolling programme, to ensure that it is available to new staff and also that existing staff can regularly have their knowledge updated and reinforced.

Box 4. General principles

In domestic violence cases, Housing Officers should bear in mind the following principles:

- the first priority is to ensure the safety of the person who is fleeing domestic violence
- respond sympathetically to the applicant ....
- believe the applicant ......
- ... people who are fleeing domestic violence should never be asked to prove that physical violence has taken place
- be non-judgmental ...
- maintain confidentiality

(From *Domestic Violence: Policy and procedures for housing staff*, Manchester City Council, April 1998: 4 & 5)

Box 5. Conducting an interview

Interviews with women who are abused are rarely straightforward. Some will first 'test the water' by presenting differing problems rather than pinpoint the violence as their main worry. Some will deny your suspicions or intuition that she is being abused. Aim to conclude a satisfactory interview for you both by using the following guidelines:

- Probe gently ask open ended non-threatening questions like 'are you having difficulties at home?'; offer examples of other clients' experiences to show that she's not alone.
- Validate her and tell her how common you know domestic violence to be; assure her that she's not to blame, that no-one should have to put up with abuse in their relationship and that he's responsible for his use of violence.
- Avoid stereotypes of language and use the words she does to describe her experience, e.g. avoid using the terms 'battered wife' or 'domestic violence' until she does.
- Explore the options with her and don't presume to tell her what she should do next, or to try and 'rescue' her by solving her problems'. Remember that she may still be trying to make the relationship work, so talk through with her how she tries to avoid being assaulted, taking care to introduce new options that may be helpful.
- Don't pressurise her into doing something or agreeing to action that she's uncomfortable with ...
- Work with difference whilst not letting it restrain your discussion of options, e.g. some Asian women will fear being ostracised by their community but there are Asian groups who will support her and challenge his behaviour.

(From *Making the Difference: A good practice guide in responding to domestic violence*, London Borough of Hammersmith & Fulham/Metropolitan Police, 1995)

Emergency and temporary accommodation

No comprehensive figures are currently available on the number of homeless households experiencing domestic violence that are living in temporary accommodation at any one time (although this information has been collected in the DTLR/DH/WU study already referred to). There are likely to be wide differences in length of stay according to the level of demand for social housing in the locality.

This section looks in turn at each of the main forms of emergency and temporary accommodation available to households experiencing domestic violence. These are as follows:

- refuges;
- bed and breakfast hotels;
- hostels;
- the private rented sector;
- staying with friends or relatives; and
- transitional or second stage accommodation.

While much of the emergency/temporary accommodation used is 'mainstream' in that it caters for all homeless applicants, some - such as refuges and special hostels or reception centres - is specifically for people fleeing domestic violence. In addition, some may be earmarked for homeless women and children only, regardless of whether or not they have experienced violence.

Temporary housing catering specifically for people experiencing domestic violence - mainly refuge accommodation - is likely to have a range of support and other services to meet the needs of residents, including supported services for children. It will also almost certainly have a far higher degree of security, in order to minimise the risk to women of further violence. Other 'mainstream' temporary accommodation may lack such services, although there are examples of local authorities and voluntary organisations providing outreach support to people living in hostels, bed and breakfast and other forms of temporary housing. These are discussed below.

Problems of living in temporary accommodation

As stated above, there is a diverse range of temporary accommodation being used for households experiencing domestic violence. While some problems are specific to particular types of accommodation, there are some general problems associated with living in any type of housing on a temporary basis. These can include:

- frequent moves from one temporary address to another;
- disruption to schooling;
- disruption to employment;
- lack of access to health and social services;
- a loss of control of one's life;
- the inability to plan into the future (which can affect children's schooling, establishing social networks, employment and health);
- poor living conditions (a particular problem in bed and breakfast hotels);
- living at some distance from the original home, away from family, friends and other support networks (not all people fleeing domestic violence will want to move away from their home area);
- a lack of support; and
- poor safety and security.

In addition, problems with living in temporary accommodation which is not self-contained can include:

- a lack of basic amenities;
- problems with cooking and preparing food;
- overcrowding (in particular where adults and children are having to share rooms);
- a lack of space for children to play and study; and
- a lack of privacy.

Length of time in temporary accommodation

Not a great deal is known about how long women fleeing domestic violence stay in temporary accommodation, although it has been suggested by Women's Aid that people in this position should not be expected to remain for any longer than three months (and a maximum of six months in refuges). Evidence from a study of four local authorities undertaken in the early 1990s showed that in some areas the wait for rehousing for this group could be anything from six months to several years. A study of the length of stay in temporary accommodation in London by homeless households generally, also carried out in the early 1990s, found that the average wait for housing was 47 weeks. However, a substantial proportion (36%) had remained in temporary accommodation for more than year before being permanently rehoused. Little is currently known about whether the length of stay for households experiencing domestic violence differs at all from that for other homeless people awaiting housing. (Malos and Hague, 1993; LRC, 1991; WAFE, 1999)

Refuge support services

Refuges are safe places for women (and their children) to go in an emergency to escape domestic violence. They provide not only accommodation but also support and other services, usually as part of a package of services by Women's Aid and other similar organisations. Local helplines, outreach, resettlement and aftercare services are also likely to be provided. Safety and security are crucially important. The addresses of refuge buildings are generally kept secret from all except those who need to know, in order to protect women from being threatened by their violent partner or others associated with their partner. Refuges are normally run as women-for-women services, unless men need to visit the refuge in a professional capacity (usually by arrangement).

The majority of refuges have communal living arrangements, although the degree of self-containment varies from one to another. Transitional/second stage accommodation managed by refuge groups tends to be self-contained.

Although most refuge buildings in England are conversions of properties built for other purposes, more recently there have been some purpose built refuges developed (usually with Housing Corporation funding).

Some refuge provision is for specific groups, such as women and children from black and minority ethnic communities and women without children. There is one refuge in the London Borough of Newham that provides safe accommodation for women with learning disabilities (not only those experiencing domestic violence). Referrals are accepted from anywhere in the UK, where funding is available.

Authorities that responded to a letter from the Minister for Women asking for examples of good practice in tackling violence against women shared widespread concern about the shortage of refuge provision nationally and in particular areas. Furthermore, many local authorities reported that they had cases in their area of women and children who could not be accommodated because the refuge was full. In some areas, the nearest refuge services were in a town at some distance and there were cases where only one refuge project was serving an entire county. In one study (in the London Borough of Hackney) it was reported that: 'For each woman in a refuge ... eight others plus their children are searching for immediate shelter from violence'. (LRC, 1998; Stanko et al., 1998:49).

Funding

Another recurrent theme is the underfunding of existing refuge services. In a study of three London boroughs, the county of Essex and the former metropolitan district of West Yorkshire, inadequate funding was found in all of the refuge projects contacted. This took three forms:

- insufficient family places to meet demand;
- insufficient funding per family place; and
- lack of long term funding.

One of the consequences of insufficient funding per family place and the lack of long term funding was felt to be overcrowding and poor conditions which, workers in the study believed, sometimes caused women to return to violent partners. (Frayne, 1994).

Refuge services are heavily reliant on housing benefit as a means of funding and, for this reason, many are simply unable to accommodate women who cannot meet the full cost of the charges.

A situation may arise where a woman is claiming housing benefit and has a permanent tenancy elsewhere, which she wishes to retain while at the refuge. The regulations state that claimants are treated as occupying two properties and are potentially entitled to Housing Benefit on both of them where they have had to leave, and remain absent from, the normal home through fear of violence in the home or from a former member of the family. Where there is an intention to return, Housing Benefit may be payable for a maximum of 52 weeks. Where there is no such intention, the claimant must be treated as occupying the former home for up to four weeks if there is an unavoidable liability to make payments on it. Actual violence need not have occurred and the claimant has only to show that he or she is afraid of violence occurring in the home or from a former member of the family. (Zebedee and Ward, 1999)

One problem with these rules is the limited amount of time for women to decide whether or not to return to the original property (four weeks). Another is that any homelessness application made to the local authority is likely to be taken by the Housing Benefit section as signifying the woman's intention never to return (even though in practice she may not yet have made a firm decision). In addition, these rules apply only where the woman herself has a rent liability on both homes (i.e. is either a joint or a sole tenant). Where she is the sole tenant, the eligible rent for Housing Benefit purposes is 100% of the rent liability, regardless of whether or not the perpetrator is still living in the property. The entitlement is also 100% where she is the joint tenant but the perpetrator has left and is not paying his share of the rent. Where the woman is the joint tenant and the perpetrator is still living in the property, or is not living in the property but is paying his share of the rent, the eligible rent for Housing Benefit purposes is 50%. However, there is no entitlement to Housing Benefit on the original home if the woman has no rent liability - resulting in the potential for arrears to accrue and the possibility of the loss of a home that a woman is intending to return to. (ALG, 1999)

Services provided

A range of support and other services are available to women living in refuges, including individual one-to-one support, support groups, counselling, benefits advice, advocacy and support in accessing local facilities and community resources.

Refuge projects also provide a range of services for children (who make up about two thirds of their residents). These include arranging group play activities, one-to-one sessions, liaising with schools and other agencies, organising outings and children's house meetings, providing outreach and aftercare services and advocacy to support children involved with social services or legal proceedings. However, due to funding problems some refuges do not have children's workers or suitable facilities for children. For example, a refuge manager spoke about the needs of the children in her refuge, where six women may have up to 18 children at any one time. The children have no play area and 'the costs of coping with children are not recognised - bed wetting, wallpaper tearing, breakages'. (Stonham, 1998:6)

Local Women's Aid and other refuge projects also provide a range of support services to women not living in refuges. These include specialist outreach, resettlement and aftercare services to black and minority ethnic women, rural outreach services, drop in centres, helplines, support groups, resettlement and other aftercare services.

The provision of support for people experiencing domestic violence (either in their existing home, in temporary accommodation or once they have been permanently rehoused) is likely to be a cost-effective intervention. Adequate support can be seen as a preventative measure in housing terms, for example by reducing the likelihood of tenancy failure (the cost of which has been estimated by the Audit Commission at £2,100 per tenancy).

Women's Aid have expressed concerns about the difficulties for refuges in accessing 'floating support' funding through the Housing Corporation; of more than 100 schemes currently running, none are earmarked for people experiencing domestic violence. (WAFE, 1999)

A recent Government inter-departmental review has considered future funding for all forms of housing with support, including refuges for women and children fleeing domestic violence. The review recognised the problems inherent in the current arrangements for accommodation and services, where funding can come from a wide range of different sources, but is complex and uncertain, and support is linked to certain types of accommodation or tenure. From 2003, there will be an integrated policy and funding framework, where a single specific grant will be paid by central government to local authorities to fund support services. As part of the consultation on the 'Supporting People' policy, the Government has set up a Practitioners' Group, whose brief includes looking at cross authority arrangements to enable women fleeing domestic violence who may not have a settled home or local connection, to receive appropriate priority in funding decisions. In addition, the Women's Aid Federation England is a member of the External Reference Group, which has been established to bring together a range of organisations to look into key issues in the development of the policy.

Ownership and management

In Britain, most domestic violence refuge projects are members of the Women's Aid Federation. Many projects own and manage more than one refuge building. A few are owned and directly managed by local authorities.

A common model for refuges is that the local authority or an RSL provides the building, with Women's Aid or another women's refuge group

Box 6. Refuge services in England and Wales. Facts and figures

England:

- there were 250 known refuge projects managing refuges and ancillary domestic violence services;
- of the 250 projects, 59 were specialist groups (including 38 Asian groups, 8 African/Caribbean/Black British/Black groups, three for young women and 10 specifically for women without children);
- there were 353 general/emergency refuge buildings and 50 offering transitional or second stage accommodation;
- there were 7,269 bedspaces in refuges - an increase of nearly 15 per cent between since 1995;
- there were 813 bedspaces in the 59 specialist properties;
- 213 (60 per cent) of English housing authorities had some refuge space in their area;
- 36 refuges had accommodation reserved for use by disabled women and children only. Half of all refuges had at least ground floor accommodation or ramp access and 16 per cent were either completely accessible or contained fully accessible accommodation.

(All figures relate to 1998, *Source*: Women's Aid Federation England survey of all refuge groups in England)

Wales:

- during 1997/98, there were 33 local groups affiliated to Welsh Women's Aid (WWA) running 38 refuges;
- almost 2,000 women and over 3,200 children were accommodated in these refuges;
- in 1998, refuges run by groups affiliated to WWA had 201 bedspaces;
- in addition, there were 32 bedspaces in refuges run by non-affiliated refuge groups.

(*Source*: Welsh Women's Aid)

providing the services. In 1998, RSLs owned 57% of refuge properties in England and local authorities owned just under a third.

The code of guidance accompanying the Housing Act 1996 recommends that local authorities 'develop close links with women's refuges in order to have access to emergency accommodation for women who have been subjected to or are at risk of violence' (para 21.28:89). 'Close links' could be in terms of making referrals, funding, providing premises or being part of inter-agency work that promotes good practice in dealing with domestic violence.

How women access refuge services?

During 1996/97, there were 54,500 admissions to refuges in England. Of these, around 32,000 were children and 22,500 were women. Refuge services may be accessed in a number of ways. In England, Women's Aid operates a National Helpline. By contacting this, a woman can be referred to a refuge in an emergency or put in touch with a local project for support. This ensures that no woman or child is at risk because they do not have a safe place to stay. Other women may self-refer to a refuge by using other services for women experiencing domestic violence that are run by local or other organisations (for example, drop in centres or helplines).

Another route to a refuge is referral by a voluntary organisation or an advice agency. Local authorities also make referrals to refuge services. Such referrals are usually women who have approached the housing department because they are homeless. However, it is not uncommon for women who already have a tenancy to be referred to a refuge (because of the threat of violence if they remain in the family home). While not all of these women entering a refuge will want to leave the family home permanently (some will want to return once the violent partner has left), others will stay at the refuge until alternative permanent accommodation is found. (WAFE, 1998a)

It is also fairly common for women to make a homeless application to a local authority once they are living in refuge accommodation.

How appropriate are refuge services?

Staying in refuges provides women fleeing domestic violence with a degree of safety and support that would probably not be available to them in any other form of temporary accommodation.

Surveys of women living in refuges have shown very high levels of satisfaction. For example, the women in the study undertaken in Surrey in 1996 were very satisfied with the help they had received from both the refuges in the county.

> Many women said that contact with the refuge had played a vital part in the process of leaving and recovering from domestic violence. Women found the

> self help and mutual support aspects of refuge life particularly important ... (and how the) experience of sharing and giving support made them realise that they were not alone. *(Dominy and Radford, 1996:97)*

The practical support, advice and advocacy and the more emotional and listening support provided by staff were also identified by women as being extremely useful. (Dominy and Radford, 1996)

A study of the needs of black women and children in refuges, which included interviews and groups discussions with women, also found that refuges were valued highly. (Rai and Thiara, 1997) Comments from residents and ex-residents included:

> They are places which you can see are like a sanctuary, somewhere you can feel safe ... the important thing for me as a Black woman living in a refuge was the security of it all, the safety. (p54)

> They help women get back on their feet and give them support and get their life sorted if they're in any trouble. It's a lot harder for Black women and its helped us a lot. ... if I hadn't been here I suppose I would have gone back home and faced my consequences. (p55)

> ... it was wonderful to be with a group of women who had been through the same situation ... it's also important because it shows women there's a way to escape and start again. (p56)

However, not all women want to go into a refuge. Some, for example, may be unwilling to live in such a communal environment or so close to other people experiencing crises. In other cases, going to a refuge may mean travelling an unacceptably long distance from where they currently live - away from children's schools, family and other support networks. Some local authorities therefore aim to give women who approach them the choice between a refuge and another form of temporary accommodation.

Another issue is the under-use of refuge services by some groups of women, in particular, those from African-Caribbean, Asian and refugee communities. Reasons for this include women relying on their own networks for help and support, concerns about confidentiality, feelings of shame and guilt, worries about racism and pressures within their own communities to stay in violent situations. For refugee women, fears of jeopardising their own and their partner's residential status may also play a part. Refuge providers have used a number of strategies to try and increase the use of their services by these groups; for example, by setting up specialist provision, by appointing black workers in mixed refuges, by producing publicity leaflets translated into different languages and by more outreach work. Outreach work has proved to be effective but because it is so labour intensive, and therefore costly, many refuge providers have been able to offer only a very limited service or none at all. (Rai and Thiara, 1997)

For other women, there are problems securing refuge accommodation. For example, some refuges would not have the resources to accommodate women with serious substance abuse problems or who have serious mental health problems. In addition, some refuges do not allow male children of over a certain age (which varies between 12 and 16). This could mean that a woman is faced with the choice of entering the refuge and perhaps leaving the child with the violent partner, of going into some other form of (less appropriate) temporary accommodation or of staying where they are in a violent situation. Policy guidelines from the Women's Aid Federation of England recommend that refuges should accommodate boys up to the age of 16, depending on individual circumstances. Another issue is the lack of refuges able to accommodate women with large numbers of children.

Bed and breakfast hotels

The poor living conditions and lack of support found in many of the bed and breakfast hotels used for homeless families generally have been well documented. In a study of women fleeing violence in Surrey, (Dominy and Radford, 1996) it was found that women disliked living in bed and breakfast, not only because it was uncomfortable but also because they did not feel safe. Another study showed that where women with children were placed in one room, there could be overcrowding, with serious implications for safety. There was often also little or no space for children to play or study in. 'Despite the high cost of the accommodation, the physical standards of these hotels are often deplorable and dangerous, lacking fire and safety precautions. Facilities for preparing, cooking or eating food may be few, bathrooms and toilets inadequate in number and dirty.' (Malos and Hague, 1993:69).

A study of the needs of ethnic minority women dealing with domestic violence in the London Borough of Camden reported that

> The use of B&B facilities as alternative accommodation for ethnic minority women facing domestic violence may not always be appropriate. The absence of support and counselling in bed and breakfast accommodation is an important gap for women who are stressed, injured or confused about their options... *(Sen, 1997:20)*

The authors highlighted the need for support services to be provided in this type of accommodation and recommended that housing, social services, refuge staff and women's groups should work together to develop these services. (Sen, 1997)

The particular inappropriateness of this type of accommodation for households experiencing domestic violence is clearly set out in the DETR's relationship breakdown guide, which states that

> Bed and breakfast accommodation often lacks the security and the support and counselling that may be needed by people facing harassment from violent partners. It can also pose special difficulties for women from some minority ethnic groups, because the use of shared facilities brings them into contact with male strangers. (DETR, 1999:61)

This is borne out by the code of guidance accompanying the Housing Act 1996, as follows:

> while circumstances may on some occasions require the use of bed and breakfast accommodation ... this will generally be as a last resort, and should not generally be regarded as suitable accommodation for families with children. (para 20.2:76)

and that:

> Authorities also need to take account of any medical and physical needs or social considerations relating to the applicant that might affect the suitability of accommodation as well as other factors such as the risk of racial harassment or domestic violence, access to and stability in schools, and access to other facilities. *(para 21.3:82)*

No figures are currently available on the extent of use of bed and breakfast hotels for households experiencing domestic violence, although this information has been collected in the current DTLR/DH/WU study. This will also explore the support provided to women and children living in this type of accommodation.

Hostels

The majority of hostels used by local authorities for homeless households are 'general' hostels, in that they cater for a variety of client groups, ages and genders. A study of local authority housing department hostels in England undertaken in 1994/95 found that of the 1,385 hostels they owned, funded or managed, 12% were for women and children only and a further 4% were for single women only (Bacon et al, 1996).

The code of guidance states that hostels may not meet the continuing needs of homeless people and that they may only be appropriate for short term use.

The London Borough of Islington uses directly managed hostels to accommodate women fleeing domestic violence. These have 24 hour security and can provide or direct residents to support, counselling and legal advice. One is for single women, but the others house both men and women (LRC, 1999).

The private rented sector

Very little is known about the experiences or numbers of women fleeing violence who are living in the private rented sector on a temporary basis. However, given that at the end of June 2001 there were almost 22,000 homeless households altogether living in privately rented accommodation, it is likely that the numbers of women fleeing violence living in this sector are fairly substantial.

While some women may appreciate the level of self-containment, potential problems with this type of accommodation for this group could include the lack of support, poor standards and conditions and high rents.

Staying with friends or relatives

Friends and relatives can often provide women experiencing domestic violence with help and support and it is likely that a high number of women in this situation stay on a temporary basis with friends and family when they first leave their violent partner. However, this is seldom a viable long term option. As with other temporary housing that is not specifically aimed at women fleeing violence, women are unlikely to be receive the level of support and advice that would be offered at, say, a refuge (unless outreach services were available in their local area). Another potential problem is that women may be fairly easy to track down by a violent partner.

Transitional or second stage accommodation

Transitional accommodation provides housing for women who no longer need intensive support, prior to being allocated permanent rehousing. This is likely to be self-contained, with no on-site staff and is usually only available to women who have been staying in a refuge. It differs from permanent housing in that women continue to have access to support and advice services. In 1998, there were 50 refuge groups offering transitional or second stage accommodation. Several refuges in the London Housing Unit study identified a specific need for second stage accommodation. (Frayne, 1994)

The costs of temporary accommodation

There is no comparative information on the costs of different forms of temporary accommodation used for households experiencing domestic violence. Nor has any work looking at the costs of other housing solutions (for example, injunctions or improved safety and security to a property). This is clearly an area where further work could be done (perhaps calculating the costs/benefits of the various forms of temporary accommodation and other housing initiatives).

There is, however, some limited information relating to refuges. It has been estimated that in 1996, the total cost of providing 36 refuge bedspaces in the London Borough of Hackney was almost £422,000. (Stanko et al, 1996) Other studies have looked at per bedspace costs. For example, Ball's study looking at the funding of refuge services estimated an annual average cost per adult bedspace in 1992/93 of just over £10,000 (Ball, 1994). Again this is an area that has been examined in the DTLR/DH/WU study.

Leaving temporary accommodation

Comprehensive information on what happens to people experiencing domestic violence once they leave temporary accommodation is rarely, if ever, collected in a useable way by local authorities. While local authoritiesmust produce figures on the numbers overall allocated permanent local authority stock or nominated to RSLs in their annual Housing Investment Programme (HIP) returns to the DTLR, there is no requirement to monitor specifically the outcomes of people experiencing domestic violence who leave temporary accommodation.

The situation is different for refuge groups, most of which keep good records of where women leaving their accommodation go. Figures from WAFE's 1996/97 survey, undertaken on behalf of the DTLR/DH/WU, show that of the women leaving refuges during that year:

- 29% were rehoused by a local authority or an RSL;
- 6% went into the private rented sector;
- 10% went to stay with friends or relatives;
- 15% went to another refuge;
- 12% returned home with an injunction against the violent partner; and
- 20% returned to their abuser.
  (WAFE, 1998a)

What these figure do not tell us, however, are the number of times that people may leave a violent partner, the various different housing paths they may take over a period of time before their situation is finally resolved (if it ever is) and their final housing outcome. Suggested further research to look at these issues could involve longitudinal studies of people experiencing domestic violence and one-off surveys which ask people to provide information about the various housing routes taken over time as a result of their domestic violence.

Long term housing for people experiencing domestic violence

In terms of permanent housing, people experiencing domestic violence may pursue the following options:

- social rented housing (local authority or RSL);
- the private rented sector;
- staying with friends or family; or
- buying a property.

The opportunity to pursue any of these options will depend on various factors, including people's personal and financial circumstances, the nature of the local housing market and levels of housing demand and stress locally.

The allocation of permanent social rented housing

Most people wanting to move into permanent social rented housing (local authority or RSL) will need to apply through the local authority housing register. In many parts of the country, RSL housing can be accessed only by joining the local authority housing register and being nominated to an RSL (although in some areas of low housing demand RSLs may operate their own direct waiting lists).

New tenants

Local authorities are required by Part VI of the Housing Act 1996 to establish and maintain a housing register. For new applicants (rather than existing tenants), local authorities must have an allocation scheme which must give reasonable preference to certain prescribed categories of people. These include families with dependent children, people occupying temporary or insecure accommodation and households consisting of or including someone with a particular need for settled accommodation on medical or welfare grounds. People fleeing domestic violence may fall into any of the reasonable preference categories and may fall into several at the same time. Additional preference must be given to households with a particular need for settled accommodation on medical or welfare grounds.

The code of guidance accompanying Parts VI and VII of the Act provides an illustrative list of criteria that might be used in the reasonable preference categories. Specific mention is made that the need to recover from the effects of violence or threats of violence, or from physical, emotional or sexual abuse, may establish a need for settled accommodation on medical or welfare grounds.

The DTLR relationship breakdown guide gives advice on how social landlords may develop allocations policies to ensure that they balance a range of competing needs and objectives and also that people with similar problems receive a similar level of service. (DETR, 1999)

Some local authorities give additional priority to households on the housing register experiencing domestic violence, often by allocating extra points. In Salisbury District Council, for example:

> The council's policy is to house mothers and children ... in the Salisbury Women's Refuge. The housing officer will then meet with them after two weeks to discuss their future needs and arrangements. Families score 10 housing points for every month they are in temporary accommodation and this usually means that they are offered housing through either the council or a housing association within six to 12 months. (LRC, 1998:20, para 3.9)

In Dover, the allocation policy recognises the 'special problems of women who are victims of violence to the extent we will give extra priority to such applicants or existing tenants when it comes to allocating property or using our nomination arrangements with housing associations'. (LRC, 1998 :21, para 3.11)

To date, there have been no published evaluations of the effects of the allocations provisions of 1996 Act, or any local authority policies relating to it, on households experiencing domestic violence. However, these have been examined as part of the DTLR/DH/WU study currently being undertaken.

Existing tenants

Some local authorities and RSLs have points schemes or operate management transfer arrangements that give priority to people experiencing domestic violence.

Tenancy agreements and domestic violence

The 1996 Housing Act created a new ground for possession of secure and RSL assured tenancies, where one spouse or cohabitee has left the home because of violence or threats of violence by the other and does not intend to return. The threats or violence may have been directed against the person who left, or against a member of that person's family who was living with them at the time. The DTLR's relationship breakdown guide recommends that, despite the existence of this new ground, there are still good reasons for social landlords to have clauses against domestic violence in their tenancy agreements:

- landlords will still need to rely on the tenancy agreement if they wish to seek possession from a perpetrator of domestic violence who is not a spouse or cohabitee of the victim, or if the victim wishes to return;
- an express clause alerts potential aggressors to the landlord's policy and to the possible consequences of their behaviour;
- landlords can use their own definition of domestic violence - for example making it clear that psychological abuse is included. (DETR, 1999:72)

Such clauses are not easy to enforce and obtaining evidence or persuading witnesses to testify can be a difficult and lengthy process (many social landlords have had clauses against racial harassment for many years, yet evictions are still comparatively rare). They will also only be addressed to the tenant and are likely to be of less value if the landlord has a policy of granting sole tenancies to a female partner.

Overall, however, the benefits outweigh the limitations; clauses against domestic violence provide a clear statement of the landlord's policy and intentions; they may provide some reassurance to those experiencing violence and a warning to perpetrators; and their inclusion in the tenancy agreement costs very little.

An example of a clause against domestic violence

You must not inflict domestic violence or threaten violence against any other person (they could be living with you or in another council home). You must not harass or use mental, emotional or sexual abuse to make anyone who lives with you leave the home.

(Manchester City Council, 1996:6, section 4.8)

Costs of permanent rehousing

In a study in the London Borough of Hackney, it was estimated that in 1996 the overall cost to the borough's housing department of rehousing households fleeing domestic violence was £242,000 (excluding the costs of repairs to council property, preparation for new tenants, moving and furnishing flats and indirect costs). This figure comprises new council lettings, housing association lettings and the cost of the Domestic Violence (Housing) Advice Service. (Stanko et al, 1996)

Resettlement and aftercare

Once permanently rehoused, people experiencing domestic violence may be isolated, lonely and still require a degree of support, advice and assistance. This need may be particularly acute for people whose new home is at some distance from where they lived before. As one women in the Women's Aid study of the needs of black women and children in refuge support services commented:

> It's very scary if you're in the house on your own for the first time in a different area and it would have been nice to have had contact. ... I think it would have been nice to have somebody who maybe checked on you for about two months to see how you were and keep you informed of schemes. (Rai and Thiara, 1997:53)

Staying in the family home

This section looks at some of the options available to women experiencing domestic violence who stay in the family home. Remaining *in situ* is likely to be the first choice for most people who experience domestic violence, with leaving seen as a last resort.

For many women, this will mean using legal remedies to exclude the violent partner and to establish property rights (these are covered in Chapters 7 and 8, which look at criminal and civil remedies). It may also mean taking steps to improve the security of the property itself and considering ways of maximising personal safety.

Some local authorities have been innovative in this area by, for example, supplying women with alarms, often in conjunction with the police. Usually, these are community alarms, used under the same system as that for vulnerable older people. In Mansfield, for example, the 'Safety Link' scheme has been introduced by the local authority and is aimed at people who wish to stay in the family home but who are frightened of threats of violence from an associated person. Alarms are held, installed and monitored in conjunction with the Nottinghamshire Constabulary and, once activated 'send a silent radio transmission which breaks into all police radio frequencies and overrides ongoing signals. There is an immediate response from all available officers to attend within four minutes' (LRC, 1998:26, para 4.26).

Other initiatives in Mansfield include:

- mobile phones;
- using close circuit television; and
- the 'Zippy Chippy' scheme, providing emergency carpentry repairs for

victims of crime (originally intended for older people but now also used for people experiencing domestic violence).

Prioritising any repairs needed to make a property secure and providing additional security measures are also mentioned in the DTLR's relationship breakdown guide for social landlords. (LRC, 1998; DETR, 1999)

Kirklees Housing Services issues people experiencing domestic violence with a Domestic Abuse Advice Pack, which includes details of the security measures that the Council will provide for its tenants, if required:

> If you are a victim of repeated attacks on you, your family or your home, your area housing officer will arrange security measures to make your home safer for you. These include regular police visits to make sure you are safe and so that they are seen to be checking your safety. There are also personal alarms and mobile phones for emergencies and alarm systems which can be monitored by the police.
>
> We can also provide door chains, bolts, spy holes, window locks, external security lighting and alarm systems. We replace broken windows with shatterproof glass and broken outside doors with solid wood doors. (Kirklees Housing, undated: 7)

Currently, such schemes appear to be confined to the social rented sector. However, they could also serve a useful purpose in the private sector, for people privately renting and for owner-occupiers. Their introduction in the private sector would require careful thought, in terms of practical issues (such as which agencies should be involved) and also in terms of how they could be publicised to ensure a good take up.

These types of initiatives are relatively cheap, when compared with the costs of providing someone with alternative accommodation (which may often mean a period of time spent in temporary accommodation followed by permanent rehousing).

Accommodation for perpetrators

Offenders and ex-offenders

In relation to abusers being granted bail, the Inner London Probation Service (ILPS) recommends in its domestic violence policy that:

> The nature and location of accommodation being offered by/to the defendant must be considered in terms of the issue of protection. Victims should not be put under pressure to allow the perpetrator to return and the involvement of other family members should be avoided. (ILPS, 1996:27, para 7.3.3)

Exclusion from housing registers

Local authorities are entitled to exclude certain groups of people from qualifying for the housing register. Some local authorities may decide that people with a history of anti-social behaviour should be excluded from the register, which may mean that in these areas perpetrators of domestic violence would be prevented from gaining access to local authority housing. No research has been undertaken which specifically looks at the implications of exclusion policies for people experiencing domestic violence. However, Wome's Aid have expressed concern that where abusers run up rent arrears, while the woman is in temporary accommodation or in a refuge, she may be expected to clear this debt before reclaiming the tenancy, or she may be excluded from joining the housing register.

Seeking possession

The new domestic violence clause in the Housing Act 1996 is likely to have an effect on perpetrators' housing options in the future - as are the clauses against domestic violence that some social landlords are introducing into their tenancy agreements.

Again, the implementation and effectiveness of these policies have been considered as part of the DTLR/DH/WU study.

Lack of information

There is a dearth of information about perpetrators and their accommodation. It would be useful to investigate the consequences, in crime prevention terms, of alternative strategies for violent partners. Research could focus on whether they would be less likely to seek to return to their ex-partners or form other potentially violent relationships if adequate alternative accommodation were made available (perhaps as part of wider perpetrator schemes).

Conclusions and recommendations

The conclusions below represent the main findings from the survey of existing literature. The next section sets out a number of recommendations for areas where further research might be necessary to understand better the issues surrounding domestic violence and the provision of accommodation.

Conclusions

- Social landlords should be encouraged to develop, review, monitor and evaluate specific policies and procedures for dealing with people experiencing domestic violence. These should encompass housing advice, homelessness, allocations and transfers, and housing management.
- The 1996 Housing Act and the code of guidance on allocations and homelessness include clauses to assist the situation of women experiencing domestic violence. A new, further revised code of guidance which is due to be issued shortly, and the proposed extension of the priority needs categories should lead to improvements in the delivery of homelessness services to women experiencing domestic violence.
- As one of their most vulnerable client groups, local authorities should aim to avoid the use of bed and breakfast accommodation for people experiencing domestic violence, as reflected in Government guidance. Temporary accommodation not specifically designed for victims of domestic violence may offer limited access to appropriate support services.
- There is a high level of satisfaction among users of refuge services. There is, however, widespread concern about the shortage of refuge provision, both generally and for women with special needs, underfunding and the reliance on Housing Benefit as a means of funding. The under-use of refuge services by some minority ethnic communities, and the lack of funding to provide the outreach work necessary to rectify this, are also identified as problems.
- Providing people experiencing domestic violence with appropriate support is considered to be a cost effective intervention. Social landlords and other agencies that work together can ensure that appropriate outreach, resettlement and aftercare services are available to people who require them.
- There is scope for more agencies to introduce schemes that assist people experiencing domestic violence to be safe and secure in their own homes (e.g. personal alarms, mobile phones and security

measures). Social landlords, the police and other agencies need to consider how they can work together to develop such schemes. It may be possible to extend such schemes to make provision available to people living in the private rented and owner occupied sectors.

Further research

Costs and benefits of various housing options

Very little information exists on the comparative costs and benefits of various housing options for people experiencing domestic violence, and the potential costs of not providing an appropriate housing response. This is an area where further research could be undertaken.

Housing outcomes

Although the annual Women's Aid surveys provide good information on where women go when they leave a refuge, there is little information on the various housing paths followed over a period of time (other than on a very small scale local basis). Again, further research could be carried out to examine this.

Accommodation and support needs

There appear to be very few practical examples in the literature of policies or initiatives that tailor the accommodation and support needs of people experiencing domestic violence to their varying circumstances. For example, peoples' needs are likely to be very different when they are in an emergency situation compared with once their immediate crisis has been dealt with. When people initially leave a violent situation, they are likely to require accommodation, intensive support and a range of services. Once past this initial stage, their accommodation and support needs are likely to be different.

It would be useful to pilot a scheme where an inter-agency approach could be taken to tailor accommodation and support provision to people's needs. This could use refuges as a first stop for women in an emergency, followed by another form of temporary accommodation combined with appropriate support for the next stage, followed by transitional accommodation, still with a degree of support, until women are rehoused. Once rehoused, women could be offered resettlement and aftercare services.

Given the dearth of information about perpetrators and their accommodation, it would be useful to undertake some research looking at alternative accommodation strategies for violent partners.

Domestic violence and harassment: An assessment of the civil remedies

Susan Edwards

This study examines the civil law remedies available to protect women and children from domestic violence, and which are contained within the Family Law Act (FLA) 1996, the Protection from Harassment Act (PFHA) 1997 and the Children Act (CA) 1989 (as amended). This review provides an overview of the civil legislation, case law and an evaluation of the application of the law through an analysis of largely unpublished statistical data made available to the author by the Lord Chancellor's Department on applications and orders made.

In evaluating the FLA 1996 and the use of non-molestation and exclusion injunctions the study found that the number of non-molestation injunctions granted remained roughly the same as under previous legislation. Whilst more occupation orders were granted under the FLA than ousters/exclusion orders under previous legislation, direct comparison is not possible as there are several types of occupation orders under the current legislation containing very different conditions only one of which is the power to exclude a person from the home. A power of arrest was attached in 75% of occupation orders and in 80% of non-molestation orders. This represents a significant improvement on previous legislation where a power of arrest was attached in only one third of both non-molestation and exclusion orders combined. In evaluating the PFHA 1997, the harassment remedy under section 3 has been used in many more cases than was originally anticipated, although it is not possible to identify from the data the injunctions which relate to domestic/ intimate related incidents. In evaluating the important amendment provided in the FLA to the CA 1989 allowing for an exclusion order to be attached to an Emergency Protection Order or Interim Care Order where children are at risk of significant harm, no statistics are currently being collected thus eschewing any evaluation of the impact of law or its application.

In evaluating the response of the courts to contact of the violent father with the child under the CA 1989 section 8, analysis of case law and available literature suggest that in public and private law proceedings the courts continue to uphold the presumption that contact is best. Analysis of recorded cases on section 8 orders for contact could not identify those cases in which the violence of the father was in issue. The figures did however point to regional variations in contact orders. There is a need for research in each of these areas to cast further light on the use and effectiveness of these remedies in protecting women and children.

Introduction

Domestic abuse takes many forms including physical and mental assault, pestering and harassment. The victims of these several kinds of abuse are usually women and children. Both the criminal and civil law provide a range of protective measures and there are arguments for the continued existence of both types of remedies (Women's Aid, 1997).

However, there is a competing viewpoint (Edwards, 1989a), critical of the civil law, which believes that the continued provision of injunctive relief under the civil law may undermine the principle that violence against women is a criminal matter. Many agree that it is the perception of domestic violence as a 'family matter' that continues to undermine the application of sanctions under the criminal law. The application and effectiveness of the civil law remedy, particularly the ouster provision which excludes the aggressor from the home is also considerably weakened by the competing and often prevailing consideration of whether it can ever be appropriate to exclude a man from 'his' home (see *Summers* v *Summers* [1986] 1FLR 343 at 497).

Notwithstanding, there are powerful arguments in support of the civil law. Women's Aid, for example, point out that many women may not wish to support a criminal prosecution and that civil protection with its power to exclude the violent partner for a period from the home provides women and children with a measure of safety and protection whilst they consider their options. The usefulness of the civil remedy is well illustrated in *Odumosu v Aiyeola* Court of Appeal (Civil Division) 16 October 1996 (Transcript Smith Bernal). In this case the appellant left her cohabitee and went to live with her mother. They received various threats from the respondent and the mother's home was ransacked and damaged. The respondent was arrested and bailed by the police, but no criminal proceedings were brought. On 26 June 1995 the appellant commenced proceedings in the court for a non-molestation order, restraining the respondent from using violence against, harassing or pestering, the appellant, which was granted ex parte until 5 July 1995. On 5 July 1995 the injunction was extended until trial or further order, as the respondent (who had been served with notice) failed to attend the hearing. On 30 July 1995 the appellant sought to have the respondent committed to prison for breach of the injunction. The judge found the incident proved and sentenced the respondent to six months imprisonment, suspended for two years (see also *A-A* v *B-B* [2001]2FLR 1]).

The civil law provides protection for adults and children from domestic violence through injunctions in tort to restrain harassment, assault and battery; in damages for personal injury and through non-molestation or ouster/exclusion orders now called occupation orders. A number of recent changes to the legislation, notably the Family Law Act Part IV (FLA) and the Protection from Harassment Act 1997 (PFHA) have introduced a new range of civil remedies available to 'associated persons' (FLA) and to any person (PFHA) seeking protection from domestic abuse and harassment. Furthermore, the Children Act (CA) 1989 has been amended by the FLA providing the courts with a power to attach an exclusion requirement where an emergency protection or interim care order in respect of a child is granted.

However, there is also concern that whilst the government has expressed a commitment to improving the protection of those experiencing domestic violence (Cabinet Office, 1999) in some instances the judicial interpretation of the FLA may undermine this objective, most notably in cases where section 8 contact orders under the FLA are granted. This particular section requires the carer to allow contact between the child and the violent father. On numerous occasions, contact has been found to place both women and children escaping from domestic violence in danger. It is suggested that an amendment to the legislation is now required to ensure that women and children are not placed in any further danger which arises from an order made for contact.

Aims of this chapter

It is the intention of this chapter:

- To provide an overview of the existing civil remedies of relevance to domestic violence and to consider their application and effectiveness in protecting women and children.
- To explore annual trends in the grant of injunctions (non-molestation and occupation) with a view to ascertaining how successful the FLA has been as compared with earlier legislation in achieving its statutory objective in protecting women and children.
- To explore whether the FLA and the PFHA are being applied uniformly in England and Wales or whether there are regional variations in the granting of orders which might need addressing to ensure that all applicants wherever they reside receive equal protection.
- To examine the effectiveness of the enforcement of these orders including the predilection of the court to attach a power of arrest to an existing injunction and the response of the courts to those who breach these orders.
- To evaluate the effectiveness of the exclusion requirement under the CA 1989 in child protection.
- To consider the impact of the judicial interpretation of granting contact orders where women and children are in danger from further violence.
- To evaluate the existing remedies through an analysis of the statistical data, available literature and case law.

Civil remedies: An overview

Prior to the introduction of the FLA 1996 the Domestic Violence and Matrimonial Proceedings Act (DVMPA) 1976 and the Domestic Proceedings and Magistrates Courts Act (DVMCA) 1978 provided protection for women and children from domestic violence.

Both Acts provided for injunctive relief prohibiting molestation and/or for an order that excluded the violent aggressor from the home. However, the ouster/exclusion order was rarely used since judges were reluctant to exclude aggressors unless the violence was severe and 'plain as a pikestaff' (*Davis v Johnson* [1978] 1 All E R 1132). Non-molestation and ouster/exclusion orders could be supported by a power of arrest, which allowed police to arrest and remove a suspect who was in breach of a court order. However, the courts regarded the power of arrest as draconian, particularly as it involved police in what was regarded a civil and family matter, with the result that a power of arrest was rarely attached. It was widely conceded, by police and those working with abused women, that injunctions which were not supported by a power of arrest, were 'not worth the paper they were written on' (Barron, 1990). Where an injunction was breached the applicant could make an application that the person breaching the order be committed to prison. Research showed that the courts were extremely reluctant to commit those in breach to prison (Edwards, 1989a). In 1987, 274 men were committed to prison for breaching injunctions. The courts also developed a practice of accepting 'undertakings' which were widely regarded by those outside the courts, as ineffective and inappropriate (see Barron, 1990; Mullender, 1996).

In response to these and other shortcomings of earlier legislation the FLA 1996 introduced some significant changes including amendments to the CA 1989 so as to allow for the exclusion of suspect abusers where children were in need of protection. In addition, the introduction of the PFHA 1997 provided a civil remedy of damages for harassment.

Personal protection and occupation of the family home under the Family Law Act 1996 Part IV

The remedies protecting women and children from domestic violence are now contained in Part IV of the FLA, which came into force on October 1st 1997. These include:

- The occupation order and
- The non-molestation order.

The occupation order

The occupation order serves two broad functions, first it secures for the applicant the right to occupy the home and second it excludes or restricts the right of occupation. Occupation orders are therefore concerned as much with proprietary entitlement, that is entitlement to occupy, as with personal protection from domestic violence. For this reason the occupation order, with its several conditions, is not directly comparable with its predecessor - the ouster/exclusion order.

In considering an application for an occupation order the court shall have regard to:

- the housing needs and resources of each party and any relevant child;
- the financial resources;
- the likely effect of any order or decision of the court not to grant any order on the health, safety or well being of the parties and of any relevant child; and
- the conduct of the parties in relation to each other.

An occupation order may contain one or more of the following provisions:

1. Enforce the applicant's entitlement to remain in occupation as against the other person ('the respondent').
2. Require the respondent to permit the applicant to enter and remain in the dwelling house or part of the dwelling house.
3. Regulate the occupation of the dwelling house by either or both parties.
4. Prohibit, suspend or restrict the exercise by him of his rights to occupy the dwelling house.
5. Restrict/terminate the respondent's rights in the matrimonial home.
6. Require the respondent to leave the dwelling house or part of the dwelling house.
7. Exclude the respondent from a defined area in which the dwelling house is included.

Given the range of situations which arise under an occupation order it becomes clear that only orders under 4, 6 and 7 above are directly comparable with the ouster /exclusion injunction under earlier legislation.

The non-molestation order

Under section 42(1) the court may make an order prohibiting the respondent from molesting the applicant. The Act does not define molestation although, under previous legislation, molestation has been taken to include violence and where harassment related conduct has been in evidence courts have generally been reluctant to grant a non-molestation injunction. It is expected that the courts will follow earlier reasoning. Although in *C v C (Non-molestation Order: Jurisdiction)* [1998] 1 FLR 554, Sir Stephen Brown P held that molestation implies

> *...Some quite deliberate conduct which is aimed at a high degree of harassment of the other party, so as to justify the intervention of the High Court.*

Ex parte orders

Section 45(1) allows a court 'in any case where it considers it just and convenient to do so to make an occupation order or a non-molestation order even though the respondent has not been given notice of the proceedings'.

In *Loseby v Newman [1995]* 2 FLR 754, this was decided justifiable 'where there is real urgency and impossibility of giving notice [and] where there is a real immediate danger of serious injury'.

In practice, however, the courts in construing the legislation seem to have ruled against occupation orders on an *ex parte* basis. In *Chalmers v Johns* [1999] 1 FLR 392, Thorpe LJ, referring to occupation orders commented

> *The order remains draconian, particularly in the perception of the respondent. It remains an order that overrides proprietary rights and it seems to me that it is an order that is only justified in exceptional circumstances.*

One solicitor's experience is reflected here:

> *In a recent case one of my clients had been raped by her partner from the beginning of the relationship. He brutally attacked her on several occasions, trying to strangle her, grabbing her by her throat and lifting her off the floor, ripping off all her clothes and making her sit naked and talk to him for hours. He would punch and kick her about the face, stamp on her head, drag her to the floor by her hair, threatening to slit her throat with a knife. On the last two occasions the client ended up being hospitalised. She fled the joint home. She was admitted to hospital as she had sustained multiple injuries, a broken jaw and multiple bruises. She came out of hospital and was accommodated at a local Refuge. I went to Court the same day for an ex-parte non-molestation order and occupation order with a power of arrest.*
>
> *The judge responded explaining that an occupation order was not necessary as she was safely accommodated in the refuge. 'I cannot make such an order on your client's version of the story alone', refusing to grant the ex-parte occupation order granting only an ex-parte non-molestation order with a power of arrest. (Source: Personal communication, solicitor, Milton Keynes).*

Balance of harm test

In considering whether to make an order to protect a woman or relevant child from domestic violence the court must apply the 'balance of harm' test in section 33(7).

The court is under a duty to make an order if the applicant or any relevant child is 'likely to suffer significant harm' attributable to the conduct of the respondent if an order is not made, unless it appears that the respondent or any relevant child would suffer, as great or greater harm (not specified) than that suffered by the applicant.

There has been considerable criticism of this test which seems to restrict a 'significant harm' suffered by the applicant to that occasioned by the conduct of the respondent. In contrast the respondent, it would appear, can rely on any harm whatsoever which might follow from the making of the order.

Undertakings

Undertakings are now specifically provided under section 46 (1). Here the respondent makes a promise to the court that he will not molest the applicant. There are restrictions, however, and the court cannot accept an undertaking in any case where the respondent has used or threatened violence. Thus, undertakings should only ever be accepted where there has been harassment or some form of conduct without violence or the threat of violence. It has been suggested that this statutory limitation placed on the acceptance of undertakings may curtail their use (Lockton and Ward, 1997), although data for this study shows that in the early inception of the Act undertakings are in fact widely used, 4710 in 1998, and 5073 in 1999 (*Judicial Statistics*, 1999).

Enforcement

Power of Arrest

Under section 47(2) of the 1996 Act, there is a presumption in favour of a power of arrest where 'it appears to the court that the respondent has used or threatened violence against the applicant or relevant child.' This presumption is operative unless the court is satisfied that the applicant or child will be protected without it. This presumption reverses the situation under previous law where the power of arrest was discretionary. Although it is to be noted that where an occupation or non-molestation order is granted *ex parte* any decision to attach a power of arrest is at the discretion of the court.

The presumption in favour of attaching a power of arrest carries with it considerable resource implications for police transforming them into a front line aid for the protection of women in civil cases. Where a power of arrest is attached to the order it is copied and kept at the police station in the area where the applicant resides. If the order is breached police are under a duty to arrest; they may detain the person for up to 24 hours before bringing them before the court. The court may then remand the abuser.

The 1997-9 statistics on the operation of the FLA show that a power of arrest was attached in 80% of all orders granted.

A power of arrest cannot be attached to an undertaking. It is suggested that this places the applicant in a vulnerable position, as it is she who must start proceedings to bring the person who has breached the undertaking before the court.

Contempt of Court

Where there has been a breach of an order the court can consider imprisonment (*Wilson v Webster* [1998] 1 FLR 1098 (CA) *Thorpe v Thorpe* [1998] 2 FLR 127, *Neil v Ryan* [1998] 2 FLR 1068, [1999] 1 FCR 241) although 'committal orders are remedies of last resort' (see *Ansah v Ansah* [1977] Fam 138:2144, *Roberts v Roberts* [1990] 2 FLR 111).

Prison can also be considered where there is a breach of an undertaking (*Cambridgeshire County Council v D* [1999] 2 FLR 42).

The Protection from Harassment Act 1997

The PFHA came into force on 16 June 1997. The PFHA is a potentially important piece of legislation offering protection to anyone in fear of violence or who is being pursued, watched etc. in a manner that amounts to harassment. Being in fear of violence and being harassed is often part of the wider violence, fear and abuse that women encounter. Women who experience domestic violence may also experience being stalked, followed, pursued, watched, monitored, intimidated and threatened by men whom they know - often by former husbands or partners. The facts in the case of *R* v *Liddle* [1999] 3 All ER 816 provide such an example.

In the past, only on rare occasions did conduct amounting to harassment result in the courts granting a non-molestation order (*Ansah, ibid)*). The PFHA is a potentially useful remedy when the molestation complained of falls outside the remit of the nature and degree of violence required for the grant of non-molestation order. Furthermore, whilst the FLA limits applicants to 'associated persons' who have lived or are living together the PFHA extends the remedy of harassment to anyone regardless of residential relationship.

The PFHA has the potential to deal with a broad spectrum of conduct, including harassment, pestering, stalking, neighbour disputes and racial abuse. The Act creates two criminal offences - a summary offence of criminal harassment under section 2 and 'putting a person in fear of violence' section 4 (1) (2) (discussed in the chapter on criminal remedies).

Section 3, the civil remedy, provides for an actual or apprehended breach of section 1 (harassment) where damages may be awarded (section 3(2)). Where an injunction forbidding harassment has been granted and a judge has reasonable grounds for believing that the defendant has done something which he is prohibited from doing by the terms of the injunction, a warrant for arrest may be issued (section 3(3)). Thus, this is a considerable advancement over previous law since a civil injunction is now enforceable by a criminal sanction.

Exactly how useful this civil remedy is in the protection of women and children from abuse requires further investigation and research. It is not yet clear what the civil law benefits are over the criminal law route. In the author's view, it is thought unlikely that this civil remedy for damages will be used in the domestic violence context since few women experiencing domestic violence in the past used the remedy of a claim for damages in tort.

Exclusion orders under the Children Act 1989

An additional remedy provided to further the protection of women and children from domestic violence is found in the amendments to the CA following the introduction of the FLA. Where the local authority or an authorised person (NSPCC) suspect that a child may be being abused they may apply for an Interim Care or Emergency Protection order under sections 38(1)(b) and 44. Where an order is granted an exclusion provision (section 38A(3) and section 44A(3)) may be attached with a power of arrest (as amended by the FLA 1996, s. 52, sch. 6 paras. 1,3). This allows for the child to remain in the home whilst excluding the suspect abuser from the home for up to 15 days. There is no need to prove violence to the child. A major limitation is that the party with whom the child remains must give consent to the exclusion.

In the past child protection could only be assured by removing children from their home whilst investigations were being conducted. The Cleveland investigation for example resulted in 174 place of safety orders being granted by a single justice (Butler-Sloss, 1988 para 10.9).

The court may also accept an undertaking in respect of the exclusion requirement if the suspect abuser agrees. The court is not restricted here by being required to consider whether a power of arrest should be attached, as there is no provision which allows a power of arrest to be attached to an exclusion orders (see *President's Direction (Children Act 1989: Exclusion Requirement)* [1998] 1 FLR 495). An undertaking, however, can be enforced by a warrant for arrest.

Research needs to be conducted to evaluate how the exclusion order is being used by the courts, whether undertakings are being accepted and how effective this provision is in achieving its purpose of protecting children from further harm.

Contact orders under the Children Act 1989: Domestic violence and safety issues

The central objective of the CA is to protect children and bring them up within their families so long as it is safe to do so. There is an overriding obligation to maintain contact between parents and children as this is considered to be in the paramount interests of the child. Section 8 of the CA allows the court to make an order for contact between a parent and a child. However, it appears that making an order for contact may undermine the safety of women and children in cases where the father is violent.

There is considerable evidence to suggest that contact is damaging not only for the mother but also for the child (Mullender, 1996; Rights of Women, 1997; Barnett, 1999). Research has shown that children are deeply affected not only as direct recipients of domestic violence but indirectly as witnesses to the violence they see one parent inflicting on another. Hughes (1992) found that in 90% of incidents of domestic violence against the female spouse children are present either in the same or next room. For some children the effects of watching a mother being abused are so great that, in efforts to protect her, children may even go on to kill the violent father (see *Pearson* [1992] Crim LR 193, *R v Maw and Another* (CA) *The Times*, 4 December 1980). Research has also shown that living in an altercated atmosphere can have a damaging effect on children (Saunders, 1994; Mullender, 1996).

In ordering contact in such circumstances, the judicial interpretation of section 8 of the CA can place the paternal right to contact above the right of the child to be free from harm, despite growing evidence that witnessing parental violence is harmful to children. This may be a consequence of the fact that the court is not bound to consider the 'welfare checklist' under section 1, which requires the court to consider a standard of harm that is 'any harm' which may not amount to 'significant harm', unless the order is being opposed. The welfare checklist would otherwise require the court to consider:

- the wishes and feelings of the child;
- his physical, emotional and educational needs;
- the likely effect on him of any change in circumstance;
- his age, sex and background;
- any harm which he has suffered; and
- how capable each of his parents is of meeting his needs.

Where contact is unopposed the court is not bound to consider these factors. There is some evidence (Rights of Women, 1997) which suggests that solicitors actually advise women not to oppose contact. In the absence of contact being opposed the courts are not bound to take into account' any harm'. In the author's view this is a factor which should be considered as of paramount importance regardless of whether an order is opposed or not.

Where the court makes an order for contact it may impose conditions (under section 11 (7)) although in practice conditions are rarely imposed (see *Re L, Re V, Re M, Re H* [2000] 2 FCR 404).

Evaluating civil law remedies

In examining these new remedies it is important:

- to evaluate their effectiveness in protecting women and children from violence;
- to determine whether the new legislation has achieved all that was expected of it; and
- to examine the cost effectiveness of the new remedies in providing enhanced safety and protection for women and children from domestic violence.

In order to achieve this, a review of case law, available literature and government statistics was undertaken.

The Family Law Act Part IV

How effective is the FLA in protecting women? Case law on non-molestation orders, occupation orders and undertakings under the new legislation is limited. It is however possible to examine any change in its effectiveness in protecting women and children by examining annual trends in injunctive relief, prior to and following, the implementation of the FLA. By examining *Judicial Statistics* produced by the Lord Chancellor's Department, one can see that there has been a broad rise in both applications made and orders granted under the Domestic Violence and Matrimonial Proceedings Act 1976 for 1981 – 1997 and the Family Law Act 1996 for 1998 and 1999.

This can be compared to the use of personal protection and exclusion orders granted under the Domestic Proceedings and Magistrates Courts Act 1978 for the years 1987-1993. An analysis of this data showed that a declining number of orders were granted for non-molestation or exclusion in the magistrate's court, falling from 8,480 in 1984 to 640 in 1993. Molestation was not included in the DPMC Act 1978, restricting the granting of a personal protection order to incidents of physical violence.

Tables 1 and 2 overleaf show annual trends in orders for domestic violence protection from 1985 to the present. Of particular interest is the impact of the FLA 1996, which came into force in October 1997. This has resulted in:

- No change in the grant of non-molestation orders when comparing 1996 at 19,707 orders before the FLA, with in 1998, 19,365 orders, and 1999, 18,465 orders - but showing a continuing downward trend since 1994.
- A dramatic increase in ouster orders (now occupation orders) granted, from 2,945 in 1996 to 9,023 in 1998 and 8,319 in 1999. This meteoric rise must be interpreted with extreme caution as the new occupation order applies both to orders made regarding proprietorial rights and to orders made regarding personal protection. Therefore only some occupation orders so called will contain a provision to exclude based on domestic violence.
- A dramatic increase in the use of power of arrest from 10,049 (44% of all orders) in 1996 to 22,472 (79%) of all orders in 1998 and 21,475 (80%) of all orders in 1999.
- A decline in proportion of ousters granted under the DVMPA from 1985-1996 from 29 per cent of all orders in 1985 to 13 per cent of all orders in 1996. There has always been a judicial reluctance to grant ousters, which have been regarded as draconian. Following the House of Lords decision in *Richards v Richards* [1984] 1 AC 174, the courts were even more reluctant to do so. The court in this case ruled that the interests of an adult in remaining in the home prevailed, unless his behaviour had been so bad as to justify the consequences to him.
- A power of arrest being attached under the DPMCA in:
  - 30% of cases in 1987;
  - 31% of cases in 1988;
  - 32% of cases in 1989;
  - 32% of cases in 1990;
  - 42% of cases in 1991;
  - 35% of cases in 1992; and
  - 41% of cases in 1993.

This shows the increasing importance attached to the power of arrest.

Table 3 shows that most proceedings are heard in the County Court suggesting that (as was the case before the FLA) the magistrates' forum is a declining jurisdiction for domestic violence cases.

There is a considerable variation of the use of the Act. For example when analysing the orders granted by region for an 18-month period. 6,954 undertakings were accepted out of 40,818 non-molestation and occupation orders showing a use in 17 per cent of all cases, a surprisingly high proportion for what is considered a derisory remedy (Barron, 1990, Lockton and Ward, 1997). In the Eastern and East Midland region undertakings are used more than elsewhere, whilst Merseyside makes little use at all of undertakings. This suggests that there are differences in the protection available for women and children according to area.

There are marked regional variations in enforcement with regard to the power of arrest. A power of arrest appears most likely to be attached to an

Table 1
Applications made and orders granted under the Domestic Violence and Matrimonial Proceedings Act 1976 for 1981-1997 and the Family Law Act 1996 for 1998 and 1999

		Orders granted			
Year	Applications	Ousters/ occupation	Non-Molestation	With Power Of Arrest	Total
1985	13,531	3,818	9,202	3,314	13,020
1986	16,046	4,759	10,826	4,005	15,585
1987	16,474	4,903	11,081	4,623	15,984
1988	19,329	5,633	13,133	4,996	18,766
1989	20,030	6,180	14,239	5,870	20,419
1990	21,023	-	-	-	25,609
1991	21,205	-	-	-	26,236
1992	20,648	5,940	25,431	9,660	31,371
1993	20,462	4,541	28,240	10,088	32,781
1994	25,034	3,946	24,566	9,793	28,512
1995	24,010	3,513	22,454	9,568	25,967
1996	21,862	2,945	19,707	10,049	22,652
1997[1]	17,064	2,666	17,169	9,409	19,836
1998	29,300	9,023	19,365	22,472	28,388
1999	26,665	8,319	18,465	21,475	26,784

Note: Figures for 1997 are estimates calculated on nine months of actuals.
Source: Judicial Statistics, LCD for 1985-1999. nb. Incomplete data for 1990-1991 is due to changes introduced by the Lord Chancellor's Department.

Table 2
Personal protection and exclusion orders granted under the Domestic Proceedings and Magistrates Courts Act 1978 for the years 1987- 1993

	Family protection or exclusion order[1]	Expedited order[1]	MCA Breach of family protection order	Total Orders
1987	3,720 (670)	2,040 (1,110)	200	5,960
1988	3,480 (650)	2,030 (1,130)	150	5,660
1989	3,140 (740)	1,860 (980)	360	5,360
1990	2,850 (610)	1,810 (890)	100	4,760
1991	2,050 (750)	1,400 (730)	70	3,520
1992	1,260 (310)	940 (480)	70	2,270
1993	640 (197)	496 (280)	29	1,165

Note: Figures in brackets refer to orders with power of arrest
Source: Domestic Proceedings England and Wales *Home Office Statistical Bulletin for the years 1987 to 1993.*

occupation order in the London region (in 86% of cases), and least likely in Yorkshire and Humberside, and the North East (in only 67% of cases). Variations in the power of arrest for non-molestation orders, however, are far less marked, the highest region (84%) in East Midlands, whilst the lowest regions- West Midlands, Eastern and South East -where a power of arrest was attached in 75% of cases. The East Midlands region is the most likely to issue a warrant for arrest whilst Yorkshire and Humberside most likely to remand in custody those who are in breach of an order.

Commentary

From the statistical analysis above, it can be concluded that non-molestation injunctions remain unchanged under the new Act halting an otherwise upward trend. The new Act may not be as effective as anticipated. There is concern that one of the factors possibly influencing the ability of the FLA to reach and protect women is the Legal Aid Criteria and Eligibility rules (Legal Aid Board, 1999) where the financial cost of seeking an injunction may have deterred some women from seeking protection.

This follows the introduction of revised legal aid criteria in 1997 for applications for injunctive protection. These include the requirement that a warning letter should have already been sent to the home in non-molestation injunctions (see Gold, J. *New Law Journal*, 9th October 1997:1431). This is a measure women might refuse for safety reasons, in addition the conduct must be brought to the attention of the police within two weeks of the incident. The new criteria also appear to be partly informed by an underlying presumption that civil protection is only necessary where criminal law remedies are not available. One solicitor explained the effect of these changes and the possible costs facing clients:

> *Normally all the work is completed during the initial six-week period before the emergency certificate expires and before the full Legal Aid Certificate (the one which requires a contribution) takes effect. At present my clients are paying between £15 to £70 per month if in work.*

From 1 April 2000 the current civil legal aid merits test has been replaced by the Funding Code introduced by the Access to Justice Act 1999. Under this Code, domestic violence cases have an increased priority for funding.

Discussions with the police, however, suggest that this plateau in non-molestation injunctions may also actually be the result of improvements in the use of the criminal law since the police are now much more inclined than in previous years to respond to domestic violence by pursuing criminal remedies. However, there is another possible, yet more invidious, explanation—now judges are under a duty to attach a power of arrest to a non-molestation injunction, any reluctance on their part to do so may

Table 3
Family Law Act 1996 part IV Domestic Violence - applications and orders by tier of court for 1998

Nature of proceedings	Magistrates	Court County	High	Total
Non-molestation orders				
Applics. ex parte	475	10,657	61	11,193
Applics. on notice	407	6,514	39	6,960
Orders with power of arrest	669	14,861	66	15,596
Orders without power of arrest	82	3,666	21	3,769
Total non-molestation orders	751	18,527	87	19,365
Occupation orders				
Applics. ex parte	174	6,278	28	6,480
Applics. on notice	145	4,487	35	4,667
Order with power of arrest	173	6,678	25	6,876
Order without power of arrest	33	2,098	16	2,147
Total occupation orders	206	8,776	41	9,023
Number of cases where undertaking accepted	183	4,495	32	4,710
Warrants of arrest				
Applics. made	12	223	7	242
Warrants issued	10	212	-	222
Remands into custody	16	330	-	346
On bail	20	495	-	515
For medical report	1	50	1	52

Source: *Judicial Statistics, LCD* Table 5.9 Cm 4371

result in a refusal of the injunction altogether. As Allison (1999) observes:

> *In Chechi, the question for the Court of Appeal was whether, having found that the applicant had prima facie established the grounds for an order and on the basis that, having established the grounds, the court was obliged to attach a power of arrest, could the court then refuse to make the order on the basis that the power of arrest would give too much power to the applicant? Butler-Sloss LJ said it could. In a reserved judgement against an order of Kenny J. on 26th August 1998 she said: 'The judge was entitled to consider the power of arrest gave the applicant an unacceptable power over the defendants. In the light of his inability to refuse to attach a power of arrest to his order, the only alternative was to refuse to grant the non-molestation order.*

The regional variations in the grant of occupation and non-molestation orders are to be treated with caution. The differences will depend on, amongst other factors, regional population size as well as any real difference in the prevalence of domestic violence, differences in the 'take up' of remedies and the response of the courts (Edwards and Halpern, 1991).

However, the percentage variations in use of power of arrest and especially undertakings are also an artefact of judicial interpretation of the legislation. Particularly with regard to the latter, it is a matter of considerable concern that in some regions courts accept undertakings to the extent that they do, given that they have been the subject of so much criticism (Barron, 1990, Lockton and Ward, 1997).

In conclusion, it appears that despite the shortcomings, bringing the remedies under one Act has produced a more effective remedy for dealing with domestic violence.

Evaluating the Protection from Harassment Act 1997

The PFHA provides an additional civil remedy under s. 3 (1) and s. 3 (3) (a) for women experiencing domestic violence. It is particularly important for those experiencing threats, harassment and other forms of intimidation that may not amount to a direct physical assault. Two courses of redress are open, the first is to pursue a charge of harassment under the criminal limb of this Act, and the second is to pursue civil proceedings. How far the civil remedies are appropriate and used by women seeking redress from domestic violence is largely unknown. There is very little literature, commentary, or case law and at the time of writing no published statistics on the civil use of the PFHA.

Data held by the LCD shows that, in a fifteen month period, 468 civil injunctions under the PHFA have been granted. The most extensive use of this remedy being made in the London and Yorkshire and Humberside regions.

Commentary

- The use of the PFHA civil injunction by applicants, solicitors and the courts is greater than was originally anticipated. Unfortunately, however, the statistics are not collated according to type of conduct or relationship of victim to suspect and cannot provide any indication of the number of cases that involve domestic/ intimate harassment conduct. This would require empirical research on a court-by-court basis.
- The variations between regions indicate that some areas, e.g. Eastern and Merseyside, use the remedy sparingly, which may amongst others be an artefact of solicitors' advice to clients seeking redress for harassment. This may suggest the need for more advice/training to

solicitors on the Act, its purpose, its application and usefulness.
- It is hypothesised that the PFHA may be being used in cases where a non-molestation order might previously have been considered, particularly in cases where there is no actual violence and where the court may well have been inclined to accept an undertaking. This might explain the fall in the granting of non-molestation orders in 1998 and 1999 over 1996.
- Legal Aid is only likely to be granted if a warning letter has been sent and the conduct complained of has occurred within the last two weeks. Legal aid is not likely to be granted if the damages likely to be granted are above £1000 (see *NLJ*, 1997:1431).
- No power of arrest can be attached to the injunction but a warrant for arrest may be applied for when disobedience is alleged (s.3 (2)).
- The cost effectiveness of the new remedy is yet to be tested.

The Children Act 1989: Exclusion orders attached to protective orders for children

There is little literature, case law and no published or indeed unpublished figures on the use of exclusion orders attached to child protection orders. However, what can be observed is that on average over the last few years over 2,000 emergency protection orders were granted.

It is argued that in many of these orders for child protection, a child will require the further protection ensured by removing the abuser from the home. This removal is provided for in law by an exclusion order or by an undertaking made by the suspect abuser to the court. In the absence of any data on this, it is impossible to make any assessment whatever on the use and effectiveness of this most significant and important provision.

The Children Act 1989: Contact orders

Whilst the various remedies already outlined provide protection from domestic violence, those professionals working with women and children share the view that in cases where the courts have been reluctant to refuse contact between the abusive parent and the child, the contact order can have the effect of locking women and children into a prospective continuum of violence.

The courts and the contact presumption

In considering whether to make a contact order where domestic violence has been directed towards the mother the courts have been guided by a 'presumption of contact' (Cantwell and Roberts, 1998). Article 8 (1) of the

European Convention on Human Rights and Fundamental Freedoms which upholds the right to privacy and family life has been used to uphold the right of the parent to contact with the child (see *Re KD (A minor)* [1988] AC 806. This suggests that the parental right to access (now contact) does exist independently of considerations of the child's welfare. Although in *M v M Child Access* [1973] 2 All ER 81, contact was regarded as the right of the child (see *Re R* [1993] 2 FLR 762).

In *Re F* [1995] 1 FLR 956, the judge stated:

> *The starting point always, is that every child has a right to be brought up in the knowledge of his non-custodial parent. This is a right which the courts are determined to preserve.*

The preservation of this right to contact has been regarded as absolute even though the harm done to the child in enforcing and preserving contact may be far greater than the harm done to the child if contact were not ordered. In some cases, the courts minimise their consideration and regard to the evidence of past violence and the prospect of future violence and maximise the benefits to the child of continuing contact as if it is some absolute residual right. The approach of the courts is that fathers should only be denied contact in wholly exceptional cases (see Weyland, 1995, Cantwell and Roberts, 1998).

In *Re H (Contact: Domestic Violence)* [1998] 2 FLR 42 a recorder's order for contact was upheld. Wall J. said:

> *As a matter of principle, domestic violence of itself cannot constitute a bar to contact. Each case must inevitably be decided on its own facts. Domestic violence can only be one factor in a very complex equation. There will be contact cases in which it is decisive against contact. There will be others in which it is peripheral.*

A survey of 56 solicitors conducted by Rights of Women (1997) found that over half the solicitors advised the women not to oppose contact, even though a third of the mothers wished to because they were afraid that their children would be abused, abducted or neglected.

In cases where there is domestic violence the mother is understandably fearful and may oppose contact. The court has construed this opposition as belligerence and regarded her reasonable and justifiable refusal as 'implacable hostility' (see below). In *A v N (Committal: Refusal of Contact)* [1997] 1 FLR 533, the Court of Appeal reaffirmed the principle that in an extreme case a mother who prevents contact which is in the interests of a child may be sent to prison and upheld a sentence of 4 weeks imprisonment.

Re P (minors) (contact: parental hostility) [1997] 1 FCR 458 at 473, the court summarised the decision of the court in *Re O (contact: indirect contact)* [1996] 1 FCR 317 in the following propositions:

- The welfare of the child is the paramount consideration.
- It is almost always in the interests of a child whose parents are separated that he or she should have contact with a parent with whom the child is not living.
- The court has power to enforce orders for contact, which it should not hesitate to exercise where it judges that it will overall promote the welfare of the child to do so.
- In cases in which, for whatever reason, direct contact cannot for the time being been ordered it is ordinarily highly desirable that there should be indirect contact.

In *Re M (Contact Order: Committal)* [1999] 1 FLR 810 the Court of Appeal set aside the order of a circuit judge who had instigated committal proceedings against a mother for breaches of an order relating to contact.

Balcombe, L.J. in *Re J (A Minor) (Contact)* ([1994] 2 FCR 741 at 749) had previously remarked

> *But before concluding this judgement, I would like to say that judges should be very reluctant to allow the implacable hostility of one parent (usually the parent who has a residence order in his or her favour) to deter them from making a contact order where they believe the child's welfare requires it.*

In the case of *Re M (minors) (contact: violent parent)* [1999] 2 FCR 56, the justices found that the mother was subjected to domestic violence and the father had a drinking problem. The justices further found serious risk of destabilising the family unit if the father were to be granted direct contact to the children. The justices refused to order contact. The Court of Appeal upheld their decision and reaffirmed what they considered the correct test to be applied in such cases as laid down by Bingham M.R. in *Re O* (above).

Hale J., sitting in the Court of Appeal in *Re D (contact: reasons for refusal)* [1998] 1 FCR 321 at 327-328, said:

> *It is important to bear in mind that the label 'implacable hostility' is sometimes imposed by the law reporters and can be misleading. In some cases the judge or the court finds that the mother's fears, not only for herself but also for the child, are genuine and rationally held . . .*

In *Re A (contact: domestic violence)* [1998] 2 FLR 171 Connell J. upheld the refusal of magistrates to order contact. In *Re L (a child) (contact: domestic violence); Re V (a child) (contact: domestic violence); Re M (a child) (contact: domestic violence); Re H (a child) (contact: domestic violence)* [2000]4 All ER 609, it was held

> *Family judges and magistrates needed to have a heightened awareness of the*

existence of and consequences on children of exposure to domestic violence between their parents or other partners. Where, on a contact application, allegations of domestic violence were made which might have an effect on the outcome, those allegations had to be adjudicated upon and found proved or not proved. However, there was not, nor should there be, any presumption that, on proof of domestic violence , the offending parent had to surmount a prima facie barrier of no contact. As a matter of principle, domestic violence could not of itself constitute a bar to contact.

There is a growing body of academic and practitioner opinion that reverses the presumption of contact so often applied by the courts and replaces it with a presumption of 'no contact'. This demands that the onus of proof be on the applicant to show that contact be managed satisfactorily (Mullender, 1996; Cantwell and Roberts, 1998; Cabinet Office, 1999). This is based on the risk factors i.e. the danger to mother in being subjected to violence and the harm to the child in witnessing violence which arises from contact with a violent father.

Case examples

There are many cases that illustrate the potential danger that flows from the grant of a contact order.

Imtiaz Begum fled to a refuge with her youngest son and applied for residence for her three daughters. On 20th January 1996 she was collecting her son after a contact visit when she was stabbed to death in a busy railway station. Her son was found strangled in her husband's car, and later her three daughters were found dead in their beds with their throats cut. Her husband was convicted in October 1996 and is serving life for their murders (Saunders, 1999).

In February 1994 Sarah Heatley was worried about her violent husband's behaviour. She had tried to stop his unsupervised visits and got three different injunctions from the court. She was persuaded to agree to contact without a court hearing. Her two children were subsequently murdered during a contact visit. On 10 December 1993, her husband was allowed alternate weekend access. On Sunday 6 February 1994 - his third weekend with them - there was a knock on the door of my flat. It was the police. 'There really isn't an easy way to say this,' said one officer, 'but your husband has killed your children.' (*Evening Standard*, September 25, 1997)

Ian Lazenby, from Humberside, killed his three daughters and himself after his wife left him because of his violence. In London, Jose Pimenta pushed his two young sons off a fourth-floor balcony and then jumped off after his estranged wife told him she had begun a new relationship. In Dorset, Mark Bradley killed himself and his two children in his fume-filled car after murdering their mother. She had told him she had had an affair and wanted a separation (*The Independent*, December 21, 1997).

Research on the risk of contact

In a study of 79 abused mothers in England and Denmark, Hester and Radford (1996) found that

- Most mothers initially wanted children to see their fathers, but contact arrangements broke down because of violence.
- 74 of the woman interviewed had been assaulted by their ex-partners when taking or collecting children from contact visits.
- Half of the 53 women from England said that their children had been physically or sexually abused by their former partners. However, contact went ahead for all but six of the families, with inadequate provisions being made to ensure the safety of the children.

A survey of 54 Women's Aid refuges found that 67 per cent reported incidents of a woman being abused during contact and 31 per cent of children being physically or sexually abused during contact visits (WAFE, 1997).

The effects on children of witnessing domestic violence should not be underestimated:

> *My worst moments were when my Dad said he was going to throw the baby out of the window and when he said he was going to cut my Mum's ears off and poke her eyes out.* (Saunders, 1999:2)

> *Patricia was attacked by her ex-husband and suffered severe concussion, a broken nose and extensive bruising. Her nine-year-old daughter witnessed the assault and was terrified. The child still suffers from trauma, sleepless nights, and loss of appetite, anxiety and nightmares. She becomes hysterical at the mention of contact visits and has refused to see her father again.* (Saunders, 1999:2)

In 1998, 49,313 private orders were made for contact and 731 public orders. The granting of private orders arise out of applications under section 8 of the CA 1989, orders which are concerned with issues of parental responsibility. Public orders arise out of applications made by local authorities for child protection. Of these 8,385 contact applications were withdrawn, 1,911 refused, and in 3,298 applications no order for contact was made.

Commentary

It is not possible to discern what proportion of section 8 orders for contact, no order for contact, or refusal involves circumstances where a father is violent. However, once again, there are considerable regional variations in the proportions of withdrawal and refusal of orders. Research is needed to determine the extent of domestic violence as it is relates to contact issues and the significance of the regional variations.

Contact is damaging for children and for women. Women have been abused and assaulted during the collection of the child by the abuser parent. The effectiveness of other civil remedies is considerably undermined where on the one hand women and children's protection is prioritised, but, where contact is an issue, their protection is subordinate. The recognition that contact is a dangerous time for women and children has resulted in the provision of number of supervised contact centres. The National Association of Child Contact Centres supports over 250 child contact centres in Great Britain although few of them provide supervised contact. The costs of these centres should be weighed against the benefits of safety for women and children. However, if the courts were more cognisant of the problems caused by domestic violence and granted fewer contact orders child protection and women's protection would be enhanced.

What is clearly required in this regard is a programme of judicial training in domestic violence and family issues particularly the issue of contact.

Conclusion

The chapter set out to examine the impact of the new civil remedies for the protection of women and children, and to consider:

- What is working?
- What remedies and provisions could work but are being underused?
- What changes need to be made?

The Family Law Act

Whilst the FLA has widened the constituency of applicants who may apply for protection, the anticipated increase in non-molestation applications and orders granted has not happened. This plateau, it is suggested, is the result of the impact of legal aid changes, which are obstructing women's protection and the result of a police response that regards domestic violence as a criminal matter. The meteoric rise in occupation orders cannot be compared with earlier years, as the ouster order and the new occupation order are not directly comparable.

If any meaningful evaluation of the FLA and ouster protection is to be undertaken then it is necessary to identify and distinguish occupation orders that involve exclusion provision. Whilst the Act allows for occupation orders to be granted *ex parte* under section 45(1) there would appear to be some judicial reluctance to issue them.

The use of power of arrest is extremely encouraging and is vital in protecting women. It is cost effective in providing a powerful deterrence and a once and for all means of dealing with the repeat offender. Although there could be heavy implications for police in their mandated involvement in domestic violence, the power of arrest will provide a quick and effective remedy where men who might not have been refused bail will be detained overnight pending a court appearance for breach. However, long term the cost to the police of the mandatory power of arrest as a long term deterrent will, it is anticipated, reduce the amount of police time spent on repeat attendance and investigation of domestic violence.

Weaknesses

The legislation does not extend to those who have never lived with their abusers, except where there has been a formal promise of future marriage. In one study, 52% (*n*=446) of women suffering domestic violence who reported to police in Streatham were not living with their partner (Buchan and Edwards, 1991). The balance of harm test is based on balancing competing interests, i.e. the need for the applicant to be protected from violence against any harm done by imposing the order on the respondent. However, it returns us to a pre-*Davis v Johnson* position where male proprietary rights prevailed over the female right to protection (Edwards and Halpern, 1988) and resuscitates the balance of hardship test originally formulated in *Bassett v Bassett* [1975] Fam 76.

Section 60 provides powers for third parties, including the police, to take out injunctions on behalf of abused women. Third party applications have been used very successfully in Australia and in the United States (with the woman's consent), and have a number of advantages, including their speed and the removal of problems associated with legal aid and a reduction in the number of cases withdrawn (Humphreys and Kaye, 1997). Section 60, has however, not yet been implemented. Because of the recognition that the victims of domestic violence often feel unable to act, the most obvious third party will be the police. Ultimately, the effectiveness of Section 60 may depend on the willingness of police to take on this new role.

Protection from Harassment

The PFHA is an important new provision for women experiencing domestic violence. The advantage of an order under PFHA over the FLA may be that a breach of an order may be more effectively dealt with under s. 3 (a). In addition, such orders under the PFHA, unlike the FLA are not limited to 'associated persons', and apply to any person who may wish to avail themselves of the remedy. It is not clear, however, how far in the domestic context the civil provision of damages will be of use. It is suggested that the civil provision in the PFHA will be of less relevance to the victim of domestic harassment than, perhaps, for those who are of some means – for example - celebrity stalking cases.

There is a need for further work that will enable the identification of domestic violence and intimate related harassment in order to ascertain the usage of this legislation in the domestic context.

Exclusion orders under the Children Act

The provision in the CA that now allows for the suspected abuser to be removed where there is suspicion of abuse to a child is extremely important. It is regrettable that the use of exclusion orders cannot yet be discerned due to the absence of published and unpublished statistics. This must be rectified if the impact of legislation is to be monitored and its application made accountable.

However, it is probably reasonable to suggest that exclusion orders should be used more widely in cases where there is an interim care order or else an emergency protection order, given that in 2000, 2,232 emergency protection orders were granted, the potential for use is enormous.

Contact orders under the Children Act

The continuing tendency of the courts to grant contact orders to violent fathers must be investigated and reviewed as a matter of urgency. Where there is domestic violence the issues of whether an order is being opposed or unopposed should be immaterial and the welfare of the child the paramount consideration.

It is to be noted that the welfare checklist must be applied where orders are being considered where the child is suffering significant harm. The violence, which may flow from contact in the domestic context and the likely harm to the child as a result, necessitates as a matter of urgency an amendment to the CA which would require courts to consider the welfare checklist where an application for contact is being made. This situation at present only requires the checklist to be applied where an order for contact is being opposed. It is also suggested that judicial training should deal with the issue of the dangers of contact in domestic violence cases.

New directions in prosecution

Susan Edwards

This study reported in this chapter examines the criminal law remedies including the Protection from Harassment Act (PFHA) 1997 available to protect women and children from domestic violence. This is achieved through providing an overview of the existing criminal law legislation, case law and literature available. The application of the law is evaluated through an analysis of largely unpublished statistical data made available to the author by the Home Office Research, Development and Statistics Directorate, on applications and orders under the PFHA. In addition, the study made use of the findings of a small scale research case study, carried out for this review, eliciting information from all police forces together with a more detailed analysis based on four site visits to pilot projects. This covers the police use of the PFHA, their use of the Criminal Justice Act (CJA) 1988 section 23(3)(b) which allows for, in appropriate cases, the use in court of a written statement made to police in the absence of oral testimony, and finally their experience of enhanced evidence gathering including the use of photographic evidence at the scene.

The study found that the PFHA is being widely used (in 1998, a total of 5,788 cases were proceeded with) with wide variations between circuits (regions) although it is impossible from the way the figures as presently collated to identify the cases which relate to domestic/intimate related incidents. The study found little use made of section 23, although some forces were looking to supporting prosecutions with enhanced evidence gathering. These included taking detailed witness statements, a complete history of the abuse, witness statements from other parties and photographic evidence.

Introduction

The criminal remedies that apply in offences involving domestic violence have hitherto been under-enforced, this has been the result of a combination of the perspectives of individuals and of agencies which have trivialised the seriousness of domestic violence (Clarkson, et al, 1994:15; Bourlet, 1990:11; Buchan and Edwards, 1991). Institutional procedures and practices have persistently and obdurately failed to protect victims and the criminal justice system has apparently been unable, or unwilling, to understand the dilemma facing an abused party. The criminal justice system has preferred instead to adopt the position of Lord Salmon who stated: '...if she does not want to avail herself of this protection, there is, in my view, no ground for holding that the common law forces it upon her' (*Hoskyn v Commissioner of the Police for the Metropolis* [1979] AC 474).

Until recently the law has remained remote from women's experiences of domestic violence and has confined its protective response to domestic abuse involving serious physical violence (Saunders, 1989). In the author's opinion, even in cases where domestic violence falls squarely within the legal definition of physical assault the law has been under-enforced. This has been partly the result of police perceptions of the Crown Prosecution Service (CPS) case determination, where police consider the CPS more likely than not to discontinue cases in which the victim might withdraw the allegation at some later stage. De facto attrition - the product of prosecutors' decision making rather than victims' refusal can only be confronted if police, prosecutors and the courts acknowledge this.

Significant changes have been introduced during the last decade in most police forces in England and Wales, Scotland and Northern Ireland. This includes establishing dedicated domestic violence units, enhanced training, improved recording of domestic incidents following the Home Office Circular (60/1990) to all police forces, and in the Metropolitan Police District establishing minimum standards of operational performance (MPS, 1996; 1999). There has also been considerable improvement in organisational structures (Plotnikoff and Woolfson, 1998) and in some forces monitoring of police performance.

Changes in police policy in respect of recording domestic violence has been reflected in the marked rise in recorded incidents of domestic violence. Greater Manchester Police and the Metropolitan Police District provide just two examples of quite significant increases in the number of recorded incidents (see Edwards 1998, and below), but this has not been matched by a proportionate increase in cases prosecuted. Care must be taken when analysing these figures since variations in definitions of domestic violence between forces and the expansion of the category 'domestic incidents' to include all incidents rather than the inclusion of criminal offences only.

The likelihood of prosecution remains poor and when defendants are proceeded against and convicted at the sentencing stage magistrates and judges continue to pass derisory sentences. Buchan and Edwards (1991) looked at 79 prosecutions where defendants were remanded in custody, only one defendant received a sentence of imprisonment.

This undermines the improvements in commitment to dealing effectively with domestic violence at other stages of the criminal justice process leaving women vulnerable and reinforcing in men the belief that they can abuse with impunity. All efforts should be directed to improving the likelihood of prosecution of domestic violence cases. Prosecution can reduce domestic violence and is instrumental in intervening in the escalation and repetition of such incidents.

Aims of this chapter

The aim of this chapter is to consider the effectiveness of recent efforts in improving the protection of victims of domestic violence. It will examine the Protection from Harassment Act (PFHA) 1997 and advances in enhanced evidence gathering to support criminal prosecutions in conjunction with the use of the power under section 23(3)b of the Criminal Justice Act (CJA) 1988. This can be used in some cases where the victim is unwilling or unable to appear in court and give oral evidence. It will consider how far and to what extent these efforts address one of the core goals recently formulated by the Women's Unit of the Cabinet Office, that of

> ...reducing attrition in the prosecution process. (Cabinet Office, 1999:11)

Methods used

In order to investigate the use of both PFHA 1997, and section 23(3)(b) CJA 1988 the following has been carried out:

- a review of the criminal remedies;
- an examination of the use made of these remedies by police and prosecutors with reference to published and unpublished statistics;
- a consideration of responses to a letter to the Chief Constables of all police forces seeking information on their use and experience of the PFHA and section 23(3)(b);
- a consideration of responses to a letter to all police forces seeking information about their experience of enhanced evidence gathering including the use of photographic evidence at the scene; and
- a review of the findings of four site visits to pilot projects in forces currently exploring and developing enhanced evidence gathering techniques: Fulham, South London, Metropolitan Police, New Scotland Yard, Hertfordshire, and Halkyn, North Wales in order to examine the effectiveness of these schemes and their impact and the costs and benefits in tackling the crime of domestic violence.

Criminal remedies: An overview

In examining the criminal law remedies that are available two limitations are worth noting. First the criminal law has historically only recognised physical assault, (although psychiatric injury has more recently been recognised), and second the effectiveness of criminal law remedies depends upon the application and implementation of the law by police, prosecutors, judges and magistracy.

Criminal assaults

The law governing criminal assault is provided for in the Offences Against the Person Act (OAPA) 1861 (currently under review) and the Criminal Justice (CJA) Act 1988 section 39 - common assault and battery.

The OAPA provides for the more serious offences of assault including assault occasioning actual bodily harm - section 47, grievous bodily harm - section 20, and grievous bodily harm with intent - section 18. Section 47 and section 20 are triable either in the magistrates or in the Crown Court, whilst section 18 is triable on indictment in the Crown Court only.

Recent case law has expanded the meaning of 'force' so as to include fear. In *Constantza* (*Times Law Report* March 31st, 1997; [1997] 2 Cr App R 492) the Court of Appeal upheld a conviction for a section 47 assault where the appellant had made telephone calls to the victim, sent more than 800 letters, and repeatedly visited her house late at night. The Court of Appeal held that it was enough to prove '...a fear of violence at some time not excluding the immediate future' and that '...an assault could be committed by words alone'. This reasoning was followed in *R v Ireland; R v Burstow* [1997] 4 All ER 225). In *Smith* [1998] 1 Cr.App.R. (S) 138. In this case, after a relationship had ended, the appellant, over a period of four years made phone calls, sent letters, gifts and offensive communications, and the police and prosecutors proceeded with assault charges. A sentence of two and a half years was reduced to 21 months for section 20 assault inflicting grievous bodily harm.

Offences under section 39 are triable in the magistrates court only and this section is frequently used in cases involving domestic violence (Edwards, 1989a; Cretney and Davis, 1997a). Its advantage is that prosecutions can be dealt with quickly, defendants are often willing to plead guilty and the cost is appreciably less than cases heard in the Crown Court. However, there is some evidence that use of this section for crimes of domestic violence lead to the trivialisation of domestic violence (Edwards 1989a; Buchan and Edwards, 1991).

Protection from Harassment Act 1997

The most recent development in the criminal law is provided in the PFHA, which came into force on 16th June 1997. The introduction of the new Act followed on from the Home Office Consultation Paper *Stalking- the Solutions* (1996). As Lord Steyn stated in *Ireland*:

> *Harassment of women by repeated silent telephone calls, accompanied on occasions by heavy breathing, is apparently a significant social problem. That the criminal law should be able to deal with this problem, and so far as is practicable, afford effective protection to victims is self-evident.* (ibid at 228b)

The PFHA has the potential to deal with a broad spectrum of conduct, including harassment, pestering, stalking, neighbour disputes and racial abuse. Two new criminal offences were created:

- Section 2 creates a summary offence of criminal harassment.
- Section 4(1) (2) creates the more serious offence of 'putting a person in fear of violence'. This offence is triable summarily (before magistrates) or on indictment in the Crown Court.

The evidence required for both these offences is that the defendant pursues 'a course of conduct' on at least two occasions (section 7(3)).

There is no definition of harassment although it is anticipated that interpretation will draw on the Public Order Act 1986, sections 4A and 5, where some attempt at definition is provided by way of examples of threatening, abusive, insulting or disorderly behaviour. The PFHA expressly provides that harassment will extend to speech, (section 7(4)).

There is no definition of what might be considered to constitute 'causing another to fear violence' although section 7 (2) refers to 'alarm or distress'. Proceedings may be instituted if the victim/complainant perceives harassment or fear. The Act provides for both an objective and subjective test whereby section 1(b) states: '....he knows or ought to know what constitutes harassment'.

It is a defence for the defendant to say that he did not know and could not have known that his conduct could be likely to cause alarm or distress or put a person in fear or constitute harassment. For example: a woman complains that her ex-husband is harassing her by standing on her street corner every day at 8am. He says he did not know his ex-wife had moved to that street and he was awaiting his daily lift to work. Unless the prosecution can prove beyond a reasonable doubt that he did know or ought to have known that his ex-wife lived in that street and would feel harassed by his conduct, the defence would succeed.

For a conviction for either of the offences named above it is necessary to prove the three elements beyond reasonable doubt. First, that there was a 'course of conduct'. Second, that course of conduct amounted to harassment/ putting a person in fear. Third, that the perpetrator knew or ought to know that his course of conduct constituted harassment (section 2), or, in the more serious section 4 offence, that his course of conduct was putting the person in fear - alarm or distress. An offence under this act is an arrestable offence. Police and Criminal Evidence Act (PACE) 1984 section 24(2) provides the power to arrest without a warrant.

Section 5 provides for the additional discretionary power to make a restraining order in addition to any sentence imposed. Such restraining orders can be in force for a specified time, and a breach of this order carries a maximum five years imprisonment.

Prosecuting domestic violence

Reporting domestic violence

Domestic violence and domestic harassment remain a grave problem affecting the lives of women many of whom may be reluctant to report the abuse or harassment to police or to voluntary or statutory agencies.

The British Crime Survey (Mirrlees-Black et al, 1996) reports that one woman in four experiences domestic violence at some stage in her life. Shame, fear of reprisals, low expectations of the criminal justice system's ability to help, and in some communities the loss of family honour, are just some of the factors inducing women's silence and apparent complicity.

Recording domestic violence

The difference in definition between forces and the Home Office will impact on any measurement of domestic violence carried out by different agencies and on any effort to compare practices as and between police forces and prosecution areas.

The Home Office and Her Majesty's Inspectorate of Constabularies (HMIC) introduced a new definition of domestic violence, from April 1999, which includes financial abuse.

> Domestic violence involves any violence between former or current partners in an intimate relationship wherever and whenever the violence occurs the violence may involve physical, sexual, emotional or financial abuse.

Individual police forces may however, use different definitions, e.g.

> Any form of physical, sexual or emotional abuse between those who are, or were, family members or partners in a relationship. It may be accompanied by other kinds of intimidation such as degradation, mental or verbal abuse, humiliation, deprivation, financial abuse, threats or systematic criticism and belittling (Metropolitan Police Special Notice, 1999:3).

Hampshire Police define domestic violence as follows:

> Domestic violence is defined as any incident involving abuse whether physical,

> sexual, emotional or psychological towards an individual by a family member partner or ex partner in an existing or previous domestic relationship regardless of gender or sexual orientation. Violence can be actual, threatened or attempted.

Recently, a further definition of domestic violence, agreed between the Association of Chief Police Officers and the Audit Commission has been adopted for the purposes of police Best Value Performance Indicators. This includes use of the somewhat vague term 'family members'. Domestic violence, for these purposes is defined as:

> any incident of threatening behaviour, violence or abuse (psychological, sexual, financial or emotional) between adults who are or have been intimate partners or family members regardless of gender.

Not only does the definition of domestic violence vary from force to force (or agency to agency) and according to purpose, but where domestic violence is reported to police, the allegation may be recorded in different ways - as a crime and entered in a crime report, as an incident and entered in an incident report or pocket book entry or equivalent. Where an allegation is recorded as a crime, the crime classification selected will depend on the details of the incident: it might, for example, be assault, rape, vandalism or breach of the peace. Subjective judgement and differences in recording practice may also affect the selection of categorisation.

The number of domestic violence cases and domestic incidents recorded has substantially increased in recent years as a result of the changes in police recording procedures and practices. *The British Crime Survey* (Mirrlees-Black et al, 1996) revealed a 242 per cent increase in domestic violence recorded between 1981-1995. The increase in 'domestic violence incidents' recorded in the Metropolitan Police area[1] provides a further example of the extent of under-recording in earlier years. In 1985, 384 domestic violence crimes were recorded by the Metropolitan Police rising to 38,465 in 1998. It is important to consider this rise in the context of the inclusion of domestic incidents and other family members in this category for recording purposes.

The volume of the domestic violence statistic has not only been affected by changes in definition but also by real changes in victims perception of police and victim willingness to support a prosecution (Smith, 1989). In the past, where victims were unwilling to support a prosecution, it has been police practice to enter the allegation on a crime sheet and when the victim later expresses no desire to support a prosecution to subsequently enter 'no crime' as the final classification (Edwards, 1989a, 1996; Smith, 1989). Whilst there is evidence of that practice diminishing it is not known how far and to what extent it is still being used (Grace, 1995).

Figure 1 shows the considerable increase in the recording of domestic

Figure 1
Domestic Violence Incidents in the MPD for selected years.

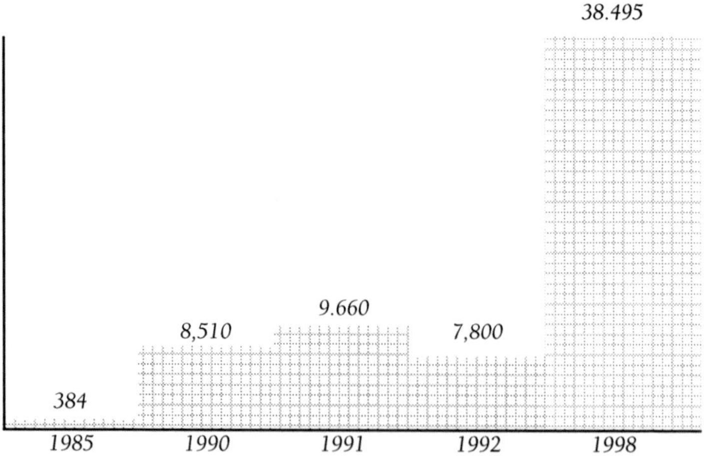

Source: Metropolitan Police-for 1985, 1990, 1991, 1992 and Performance Information Bureau Metropolitan Police for 1995,1996,1998.

violence incidents in the Metropolitan Police District. A general upward trajectory can be noted, probably facilitated, by the *Home Office Circular* 60/1990, and by the recent introduction of *Minimum Standards of Operational Performance* (MPS, 1996).

The minimum standards require:

- the effective handling of a telephone report;
- the proper investigation of an incident at the police station;
- that incidents are correctly recorded in accordance with the current Metropolitan Police Service policy;
- the actions to be taken in support of a prosecution; and
- a partnership approach to tackling domestic violence.

A further Special Notice 7/99, issued in April 1999, established minimum standards of investigation for community safety units and domestic violence units. However, fluctuations in the figures are the result of a multiplicity of factors including internal changes in counting and definitions of domestic violence.

It is clear that improvements in police recording practice and the provision of a more accurate statistical record of the problem is important in raising awareness and ensuring that the necessary resources are committed to effective policing and crime prevention in this area.

Prosecuting domestic violence

The meteoric rise in recorded domestic violence incidents in the Metropolitan Police district (see Figure 1), however, is not reflected in a proportionate increase in the number of cases prosecuted. This high attrition rate is one experienced by all police forces. Despite the fact that witnesses are fearful of giving evidence in court (Edwards, 1989b), the little use of section 23(b) of the Criminal Justice Act 1988 could suggest that prosecutors, the courts and the police are reluctant to find alternate ways of supporting these vulnerable prosecutions. It may also be the case that the strict requirements of s.23, in particular the need for the court to be satisfied that admitting the evidence is in the interests of justice and will not be unfair to the defendant, may deter police and prosecutors from placing such cases before the courts.

Evidence elsewhere, in the US for example, suggests that effective prosecution of domestic violence suspects has a dramatic impact on reducing the escalation in repetition and severity of domestic violence and can be measured through a fall in the spousal homicide rate. In Duluth, Minnesota, reported homicides fell from seven domestic murders per year to none (see Edwards, 1998, and Hague, this volume) as a result of an increased prosecution rate in domestic violence cases and the development of an inter-agency co-ordinated approach. In San Diego an increased emphasis on prosecuting violent abusers reportedly reduced the domestic homicide rate for the city by 61% (*New York Times*, July 9, 1995). Homicide statistics for England and Wales show a marginal fall in the number of female intimates killed. This may in part be the result of improved policing of domestic violence in recent years

Prosecuting domestic violence: The criteria

In accordance with the Prosecution of Offences Act 1985 (POOA), once the police have preferred charges, the prosecutor is responsible for determining whether charges should be continued or discontinued. In making this decision the Crown Prosecution Service (CPS) apply two criteria:

- whether there is a sufficiency of evidence to afford a 'realistic prospect of conviction'; and
- whether 'it is in the public interest' to prosecute.

Sufficiency of evidence

In consideration of this requirement the prosecutor will evaluate 'all the evidence' including witness statements, photographs and medical statements, and other factors influencing the conviction potential of a case, for example, what impression a jury may form of the evidence and of the witness(es). The evidential test is objective. This means that a jury or bench of magistrates is more likely than not to convict the defendant of the charge as alleged (Blackstone's, 1999 Appendix 4:2328).

The public interest

In applying the second criteria of 'public interest', the CPS balance factors for and factors against a prosecution. The Code for Crown Prosecutors (1996) outlines a list of factors which would weigh against the public interest in prosecution and the factors they have identified in support of a prosecution (Blackstone's 1999, 2329 para 6). Both of these are discussed below in the 1995 policy document on domestic violence.

CPS policy on prosecuting domestic violence cases

Prosecutors have been widely criticised for failing to prosecute in domestic violence cases (Edwards 1989; Home Affairs Committee, 1992-93). In response to this criticism the CPS have published two statements outlining best procedure in such cases.

In 1993 and 1995, the CPS published their policy on prosecution in cases of domestic violence. This addressed the application of the codes, as well as reviewing the issues of compellability of witnesses and the bringing of prosecutions where witnesses are reluctant to give evidence (CPS, 1993).

The policies provided that where a complainant wished to withdraw an allegation a prosecutor of at least Principal Crown Prosecutor (PCP) level would be assigned to supervise the case. The following options should be considered for continuing with the case:

1. whether is it necessary to call the victim;
2. whether the victim should be compelled; and
3. whether the victim's statement can be admitted under section 23 CJA 1988.

In addition, the parameters of the meaning of 'sufficiency of evidence' and 'public interest' criteria were defined including cases where the complainant changes her mind about giving evidence. Where the victim still wishes to withdraw support then the CPS is to consider whether it is possible to pursue a prosecution.

The 1995 document gives the definitions of the 'public interest' criteria. Para 5.2 states that

> there may often be difficulties in striking this balance. For example, there is one side of public interest which condemns all personal violence, and another which recognises the benefit of keeping a family together. (CPS, 1995:4)

Para 5.4 lists the 'public interest' factors against prosecution. These include the chances of the abuser offending again, the victim's continuing relationship with the abuser, and the effect on that relationship of continuing with the prosecution against the victim's wishes. Public interest factors in support of a prosecution, (despite the victims wishes) include:

- the history of the relationship, particularly if there has been any other violence in the past;
- the seriousness of the offence;
- the victim's injuries;
- whether the abuser used a weapon;
- if the abuser has made any threats since the attack; if the abuser planned the attack; and
- the effect on any children in the household.

(*Source*: CPS,1995:5; CPS Inspectorate, 1998:31).

Discontinuance

There is some evidence, however, that the CPS has not lived up to its own promise to always explore all possibilities before abandoning a prosecution. In one case, *DPP ex parte C* [1995] 1 Cr App R 136, the Divisional Court reviewed a decision of the DPP not to prosecute. The complainant was forcibly buggered and assaulted on several occasions by her husband. However, the CPS prosecutor, said in evidence:

> *Approaching the case on the basis that the alleged buggery could not have been proved to have taken place without the complainant's consent, I concluded [that] in all the circumstances the complainant's grievance could be more appropriately dealt with in the matrimonial court, and that the public interest did not require the institution of criminal proceedings....* (142C)

In fact, the Crown Prosecution Service Annual Report (1991-2:20) cites discontinuance as a performance indicator for all criminal cases.

> Earlier decisions to discontinue cases will reduce unnecessary court appearances, and monitoring the timing will identify our progress.

In accordance with section 23(4) POOA, (which provides for those occasions when a suspect has been charged, but the court has not yet received papers), the CPS may discontinue any case without reference to the court, provided that charge sheet information has not been sent to the court. This is used where there is prior dialogue between the police and prosecutor before the police decide whether to charge a suspect.

In a survey of all cases discontinued during November 1993 the CPS found that 17% of discontinuance occurred because the prosecutor was 'unable to proceed.' This included 13% of cases where 'an essential witness was missing or refused to give evidence and we had no option but to discontinue' (Cretney and Davis, 1996:166 nb 25 quoting from CPS, 1994:15). Thirty one percent of all cases were discontinued on public interest grounds.

In examining discontinuance in domestic violence cases, Cretney and Davis (1997)found a 30% victim withdrawal rate. However, 52% of domestic cases were actually discontinued, suggesting that prosecutors were withdrawing domestic cases for reasons other than victim withdrawal, reasons which are likely to include evidential insufficiencies.

Statistics show that the discontinuance rate for all criminal offences increased in the first few years of the inception of the CPS. The proportion of terminated cases increased from 7.7% in 1987 to 13.2% of magistrate's cases in 1992 (Crisp and Moxon, 1994:2) and 11.9% in 1998-9 (*CPS Annual Report,* 1998-9:39.) It is not known what proportion of these discontinuances relate to domestic violence cases.

Pre-trial advice

The declining discontinuance rate indicated in the 1998-9 figures to 11.7% over previous years (CPS, 1999:34) must be evaluated, however, alongside the role pre-trial advice plays in the police decision to charge. The relationship between police administrative support units and their perception of CPS practices and requirements is another factor influencing pre trial advice and discontinuance. From 1993 the CPS have been encouraging police to refer cases to them for advice prior to charging. Pre-trial advice referrals rose from 57,000 in 1987 to 73,337 in 1991 and in 1998-9 fell to 57,351 (CPS, 1999:38). The intention however is to increase substantively pre -trial advice referrals. The 1997-8 CPS Annual Report (CPS, 1998:35) lists as one of their corporate performance measures the increase in the proportion of pre-trial advice cases.

Crisp and Moxon examined the inter-relationship between Crown prosecutors and supervising police officers in decisions to charge and found that police were loathe to 'send cases across to the CPS when they thought that termination was the likely outcome' (1994:9). It seems clear that the types of cases which in earlier years were highly likely to have been discontinued by the CPS are now the very cases which are not reaching the CPS, since the police are either not putting such cases forward or else seek pre-trial advice wherein prosecution is not advised.

The impact of pre-trial advice then is to substantively reduce the discontinuance rate and the rate of cases withdrawn or not proceeded against in the magistrates' court. These issues are crucial in the interpretation of the prognosis of domestic violence cases and if the attrition rate is to be monitored it must be set against these two considerations.

Deciding the charges

There is evidence that the CPS engage in 'plea-bargaining' especially in domestic assault cases. (Sanders, 1998). The author saw evidence of this first hand in the Streatham study (Buchan and Edwards, 1991) where some assault cases were reduced to the lesser offence of common assault and battery under section 39 CJA 1988. The reluctance by the CPS to prosecute in *DPP* ex parte C (*ibid.*) suggests that there is a need to ensure that the policy statements of 1993 and 1995 (although introduced after the original decision made in 1992 not to prosecute was made in this case) is implemented and its implementation closely monitored. The author argues that such case experience continues to minimise the offender's behaviour, reinforcing his and society's belief that domestic violence is not serious, thereby undermining efforts in other parts of the system to treat domestic violence seriously.

Pre-trial and trial issues

Compellability

In accordance with the Police and Criminal Evidence Act 1984 section 80 (8) spouses are compellable to give evidence against each other in all criminal trials excepting those in which they are co-defendants. This overrules *Hoskyn* where the House of Lords quashed a conviction for grievous bodily harm, on the ground that the victim had been wrongly compelled to give evidence. Making spouses compellable witnesses (Cretney and Davis, 1997a, 1997b) was thought to be a positive step in ensuring the prosecution of husbands for violence against wives.

Spouses can be called as witnesses without right of refusal. Yet, despite this change in the evidential status of spouses, legal compellability does little to address fear of the violent spouse. Witnesses who refuse to give evidence can be charged with contempt of court and imprisoned (see *Renshaw* [1989] Crim LR 811).

The Criminal Justice Act section 23 (3)(b) allows in some circumstances, witnesses who are in fear the opportunity of presenting written evidence to the court in place of oral testimony. It is important to develop research and policies on what can be done to help, assist and support witnesses by drawing on their experiences. This may involve providing, where appropriate, police protection for the victim and/or this may involve refusing the suspect bail and/or imposing rigorous bail conditions. Above all the frightened witness should be asked - what does she want and need of the criminal justice system?

Evidence at trial section 23 (3) (b): Documentary hearsay

Since 1988, section 23(3)(b) CJA has provided for the submission of a written statement in the absence of oral testimony where the witness is in fear or kept out of the way – that is prevented from giving evidence. The rules governing the admissibility of such a written statement require that it is in the interests of justice to admit it and that admitting the statement would not be unfair to the defendant.

Fear must be of sufficient weight before the judge may conduct a balancing exercise to determine whether it is in the interests of justice to admit the statement. Although the fear itself need not be reasonable, as laid down in *Acton Justices* [1991] 92 CAR 98.

Whether it is of sufficient weight is a matter for the court and hearsay would be admissible as oral evidence to prove her state of mind. It has been suggested that what constitutes fear should be assessed against the battered woman's perception of fear (Edwards, 1990). In *Martin* [1996] Crim.L.R. 589, the court took the view that no limitation on the words should be imposed given that witness intimidation is a subject of such concern. It is worth noting that only admissible evidence can be employed to determine whether a witness was in fear or kept out of the way (*O'Loughlin and McLaughlin* [1987] 85 Cr App 157).

This section has however been very rarely implemented and there are a limited number of reported cases. Reported cases on the point tend to arise where one party or another can find legal grounds to support their grievance at the decision whether or not to use the section. (see *Ashford Magistrate's Court ex parte Hilden*, [1993] 2 All ER 154, and *McGillivray* [1992] 97 Cr App R 232, *R v Glen William* [1999] LTL 18.3.99). The Court of Appeal in *Bird* and *Holt (supra,)* has provided guidance on the circumstances under which it considers the use of section 23 appropriate.

The required standard of proof when the statement is being tendered by the prosecution is beyond reasonable doubt (*see R v Waters* [1997] 18/2/9).

However, where such a statement is being tendered as part of the defence case the Court of Appeal in dismissing the appeal has held that the proper standard for a defendant should be the balance of probabilities (*R v Mattey &Queeley* [1995] Crim L.R. 308). As Blackstone (1999) F3.20 at 1919 asserts:

as a matter of principle, when the burden of proving the admissibility of a particular item of evidence is borne by the defence, the standard to be met should be proof on a balance of probabilities.

The Protection from Harassment Act, 1997

In this section the case law, criminal statistics and police responses to PFHA will be reviewed.

Case law indicates that the act has been used in a wide variety of situations, although in (*Huntingdon Life Sciences Ltd.* v *John Curtin & Ors* [1997] TLR 11/12/97) where there was an application to use the Act to restrain animal rights protestors the judge said:

> *... [the] legislators who passed the 1997 Act would no doubt be surprised to see how widely its terms are perceived to extend by some people. It was clearly not intended by Parliament to be used to clamp down on the discussion of matters of public interest or upon the rights of political protestors and public demonstration which are much part of our democratic tradition. I have little doubt that the courts will resist any such wide interpretation ...* [and] ... *lawful protest does not constitute harassment'.*

As mentioned above, for a successful prosecution, it is necessary to prove the three elements beyond reasonable doubt:

1. that there was a 'course of conduct';
2. that it amounted to harassment/ putting a person in fear; and
3. that the perpetrator knew or ought to have known that he was harassing or causing a person to be alarmed distressed or put in fear.

Construing the phrase 'course of conduct'

In construing the Act the courts have ruled that 'course of conduct' does not restrict conduct towards one person. In *DPP v Michael Williams* [1998] QBD, 27/7/98, (unreported. *Lawtel*) Lord Justice Rose and Bell J, ruled that the Act did not limit conduct towards one person and a 'course of conduct' could be established if that conduct was directed to others whereby the named person became alarmed or distressed. In this case the conduct involved the appellant putting his hand through an open bathroom window and looking though the window at the female occupants.

However, a conviction was quashed on appeal in *Lynne Elizabeth Mills v DPP* [1998] QBD, 17/12/98 (unreported) where two separate victims had made allegations against the appellant. The court ruled that although the complainants were neighbours there was insufficient nexus between them, as the complaints had been almost entirely unrelated.

The PFHA in domestic violence cases

Stalking, harassment in its many forms, and putting a person in fear of violence constitute some of the many manifestations of domestic abuse. In *R* v *Liddle* [1999] 3 All ER 816, for example, the appellant constantly harassed his ex-wife.

However there is still considerable ambiguity about the PFHA and its intended application in domestic violence and domestic related harassment. This is indicated by the responses from police forces and is also suggested by the regional variations in persons proceeded against under the Act (see below). Whilst the unpublished statistics for 1997 relate to a six-month period only, it is also to be noted that as harassment was not a notifiable offence until April 1st 1998 police forces were not bound to submit statistics to the Home Office on cases recorded and proceeded against.

The Home Office has recently published research (Harris, 2000) on the application of the PFHA. This found that the act is being rarely used for stalking (for example of celebrities) as frequently portrayed by the media, but is being used to deal with a variety of behaviour such as domestic and inter-neighbour disputes. The most common reasons given for harassment was that the complainant had ended an intimate relationship with the suspect (43% of all cases reviewed).

The statistics available for this review indicate a much greater use of the harassment remedy under section 2 than putting a person in fear. In 1998, a total of 5,788 defendants under both sections were proceeded against.

There is a wide variation in the number of defendants proceeded against by circuit. This suggests either that there are more harassment related offences in one area than another, or as is more likely the case, there are variations in police and prosecutors' perceptions and use of the Act. The data also shows that defendants plead guilty in 91.4 % of cases. Clearly, where there are so few contested cases the remedy is effective in dealing with harassment including domestic harassment cases.

Summary of data.

- There has been an increase in the use of the PFHA since the inception of the Act. This applies to offences under section 2 (harassment) and section 4 (putting a person in fear).
- There are six males for every female being proceeded against under the legislation. It is hypothesised that it is likely that a significant proportion of males proceeded against arise from domestic type incidents.
- Variation between Crown Court circuits indicates an underlying

difference in the predilection of police forces and prosecutors in those circuit areas to use the new legislation. With respect to section 4 cases in the Crown Court there are even wider variations, with the Western Circuit appearing particularly low in the use of this section.

- Variations between court circuits in the grant of restraining orders should be examined by looking to police perceptions, responses to and 'take up' of the new legislation. Take up depends also on prosecutors' perceptions and their willingness to use the Act. The shadow of the law is important and complex. Where police and prosecutors have put cases before the courts the response of magistrates and judges to the new legislation will also determine the predilection of police and prosecutors to put cases forward in the future.
- Variations between circuits and courts reflect the attitudes of judges and magistrates to this new legislation.
- Overall, use of enhanced evidence gathering and tagging by police forces at the onset of any conduct, which falls within this Act, should lead to an increase in the successful prosecution of cases that depend upon establishing a course of conduct.

Sentencing and PFHA

Little is known about the judicial approach to sentencing in domestic violence harassment cases. However, there are some case examples:

Julian Webster

Julian Webster pleaded guilty to harassment. He harassed his former girlfriend by repeatedly telephoning her, writing her letters and turning up her flat after she had broken off their relationship He was ordered to pay £1500 compensation and made subject to a restraining order (*The Lawyer*, 11/1/99:2).

R v Liddle, R v Hayes

In *R v Liddle, R v Hayes* [1999] 3 All ER 816, the Court of Appeal laid down sentencing guidelines in harassment cases. Liddle's sentence of 21 months imprisonment for harassment of his ex – wife was reduced to 15 months and Hayes who harassed a woman who was a stranger to him had a two-year sentence reduced to 11 months.

The Police and the PFHA

The survey of police forces conducted by the author revealed variations in police perceptions of the appropriateness of the use of the Act in domestic violence cases. In some forces police were unsure of their powers and ambivalent about using them. At the same time there are instances of good practice pointing to 'what works in reducing domestic violence'. Whilst all police forces which responded to the police circular appeared to have used the Act, police forces varied in the extent to which they used it in incidents involving domestic violence, their methods of recording and the extent to which recorded data was readily retrievable.

Box 1: First Contact

There is an innovative scheme in the Flintshire Division, North Wales. This monitors and records domestic harassment and fear incidents.

First Contact was established in 1998, under the scheme the following steps are taken.

- A call is received at the police control room. An officer attends the scene and if he/she is satisfied that an incident of harassment has occurred the victim will be issued with copy of the Form CID 61 on which is written the incident reference and the officer's details. The suspect is located and a Warning Notice is served on the suspect following the first contact with police.
- 'This is an Official Warning. You are suspected of having committed an act of harassment against.... If police are called to a second incident you may be arrested and charged with an offence under the Protection From Harassment Act 1997'.
- The scheme ensures early intervention whilst sending a powerful message to the suspect about his conduct. The Warning Notice is personally served and provides evidence in writing of the first offence which allows the 'course of conduct' necessary to a prosecution under the PFHA to be established.

The scheme is effective in inducing guilty pleas, if the conduct continues, as the Warning Notice is signed both by the officer and by the suspect and has clear evidential value. Another copy of the notice is filed with the Domestic Violence Officer.

In one of the cases dealt with under the First Contact scheme, a defendant who had intended to plead not guilty changed his plea to guilty and made a full admission when the signed warning notice was introduced as evidence of an earlier occasion of his conduct. He was convicted of criminal harassment.

During the pilot period, the scheme was implemented on 73 occasions.

Only two cases have re-offended and committed the full offence of harassment or putting a person in fear. The scheme's devisor argues that the warning notice is effective in deterring future offending (see Taylor and Tipton, 1999; Tipton, 1999). This pilot scheme is now instituted as regular practice.

Box 2: The 'First Contact' Response

Warning letter
Thames Valley Police is one of several forces that send out a warning letter to those committing a first incident identified as harassment. A sample letter contained the following:

> I write to inform you that on .... we received from ....a complaint against you that might put you in Breach of The Protection from Harassment Act 1997. May I assure you that this letter in no way indicates any prejudgment on the part of the Police, but the alleged behaviour, namely making unwanted and nuisance telephone calls and attending her home address in a violent manner without invitation appears to be contrary to the legislation.

Data recording and retrieval of use of PFHA

Few forces were able to provide any information of the use of the PFHA in domestic related incidents. Two problems arise here. Firstly, forces have different definitions of 'domestic' and secondly these definitions are not always congruous with the definition used by the Home Office and HMIC. There is evidence that some police forces are gathering figures for the Home Office in respect of its classification of domestic violence and for themselves in respect of their own domestic violence definition. Few forces able to provide any information on prosecutions under the PFHA in domestic related incidents. Avon and Somerset Constabulary reported for the period October 1998-March 1999 approximately 154 crime reports under the PFHA relating to domestic violence/quarrels. Thames Valley Police for the period 1st April 1998-23rd June 1999 reported a total of 2,211 PFHA offences recorded of which 168 related to domestic incidents. In Northern Ireland, the Royal Ulster Constabulary has used the Protection from Harassment (NI) Order 1997 in giving 86 advice and warnings and 14 prosecutions in domestic-related incidents of harassment/fear. West Yorkshire police recorded 230 uses of the PFHA in domestic violence related incidents up to June 1999, this was for only those divisions that recorded such incidents.

Other forces, whilst recording harassment offences, were unable to determine how many cases recorded related to domestic /intimate related incidents.

Evaluating the use of the Criminal Justice Act, 1998, section 23

The CPS: Implementing section 23(3)(b)

The effectiveness of the CPS in prosecuting domestic violence has been the subject of recent criticism by the Crown Prosecution Service Inspectorate (1998) who have remarked both on discontinuance and little use of section 23 (3)(b). In their file sample of 180 magistrate and 52 Crown Court cases they found:

> The quality of decision making is good. We found very few cases in which we disagreed about whether the case should proceed. In some, however, we disagreed with the decision [of the CPS] to terminate the prosecution, after the victims indicated that they no longer wished to give evidence. We considered there was sufficient other evidence to allow these cases to continue. (para 2.3 p. 3)
>
> Our evidence suggests that decisions, both to prosecute and to terminate domestic violence cases, are often taken without the benefit of important information that might have an impact on those decisions. By this we mean information about the ability and willingness of the victim to give evidence; the history of the relationship and any previous incidents; the existence of civil proceedings; the composition of the family and current domestic arrangements; the future of the relationship; and the likelihood of violence recurring. We found that CPS passively accepts the background information supplied by the police and very rarely seeks to implement it. Background information may not be conclusive in the decision whether to prosecute, but it is helpful in putting the case in context. In our view, such information is essential in ensuring that prosecutors comply with the CPS' published policy for dealing with domestic violence cases. (para 2.4.p. 3)
>
> We are concerned that CPS policy is not being complied with in a significant number of cases in which the victim wishes to withdraw her evidence. In such circumstances, prosecutors should consider whether any of the alternative options of proceeding without the victim, using section 23, Criminal Justice Act 1988, or compelling her to give evidence, ought to be pursued. The case should only be discontinued where none of these alternative is appropriate. (para 2.6. p. 3)
>
> We found, however that on over 75% of cases where the complainant withdrew her support for the prosecution, the case was terminated as a result. It is rare to find any evidence of the lawyers' thought process, prior to that decision to terminate. It appeared to us that, in too many cases, there was scant, if any consideration of the alternative courses of action, once the statement of withdrawal was received. To some extent, this is a file endorsement problem. However, it was clear from the comments of several external interviewees, that there was a

perception that the withdrawal of the victim's support for the prosecution inevitably meant the termination of the case, as far as the CPS was concerned.

However, the CPSI agreed with the decision to terminate proceedings in 89% of victim withdrawal cases in the file sample. (para 2.9 p. 3).

Criticism of the CPS has also come from other quarters, for example their failure to use documentary hearsay under section 23 was criticized in *Holt and Bird* by Roch LJ, Jowitt J and Judge Ann Goddard (QC).

Case Example: Holt and Bird

Sarah Holt suffered serious injuries inflicted by her partner, Alex Fryatt Holt and her friend Sophie Bird refused to give evidence against Fryatt.

The Court of Appeal found that the CPS procedure (cited in 1995 Domestic Violence Policy Document) was not followed, despite the fact that the appellants had, in the week preceding 16 September 1996, indicated their wish to withdraw the complaint and not to give evidence. This should have then sent the CPS down the route of considering whether to proceed with a prosecution applying compellability or alternatively without a witness by applying s 23 (3)(b). There was a further failure, said the CA - that despite indications by the appellants in the week before the trial that they wished to withdraw their statements, the Crown Prosecution Service's sensible procedure did not operate. The Court of Appeal considered that such a case might be one for a prosecution application under s 23(3)(b) of the Criminal Justice Act 1988 for the witnesses' nine statements to be used as evidence, because the appellants were witnesses who did not give oral evidence through fear. The judgement stated: *'We would draw attention to this provision and express the hope that greater use will be made in future of it in cases like the case from which these proceedings emerge.'*

Section 23: Judicial attitude

The use of section 23(3)(b) will depend on the sufficiency of evidence gathered by the police and the willingness of prosecutors to consider use of the provisions. Ultimately it will remain a matter for magistrates and judges to decide whether the victim's fear is beyond reasonable doubt and whether it is in the interests of justice to admit the evidence. The Crown Prosecution Service Inspectorate Report notes:

> It is less likely that a court will allow an application under section 23 to succeed in a case of domestic violence than it would in other types of case. This is because there is, more often than not, only one witness to the offence, the victim herself. It is more difficult to argue successfully that it is in the interest of justice to deny a defendant the right to cross-examine the only prosecution witness. The onus is on the prosecution to satisfy the court (*R v Patel* [1997] Cr. App. R. 294.).

Admissibility

Whether a document is admissible under section 23 depends upon the court's assessment whether it is in the interests of justice. In exercising its discretion the court must look to the nature and source of the document and to the extent to which other evidence on the issue is available. Where such statements are admitted they are frequently the subject of appeal. In *R v Amersham Magistrate's Court* [1997] 7/7/97, where the applicant applied for judicial review of the decision of the magistrates to admit evidence under section 23 as being prejudicial to his case. The Court held that the justices were entitled to take the view that they did in allowing the evidence to be presented.

> *The justices were entitled to take the view they had, having been impressed by the plausibility of A's statement and as such the decision to commit the applicant was the only correct one for them to have made. In any event the applicant would be fully protected in the Crown Court, because it did not follow that the Crown Court would necessarily admit the statement in the absence of oral evidence from A as the justices had done.*

In *R v Rutherford* [1998] 19/9/97 a conviction was upheld where the judge had carried out the correct balancing exercise before admitting a written statement in directing the jury as to the draconian effect on the defence (*see R v Waters* [1997] 18/2/97, *R v Li and Ors* [1997] 25/7/97, *R v James Greer* [1998] 11/12/97, *R v Christopher Thomas* [1998] 19/6/98, *R v Lynch* (1997) 23/4/97).

However in *R v Wood* [1998] 10/10/97 and *R v Williams* [1999] 18/3/99 the convictions were quashed.

Section 23: Police perceptions

Police responses to the letter requesting information on their use of section 23 in domestic violence cases revealed:

- very little use of section 23 (3) (b) constituting a mere handful of cases; and
- variations in the use of enhanced evidence gathering to support section 23;
- the reasons given were that prosecutors were cautious in allowing this evidence and that few forces had any experience of using section 23 (3) (b).

Of the forces that responded Wiltshire, Suffolk, Hertfordshire and West Midlands reported at least one such prosecution for domestic violence. Coventry division had used section 23 where the deceased's statement was used in evidence.

Fair trial and documentary evidence

Section 23 is draconian in its effect on the defendant's case with the result that it has been given a narrow interpretation by the courts. As in *Iqbal* [1990] 3 All ER 787,795, per Ward J ' the court will be vigilant to ensure that any relaxation of the rules of hearsay evidence does not lead to any abuse of the due process of law.' Article 6 of the European Convention of Human Rights provides that:

> (1) In the determination of .... any criminal charge against him, everyone is entitled to a fair and public hearing within a reasonable time by an independent and impartial tribunal established by law ....

and

> (3)(d) to examine or have examined witnesses against him and to obtain the attendance and examination of witnesses on his behalf under the same conditions as witnesses against him.

It has been argued by the defence that the admission of such written statements deprives the defendant of an opportunity to cross-examine a witness and is an abuse of due process. In the balancing exercise judges have in their deliberations had particular regard to the Convention (see *Li and Others* Lawtel 25/7/97) Indeed in *Thomas, Flannagan, Thomas and Smith,* Lawtel 19/6/98 the court held that the provisions of ss. 23 to 26 of the Criminal Justice Act relating to the admission of documentary evidence did not contravene Art. 6 of the Convention and held that the 1988 Act should not be construed in such a way as to exclude cases where the statement of the fearful witness is the only evidence in relation to a particular offence:

> *Article 6 (3)(d) amounts to an express prohibition on the admission of*
>
> *hearsay evidence adduced by the prosecution. But it does not necessarily follow that the admission of hearsay evidence ... for example under ss. 23 and 24 of the CJA 1988 will amount to a violation of Art 6 (1).*

As Emmerson (2000) writes:

> The effect of Art 6 (3)(d) on ss 23 to 26 of the 1988 Act can be seen in the case of *R v Abbas Gokal* [1997] Cr App R 267. The Commission recently declared the first application based on CJA 88 s 23 inadmissible. In *Trivedi v United Kingdom* ([1997] EHRLR 520) the Commission attached particular importance to the fact that the disputed evidence was confirmed by independent admissible evidence and to the fact that evidence relevant to the credibility of the absent witness had also been admitted.

Enhanced evidence gathering

Several police forces responded to the circular letter sent by the author and provided details of enhanced evidence gathering practices operative in their forces. These included taking detailed witness statements, a complete history of the abuse, witness statements from other parties and photographic evidence. Photographic evidence and the use of Scenes of Crime Officers appear to be crucial elements in evidence gathering and prosecution of incidents of domestic violence. Photographic evidence can clearly be very useful as evidence of the assault.

There was a strong consensus that developments in enhanced evidence gathering were constructive in increasing the number of cases proceeded with and that it was cost effective.

A number of police forces have been identified as using instant cameras in an attempt to provide further supportive evidence at the scene. Of those police forces responding to the circular letter at the time of the research, the following said they were using photographic evidence at the scene:

- Royal Ulster Constabulary,
- Hampshire
- Cambridgeshire
- Devon and Cornwall
- Hertfordshire
- West Midlands police
- Thames Valley
- Tayside
- Avon and Somerset
- Suffolk

Each of the above projects noted above are at different stages of development. Research should be conducted to examine the outcome, practice and experience of these projects.

The use of instant cameras allows a more pro-active approach to be used. It also allows the prosecution to proceed without relying solely on witness appearance in court and provides a record of repeat incidents that can increase the number of successful prosecutions. Several forces reported that such enhanced evidence gathering had a significant impact in inducing guilty pleas. Some forces also reported that photographic evidence also assisted the complainant in continuing with a prosecution. For example the superintendent managing the Suffolk pilot noted that where photographic evidence was used only two victims expressed a desire to withdraw the complaint. Police in Dudley and Sandwell had a case where a photograph was produced showing injuries to the complainant. This was available at the initial remand stage and supported the prosecutor in a request for a custodial remand. The application was successful. However, it should be noted that photographs can only be relied on by the prosecution if there is other evidence to support their admission in evidence.

Good Practice - At the Scene pilot projects

Law Enforcement Kits (LEK) Pilot Scheme: Hertford, Hertfordshire Constabulary

The Hertford project was piloted from 1st February 1998 to 30th October 1998. Three law enforcement kits were located in the Instant Response Vehicles, two initially at St Albans and one at Harpenden. The Law Enforcement Kit was to be used primarily for domestic incidents.

During this period 517 incidents of domestic violence were recorded. Camera evidence was used in 28 cases producing 82 photographs. The force reports that this has facilitated successful outcomes in inducing guilty pleas from defendants who were shown the photographs as exhibits at the interview stage in cases which would otherwise have proceeded to trial on a not guilty plea thereby incurring considerable time and expense. The photographs can also be used as an aide memoire documenting previous assault details that can provide important information and intelligence.

Since the implementation of the scheme domestic violence reporting has increased by 106 per cent and there has been a 30 per increase in arrests. A fuller and more detailed study needs to be commissioned to examine the impact on prosecution prognosis. (Hertfordshire Constabulary: *Polaroid Instant Evidence and Domestic Violence* unpublished final report 13th November 1998).

R v Simmonds

On 6th February 1998 a St. Albans officer attended a serious domestic violence incident. The officer found the victim near her home barefooted in abject terror and seriously assaulted. She had jumped from a first floor window to escape her attacker. Simmonds was arrested and instant photographs were taken and used in interview with him. Police had been to the victim's home on 22 separate occasions since 1996 and although she made a statement on the night, in fear of her attacker she withdrew her statement the next day. With the support of the Crown Prosecution Service in a case that relied on, in part, photographic evidence after she withdrew her complaint it was decided to proceed. Simmonds pleaded guilty and was jailed for six weeks *The Guardian* October 16, 1998).

The London Project - ICEFLO

The ICEFLO project (Immediate Capture of Evidence by Front Line Officers) is designed to provide immediate evidential capturing techniques for front line officers. The aim of the project is to pilot the feasibility and usefulness of photographic evidence to assist the prosecution of a range of criminal offences including domestic violence. The pilot project commenced on August 2nd 1999 for a period of six months in five pilot site locations

- Bromley using Kodak APS cameras and Polaroid cameras.
- Belgravia using 35mm cameras
- Islington using Kodak APS cameras
- South Norwood using digital cameras
- Chingford using Polaroid cameras

The objective is to compare and contrast different types of photographic equipment and to assess their effectiveness and evidential value in at the scene investigation.

The Fulham project

New developments in the United States (for example, San Diego and Duluth) have shown how a focus on survivor/victim safety and offender accountability within a multi-agency response can significantly improve victim protection from domestic violence, including reduction of domestic violence homicides.

Hammersmith and Fulham Domestic Violence Forum has initiated a pilot project called *Standing Together Against Domestic Violence* (Community Safety Unit, London Borough of Hammersmith and Fulham, 1999). This is a multi-agency co-ordinated programme where women, police, CPS, local magistrates, probation and women's aid and women's advocacy work and domestic violence prevention treatment programmes work together to protect women from abuse. The Forum prioritises women's safety and focuses on providing support for women throughout the process emphasising both the importance of prosecuting domestic violence and treating/educating violent men (Edwards, 1998).

At the pilot project at Fulham Police station enhanced evidence gathering is part of a co-ordinated approach involving use of instant photography by police when attending the scene. The officer who attends the scene asks the victim if she would like an advocate. The advocate is funded by the Fulham project and working under the auspices of Women's Aid. The advocate works closely with the police and both advocate and police have common training in domestic violence. The function of the advocate is to support the woman throughout the prosecution process. The police then liase with CPS, establish if any further evidence is required and provide regular communication and information to the victim regarding the progress of the case. The Fulham experience has resulted in several successful prosecutions.

> *Now we regularly get cases to court - nine cases have gone to court and we have had nine successful prosecutions. I can put the picture in front of the suspect and ask him what comments he has to make on it. The Fulham experience is that photographic evidence is effective in getting suspects to plead guilty.* (In interview for this report).

Conclusions and recommendations

- There is the need for a review of the operation of the PFHA specifically in cases involving domestic incidents in order to see how and in what kinds of cases it is being applied. Sentencing needs to be reviewed, particularly the use and effectiveness of the restraining order.
- There is a need to more fully implement section 23 (3) (b) at the prosecutorial and court levels by delivering common training packages in order to achieve a co-ordinated and consistent resolve to prosecute cases even where the victim is reluctant to support a prosecution.
- There is a need to evaluate more fully and where successful to extend to other police forces 'good practice' pilot projects where there has been a significant improvement in prosecution and in the protection of victims.
- Improving police accountability - Under the Crime and Disorder Act 1998 section 6(2), local authorities must embark on a crime audit. Clear performance indicators agreed upon by all agencies including police and a clear monitoring and ongoing evaluation to include a focus on domestic violence increased prosecution and victim protection.
- Where enhanced evidence gathering has been proven to assist in bringing successful prosecutions there is a need to consider extending such strategies across all forces. This will require the training of officers in enhanced evidence gathering to include routine recording and use of 999 calls, use of photographic evidence at the scene. The complainant should be encouraged to make a fuller statement of all aspects of the abusive relationship.
- This includes the need to identify domestic incidents at the point of the first call on computer aided dispatch systems since this provides the first stage of evidence gathering to establish a course of conduct for prosecution under the PFHA.
- One of the major deterrents to effective prosecution has been the time from the date of the offence to the court hearing. A recent study found that the time interval from date of offence to completion in magistrates' courts was in June 1998 was 126 days (LCD, 1999a) falling to 122 days in June 1999 (LCD, 1999b). In the USA jurisdictions, offenders are taken back to court within 24 hours of arrest. Plymouth police and the CPS are working together on a 'fast track' project that is assisting women in staying with the prosecution process instead of withdrawing.
- There is a need for magistrates training and judicial training on what constitutes 'fear', 'course of conduct' and 'harassment' and training regarding admissibility of documentary hearsay in order to ensure that the PFHA is fully implemented and evidence admitted under section 23(3)(b).

Note

1. Any incident involving assault, disturbance or potential breach of the peace between parties which could generally be described as married or having a family relationship and including cohabitors or lovers or those separated or divorced.

Supporting women and children in their communities: Outreach and advocacy approaches to domestic violence

Liz Kelly and Cathy Humphreys

The systematic development of outreach and advocacy projects, and widespread recognition that they are essential rather than marginal to responses to domestic violence, is still to occur in the UK. While Women's Aid and the refuge movement have a long history of service provision in this area the work has frequently been given little public profile. However, in the past five years significant developments have occurred both within mainstream provision and specialist Women's Aid and refuge services. This chapter will include: a discussion of the history of advocacy and outreach responses to domestic violence; definitions, tensions and debates and an overview of research evaluating theses approaches; a discussion of pro-active responses and safety planning; reflections on the value added by use of advocacy and outreach; and suggestions for how these approaches could be developed further in explicit crime reduction strategies.

Introduction

In the last five years advocacy and outreach responses to domestic violence have become more evident (Mullender, 1996), although an argument could be made that these are elements that have been present since the first refuges opened in the early 1970s. Outreach services broadly comprise responses that support domestic violence survivors in their homes and communities providing accessible and flexible points where information about service provision, and follow up contact are available. Advocacy incorporates a similarly wide range of activities. At an individual level, advocates provide women in situations of domestic violence with support, information, and advice and often act as liaison between women and various agencies and organisations. At a structural level, advocacy involves taking collective issues forward to create legislative and policy changes that will enhance the safety and well-being of women and children[1] in situations of domestic violence. Originally these activities were associated with the broader, though often invisible aspects of work within women's refuges. However, as other agencies have begun to address domestic violence more directly, and multi-agency work proliferates, elements of these responses can also be found in a wider range of locations.

This chapter will include:

- a discussion of the history of these responses;
- the associated definitions, tensions and debates;
- an overview of research evaluating these approaches;
- a discussion of pro-active responses and safety planing;
- reflections on the value added by use of advocacy and outreach; and,
- suggestions for how these approaches could be developed further in explicit crime reduction strategies.

A key question which has informed both our thinking and research is whether the language of advocacy and outreach represents a significant shift in orientation, or whether it is little more than a new terminology for earlier concepts such as 'access', 'self-help', 'empowerment', 'community development', 'support, advice and information services'. In other words are we looking at 'old wine in new bottles' or at the emergence of more differentiated, targeted forms of provision and response?

Answering this question proved complex, since we encountered considerable confusion about the precise meaning of these terms, particularly advocacy, with some projects embracing and others resisting it. Even in the USA two decades of explicit reference to advocacy has failed to produce any literature which either defines or outlines its parameters with respect to domestic violence (Peled and Edelson, 1994). Whilst there is less unease about the term 'outreach', there is little consensus about what forms of provision it encompasses: for example are helplines, drop in centres and one-stop shops types of outreach?

A key aspect of this chapter, therefore, is to explore the contours of these approaches, since without greater clarity about the features of advocacy and outreach it is virtually impossible ascertain what they are able to add to a crime reduction strategy. The absence of a developed knowledge base, especially the extremely limited research literature, means that of necessity this chapter will be more conceptual and exploratory than others in this volume. Our intention is to lay out some basic groundwork, in the hope that this will facilitate those interested in developing such approaches to be more precise about the intervention, intended outcomes and appropriate evaluation.

Methodology

From the outset it was evident that there was simultaneously a limited research and evaluative literature[2], and a rich practice base on these approaches. Our methodological approach, therefore, had to encompass more than a conventional literature search and review. It contained three additional elements:

- negotiating access to data currently being collected in two research projects;
- identifying and contacting services which focus specifically on advocacy or outreach; and
- in-depth interviews with representatives from a selected group of organisations.

Our literature searches involved accessing several social science abstract services and databases, an Internet search and detailed examination of the journal Violence and Abuse Abstracts (Sage) from 1996-99. Significantly, although both advocacy and outreach are key words for the journal indexing system, very few entries were found; and even looking in detail at the sections on the criminal justice system failed to produce much additional material. Only five publications that combined our themes and domestic violence were found through these processes. The Internet search produced more material, but the vast majority comprised little more than descriptions of projects based in the USA.

Three continuing and overlapping research projects ask questions directly relevant to this chapter. The Department of Environment, Transport and the Regions (DETR) survey, being conducted by Women's Aid Federation, England (WAFE) of refuge accommodation and support services includes a questionnaire focused entirely on 'outreach, support and other support services'. Within this, the term advocacy is explicitly used (although usually alongside 'support' as an alternative meaning). This information will also be used in a mapping project, funded by Joseph Rowntree in charting good practice in domestic violence across a range of agencies. The third project is funded by the Women's Aid Federation of England and explores 12 outreach projects in depth (Humphreys and Thiara, forthcoming). This data will provide further information in the future to supplement this discussion of outreach and advocacy.

Consultation was undertaken with WAFE and Welsh Women's Aid to identify groups with strong outreach and/or advocacy projects. The Domestic Violence Information Datasource (DVIDs) conducted a search of their database for groups using outreach and advocacy, and current research projects. The results were limited to two organisations, one of which had already been evaluated by one of the authors. The administrator of the database reported that in their recent trawl of local Crime and Disorder Act crime audits, for evidence of how domestic violence was included, little if any reference was made to advocacy or outreach. Our intention of contacting a significant number of organisations for descriptions of their projects was undermined by this lack of information.

In depth interviews were conducted with three national workers at WAFE with varying roles, the outreach workers at three refuges - Halton, Bangor and South Devon and workers in the HALT project in West Yorkshire; and Newham Action Against Domestic Violence. These workers were chosen as women with expertise from the field who were actively involved in well established and well recognised outreach and advocacy projects.

What's in a word? Definitions, descriptions and debates

In this section we explore various ways in which advocacy and outreach have been defined, a brief history in relation to domestic violence responses and the critical debates and questions that arise in the provision of these services.

Advocacy

Within the UK, the use of the word 'advocacy' in relation to women's services is relatively new; and the term itself is neither widely understood nor universally accepted. Exploring the contours of advocacy meant that we had to look for a more developed literature: two obvious areas were the law and disability. The connection between these two areas is their understanding of an advocate as someone who acts on behalf of another in order to ensure that their rights as citizens are safeguarded. This literature is then used to sharpen the definitions of advocacy in relation to domestic violence services.

Within the legal literature, advocacy refers to the conduct of lawyers in court, and how they present cases on behalf of their client. Several recurring themes have a wider application, such as the importance of having all the relevant information, being clear and avoiding jargon and pleading the case effectively.

The disability literature provides a slightly different model of advocacy that does not presume that it involves acting on behalf of someone else. The link between advocacy and the notion of rights - legal, citizenship and human - is central in the disability literature, and also in explorations with

Box 1: The tasks of an advocate

Task	**Activities**
Nurturance:	appreciation, listening carefully and taking seriously, providing emotional and practical help.
Witnessing:	acknowledging suffering and maltreatment protest at bad/poor treatment, being a whistle blower if necessary, ensuring person knows they are not alone and that they have an articulate defender.
Translation:	making the person's suffering and needs understandable to those who have power, making professional terms and processes accessible in ordinary language.
Support:	recognition of the person's inner advocacy and creativity and creating a belief that things can get better.

respect to age (see Dalrymple and Hough, 1995 on children and Dunning, 1995 on older people). It is the emphasis on rights, in a context of fighting to secure justice and redressing abuses of power, which marks one key difference between advocacy approaches and those that use the concepts of support and/or empowerment. The latter focuses on the individual, whereas the former locates individuals within a social context in which they are understood to be connected to various agencies, organisations and systems, and from which in turn they have entitlements. Thus advocacy can be understood as including support/empowerment but extending beyond this. Definitions of advocacy include the following:

> Advocacy affords protection from abuse, assists in decision-making at transitional points, ensures that legal rights are observed, quality services received and preferences respected. (Killeen, 1996:11)

> [Case advocacy is] partisan intervention on behalf of an individual client or identified client group with one or more secondary institutions to secure or enhance a needed service, resource or entitlement. (Brandon, 1995:29)

The model offered by Southgate (cited in Brandon, 1995:9) of the five tasks of an advocate illustrates an approach to advocacy based on the development of partnership between advocate and client (see Box 1).

There is also considerable emphasis in some of the literature on the skills, stages, processes and techniques which advocacy requires. A composite of these is presented in box 2. This is not intended to be prescriptive, but rather illustrative, of the ways in which advocacy can be understood.

Box 2: Skills requirements, stages and techniques of advocacy

Interviewing:	To be able to listen, probe and elicit relevant information.
Assertiveness:	To be direct, honest and non-manipulative with clients, present their case forcefully, be persistent and resolute.
Negotiation:	To be creative and adaptable, whilst determined to achieve the best possible result.
Self-management:	Time management is important.
Legal research:	It is essential to be knowledgeable about rights and entitlements.
Litigation:	The last resort.

Stages of advocacy

1. Clarifying the problem.
2. Information gathering.
3. Legal research.
4. Interpretation and feedback to client.
5. Active negotiation and advocacy.
6. Litigation.

Techniques used:

- put everything in writing, keep a copy, give a copy to client;
- use a formal tone in negotiations;
- place an individual's problems within a wider picture;
- present complaining as positive, it offers an opportunity for improvement;
- ensure you have a good grasp of the facts;
- develop understanding of the relevant technical, procedural legal aspects; and
- where relevant use (or threaten to use) publicity as tool.

Distinct models of types of advocacy have been proposed (Dunning, 1995) Some of the most common are:

- 'citizen advocacy' whereby a volunteer acts as the advocate for an individual (usually with a disability) to ensure that their needs are met and that they are treated with respect;
- 'self advocacy' where individuals and groups act on their own behalf in pursuit of their own needs and interests;
- 'peer advocacy' in which members of disadvantaged social groups act as each others advocates;
- 'active advocacy' highlighting bad practice, whistleblowing; and

- 'principled advocacy' acting always from the interests and wishes of the client rather than an organisation/agency.

Within these variations two demarcations are common: self-advocacy and advocacy by others; individual/case and system/policy advocacy. The first tension represents, at least in the disability field, the desire for independence from supporters and taking more responsibility for, and power over, one's own life. The second key difference marks a distinction between advocating for an individual and a group/collective.

Advocacy and domestic violence

There are both similarities, and differences, in the outline of advocacy approaches above and the early principles developed in the refuge movement. Women's refuges developed internationally with a strong commitment to democratic and participative structures. Collectives frequently provided the organisational structure for the service, unlike the 'self-advocacy' movement which sought differentiation and autonomy from their institutional carers, the ambition was to make connections between women who used the service and those who provided it. Within feminist discourse, 'self-help' and the promotion of strategies for helping women to help themselves and each other were common aims. Self-advocacy or even advocacy by women's supporters were not terms which were used in relation to survivors of domestic violence at that time, and continued resistance to these terms is illustrated by this comment from an experienced Women's Aid worker interviewed for this study:

> *At some level, advocacy implies doing something on behalf of, or for another from a position of expertise or power. This is in the traditional legal sense and is really the opposite from the ideals we had, or have, for women leaving situations of domestic violence.*

The use of the word 'ideals' is significant here, since there is an argument that this perspective is over-optimistic about the extent to which women in crisis can be their own 'advocates' with a range of complex systems and organisations. The reality is that in many refuges, staff and volunteers have always acted as advocates, especially where the issues are complex or there is non-co-operation or hostility from the other organisations.

A different pattern in relation to the term advocacy is evident in the USA. During the 1990s, the use of the term advocacy became ubiquitous, to the extent that it is sometimes interchangeable with any work from an organisational base with women who have experienced domestic violence (Davies et al, 1998). Distinctions have been drawn between 'service-led advocacy' (fitting women into currently existing services), 'women centred advocacy' (allowing women to define their own needs for safety and the services they require), and 'policy advocacy' (directed at change which will benefit the group, rather than an individual) (Davies et al, 1998:3). Peled and Edelson (1994:295) studied 379 domestic violence projects that used advocacy. They expressed some surprise at the lack of policy advocacy, (which they term 'systems advocacy'), in light of the emphasis in the battered women's movement on the need for social change. They raise the question of whether women's services have become too close to the systems that they were attempting to change. However, findings from research in the UK on the Domestic Violence Matters project (DVM) (see later) raise questions about making too stark a distinction between case and policy advocacy.

Tensions and debates

In addition to the debate that surrounds advocating on behalf of someone else, there are a series of other issues referred to in the advocacy literature. Two are particularly relevant in relation to domestic violence: a) whether advocacy can be undertaken by workers within their own organisation and/ or statutory agencies; and b) the potential conflicts between advocacy and multi-agency working/partnerships.

Clearly many workers advocate at times on behalf of people they are working with; for example, social workers may ensure access to certain resources, refuge workers may negotiate benefit and housing entitlements and a range of workers may provide support and undertake the translation role with respect to legal proceedings. These all involve *taking the role* of advocate about specific issues, and in some cases (refuge workers in particular) involve *being an advocate* for an individual. The question that remains is what distinguishes these activities from what might be designated advocacy projects. The issue of *independence* is critical here, as advocates need to be willing to question and challenge the actions and inactions of all the agencies with which their client might be in contact. This connects directly to the second area of potential tension.

The ability of advocates to be effective in relation to individual cases, and system change, often turns on their ability and willingness, at all times and in whatever ways are necessary, to represent the interests of those they are advocating for. This may mean using strategies such as threats of adverse publicity or litigation. Statutory workers are far less likely, or even able, to use such strategies, and voluntary sector groups may be compromised in relation to their sources of funding, and current positive working relationships. Advocacy in its purest forms can, therefore, constitute a serious test of many of the comfortable representations and relationships that are accepted as necessary aspects of inter-agency working. It is the emphasis on rights and entitlements, alongside a recognition that negotiating with powerful organisations can be anything but empowering, which distinguishes advocacy from other more familiar concepts like support. Whilst aspects of advocating for individuals are evident in both the responses of some statutory and refuge groups, the adoption of advocacy as the core method of approach to domestic violence is a relative new form of provision.

Some of the most compelling arguments for advocacy projects include the following:

- systems are complex and intimidating;
- most people have limited skill, confidence and knowledge to advocate on their own behalf;
- some groups of people may be particularly disadvantaged, such as those with mental health problems, where there are language and cultural barriers and disabled people;
- empowerment is a process that takes time, many people need access to services and justice quickly, and advocacy means they are likely to get more, faster; and
- advocacy can make systems more accountable as advocates build knowledge of typical responses.

In short, recognition needs to be given to different forms of advocacy – individual advocacy and policy advocacy, though acknowledging the links between the two. Advocacy with domestic violence survivors can therefore occur through workers in a range of different locations – statutory, voluntary and independent organisations and within specific advocacy projects or within more generalist work with domestic violence survivors. However, it also needs to be acknowledged that in some cases there will be tensions and limitations to both individual and policy advocacy by workers within statutory and some voluntary organisations, and the on-going debate between self-advocacy and advocacy by others will continue.

Outreach

Outreach is a term used to describe domestic violence services extended to women, and sometimes children, based in their homes and communities. Outreach in the UK has two different aspects which can overlap: outreach to women who are currently living in, or moving out of violent relationships but not using a refuge; and re-settlement[3] support for women, and to a lesser extent their children, when they leave a refuge.

Interestingly, outreach is a term often juxtaposed with refuge or safe house provision that historically, has been the primary, domestic violence service in the UK. In the early seventies, when the second wave of feminism gained momentum, domestic violence was named as a significant cause of women's oppression and refuges in which women and children could hide from their violent abusers, the key service response. It is undoubtedly the case that refuges will remain a central and primary service. Consistently high homicide rates against women in situations of domestic violence and high levels of post-separation violence point to the importance of this provision. Similarly, the difficulties of rehousing and the significant support that refuges provide for women and children recovering from the terrors of being trapped in a situation of violence will continue to make refuge provision essential.

However, twenty-five years of refuge provision has shown that broader responses are also required. Firstly, many women and children for a wide variety of reasons do not access refuge provision when they are in situations of domestic violence. Secondly, women leaving the refuge to live in situations of poverty, isolation and hardship are vulnerable to either returning to violent partners or further abuse unless there is an added layer of support that assists them with the process of resettlement.

It is the refuge sector which has been most obviously involved in developing outreach, and the WAFE Agenda for Action (WAFE, 1998b) names outreach services as a priority need which requires on-going recognition and funding. Although not minimising the continued demand for the provision and adequate resourcing of safe houses, the document acknowledges the urgency of extending services which are accessible and supportive for women in their homes and communities. Naming outreach services has, in part, been a political move to acknowledge the broad range of services which are being provided by refuge based workers, who are not explicitly funded. Seventy-one percent of Women's Aid refuges in England and 88% in Wales, Scotland and Northern Ireland now offer outreach services (Humphreys et al, 2000). One of the earliest funded outreach projects we have discovered is Bristol Women's Aid, which gained funding in 1987 for an Asian women's outreach worker, since this group of women had not been using the refuge.

Nicola Harwin (WAFE national office: personal communication 1999a) regards a workshop by Ellen Pence from the DAIP, Duluth, Minnesota at Stirling in 1988 as a turning point. Here an integrated community based model of response to domestic violence was outlined in which outreach services were a significant component. These developments in the United States linked to the ideas and provision already becoming established in the UK provided further momentum and legitimacy for the development of these services.

Responses to the 1999 DETR research indicate that the terminology in this area is varied and changing. Respondents to the questionnaire focused on the importance of a public access point in the community; the absence of which was seen as a serious gap in local services. Respondents also associated the term 'outreach' with specific funded services whether they were helplines, women's advice service or drop-in centres. Definitions of outreach include the following:

> *Reaching out to women affected by domestic violence by responding to their defined needs whatever they might be. This means not necessarily in the traditional way through refuge provision, but extending to women in their homes and communities.* (Women's Aid Federation, England: interviewed 1999)

> *A key feature of outreach is the flexibility to meet women's needs... there are two main aspects to the job: support for women and children still in their homes, or women who have left the refuge and are re-housed locally.* (Bangor Women's Aid: interviewed 1999)

Given the developments in this area, and the emphasis in public policy on the importance of access to services, the lack of explicit reference to outreach provision in many recent policy and strategic planning documents, locally, nationally and internationally is surprising. For example, the key government document, *Living Without Fear: An Integrated Approach to Tackling Violence Against Women* (Cabinet Office, 1999), mentions outreach services, but only in the good practice guidelines provided by the organisations associated with refuge provision. An overview of the 17 domestic violence strategic plans for New South Wales, Australia found only two mentions of outreach, and both referred to services for rural women (New South Wales Strategy to Reduce Violence Against Women, regional plans 1998/99).

Several questions arise from this exploration: is this simply an issue of terminology? Or are outreach services for women and children in situations of domestic violence being over-looked? One way of approaching these questions is to explore the key features of outreach as described by workers interviewed for this chapter. These have been identified as follows:

- Accessible services based in communities, staffed by people who are specialists in domestic violence.
- Access to information and support as early as possible.
- Targeting groups of women who are hard to reach.
- Developing links to support and maintaining connections.
- Service users defining their own needs rather than provision being 'service led'.
- Active support in the community during separation or leaving a refuge.
- Pro-active methods are sometimes, though not always a feature.

When looked at in this light, it is clear that there are a range of services which could be designated as forms of outreach. Potentially, specialist telephone helplines, women's information and support services, drop-in centres or groups, 'one stop shops', and designated outreach projects contain a number of the features outlined above.

Creating accessible services and information

The most distinctive feature of outreach services, and one that unites a seemingly diverse range of activity, is the issue of accessibility. Survey figures suggest that between one in eight and one in ten women will have experienced domestic violence in the past year (Mooney, 1994; Dominy and Radford, 1996). The most comprehensive survey of disabled women undertaken in Canada showed that they were experiencing abuse at approximately the same prevalence rate as women without disabilities, though the duration of both physical and sexual abuse was significantly longer (Young et al, 1997). While very high numbers of women and children use refuges services each year (69,634 women and children accommodated in 1998/99)), this does not come close to matching the prevalence figures for the UK. This is particularly true for groups with special needs such as disabled women. Australian research suggests that only 10-20% of women in situations of domestic violence contact a police or crisis service (Robyn Holder, Victims of Crime Co-ordinator, Canberra, Australia: personal communication, 1999). Thus, very significant numbers of women are not accessing the most well known domestic violence intervention services.

Asian, African and Caribbean women were the first group who were recognised as not accessing refuge services. Black women's advocates as well as research evidence (Mama, 1989; Sen, 1998) outlined a complex array of reasons for the limited refuge use, including provision failing to recognise cultural differences, and the anticipation and/or experience of racism. Language barriers, poverty and isolation (often created by the abuser) compounded the problems for Black women in finding out about the range of options that might be available (Rai and Thiara, 1997). Responses to the additional needs of Asian, African and Caribbean women and children include specialist refuges, as well as the development of outreach services. Outreach to recent migrant women, including refugees and asylum seekers is less well developed.

As outreach services grew it became clear that leaving their community, or even their partners, was not an option many women necessarily identified as positive. For Asian women in particular the shame associated with separation affected not only the woman's standing within the community, but also that of her daughters whose prospects for marriage can be significantly affected by such a radical step (Imam, 1994). Similarly, the protection from racism, the family support, the ability to participate in particular cultural and spiritual practices, and the ease of being able to speak one's first language are significant reasons for women preferring to stay within their communities wherever possible. The added problems for recent arrivals of the 'one year rule'[4] in which women risk deportation if they leave a relationship, even a violent one, before they have been resident for a year also highlighted the problems in separation and moving to a refuge for migrant women. A UK study on the needs of ethnic minority women (Sen, 1998) concluded that their needs could best be met through a local outreach and advocacy project.

Similarly complex stories, which point to the need for more variation in the forms and content of services, can be traced to other groups of women and children, most particularly for women living in rural areas, disabled women, women with mental health difficulties, and those with drug/alcohol problems. Disabled women, for example, found themselves confronted with refuges, which, unlike their homes, were not specially adapted to their needs. Community-care services, sensitive care assistants, and group and individual support networks are not usually transferable to a refuge, or another area. These issues applied equally for women with a disabled child/children.

Other factors are now also coming into play that may also be significant for outreach provision. Twenty-five years of active work to bring the problems of domestic violence into the public domain, alongside perceptible shifts in the roles and the opportunities for agency available to many women has led to a changes in expectations. The idea that the offender should be the one to move, and that women and children are entitled to protection in their own homes has gained increased currency. Safety alarms, stronger civil and criminal legislation (The Family Law Act 1996, Part IV and the Protection From Harassment Act 1997), more active policing, offender programmes, are a few of the measures introduced to increase this possibility. Clearly, these strategies may have minimal effect in preventing domestic violence in cases where an offender is persistently violent and threatening. However, they are strategies unavailable until recently, and their effectiveness in preventing violence, and allowing domestic violence survivors to follow less disruptive routes out of violence are yet to be evaluated.

The tasks and skills of the outreach worker

The range of roles and skills entailed in outreach work parallel the discussion of the diverse activities involved in advocacy work. Work with individual women is frequently the key demand both in re-settlement work and supporting women living in, or leaving situations domestic violence. This need is well established and evaluated very positively by the women (Humphreys, 2000). However, a problem mentioned by all outreach workers who were consulted, lay in finding a balance between individual work and more broadly based community development, group work, prevention and training.

Many outreach projects in the UK have only one part-time worker. When the need for services is high, there is clearly pressure to undertake work that will create maximum impact with minimal resources. While there are some clear patterns emerging particularly in re-settlement work, there is a much greater variation in local service priorities. The service development required to reach Asian women may be very different from that for rural women, young women, older women or disabled women.

A particular response, consistent across several projects is to use the resource of the outreach worker to train volunteers who can then participate in the provision of a service. South Devon Women's Aid provides a particularly well developed example of this model, with two co-ordinators allocating a significant amount of their time to training volunteers to provide a help-line service in this area. Other local factors may be of particular significance. For instance some areas have skilled, inter-agency trainers who can mainstream awareness and skills into professional networks including health visitors, interpreters, police, GPs, social workers, housing officers and court welfare officers. This training is an attempt to ensure that women and children are offered sensitive, informed and responsive services whichever agency they initially contact. Where experienced trainers are not available, outreach workers may define training as one of their service priorities. A similar case can be made for drop–in groups, local prevention, and the provisions developed by children's charities in a few areas (for example, The Children's Society, Wylie Birch Park in Birmingham, and the Wellingborough NSPCC).

While there is a strength in outreach work responding flexibly to local needs, there is a danger of the role becoming diffuse, in an attempt to fill all the gaps in provision that are identified locally. There seems to be a role here for more strategic planning in establishing priorities; there are a few examples in the UK of this (Leeds Inter-Agency Project in Leeds, Hammersmith and Fulham Domestic Violence Forum and at national level, the Scottish Partnership on Domestic Violence). In Australia, the New South Wales Reducing Violence Against Women Strategy also has a well developed model. The limited research and evaluative knowledge base on outreach remains a barrier, not only to informed strategic planning, but also assessing the crime reduction potentials of particular strategies, and the best value for scarce resources.

Outreach and advocacy in context

The demand for advocacy and outreach work with women and children experiencing domestic violence has been created by a complex set of factors. Superficially, some of these factors are contradictory. However, closer exploration shows that they reflect the diversity of survivors and their circumstances, an issue that highlights the need for a wide range of flexible services.

The rationale for advocacy and outreach responses can be summarized as including:

- Research and practice show that leaving a violent and abusive relationship is both logistically and emotionally complex, not to mention dangerous (Kirkwood, 1993; Hoff, 1990).
- As more women have greater personal and material resources, they are demanding their right to be protected within their communities and that more effective crime reduction responses are found which disrupt the lives of the perpetrator, rather than the victims (Davies et al, 1998).
- The level of losses, and sometimes abuse that, in particular, ethnic minority women and children (Iman, 1994) and disabled women may experience if they re-locate, or move to a refuge.
- Recent changes in legislation and policing which may provide viable protection from domestic violence that was not previously available.
- Negotiating legal systems, benefit entitlement, housing services, health and welfare systems is increasingly complex.
- Many domestic violence survivors (women with mental health or drug/alcohol problems, women with older male children, men, disabled women with specialist needs) are not eligible, or able, to be well supported in a communal refuge.
- The ability of women and children to hide from their abusers has become increasingly difficult as 'seek and find' orders, nationally computerised records, and court ordered child contact make 'disappearing' into a refuge and then a secret location a less effective strategy than hitherto.

Advocacy in practice

In this section our focus is projects that have been evaluated which use advocacy as their framework for intervention. There are two from the UK that use versions of pro-active advocacy - Domestic Violence Matters (Kelly, 1999) and the Domestic Violence Intervention Project (Burton et al, 1998). The advocacy service that comprises a core element in the recently established Hammersmith and Fulham co-ordinated community response pilot project, Standing Together, draws on the lessons from both these projects. Southall Black Sisters are a UK example of a project that explicitly and successfully combines case and system advocacy.

Two demonstration projects

Domestic Violence Matters (DVM) was a unique, three-year demonstration project funded by the Home Office Programme Development Unit. It involved siting a team of four civilian workers and a co-ordinator in a police station, providing a service 16 hours a day, seven days a week. It used crisis intervention case advocacy[5] as its key method of work.

The project had five key aims:

- to establish the fundamental principle in the local area that domestic violence is a crime;
- to follow up police responses;
- to contact all victims within 24 hours of the call to the police;
- to use immediate crisis intervention to decrease repeat calls and increase the likelihood of referrals to other agencies being taken up; and
- to improve communication and increase the immediate and effective response of all agencies in the borough to domestic violence.

During the 32 months of service provision covered by the evaluation DVM supported 1,236 victims in relation to 1,542 incidents. A third of police calls and DVM cases involved women who were already separated from the violent partner; further confirmation that leaving does not ensure safety.

One of the key differences between DVM and other services was their 'out of hours' availability: two-thirds of referrals took place out of office hours. A swift contact was considered imperative, as it is at the point of crisis that change is most possible. The workers made contact within 24 hours in 90% of cases, and over a third of first contacts took place immediately following an incident. The significance of this was confirmed by service users, many of whom noted that this was the most important factor enabling them to take actions which increased their safety and accelerated the process of change. The closer the intervention was to the original model (offering support after an incident and acting as a temporary advocate) the more likely it was to accelerate the process of change, including ending relationships and proceeding with legal action.

DVM was successful in decreasing repeat calls to the police, and by inference repeat victimisation. Within the pre-DVM data (covering a six month period) 22% of victims made a repeat call, and 11% made three or more. The DVM data covers a period five times longer, 33% made a repeat call, 15% three or more, and the proportion making six or more calls is the same for each data set. There was also evidence of decreasing repeat calls as the project developed: the evaluation questionnaires for women returned in the first year revealed 66% had called the police before, whereas this had decreased to 40% in the final year.

The pro-active and case advocacy approach enabled a significant number of women to create safety for themselves and their children. One element that contributed to this was DVM's advocacy role in making effective and co-ordinated referrals. Over two-thirds (70%) of the service users had never approached a formal agency other than the police, and of the remaining 30%, half had only made one such approach. Thus DVM created new access to services - these ranged from refuges and local authority housing departments, through specialist firms of solicitors to support and counselling groups. Referral was always tailored to the needs of the woman, and the stage she was at in dealing with the violence; altogether over 70 statutory and voluntary agencies were used as referral points, but 30 were used regularly. The case advocacy method prompted change more generally in other local agencies; two-thirds of the agency workers interviewed at the end of the pilot reported that they thought DVM had made a difference to local responses. This was achieved in two ways: through an insistence that DVM clients got swift and appropriate responses to their entitlements; and by co-ordination of linked and appropriate referrals. For example one housing worker commented: 'It hasn't changed our policies, but it has affected our attitudes and encouraged a more co-ordinated approach and liaison'.

One of the key lessons from DVM was that pro-active responses were welcomed by service users, as was the uncompromising focus on violence and safety. What women defined as helpful were clear messages that: abuse/violence was not acceptable; they were not to blame; and that they had a right to lives free of violence.

The majority of DVM's users (90%) thought domestic violence should always be treated as a crime. However, the project also confirmed that 'pro law enforcement' orientations need to be backed up by appropriate support and effective protection if they are to be translated into an increase in prosecutions.

The Domestic Violence Intervention Project (DVIP) was the first voluntary sector project in England to work with domestic violence perpetrators. It used a model that combines an education programme for violent men (Violence Prevention Programme, VPP) with pro-active responses and advocacy with partners (Women's Support Service, WSS, which also provided support to any woman who contacted the service). Drawing on the emerging international literature on work with perpetrators of domestic violence a linked advocacy project with partners was considered an integral and necessary part of the project because:

- men's involvement in a programme has been found to be the most significant factor affecting women's decisions not to leave violent relationships;
- where programmes have no direct contact with partners some men deliberately misinform their partners about the programme content, their attendance, and other significant matters; and,

- without contact with partners there is no external validity check on men's claims that they have not used violence.

WSS, at the time of the evaluation, was staffed by two part-time workers and a group of volunteers. The services offered were: telephone advice and support (including out of hours evening calls); short term problem-solving counselling; support groups; and advocacy with other organisations. The pro-active contacting of current and ex partners of men on the programme could also be seen as a form of outreach. The advocacy elements involved intervening for women in relation to legal cases (both criminal prosecutions and civil matters), housing and accommodation, and frequently with respect to post-separation abuse in the context of contact arrangements.

Over two years, with a small resource base, WSS was in contact with 796 women. A third were partners of men on the VPP programme, the majority made contact independently. WSS was effective in reaching women from ethnic minorities and women with professional qualifications, two groups which currently under-use other forms of provision. The pro-active aspects of the service had several elements:

- the project made initial contact with women whose partners are on VPP;
- for all women WSS was persistent about making and continuing contact (this could involve making numerous telephone calls and/or following women up at regular intervals); and,
- the model used was goal oriented and directive crisis intervention, using a strategy called 'safety planning'. This tool aims to enable women to move from reacting to events as they happen, to anticipating and planning ahead (see later section for more detailed description). This could be defined as enabling a form of self-advocacy.

In assessing 'what works' in the WSS approach and why, there is no simple answer, other than that the service is flexible enough to respond to the particular and changing nature of each woman's needs. What made a difference for women, therefore, varied. For some it was that there was a place where their sense of victimisation was validated, for others that there was a single location where they could access advice and support, and still others found solutions to what had appeared intractable problems through WSS's advocacy on their behalf. What was also evident was that many women benefited from the combination of possible forms of support and intervention which WSS made available, with support groups being thought the most effective in combating the shame, self-blame and the destruction of self-belief which strongly inhibit women's attempts to end violence.

Both evaluations made clear that rather than resenting pro-active interventions, women living with domestic violence welcomed an outsider making the first move, and saw the offer of support as enabling them to make changes sooner and/or more definitely than they would have done otherwise. The potential of pro-active work is that through earlier intervention some women and children will suffer less violence and fewer consequences. In other words that they reduce the extent of repeat victimisation which is so commonly a feature of domestic violence. It is also worth noting that both projects worked with relatively large numbers of women compared to other forms of specialist provision, such as refuges.

There are other implications that can be drawn from these projects. Pro-active advocacy projects such as DVM and WSS combine a 'one stop' location for information, advice and co-ordination of responses with an interventionist pro-active response to recent incidents of violence. For many women this speeds resolution, and decreases the 'lottery' aspect of agency response, with chance and luck being replaced by more considered and connected responses. The positive evaluation of both projects by service users is food for thought for localities considering some form of 'one stop shop' provision[6]. Other chapters in this volume point to some of the things that we do know about the extent of domestic violence, including its frequency, the risks and costs involved and the missed opportunities in agency responses. Drawing on this work and our own for this chapter, it is our view that independent, well resourced advocacy and outreach projects have much potential. They may, in fact, prove more effective than many of the proposed models for 'one stop shops' which site workers from a range of statutory organisations in one central location. Our argument is based on the fact that advocacy projects are flexible and can design 'packages' of provision based on women's current and changing needs, which combine advice, support (including support groups and out of hours telephone contact), coordination and advocacy (intervention on their behalf with agencies).

The DVM evaluation also raised interesting questions about the distinction made in much of the literature between case and systems/policy advocacy. A local advocacy project that has a substantial caseload means that there are regular and recurring contacts with the same agencies/workers. In using assertiveness to ensure that women receive their entitlements, local practices changed, becoming more consistent and in keeping with general policy frameworks. Thus case advocacy can have a direct influence on the implementation of policy. It may also serve the function of highlighting gaps in local policy and provision.

Southall Black Sisters

The work of Southall Black Sisters over two decades demonstrates the connections between case and policy advocacy even more powerfully.

Established in 1979, SBS provides a comprehensive and holistic service to Asian and African-Caribbean women. Responses include crisis intervention, casework (case advocacy), and campaigning locally and nationally (system/policy advocacy). The resource centre provides: information, advice, support (including groups), counselling and advocacy on a range of forms of violence against women and their connections to racism, immigration and asylum, children's welfare, and mental health issues.

The most recent example of 'system/policy' advocacy undertaken by SBS has been their campaign against the 'one year rule', which effectively denied migrant women the same protections against domestic violence as other residents in the UK. Persistence over many years, in the face of extreme reluctance by governments to consider changes in the vexed area of immigration, resulted in June 1999 of an announcement that new guidelines were to be issued. These increased the rights of migrant women to protection, justice and support when they were facing domestic violence. The requirements that women be able to provide some kind of evidence, such as police or doctor's reports, to prove violence, means that not all women are able to avail themselves of the new provisions.

Advocacy projects in other jurisdictions

There are also examples of advocacy projects in other jurisdictions, which have direct links to the criminal and civil justice systems and which link child protection, domestic violence and health provision. One of these is the New South Wales Domestic Violence Court Assistance Scheme

The Women's Domestic Violence Court Assistance Scheme, New South Wales, Australia (WDVCAP) began in 1996 with an allocation of recurrent funding of $1.5 m for court assistance schemes. This provides women and their children with support, advocacy, referral and information and facilitates their access to appropriate legal representation with the aim of using the justice system to end the violence they are experiencing. By 1995, there were 35 schemes in New South Wales. Secure funding is now available for 16 schemes based in the courts handling the highest numbers of protection orders. An evaluation of the programme (Bradfield and Nyland, 1998) shows that it has met with high levels of success. The programme successfully assisted 16,000 women in its first year of operation; the majority of clients gained a protection order (Apprehended Domestic Violence Order) or interim order. Only 2.4% of clients had applications dismissed or denied, and only 8% of clients withdrew applications. Almost all (97%) clients surveyed reported that the court support scheme made a positive difference to their situation.

Humphreys and Kaye (1997) carried out an evaluation of third party applications for Protection Orders in Australia. Australian jurisdictions allow police to act as third party applicants for protection orders on behalf of women and children experiencing domestic violence. This practice is particularly well developed in Queensland (39% of applications between 1989-1996) and New South Wales (52% in 1995). It is a particular advocacy process that takes the burden of making the application and taking it through the court, away from the woman, although she is still required to be present at court and to give evidence if required. The evaluation which involved semi-structured interviews with more than 50 people from 28 organisations was overwhelmingly positive about the benefits for women and children involved in this process.

Outreach services: an audit and assessment

In this section we will discuss current provisions and explore what these projects 'add' to domestic violence responses. There will be two main emphases; outreach, which seeks to make contact with women and draw them into supportive networks, and outreach which, seeks to support women post-separation. A range of creative projects is developing to provide accessible points of contact for domestic violence survivors. A recent mapping exercise showed that they provided a service for more than a quarter of a million women (*n*=262,279) in 1999 (Humphreys et al, 2000). A number of other service initiatives will be discussed: the use of helplines, outreach services for Black and Asian women and re-settlement provision.

Helplines

Helplines are proving to be a key outreach initiative. High rates of usage and demand which exceeds the ability to resource the line (shown by BT records of attempted calls) suggests that this is an area in which resources can be effectively extended to increase access. There are several national lines (Women's Aid National Domestic Violence Helpline, Refuge 24 Hour National Crisis Line, Victim Supportline and Childline) as well as local helplines (e.g. South Devon Women's Aid). Many local women's refuges actually provide helpline support through their refuge public phone lines and the 24-hour on-call service that they provide. However, this work is generally unresourced and part of the 'invisible' work undertaken by refuge workers.

Women's Aid National Domestic Violence Helpline

This national helpline received 20,000 calls in 1998 (100,000 attempted calls as recorded by BT). 1999 showed an increase in calls between January – June. A third phone line and increased publicity on domestic violence may account for this increase. From July 1999 the phone line was open on the weekends. The helpline is resourced through paid staff and volunteers and provides access to a wide range of information and support. The use of volunteers and the huge demand on the line suggests a very effective use of limited resources (Cabinet Office, 1999).

Helplines and children

Children are also using helplines to voice their concerns about domestic violence, for example children and young people are constantly ringing ChildLine, the national helpline for children, to report the problems that they encounter (115,146 'first time callers' in 1997/98). Of these calls there were 2300 children and young people who talked about domestic violence. Of this group, 38% reported that they had been physically assaulted as well and a further 8% reported sexual abuse. Most of the violence they reported (84%) was violence towards their mothers by a male partner or ex-partner. Only 4% reported that it was violence by mothers or stepmothers towards a male partner or ex-partner (McCleod, 1998).

Community based services

Creating accessible community based services, often using already existing fora or meeting points for women has been a key strategy and one pioneered by Black and Asian women. It is now being more widely used as a general outreach strategy. One example of this is Newham Action Against Domestic Violence (NAADV). NAADV actively works to provide access to information, advice, support and advocacy at points where women and children are already using other services. Outreach workers, including children's workers attend women's support groups, several drop-in centres in different parts of the borough, the community centre, the council 'one-stop shop', and schools. The project is also actively involved in training other professionals about domestic violence and children.

Creating accessible points in the community has stemmed from the recognition that particular groups of women are not accessing refuge services and that other forms of provision are required to meet their need for information, advocacy and support in relation to domestic violence.

Re-settlement services

> They shouldn't have a refuge without an outreach service - it is that simple
>
> It is about getting a normal life back. I couldn't have done without it. Without outreach I would have had nothing. I didn't have to start from Square 1.
> *(Comments from participants in an evaluation of an outreach project)*

Re-settlement support for women leaving refuges has been identified as a need from the outset of safe house provision. Refuge workers quickly became aware of the 'revolving door' which involved women leaving a violent relationship, making attempts at re-settlement, returning to the relationship where the crimes against her continue and then returning to the refuge. This is a disruptive and expensive process for the women and children involved. Women and children have particular vulnerabilities in the re-settlement period, these include:

- Poverty associated not only with being a single mother, but having to start again from scratch buying household furniture, appliances, curtains, clothes, and children's toys.
- Isolation and loneliness connected with leaving a partner, networks of families and friends to live in areas in which they know no-one and have no immediate avenues of support.
- Fear, anxiety and health problems for women and their children who may be accommodated in poor housing stock on estates with high rates of crime, and/or as a consequence of ongoing harassment and abuse from the perpetrator.
- Pressures from ex-partners (and sometimes also family members) to return using either promises of reform or intimidation through post-separation violence.
- Pressures from children who wish to return to their homes, previous school and communities.
- Problems of racism for Black and ethnic minority women moving onto predominantly white housing estates.
- Overwhelming problems negotiating government bureaucracies (housing, benefits agencies, social services and legal systems).

In response to these vulnerabilities refuge workers have often continued to offer a range of assistance to women when they leave the refuge as a means of 'adding value' to the refuge provision for women and children

Milton Keynes Women's Aid has undertaken a consultation and evaluation of the re-settlement aspect of its outreach service currently provided by one part-time worker. There are a number of elements within the forms of support and assistance identified by women. These are considered typical of this kind of outreach work (Humphreys, 2000).

- Facilitating contact and support networks with other ex-residents.
- Confidence building and assertiveness training.
- Individual support.
- A leisure activity programme for women and children.
- Information on local services, training and courses [7].
- Material and practical assistance, such as second hand furniture,

clothes, toys, DIY assistance and charity applications.
- Advocacy in relation to the legal process.
- Christmas hamper and gifts.
- Drop-in group.
- Moving on to be a volunteer and helping other women and children.

Women consistently reported the most valuable aspect of the service was the individual support from the outreach worker and many said that they would have returned to violent relationships without her support. However, all aspects of the service were highly valued by a proportion of the women service-users consulted. Some services in the UK provide a drop-in centre facility, however, over a two-year period when this service was provided at Milton Keynes it was under-utilised and time consuming. The telephone line contact to the outreach worker is now being used more successfully for flexible contact and support.

Outreach services for children

Outreach services for children are relatively underdeveloped, yet this was the most important service priority the Milton Keynes participants identified. As a direct result of this Milton Keynes Women's Aid successfully applied to the National Lottery for a children's outreach worker, and several other groups are moving in this direction. The Children's Society through its project at Wylie Park provides a well-developed model for outreach with children. Similar gaps were noted by women with children in both the DVM and DVIP evaluations.

While there is evidence of the development of outreach services both for women and to a lesser extent to children, this work is still in the early stages of development in the UK and many areas lack even minimal provision. Moreover, most outreach projects have only insecure, short-term funding from the Lottery Board – a factor which will continue to place this essential service on the margin of domestic violence responses.

Pro-active responses and safety planning

One of the connections between advocacy and outreach responses is that they both tend to draw on the practices of pro-activity and safety planning. These are outlined in some detail as they provide a means through which advocacy and outreach responses can be mainstreamed into the work of organisations that work with domestic violence survivors. This can include workers within statutory agencies (police, social services, housing) as well as workers within the voluntary sector.

Whilst concerns have been expressed by some women's organisations about whether pro-activity undercuts women's self-determination, the assessments of women in the DVIP and DVM projects point to a number of positive contributions:

- someone else takes responsibility for naming the violence;
- the first contact can be one in which belief is established very quickly; and
- women can be invited into a support network at a much earlier point than they might otherwise choose.

Both DVM and DVIP have outlined some aspects of pro-active approaches within the UK. Buzawa and Buzawa (1996) identify further examples of ways in which pro-active responses have been used in justice system responses in the USA.

Police departments in Pennsylvania have instituted a follow up system, making phone or house calls the day after a reported incident. They conduct further investigation into the history of violence, and explore issues with respect to bail applications, and clarify current legal options. Women are provided with a named contact, and a safe contact point for her is agreed. Assessment of the scheme concludes it

> enables battered women to learn about legal options and community services in a context that is supportive, fosters an exchange of information, and engages a battered woman in critical thinking about safety strategies. Outreach thus often facilitates victim participation in, and commitment to, the criminal justice process. (p.106)

Some prosecutors' offices use pro-active contact to inform women about the outcomes of first hearings and their rights. This encourages dialogue and an early relationship in prosecution process and facilitates linking criminal with civil remedies and other support services. It also often has the spin off of substantially increasing prosecutor's information about the reported crime.

Some areas have established victim-witness clinics, linked to prosecutors and/or courts. They ensure that women have information on the legal system, and how to think about their own danger. They are intended to ensure that victims are effective witnesses. Some include support groups or networks with other victims which decrease isolation, a factor which is considered significant in withdrawals. Some also pro-actively advocate with/educate family, friends and employers to encourage them to support her 'safe participation in the Criminal Justice System'. Such specialist and targeted services have improved the rate of successful prosecutions (p108), and resulted in a range of new and creative strategies for 'victim engagement'.

Table 1
Safety strategies routinely used by women

Form	Self	Children
Protection strategies	Fleeing Seeking intervention by others Self-defence	Sending them somewhere else Sleeping in their room Feeding and putting to bed early Not leaving them alone with him Increasing outside activities
Staying strategies	Getting a job Increasing outside activities Doing self-defence, fitness Seeking solace in religion Calling a helpline Having therapy Keeping him sweet Maintaining a friendship network Not involving family Developing complex ways keeping in touch with kin	As above
Separation strategies	Planning Setting goals Obtaining a protection order	

(*Davies et al*, 1998)

Safety planning

Safety planning is a relative new concept in the UK, and should be contrasted to conventional models of risk assessment, which tend to be conducted by someone else from a position of professional expertise. In this section we outline the basic philosophy and methods of safety planning, drawing on a recent book (Davies et al, 1998) since it underpins much of the provision we have highlighted as current good practice.

The orientation for using safety planning is termed 'women-defined advocacy', which acknowledges and builds on women's perceptions and responses and 'seeks to craft alternatives that will enhance women's safety' (p.4), in the context of the limitations and realities of women's lives. There is a strong critique of the new stereotypes of abused women and their needs, which have in turn been based on over-generalizations and reduced to service categories, such as safe accommodation or a 'one stop shop'. One consequence of this has been the loss of the unique context and subjectivity of each woman.

> Quick fixes and one-size-fits-all solutions will be replaced by long-term strategies more responsive to the diversity and complexity of each battered woman's needs. These strategies will provide battered women with better options. (p.165).

The basis of safety planning is to explore in detail with women the risks they and their children may be facing. Table 1 (above) outlines the kinds of safety strategies women are most likely to use in relation to protecting themselves, deciding to stay in the relationship and leaving. A women's advocate works alongside the woman to ascertain the range of options she is currently using or could explore using in the future. These are not, and need not be confined to strategies for separating.

The key to successful safety planning is to build a partnership between the woman and the advocate. It then becomes possible to combine two perspectives, two sets of information and knowledge with the explicit goal of decreasing risk. Whilst most abused women are not killed by their abuser, it is important to address life threatening risks, and where this is an explicit concern 'enhanced advocacy' will be needed. One such model for assessing the increased risk of lethality (and therefore the need for enhanced advocacy) posits that each of the following factors is connected to increased risk of lethal violence. The more of them that are present the greater the risk.

- presence of guns (increases risk by eight times)
- previous use of a weapon
- threats with weapons
- threats to kill
- previous serious injury
- threats of suicide by the man
- drug or alcohol misuse by the man
- forced sex
- obsessiveness/extreme jealousy or dominance
  (Campbell, 1995)

A number of additional factors are used by Pennsylvania Coalition Against Domestic Violence:

- centrality of woman to abuser's life, is he isolated?;
- depression in the offender;
- repeated intervention by law enforcement;
- escalation of risk taking;
- separation by the woman; and
- hostage taking.

Davies et al conclude that consistent use of safety planning results in a different perception by professionals of women suffering domestic violence,

Box 3: The process of safety planning

1. Begin to build partnership.
2. Review her current risk analysis. Pay particular attention to
   - life threatening violence
   - risks to children.
3. Work to improve her safety planning:
   - identify options and resources
   - analyse together how each might affect her risk with her
   - develop and implement a revised plan
   - provide enhanced advocacy when needed.
4. Enhanced advocacy (means doing more):
   - make more time
   - ensure more frequent contact
   - make more follow up calls
   - find immediate protection strategies
   - encourage systems to respond quickly
   - make referrals for her to ensure a positive response
   - make safety plans with children.

(Davies et al, 1998)

and different relationships between them and workers/advocates.

The process involved in safety planning is outlined in box 3 above.

The Connecticut model is one example of how safety planning is being used in the US. There, mandatory arrest was introduced in 1985. This legal reform was more comprehensive than many in other areas of the USA, and included the creation of Family Violence Victim Advocate (FVVA) posts.

Evaluation revealed that half of the FVVAs made distinctions between what battered women wanted and what they 'really' needed. It became clear that it was the legal system, and what it had to offer, which was defining responses, rather than them being fitted to women's needs. What women said they wanted was more support and understanding. The advocacy model was adapted following the evaluation, using safety planning as the primary form of action. The basic framework became:

- understand her perspective;
- assess risk;
- build on the woman's plan; and
- review and implement.

Subsequent training expanded and developed the model, and it has increased the number of re-contacts with the service. Later training increased emphasis on advocates having to 'let go' of feeling responsible for women's safety.

A number of commentators argue (see for example Davies et al, 1998; Buzawa and Buzawa, 1996) that if criminal justice responses focus on women's safety they are likely to be more effective.

Making a difference: The relevance of advocacy and outreach to crime reduction

Outreach and advocacy combined with the key elements of safety planning and pro-active responses to domestic violence can add value to existing provision by making responses more effective. Current estimates are that women experience between 20-35 incidents of domestic violence before seeking help (Dobash and Dobash, 1979; Kelly, 1999.) Outreach and advocacy services that can decrease this figure have strong crime reduction potential. Effectiveness as a crime reduction strategy lies in the following areas:

- preventing repeat victimisation;
- earlier intervention which may prevent lengthy histories of domestic crime; and
- more effective intervention which is 'in tune' with the woman's needs and priorities.

This section will summarise key aspects of work in this area. It will also suggest that whilst there is a strong research base on domestic violence in the UK, some areas have been under-explored, and new questions have arisen as policy and practice changes have come on stream. There are several research areas, therefore, which would merit attention.

Advocacy and outreach programmes to prevent repeat victimisation

Innovative projects in the UK and overseas have shown that advocacy and outreach projects can minimise repeat victimisation.

A variety of forms of advocacy interventions make the use of the criminal and civil justice systems both more effective and more responsive to women's needs and experiences. This reduces expenditure on investigations and case preparation by police and CPS where there was no prosecution, and civil justice costs for protection orders where applications are either withdrawn or the order made void because women succumb to pressure to reconcile. There is also the possibility that resoluteness on both the woman's part and the justice system may operate as an increased level of deterrent with regard to further assaults. In the case of protection orders it would be an important component to use pro-active contact to ensure that breaches are reported and dealt with.

Court advocacy schemes in particular, aim to support domestic violence survivors in gaining effective civil remedies to prevent further violence and to allow more rapid police and legal intervention should violence continue. The figures from the NSW Domestic Violence Court Assistance Scheme suggest that with relatively limited resources (one medium size court support service costs approximately $36,000/£18,000) that there were very high rates of success in gaining appropriate orders, few withdrawals and high satisfaction expressed by clients surveyed. The pro-active use by police of third party applications in conjunction with these court assistance schemes has also been an element in streamlining the advocacy process and access to civil protection. Evaluating the effectiveness of advocacy within the developing UK court assistance schemes (and the development of further schemes) under the current Family Law Act (1996) and the Protection From Harassment Act (1997) are areas for future research.

Outreach re-settlement support is also an area where attempts are being made to prevent re-victimisation. Support for women when they are initially re-housed either through a refuge, or when leaving a violent relationship potentially adds value to previous intervention. Many of the women interviewed in outreach projects said that without the support of the outreach worker that they would have returned to the previously violent relationship (Humphreys and Thiara, forthcoming). The cost benefit of an outreach worker could be evaluated. Stanko et al (1998) examined the costs per service sector (police, GP, health visitors, accident and emergency, refuges, social services, civil justice and housing) for a borough. Evaluating both the crime reduction potential and the cost benefit of a resettlement worker may necessitate a more individualised approach – tracing retrospectively the costs of violence and relocation incurred by a group of women and children, comparing those who did and did not have access to resettlement support.

Early intervention

Earlier intervention that may prevent lengthy histories of domestic violence is a key element in crime reduction. The creation of easily accessible points where domestic violence survivors can be assured of information, support, and advocacy are an important aspect of this strategy (see Domestic Violence Matters and the Domestic Violence Intervention Project).

Whilst inter-agency work has been mapped, there is a dearth of evidence about how far local networks are involved in the following:

- strategic planning;
- working together to fill gaps in local provision; and

- how these activities are, and are not, connected to government policy, especially crime audits and crime reduction strategies and the Women's Unit recommendation that integrated approaches to all forms of violence against women are developed.

Although we now have a better sense of the parameters of outreach work, there has been minimal evaluation of the various models and patterns of provision, particularly in relation to strategic planning. A research project that explored in more depth the process of ending violence would inform further work on advocacy and outreach. This would seek to establish and understand:

- how the relationship shifts and changes;
- the connections with help-seeking;
- the timing of contact with various services (for example, are women making contact earlier than previous research suggests);
- the precise ways in which interventions are and are not helpful;
- whether women want solutions which enable them to remain in the family home and if so what factors enable or inhibit this; and
- post-separation violence.

Tuning interventions to women's needs

Women-centred advocacy and safety planning which focuses upon the joint pooling of information between advocate and domestic violence survivor may also bring both cost savings and crime reduction. Women who are prematurely pressured into legal action, refuges or rehousing frequently return to their partners. A more sensitive, less service-led approach to the range of options may provide more effective long-term strategies. Particular attention could be given to women at the point of separation where research tells us that the risks of violence are highest (Wilson and Daly, 1996; Kelly, 1999). A project which focused on safety planning and the development of interagency 'safety packages', much in the way a child care plan or community care package is negotiated may provide an effective way forward in this area.

New wine in old bottles?

In answering the question with which we began this piece of work, we find ourselves having to say 'yes' and 'no'. 'Yes', in the sense that elements of outreach and advocacy can be tracked back throughout the history of refuge provision. 'No', in so far as the kinds of projects and forms of provision we have outlined in this chapter do represent innovative practice. Many of the examples cited in this chapter reveal more strategic, targeted interventions, which draw directly on what we have discovered over the last two decades. They include what women value and rate as effective, the barriers to seeking help and the points where support is most relevant (Gevers, 1996; Kelly, 1999; Sen, 1998). Safety planning and pro-activity are approaches which focus explicitly on violence, giving a clear message that this is taken seriously, it is not 'just a domestic', and that women and children's safety is a priority. Issues of safety planning resonate with many aspects of feminist 'self help' and support found amongst women's refuge workers, and women-centred counsellors. However, the partnership in the systematic analysis of risk, the lack of presumption about the 'best and safest options' for a woman and her children and the drawing from a 'rights based focus', all provide new 'edges' to old practices.

Outreach and advocacy through their flexible approaches, variously and in combination, are able to accommodate, respond to, and take account of the following issues.

- Ending a relationship is a process. Before it can be contemplated women need the space and opportunity to name violence, allocate responsibility to the abuser, and reassess the relationship in this light.
- Ensuring access to services requires paying attention to both differences between groups of women, and individual differences in terms of preferred solutions.
- Separation is not a panacea.
- Leaving a violent partner involves taking risks and involves material, social and emotional costs.
- Criminal and civil justice processes are more effective with specialist support and advocacy.
- The break down of resettlement is often linked to the absence of support.

Through the process of conducting this review, and what we have learnt from previous research, it is possible to highlight several key intervention points in domestic violence and the kinds of intervention/services which are most relevant to outreach and advocacy approaches. These are outlined overleaf.

Pro-active outreach and advocacy strategies provide opportunities for interventions which are timely, and appropriate, and which facilitate access to services and support for currently under-served groups. Taking services to women, rather than waiting until they discover them, offers the possibility of early intervention. Many of the outreach services provided by refuges are also focused on resettlement, continuing to provide support after women and children have left refuges, thus addressing the issue of isolation which some women have identified as a critical factor in their decision to return to a violent partner.

There is also an emerging argument that these forms of provision may be more effective in reaching certain groups of women, some of whom have additional needs and/or specific vulnerabilities. They include Black and ethnic minority women; disabled women; women in the sex industry; women living in rural areas and professional women. The evidence we currently have also suggests that outreach and advocacy projects are 'cost-effective' in that they work with relatively large numbers of cases compared to other forms of specialist provision.

The systematic development of outreach and advocacy projects and widespread recognition that they are essential rather than marginal to responses to domestic violence is still to occur in the UK. Nevertheless, the development of new projects and the incorporation of outreach and advocacy responses into the mainstream of organisations which are in contact with domestic violence survivors represents both recognition and a steady broadening of the range of service provision required in this area – more wine and more bottles!

Intervention Point	Key Needs and Provision
First contact/ early intervention	Space to define and understand violence Break isolation and self-blame *Appropriate provision:* Helplines Drop-in/Women's centres Support groups Targeted outreach programmes
Involvement of legal process	Support for decision to take action Prioritising protection Information and advice *Appropriate provision:* Advocacy projects Court/witness assistance Safety planning Pro-active follow up
Separation	Advice and information Protection *Appropriate provision:* Advocacy projects Refuge/safe houses Safety planning and risk assessment Pro-active follow up Support groups
Re-settlement	Practical and emotional support Support for children Social networking Advice and information *Appropriate provision:* Re-settlement outreach (including advocacy) Support groups Outreach with children

Notes

1. We use the terms victims and women and children interchangeably in this chapter. We are, however, aware that a small proportion of domestic violence involves men as victims, and that it occurs in same sex relationships.
2. In fact much of the evaluative work has been conducted by the authors themselves
3. Frequently, the word 'aftercare' is used for forms of post-refuge support. However, in this chapter we are using the word resettlement as we consider it has less medical and benevolent connotations.
4. The government have recently announced a relaxation of these rules, though it is too early to assess the impact. (See also section on SBS.)
5. Siting civilian support in or linked to police stations has been used in Australia and India. A new law in Austria also gives police the power to remove perpetrators from the premises for 10 days. Protection orders, which can be extended if the woman applies to the court. During this period the woman is supposed to receive support from an Intervention Project, which uses pro-active and advocacy methods (Dearing and Forg, 1999)
6. Other international models can be found in Singapore and Spain. Both involve creating specialist institutions, akin to women's centres in local communities that will house comprehensive services. In Singapore a doctor is on site, and a legal service which has a video-link to court so protection orders can be obtained immediately. In Spain, the local women's centres will respond to all forms of violence against women, not just domestic violence. Neither has been operating long enough to be evaluated.
7. Refuge groups in the North and South of Ireland have created women's community personal development and re-training courses, using EU funding, as extensions of their service provision.

Multi-agency initiatives

Gill Hague

The multi- or inter-agency approach as a response to domestic violence forms a major plank of government domestic violence policy and is the subject of important Home Office Circulars. The approach includes both specific multi-agency projects (e.g. to develop practice guidance or a particular policy) and on-going domestic violence forums (which bring together all relevant agencies to build joint responses, to promote good practice and to conduct preventative and educative work). However, there is no single model of inter-agency working, and local circumstances play an important part. Creative liaisons include the development of domestic violence strategies across a whole locality, joint protocols with Area Child Protection Committees, and the adoption of multi-agency training and practice guidance. While statutory agencies have been important players in multi-agency work, it is essential to ensure the central involvement of Women's Aid, the refuge movement and independent women's services. Equalities issues also need to form an integral part of all work done, including effective consultation and involvement of domestic violence survivors.

Unfortunately, multi-agency work is critically hampered by lack of resources; there is little information on cost effectiveness; and evaluations are currently conducted only rarely. While many agencies are enthusiastic about the potential of inter-agency work, increased co-ordination is of little use if the resources and services needed are not already in place. There is a need, for example, for better provision of refuges and housing services, and co-ordinated, systematic funding for these services. Without these developments, inter-agency work on its own can achieve little. In fact, inter-agency forums can easily become talking shops or smokescreens disguising inaction. To avoid these outcomes, initiatives need to engage in work that results in perceivable changes and which is evaluated using concrete (but not simplistic) measures relating to improvements in women and children's safety. Importantly, the multi-agency approach can particularly act as a helpful way forward if it is strategically situated within a supportive, overall policy and practice framework at both local and central government level. *Local domestic violence policy and practice has been transformed in some areas by multi-agency work. There is much creativity, but it can also become a blind alley, indicating that an uncritical adherence to the inter-agency approach would be unwise. At best, the approach can form a creative 'next step' after the provision of sufficient basic services.*

Introduction

Refuges and support projects for women who have experienced domestic violence and their children have been set up all over the country since the 1970s under the impetus of the women's movement against domestic violence. For many years, however, theirs was a lone voice, advocating ceaselessly on behalf of abused women and children. Few agencies in either the statutory or the voluntary sectors made attempts to deal with the issue, often demonstrating appallingly negative attitudes to women who had experienced domestic abuse (see for example, Dobash, Dobash and Cavanagh, 1985; Pahl, 1985), although refuges themselves have always engaged in inter-agency work with other organisations wherever possible.

Studies such as those cited above exposed time and again inadequate provision, which failed almost entirely to meet the needs of abused women and their children (for further information on this research, see the chapter on women survivors' views in this review). The lack of effective services, and their lack of co-ordination with each other, led to demands from women's projects and concerned practitioners for better co-operation between agencies, but, through the late 1970s and most of the 1980s, these demands tended to fall on stony ground. Towards the end of the 1980s, however, under pressure from the refuge movement, and as a result of changing agency and public attitudes and the advent of council women's equality and other special units, things began to change.

As it became clear that further co-ordination of services and improvements in the policy and practice of both statutory and voluntary sector agencies needed to be put into place, the idea of operating specific projects to co-ordinate and develop services came into being. In the late 1980s, the first multi-agency domestic violence initiatives began to be set up in a rather experimental way, attempting to bring together relevant agencies in order to build an effective and co-ordinated approach (see Harwin, Hague and Malos, 1999). Most of these pioneering projects were established as a result of initiatives put in place by the local authority, by Women's Aid and the refuge movement, or by the police. They were often inspired and nurtured by domestic violence activists working in local authority departments (e.g. housing) and specialised units (e.g. community safety or equality units), together with women's organisations. Examples include the original multi-agency work in Hammersmith and Fulham, Wolverhampton, Nottinghamshire and Leeds, the latter remaining the most developed domestic violence inter-agency project in the country. Most of these pioneering initiatives were guided by a charismatic innovator.

The approach was recommended in the 1989 Home Office overview report on domestic violence, which was very influential (Smith, 1989). It was also recommended in the publication from the (then called) National Association of Local Government Women's Committees, *Responding with*

Authority (NALGWC, 1989), and by the 1992 National Inter-agency Working Party Report, *Domestic Violence*, published by Victim Support with input from a wide variety of organisations including the Women's Aid Federation of England (National Inter-agency Working Party, 1992). Further official encouragement followed with the report of the 1993 Home Affairs Committee Inquiry (House of Commons Home Affairs Committee, 1993). Inter-agency approaches were particularly recommended as a policy direction for police services (as part of an overall improvement in police responses) in the influential Home Office Circular 60/90, and in other pieces of government guidance. In 1991, the Women and Violence Working Group of the Convention of Scottish Authorities (COSLA, 1991) reported the need for multi-agency co-ordination as a matter of urgency. As a result of these various developments, the initial projects in the 1980s were followed by similarly pioneering multi-agency projects in Islington, Derby, Liverpool, Cleveland and elsewhere. These originators then gave rise to a considerable number of others.

By the mid-1990s, the approach had moved from the fringes of policy development to the mainstream and many inter-agency domestic violence projects and forums had been set up across the country. In 1995, the Inter-agency Home Office Circular, *Inter-agency Co-ordination to Tackle Domestic Violence*, was issued after much anticipation. This Circular offered detailed guidance on the multi-agency approach and has contributed to a further increase in the formation of inter-agency domestic violence forums. It has now been followed by a new guidance Circular published in March 2000 (Home Office, 2000)

The present author was part, with Ellen Malos and Wendy Dear, of the only national study of domestic violence multi-agency work so far conducted. This study was carried out between 1994 and 1996 and was supported by the Joseph Rowntree Foundation. It found that, at the time, there were more than 200 inter-agency forums up and down the country, and more have been set up since. However, others have gone out of existence due to the documented difficulty of keeping inter-agency initiatives going in the long term (see Hague, Malos and Dear, 1996b; Harwin, Hague and Malos, 1999).

This chapter will describe and review these developments, starting off by looking at multi-agency work in general, and then leading on to the specific field of domestic violence. The latter will include a consideration of structural and operational issues, who takes part and at what level, work done by inter-agency projects and forums, wider strategies and liaisons, resources, employees, and cost-effectiveness. The subsequent sections will deal with both the positives of the approach and the difficulties and tensions within it, and will include a consideration of power differences in relation to statutory agencies and to the voluntary sector and women's services, equality issues and the participation of domestic violence survivors.

After warning against the possible 'talking shop' outcome of inter-agency work, the chapter concludes with recommendations for future development. While the approach to domestic violence co-ordination work described herein should properly be known as `multi-agency', the terms `multi-agency' and `inter-agency' are used interchangeably in the field, and this approach is therefore followed throughout this chapter. It should be noted that there are, broadly speaking, two ways in which these words may be used to refer to a) domestic violence forums overseeing work in individual localities and b) specific multi-agency pieces of work, projects and practice developments which will vary from area to area.

Methodology

The methodology used to conduct this review was based on the following:

- The Joseph Rowntree Foundation-funded national study of multi-agency initiatives conducted by the Bristol Domestic Violence Research Group and cited above. This general evaluation of the multi-agency approach consisted of two stages: i) a national mapping survey (by telephone and postal questionnaire) of inter-agency forums in Scotland, Wales and England; and ii) in-depth fieldwork in eight local authorities, three of which were principal research sites. Stage 2 included depth interviews with agencies, with inter-agency forums, with other multi-agency projects and with relevant national bodies; the collection and analysis of documents, procedural guidance etc.; and observation at inter-agency meetings. In the three main research areas, qualitative work conducted included a data set of interviews with women who had experienced domestic violence;
- The initial impressions arising from a new study within the Economic Social and Research Council *Violence Research Programme* of multi-agency initiatives and the views and perspectives of domestic violence survivors;
- A review of the literature, including academic publications, research, policy and practice documents, and evaluations of existing inter-agency projects, often conducted as part of wider local studies (e.g. Clifton et al, 1996; Dominy and Radford, 1996)
- Consultancy and training work with a range of multi-agency initiatives around the country and, additionally, a series of national seminars facilitated by the author and colleagues at the Domestic Violence Research Group for inter-agency forums, policy-makers and practitioners;
- Consultation with the National Director of the Women's Aid Federation of England;
- Investigative research for this review of current good practice examples.

While the author was part of the main study on which this chapter is based, there is no other national work on which to draw. Specific references for each issue raised are not used repetitively, when this study is mentioned, but can be found, throughout, in: Hague, Malos and Dear, 1996b, *Multi-agency Work Domestic Violence: A National Study of Inter-agency Initiatives.*

It should also be noted that the multiple issues involved in developing good practice in inter-agency domestic violence work can only be touched on in a brief review such as this. Further information on all the issues raised is available in the research report, together with a practice guide relating to the national study (Hague and Malos, 1996) and in an overview book (Harwin, Hague and Malos, 1999) all available through the research team.

A further issue is that detailed information of numbers of inter-agency projects developing, for example, terms of reference or engaging in various pieces of work, do not exist, and, in any case, change constantly. Thus, this paper refers frequently and rather imprecisely to 'many' or 'some' initiatives, basing the use of these adjectives on the findings of the literature review conducted and on the documentation from the national 1996 study.

Multi-agency work in general

Multi-agency initiatives as a response to social problems are now a popular policy and practice option, operating in many areas of work, including crime prevention, community care, health services, child protection, and drug and youth services. The idea behind these initiatives is that, by bringing agencies together, hostilities and difficulties between them can be broken down and joint partnership policies and practices can be developed, so that the service user receives a better deal, effective, co-ordinated and to the point. However, despite these very good intentions, research studies and analyses, together with other publications about the issue (e.g. policy and practice guidance), demonstrate that inter-agency collaboration is a complex task with many potential difficulties. It has been suggested that collaboration of this type may be very limited in terms of its practical outcomes or may lead to rather sporadic attempts to improve services, which often then peter out (Gill and Pickles, 1989). While the potential for working across agencies to build a seamless and co-ordinated response is an excellent idea when it works, difficulties to be overcome include a frequent lack of multi-agency strategic planning, conflicting legislation influencing how various agencies respond, financial constraints imposed by different budgetary requirements, and uncertainties about the roles and responsibilities of different agencies (see e.g. Lloyd, 1994: 34-35). Despite these difficulties, there is a certain enthusiasm currently for the multi-agency approach, both locally and nationally. 'Multi-agency', like 'partnership', has become something of a buzzword.

Work over the last few years, produced by the Home Office and others, has been useful in analysing the complexity of the issue. Liddle and Gelsthorpe (1994a, 1994b, 1994c) produced three reports in a series on the subject of inter-agency crime prevention, addressing a wide range of issues, including a consideration of ethnicity and gender factors. In common with Sampson et al (1988; 1991) and other researchers (e.g. Blagg et al, 1988), they point out that inter-agency relations are 'highly complicated, seldom static, and influenced by a variety of institutional, individual and local / historical factors' (Liddle and Gelsthorpe, 1994b: 26). They describe five possible models of inter-agency co-ordination (Liddle and Gelsthorpe, 1994b; Gelsthorpe, 1985) as follows:

- The communication model;
- The co-operation model;
- The co-ordination model;
- The federation model; and
- The merger model.

Many multi-agency initiatives oscillate between these various possibilities. Liddle and Gelsthorpe also discuss the need for inter-agency projects to have some sort of structure (Liddle and Gelsthorpe, 1994a). They suggest that different agencies may adopt different forms of participation in multi-agency work varying from 'prime movers' to 'sleeping partners', but that the most effective style of working for inter-agency projects appears to be task-oriented and could be known as 'multi-agency problem solving' (ibid, 1994b). Liddle and Gelsthorpe (1994a; 1994b) propose that strategy-level crime prevention groups need to consist of higher managers and policy-makers, but that grassroots level groups can be very effective and dynamic, especially if they have the active support of, and effective lines of communication with, senior level staff.

Sampson et al (1991) continue this analysis, describing the importance of addressing power differences between agencies, of gender and ethnicity factors, of different perceptions, analyses and understandings of the problem being addressed and of conflict over tasks and priorities. They, and other researchers, flag up the important problem of agencies having a marked tendency to 'defend their own turf', and also point out the need for a core working group with the power to make decisions.

Various research studies have found that inter-agency projects are generally poor at conducting evaluations and at monitoring their work (Home Office, 1991: 22; Liddle and Gelsthorpe, 1994c: 16). A lack of resources to finance multi-agency responses has also been a finding of many studies. This has resulted in much debate in terms of the hampering effect of this resource lack on efforts at co-ordination and joint work, despite the possible enthusiasm of member agencies for the task (e.g.

Arblaster et al, 1998). There is, however, considerable variation in resource levels for different types of inter-agency work As might be anticipated, many of these general positives and problems which occur in multi-agency work also manifest themselves within specific domestic violence inter-agency initiatives.

Domestic violence multi-agency initiatives: Structures and organisation

From the variety of studies reviewed it is very clear that there is no one way of conducting inter-agency work on domestic abuse, no one strategy for action. Local circumstances play a large and crucial part in how this work develops. Thus, no single policy model can be followed. In fact, in many areas, inter-agency domestic violence work proceeds informally, and may have done so successfully for many years. Informal arrangements of this type can be examples of excellent local practice so that, in such circumstances, there may be no need for the setting up of more formalised initiatives. Nevertheless, specific inter-agency domestic violence forums have now been established all over the country. The 1996 study found that, generally, these forums operate initially as networking meetings of relevant agencies, and this stage may last for a year or more and be greatly valued by participants. Being able to put a face to a name and getting to know each other were constantly mentioned in the research in positive terms in regard to improving liaison and efficiency, as were sharing problems and educating each other about each agency's contribution.

Moving beyond networking: steering groups and task groups

As they develop, according to various studies, multi-agency forums often set up some sort of organisational structure, for example, establishing a steering group to oversee and manage the initiative. Many forums also set up task groups to operationalise agreed pieces of work. Such subgroups work best where they have an agreed and achievable task to perform, and where they are time-limited so that participants can plan the extent of their work commitment.

The national study quoted above found that the major rationale for setting up domestic violence forums needs to be to improve and co-ordinate services so that the safety of women and children experiencing violence can be improved - in other words, that positive change occurs. A finding of the study was that, while networking is important, in good multi-agency practice, forums need to move beyond this stage in order to engage, on some level at least, in action to increase safety and protection against domestic violence. If this does not happen (as is quite often the case), then it could be suggested that the relevant agencies should better use their energies in other activities to combat domestic abuse. There is nothing magic or prescriptive about the multi-agency approach. If it does not appear to be resulting in concrete, observable changes and remains a 'talking shop' in the long term, then it is better for those involved to do something else instead. The study found that inter-agency projects sometimes become caught in a cycle of meetings and procedures which result in few, or no, perceivable activities or improvements in policy development and service provision, at considerable expense in terms of time and salaries of participating officers.

Terms of reference and action plans

Formally agreed *Terms and conditions* are of some assistance in avoiding forums becoming talking shops and falling victim to a 'lowest common denominator effect' (see the later section on *Difficulties and tensions*). As noted in Home Office and other studies of multi-agency work of various types discussed previously, participating agencies often have a tendency to protect their own situation and practices, and to have conflicting views about the issue which is the subject of their work.

There are many possibilities for lack of clarity to arise when so many agencies with different agendas, attitudes and working practices have been brought together. *Terms of reference* can assist forums to address this lack of clarity and can usefully include *Guiding principles* negotiated between, and agreed by, all participating agencies to provide an overall framework. These will usually lead on to, or include, agreed *Aims and Objectives*. For many forums, the *Aims* include definitions of what the forum understands domestic violence to mean and general principles to increase the safety of women and children exposed to violence, to view domestic violence as a crime and to decrease its incidence. Such overall agreements as to the *Aims* of the forum may be followed by more achievable *Objectives*, which can then form the basis of practical, time-limited *Action plans*, reviewed regularly, and longer-term *Strategic plans*. The development of such *Action plans* can assist to avoid the afore-mentioned outcome in which forums do little except provide an arena for professionals to get together and exchange information.

Terms and conditions vary according to local need and circumstances. Nevertheless, good practice currently (as identified in various documents and policy guidance) is that *Terms of reference* should include an *equal opportunities policy*, *mission statements* (or some other kind of over-arching vision for the work) and, if possible, brief information on understandings of domestic violence, on agreed practices to be followed and on what is expected of member agencies. While it is not possible to include model examples in current use in a short chapter such as this, advice on drawing up *Terms of reference* is available from many sources. These include; the Women's Aid federations, research groups such as our own Domestic Violence Research Group, consultants and domestic violence trainers, and the more established inter-agency forums, all of whom are very happy to assist newcomers to the field.

Who takes part and at what level?

Participating agencies include refuges and women's support and outreach projects, the police (often through domestic violence officers or units), local authority specialist units and departments (e.g. housing, social services and education), probation, health services, community projects and the voluntary sector. The national study found that the two agencies, which participate most frequently by far, are the police and refuges. Refuges and women's outreach services (as described by Humphreys and Kelly in this volume) have a key role to play and will be further discussed later.

The police have taken a particularly active part in inter-agency co-ordination since the development of specialist domestic violence units in the 1980s (as discussed by Hanmer and Griffiths in this review). Of considerable significance has been the issuing of Home Office and other guidance, suggesting that the police should conduct inter-agency work on domestic violence as a routine part of their domestic violence response (Home Office, 1990; 2000a). Many forums have been initiated by the police, and a great deal of careful multi-agency work has undoubtedly been conducted as a result of police action. The evidence from the study is that committed and active participation by the police is vital. However, for an initiative to be most effective, it is also of crucial importance in the majority of cases that the police do not lead or dominate it, and that meetings do not take place in police premises. This is due to the sensitivities involved and the possible difficulties of equalising relationships with other agencies, for example, small women's refuges, black women's groups etc.

According to the national study, probation, housing departments and social services departments often take an active role in multi-agency work but, even so, these agencies participate less often than would have been anticipated. For inter-agency work to be effective, there is some agreement that, from the statutory side, the full range of health, social and housing services, education authorities, the police and other criminal justice agencies all need to take a full part, and that the work done is held back if they do not.

During the national study reported here, however, criminal justice agencies (with the notable exception of the police and probation), education departments and health services were often marked principally by their absence. The study concluded, as discussed below, that further local and national guidance to these agencies to encourage them to take part would be of assistance.

Health services

These are often the first port of call for women and children experiencing domestic violence, and their relative lack of participation in inter-agency co-ordination in many localities is a cause of concern. However, there is some evidence that health services are beginning to take the issue on to a greater degree than previously, with the increased development of domestic violence protocols with multi-agency input, for example (see Davidson et al, this volume and the recent Department of Health resource manual which brings these various protocols together, DoH, 2000). A current survey by Women's Aid nationally is revealing a mixed picture with inter-agency health work developing in some areas.

The criminal justice system

The Criminal justice system, similarly, has a vital role to play in any co-ordinated response, due to the now widely accepted criminality of domestic violence and the necessity for (and the complexities involved in providing) a strong and consistent justice response. Police and probation services cannot achieve this without the participation of the rest of the justice service.

Education

Educating the next generation that domestic violence is not acceptable is also an essential part of any co-ordinated strategy and needs to form part of educative and awareness-raising multi-agency approaches.

The absence, or sporadic, participation, of these various agencies in inter-agency approaches is clearly a matter that needs to be addressed, despite some improvements in recent years. Some other specialist agencies whose work includes domestic violence are also often absent from inter-agency initiatives (for example drug and alcohol agencies, see Jacobs, 1998).

There is some debate in the field about the level of seniority of participating officers. Ideally, forum members should be able to represent their agency formally, rather than attending solely out of personal commitment and interest, although the latter factors are of course important to the continued vitality of the project. Officers need to be at a senior enough level to be able to influence the policy of their agency. Conversely, however, one of the strengths of domestic violence inter-agency work is often its creative and grassroots dynamism and connection to the voluntary sector, which can be compromised by senior officer participation.

Some localities have experimented with a two-tier system of senior level strategy groups, plus local practitioner inter-agency forums feeding into them, although there can be difficulties in this approach in terms of duplication of work and effort between the groups, over-bureaucratisation etc. Aware of these problems but in specific relationship to evolving a wider domestic violence strategy, the 1998 publication from the Convention of Scottish Local Authorities (COSLA), *Guidance in Preparing and Implementing a Strategy to Tackle Violence Against Women* discusses some of the following points.

Inter-agency projects, that may not be specifically engaged in evolving a local authority-wide strategy, very often contain both policy-makers and practitioners in one group, with agencies sometimes being represented by more than one officer in consequence. Such initiatives often work hard to establish a local standing and to achieve a strong position for the issue of domestic violence on the agendas of their participating agencies. While it is vital that such domestic violence forums develop a strong local profile, and are influential enough to be in a position to have an effect on policy and practice development and on senior agency management, the strength of their grassroots and relatively informal approach (compared to child protection, for example) cannot be over-emphasised, together with the committed, activist stance that some forums adopt (see Hague, 1998).

What work do inter-agency domestic violence forums do?

Once regular meetings of participating agencies have been achieved, and *Terms of reference* and some sort of operating structure have been agreed, many forums then attempt to engage in a variety of activities, usually following an agreed (and regularly reviewed) *Action plan* (as above). Apart from networking and exchanging information, the national study found that this work on a general level usually includes:

- *Co-ordinating the domestic violence practices of local agencies and service delivery.* This work can include such activities as monitoring domestic violence referrals and the services offered by different agencies; drawing up directories of local services; evolving joint multi-agency policies and good practice guidelines; making improvements in liaison and referrals between agencies (without breaching standard confidentiality protocols) and so on;
- *Enabling member agencies to improve their own internal service provision and delivery.* This work can include assisting member agencies in evolving their own policies and practice guidance; monitoring and auditing the services offered; engaging in consultation exercises with local agencies; and developing a range of domestic violence training programmes for agencies on either a single or a multi-agency basis (often utilising a 'training the trainers' format);
- *Public education and awareness raising initiatives.* This work may include initiating public education and awareness campaigns; developing education packs for use in schools; engaging in community

development projects and in domestic violence training of a variety of types; and initiating, or contributing to, preventative work, for example outreach projects and perpetrators programmes.

Thus, inter-agency initiatives usually specialise in co-ordinating work and in preventative or awareness-raising initiatives. Only rarely do they set up direct service provision, although they generally have as one of their main objectives the establishment and maintenance of adequate emergency refuge, advocacy and outreach services for women and children experiencing domestic violence, including specialist provision for women and children from minority ethnic and other communities.

Some forums act as a 'watchdog' on the quality of local services and may conduct service and institutional audits to establish the quality and efficiency of each agency's contribution, and to track responses in order to monitor both good and poor practice. Tracking domestic violence cases through the system in order to check on and maintain good and consistent practice (without compromising confidentiality), and conducting institutional audits of the effectiveness of services provided, are new ideas in this country. They are widely viewed as good practice, but as yet are little developed here. Tracking and institutional audits build on the procedures used by some domestic violence intervention projects in the US and a variety of other countries, and refer most particularly to the Duluth model developed in Duluth, Minnesota, currently regarded as a world leader in this respect.

This project offers a multi-faceted domestic violence programme, co-ordinated through the Duluth Domestic Abuse Intervention Project. Cases are monitored daily as part of a range of interlocking procedures and services, which include perpetrators' programmes, women's support groups, comprehensive training initiatives, and provision for the conduct of institutional audits to monitor each agency's practice and adherence to agreed protocols. All of these services are integrated into a whole. The Duluth project grew out of the women's movement against domestic violence and was originally initiated by activists from the shelter (refuge) movement. The services provided and systems in operation are held informally accountable to groups of women who have experienced domestic violence (see Pence and McMahon, 1999; Pence and Shepard, 1999).

Internationally, other multi-faceted domestic violence intervention projects have developed in Australia, New Zealand and Canada, in particular in London, Ontario, and are touched on, not only in this chapter, but in various others throughout this review. These projects usually have a strong policing and justice element within a co-ordinated range of services including diverse support for survivors of abuse, provision for children living in situations of domestic violence, and key input from women's services and activists.

Wider strategies and creative liaisons

Along the lines of developing broad, co-ordinated, multi-faceted interventions of the types noted in the previous section, various possibilities have been tried in the UK. It is not possible to completely duplicate international comparisons in this country due to differing justice and social welfare systems, traditions of work, etc. However, the Duluth model is currently being replicated as far as possible in various areas of the UK, most comprehensively so far by the innovative project in the London Borough of Hammersmith and Fulham, *Standing Together*.

A development in recent years in the UK has been the formulation and operation of wide-ranging domestic violence strategies across agencies. Thus, domestic violence forums may be able to develop work through or with the local authority at a corporate level, with the police and with other agencies, to evolve an overall and comprehensive domestic violence strategy for the locality in question. Once adopted, strategies of this type, endorsed by local policy-makers and chief officers, may then be implemented with the help of domestic violence training initiatives for agency participants and phased pieces of work in individual agencies. Such wide-ranging strategies may cover a local authority area, or extend even more widely, and can give a structural 'backbone' and direction to detailed local developments. Several areas have such strategies (for example, the London Borough of Newham, Newcastle, and Surrey).

Some inter-agency forums have made particular use of new developments in legislation and government policy. The Crime and Disorder Act 1998, in particular, has given rise to new opportunities and also to new challenges, and is discussed in the next subsection.

The Crime and Disorder Act 1998

The Crime and Disorder Act is having, and will have, major impacts on utilisation of resources with attendant implications in terms of who has the power over these resources, of the role of independent women's services in local crime and disorder strategies, and of how domestic violence is dealt with under the Act.

The legislation has resulted already in a great deal of local activity on domestic violence through local crime and disorder audits, partnerships and strategies (and can act as a starting point for the development of wider domestic violence strategies of the type discussed above). In some crime and disorder strategies, domestic violence is well-profiled whereas, it appears, from what evidence is currently available, that in others, it is less so. These differences may reflect local awareness of domestic violence and whether there are refuges and domestic violence forums in the locality.

Measures taken also vary from enhancing previous provision to potentially detracting from it, in that, in some cases, previous work has been marginalised. There is evidence emerging in the current ESRC project on service users involvement in inter-agency initiatives that, in a few areas, crime and disorder partnerships have over-ridden previous grassroots multi-agency liaison. This tentative evidence can, perhaps, act as a warning that such an outcome should be avoided. There is also an additional issue of avoiding the potential marginalising of practitioners or of women's services and the voluntary sector in favour of those services with operational and policy-making briefs.

However, in various areas, it seems that the Crime and Disorder Act has led to positive developments. For example, Middlesbrough Domestic Violence Forum has recently produced a particularly detailed study of prevalence of, and responses to, domestic violence, under the Act. The publication produced was launched at a major local event in 1999 (Middlesbrough Domestic Violence Task Group, 1999). Similarly, in response to the Crime and Disorder Act, the Bristol Domestic Violence Forum formulated a wide-ranging strategy for the Bristol Community Safety Partnership. Such partnerships include the police, local councils, the probation service, and the health service. As part of this strategy, broad performance indicators related to domestic violence are being developed to measure the effectiveness of future interventions. The City Council in Bristol has also developed a corporate strategy on domestic violence (as have a variety of other local authorities in recent years).

Further examples of inter-agency liaison

A further example of a good practice co-ordinating response has been the operation over the last few years of the Greater London Domestic Violence Project, and the employment of a co-ordinator by the consortium of agencies responsible for the project, to develop and facilitate its work. A part of the over-arching job remit of this post is to improve the effectiveness of inter-agency working in boroughs within Greater London. One of the many initiatives that the co-ordinator has been able to facilitate is to act as a consultant to London domestic violence forums in regard to the Crime and Disorder Act, and to assist them to develop a framework, including a set of agreed criteria, to form the basis for their local crime and disorder strategies in relation to reducing domestic violence, which is then common across the local authorities concerned.

Other innovative recent liaison work includes the development and piloting of a variety of protocols and policies on good practice in health services, and also in the housing authorities in several local areas. Inter-agency liaison can also assist in developing new initiatives of benefit to abused women and children. For example, multi-agency work in the London Borough of Lewisham has resulted in the setting up of a new scheme in which women pursuing legal action on domestic violence can access a certain amount of free child-minding through social services.

The new procedures for conducting fundamental performance reviews in local authorities within the 'Best Value' regime can also be of use. The London Boroughs of Croydon and Haringey, for example, have conducted best value reviews with input from local domestic violence forums and all relevant agencies, and with extensive consultation with groups of women who have experienced domestic violence.

Domestic violence forums may also work in consultation with local authorities and health authorities in other ways, for example, in relation to children's services plans, community care plans, primary care groups etc. In some cases, beneficial liaison has been established between Area Child Protection Committees (ACPCs) and domestic violence forums, working together to conduct joint training, to include domestic violence within child protection protocols, or to evolve detailed 'child protection and domestic violence' policies and procedural guidelines (see also DoH, 1999). For example, Hereford Women's Aid and a group of local agencies have developed an inter-agency protocol on domestic violence, part of which has also been incorporated into ACPC guidelines. The Women's Aid Federation of England has developed a model child protection policy for use in all member refuges to facilitate liaison between statutory and voluntary services in this respect. Also, in a few areas, ACPCs and domestic violence forums have worked together to establish a children's sub-group of the forum in order to develop local policy and practice about children in relation to domestic violence. The Liverpool Domestic Violence Forums, for example, has operated such a group successfully for several years.

This type of liaison can assist in general in developing good policy and practice in relation to child abuse, now that domestic violence has finally been recognised as a child protection issue (see Mullender, this volume, and the guidelines produced by Audrey Mullender and Cathy Humphreys for the Local Government Association: Mullender and Humphreys, 1999; also the reader and training materials produced in 1998 by the Department of Health, in conjunction with the Domestic Violence Research Group, NSPCC and Barnados, and with input from Women's Aid; Hester et al, 1998a). The Women's Aid refuges and federations are also developing innovative liaisons and joint projects, together with local forums in some areas. A further example of creative work involves the domestic violence forums across South London which are collaborating currently to set up a replication of the St. Mary's Centre, Manchester. The latter project is a joint venture between the police and the local Health Trust in Manchester and offers a co-ordinated, comprehensive response to adults who have experienced sexual violence.

Statutory sector contributions

In recent years, research studies have documented a definite improvement in the response of many statutory agencies to domestic violence, albeit uneven and patchy across the country (Grace, 1995; Mullender, 1996; Hague and Malos, 1998; Hester et al, 1998a). Many statutory agencies led, perhaps most particularly, by local authorities and the police but including some probation and health services, have supplemented these policy and practice developments in their individual agencies with a strong commitment to multi-agency working. They may contribute, for example, to the development of corporate policies and strategies on domestic violence, as noted above, or promoting specific pieces of multi-agency practice.

Many individual officers of statutory agencies have devoted large amounts of time, dedication and energy to developing inter-agency initiatives and domestic violence forums, and to winning their own agency to a 'multi-agency position'. This, often thankless, work is deserving of appreciation and respect, both often slow in coming. Statutory agencies have made enormous contributions to multi-agency forums, in some cases keeping the initiative going almost single-handed. These observations are derived not from research evaluations but from consultancy with forums and the investigative work for this chapter. The effort put into inter-agency co-ordination by statutory agencies (sometimes because they have more resources than the voluntary sector) has given the approach life in many areas, and has been a major policy direction in recent years.

Thus, multi-agency initiatives can lead to the development of innovative projects associated with statutory agencies, improved co-ordination within the statutory sector and between sectors, and historically unprecedented domestic abuse policies and strategies between and across agencies. These are particularly successful when developed in conjunction with the voluntary sector, with Women's Aid and the refuge movement and in consultation with domestic survivors.

Resources

One of the findings of the 1996 national inter-agency study was that, despite all these many innovative endeavours, a lack of resources was a major factor holding back the development of inter-agency domestic violence initiatives. Many interviewees during the study pointed to the lack of provision for resourcing in conjunction with the 1995 Home Office Inter-agency Circular. This lack was seen as a disappointment, in a Circular filled with guidance on the practical development of multi-agency domestic violence initiatives. A question frequently posed to interviewers in the national study, and in later consultancy work, asks how agencies can follow the guidance and develop innovative responses, if there is no way for them to access resources with which to do so.

During the recent investigation of multi-agency forums conducted for this chapter, it was suggested that the current Crime Reduction Programme on domestic violence should be particularly vigilant in recognising the need to fund projects in a precarious financial position. Many of these may have been struggling for a long period, with no resources whatsoever and little support, doing the groundwork and slowly building inter-agency responses, against the odds. (In fact, the overriding requirement of CRP funding is to demonstrate the cost-effectiveness of interventions, and a variety of projects were considered for funding, subject to this proviso.)

Looked at overall, domestic violence multi-agency initiatives are characterised by resource shortage, although there is great variety from initiative to initiative, and this lack relates to wider work pressures and resource contraction across the board. On a broad operational level, the majority of statutory agencies participating in the inter-agency initiatives studied during the national research study on which this chapter is based were themselves facing considerable funding cut-backs and contraction of services, and sometimes could only justify involvement in forums if this could be designated as 'core' work, which it characteristically was not. Many statutory agencies attempted to donate resources, providing venues or rotating the forum secretariat between them, but in numerous cases this work placed a great strain on the agency or workers in question. In general, voluntary sector agencies are rarely in a position to donate resources. Nonetheless, all agencies tend to contribute whatever they can in kind, if not directly.

Thus, it is important to recognise that most initiatives have no resources, apart from what agencies can share out of good will and commitment. During the research study, it was clear that individual participating officers from both statutory and voluntary sector agencies were usually already at their limit as regards their work programmes and found it hard to take on additional duties of any kind. Many were inspired by the potential of inter-agency co-ordination and development of services, but lacked the time, energy or resources to take their inspiration forward. Officers interviewed in the study were unanimous that there is little that domestic violence forums can achieve unless they have some resources with which to work. While a lack of resources should not be routinely used as an excuse for inaction when at least some limited changes can be affected with little funding (see also Liddle and Gelsthorpe, 1994c: 15), our study found many examples of inter-agency forums losing their momentum and gradually also losing support. Fewer and fewer people were coming to meetings, and disillusionment and weariness were setting in.

Funding and the employment of workers

Some forums have obtained a measure of funding support, often after considerable time-consuming fund-raising effort. Sources of resources are various, but may include specific grants from local organisations (such as the police or the police authority), from various partnership programmes (and increasingly as a spin-off of crime and disorder partnership strategies), and very frequently from the local authority itself. Grant-aid through the latter may be via social services or housing committees, community safety or equality initiatives, and a wide variety of other sources of council funding, depending on circumstances and the specific focus of the work to be done. Much-used, but usually time-limited, sources of funding are provided by special government crime reduction and other programmes of various types (over different time periods).

In some localities, the availability of such resources has meant that inter-agency projects have been able to employ workers and to fund work e.g. the production of directories and public education material, the provision of domestic violence training etc. However, during the 1996 study, financial support obtained was almost invariably short-term, which precipitated recurring funding crises. Thus, financial uncertainty and insecurity prevailed in many funded initiatives, according to the study evidence. While the availability of any resources at all for inter-agency work is to be welcomed, this uneven and uncertain funding situation may militate against constructive forward-planning and project development, and, on a general level, against inter-agency domestic violence initiatives fulfilling their potential. Even where forums have paid workers, there is evidence that raising funds to resource activities undertaken as a direct result of the worker's efforts frequently continues to be an ongoing problem.

Most research respondents in the study believed that local funding for refuges and women's emergency, support, advocacy and outreach services should take priority over inter-agency co-ordination. Current best practice (from policy documents, e.g. by the Leeds Inter-Agency Project, and from the 1996 study) is clearly that multi-agency projects should not compete with Women's Aid and other refuge and outreach service providers for grant-aid. Instead, they should engage actively in attempting to ensure that these services are adequately resourced.

Ideally, study interviewees in the national research pointed out that the provision of direct services, and the development of educational and preventive work and inter-agency co-ordination, should go hand-in-hand as different sides of the same coin. It would appear to make no sense if they are competitors. In addition, the point was made that the conducting of inter-agency awareness-raising work in a locality can act as a vital catalyst to increase the funding for the provision of refuges and direct services. Nevertheless, the current lack of resources, and the need to compete for them, has introduced a difficult situation. During the course of the research, the inter-agency projects in two of the main study areas found themselves to be in direct competition with local refuge providers for small (but essential) amounts of voluntary sector grant-aid. Since the study, one of the very successful forums studied has closed down due to lack of funding.

The roles of co-ordinators and development workers

This is not, however, to belittle the considerable amount of productive work which multi-agency projects can do when they have some back-up and resourcing. Most often, when inter-agency forums have obtained some funding, they employ a specialist co-ordinator. In some other cases, a domestic violence co-ordinator for the local area as a whole is in post, most commonly council-funded, who might be able to co-ordinate the local forum as one part of their wider duties. Alternatively, council community safety or equality officers can sometimes do this work on behalf of the inter-agency initiative. The national 1996 study accumulated strong evidence from many areas of the country, supplemented by later research and consultancy work, that the availability of a co-ordinator or a development worker was of key importance in progressing inter-agency domestic violence work. Research interviewees were unanimous throughout the study that, while agencies can work together to co-ordinate their services and to engage in some limited work without the assistance of a paid worker, the employment of a co-ordinator almost invariably has a transforming effect upon the project. Even so, it should be noted that most forums across the country do not have employees.

According to agency interviewees, co-ordinators were able to initiate projects and develop the work in previously unimaginable ways. A co-ordinator or development worker can be expected to give a domestic violence forum presence, focus and direction, and to do behind-the-scenes networking and contacting to 'oil' or 'broker' the inter-agency process, an essential task given the possibilities for disagreement and confusion between so many agencies. Work done, in addition to agency co-ordination, often includes specific projects to monitor domestic violence, to research local needs and gaps in service, and to develop new initiatives to meet these needs. Inter-agency workers usually provide servicing and development for their inter-agency forum and may assist in developing good practice guidelines, domestic violence training, and awareness and education initiatives.

Many interviewees in the 1996 study suggested that it is helpful if the person employed has some experience of Women's Aid and the refuge movement, a background in women's organisations and services, and an understanding of the gendered power dynamics of domestic violence. However, study interviewees also noted that the co-ordinator's role is to support and facilitate the project, rather than to lead it. The ideas fuelling the forum need ideally to come from service providers and practitioners, together with domestic violence survivors, rather than from the co-ordinator, so that the steering committee, where there is one, leads the project, informed by the forum membership and by abused women.

Interview evidence, accumulated from various parts of the country in the mapping stage of the national study, indicates that the employment of a co-ordinator alone, without any administrative support, is often insufficient to enable the initiative to develop effectively. The employment of an administrator or administrative assistants, or the provision of administrative or secretarial help for the co-ordinator, was viewed as vital in this context.

Employment structures vary for domestic violence forums. While, for some, co-ordinators may be direct local authority employees, in others the project may be based in probation or in the voluntary sector. In some areas, the post may be 'hosted' by the local authority (for example, through its social services committee as in the Middlesbrough area, formerly part of Cleveland) or by another agency.

Despite this variety, good employment management policies need to be in place. In general, domestic violence forums have a relatively participatory and collective management system, and structure, in keeping with wider ideas about equalising power differences between member agencies and evolving collective, co-ordinated practice and policy responses.

Cost-effectiveness

There is very little work on the cost-effectiveness of multi-agency domestic violence forums in this country. Are they value for money? In the context of the lack of resources discussed above, the fact that they often do not cost very much needs, perhaps, to be scrutinised. Cynics have been prompted to suggest that the enthusiasm of at least the last government (but hopefully not this one) for inter-agency domestic violence policy options was partially, or mainly, because they entail little expenditure, but could give the impression of promoting a co-ordinated, multi-faceted response.

The most basic expenses entailed by inter-agency domestic violence initiatives are for the servicing of the initiative (venue, secretariat etc) and, more substantially, for the salaries of participating officers. This can be a considerable amount, - and calculating the cost, for example, of the attendance of forty agencies at a two-hour meeting, can be a financial eye-opener. Otherwise, there is little information on which to draw. The different activities of a domestic violence initiative clearly need to be costed separately and will vary widely according to work undertaken and how the resources needed are raised and shared between agencies. (See Crisp and Stanko, this volume and Stanko et al, 1998).

Effective inter-agency work: Difficulties to be overcome

The COSLA guidance suggests the following advantages of the multi-agency approach:

> Thus, multi-agency approaches to domestic violence work can work towards a co-ordinated, seamless response to the needs of abused women and their children so that effort is not duplicated. They can facilitate the possibility of joint initiatives on specific issues, for example, the development of child protection and domestic violence strategies, or the setting up of co-ordinated services on one site. They can lead to improved practice in individual agencies, including co-ordinated domestic violence training, and to educative and preventative initiatives across a locality. They can then become the next step forward after the provision of services.

In order to achieve this potential, however, inter-agency initiatives need to overcome a variety of hurdles, some of which were findings of the 1996 study and are discussed in subsequent sections, in order to identify possible ways forward as to 'what works' within the multi-agency method.

Difficulties and tensions

Difficulties identified in the 1996 study, include:

- Keeping the momentum going once initial enthusiasm has worn off, and the vast volume of work to be done, given the lack of previous co-ordination of domestic violence provision historically in almost all areas of the country, makes itself felt.
- Combating the 'lowest common denominator effect', as previously noted, in which the initiative is held back by agencies with little experience of domestic violence work or with the least developed views about it.
- Lack of clarity and consistency with different workers, perhaps, attending each session, with varying degrees of clarity about who is doing what and when, and with the very common situation of two or three officers doing all the work with little support or assistance from anyone else.
- Power and equality issues. These constitute a complicated body of potential sources of difficulty, and include power differences between participating agencies, between the statutory and voluntary sectors, and between service users and service providers. These complex issues form the subject of the next section.

Power differences: The problems

A thorny question within all multi-agency work, to which domestic violence work is no exception, is how to equalise power differences between statutory and voluntary sector agencies, and to encourage the statutory sector not to 'take over'. Such taking over may happen almost by default, even where there is a commitment to equal participation, due to different working practices and work expectations, greater resources in the statutory sector, and recurring crises and pressure on time commitments in the voluntary sector. The national study concluded that forums need to have concrete strategies in place to attempt to deal with these difficulties, or at least to have discussed the issues, rather than merely hoping that they will not arise. Its findings in this respect are reported in the next three sub-sections.

The participation of voluntary sector and community groups

From the study evidence, while local voluntary sector groups are represented in most inter-agency domestic violence forums, in some they are under-represented or absent, both from the membership and, importantly in terms of who has the power, from the management structure. There can then appear to be a skew towards the statutory sector. Resourcing difficulties often militate against voluntary sector involvement, and statutory agencies may be dominant even when they are not intending to be. However, the voluntary sector participants also need to make a recognisable commitment to the multi-agency process - to take responsibility for 'signing up' to it, rather than leaving it to statutory bodies.

Potential marginalisation of Women's Aid and women's services

The central focus of multi-agency work is to improve services for abused women and children and to prevent or reduce the incidence of domestic violence. While Women's Aid is accepted as the lead national agency in both these respects, and in terms of representing women and children experiencing domestic violence, the Women's Aid federations and member projects, and other refuge service providers, are, in fact, relatively small and under-funded organisations, compared with statutory bodies. Thus, one of the most pressing difficulties faced by inter-agency projects can be how to equalise power differences between Women's Aid and other women's organisations on the one hand, and large statutory organisations on the other, and how to maintain the central position of the refuge movement, as more objectively powerful agencies such as the police and the local authority, become involved in multi-agency co-ordination. Women's Aid interviewees in the national study often felt marginalised or pushed to one side, as inter-agency initiatives took off.

Even where a commitment to the involvement of refuges exists, however, their full participation is not always possible due to the continuous crisis work which they undertake and, frequently, their poor staff ratios, so that outside co-ordination work may become an impossible luxury. Nevertheless, Women's Aid, nationally and locally, has a commitment to participate in multi-agency co-ordination, and the national federations can offer advice, consultancy and assistance about the issues involved.

Of some importance is the independence and autonomy of refuge services and Women's Aid, which can be compromised by inter-agency developments which overlook this, and by the encouragement by some multi-agency initiatives of new projects outside the refuge movement which duplicate its work. Thus, multi-agency initiatives need to be aware of these issues and to promote autonomous provision of women's services within an overall inter-agency framework.

In some cases investigated during the national study and as part of subsequent research work, however, Women's Aid and local women's service providers, far from being isolated or marginalised, have clearly taken a very active - or, indeed, leading - role in their local forum in order to initiate, enable and assist its development, sometimes to the detriment of the rest of their work-load. They have frequently found themselves educating other agencies about domestic violence and giving their expertise for free in this respect, which they can often ill afford to do. The informal leadership on the issues in question that they are in the position to provide may be valued greatly by other agencies and may have a catalytic effect. Thus, the picture appears to be a mixed one for women's refuge and outreach services, varying between having too much of the inter-agency work to do, on the one hand, to the more commonly-occurring tendency within multi-agency initiatives towards the marginalisation of the refuge movement, on the other. However, a variety of forums have built creative and profitable relations, breaking down previous suspicion between refuges and other agencies, and resulting in enhanced services for abused women in the locality concerned.

In general, the central involvement of local refuge, support and outreach services in inter-agency work is of crucial importance to allow the voices of the refuge movement, and of the women and children experiencing domestic violence for whom they advocate, to be raised, and to retain funded and autonomous women's services, independent of statutory agencies. Interviewees in the national study pointed out that it can be a constant struggle for these voices to be heard in a meaningful and empowering way (see Mullender and Hague, this volume). Additionally, it can be an isolating experience when only one or two representatives from refuges and other women's services in the voluntary sector are involved in an inter-agency initiative, attempting to represent abused women's views. They may also feel compromised by having to accept multi-agency policies with which they disagree but which they are powerless to influence, even though they may be a central provider in the locality. The study found that it is important for domestic violence forums to take on these issues in a sensitive, constructive way, on both sides, and to put in place mutually agreed strategies to ensure the central role of the refuge movement - which has led the struggle against domestic violence for so long - now that the issue has entered the mainstream.

Equalities issues

Similar issues of potential marginalisation can also affect small minority agencies (such as black women's groups, community self-help groups etc), as domestic violence is mainstreamed. Domestic abuse, however, affects all communities and there is some agreement that responses to it need to be aware of equality and diversity, and available to all. Nevertheless, many inter-agency initiatives surveyed in the national mapping study (which formed the first part of the overall study) had not begun to take on issues of equality of opportunity on the grounds of ethnicity, class, religion, culture, sexuality or disability. In a large number of these initiatives, small community groups and minority organisations felt excluded and unable to attend. Some of the inter-agency initiatives in the in-depth study areas in the second part of the study had developed this work to a considerable extent, whilst acknowledging that there was still a long way to go.

The involvement of black women's organisations, groups of disabled women and other disability agencies, lesbian groups, children's charities and small community organisations is an essential part of the equality process. This can be facilitated if representatives from these groups attend the meetings and, where possible, have some realistic power in the inter-agency initiative, perhaps sitting on the steering group or becoming officers of the forum. However, the study showed that it was very rare for steering or management groups to reflect this diversity.

In conclusion, despite considerable progress in some localities in regard to at least some equality areas (and, typically, more work had been done at the time of the national study on ethnicity and disability, and less on, for example, sexuality), the issues involved remain contentious, difficult and personally painful in many cases. Study respondents pointed out that it can be hard to keep equalities on the agenda and progress may be extremely slow. Small leaps forward were often followed by long periods during which the issue seemed to have been completely forgotten again.

Accountability to abused women and their children

The involvement of women who have experienced domestic violence and their children is presently a matter of debate, and is the subject of the current study within the ESRC *Violence Research Programme,* cited earlier. There is much current interest in service users' views in all fields of social policy, and best practice in a wide range of caring services and research initiatives includes the involvement of user groups and informal accountability to them. This interest extends to domestic violence work where the women's movement against domestic violence has always attempted to raise the voices of abused women and children. As regards multi-agency developments, while service users might not necessarily be expected to know in detail about such initiatives, some process needs to be in place for groups of users and other domestic violence survivors to inform service and policy development (see Mullender and Hague, this volume).

In the national study quoted throughout this chapter, only 5 out of 70 women interviewed who had experienced domestic violence had any idea that there was a multi-agency initiative in their locality, even where this was a particularly active one. Further, a perhaps surprising research finding was that almost none of the women who were living in refuges which were very actively participating in the local domestic violence forum knew about it or were involved in it, in any of the study areas. The new study has just reported findings from which it is clear that women who have experienced domestic violence are rarely part of, or adequately consulted by, inter-agency developments except where they participate, either disclosed or undisclosed, as professionals (ESRC, 2001). It may be inappropriate for single individuals who have experienced violence to participate unless they are representing a support group or some other organisation, but clearly the voices of women service users should be heard. This issue needs to be addressed so that consultation and advisory systems can be put in place involving domestic violence survivors, and so that forums and services set up are responsive to abused women and children's needs and views.

Power differences - some positive suggestions

As can be seen from the preceding sections, many difficulties in multi-agency work revolve around differences in power, working practices and attitudes to domestic violence among participants. Some of these can be resolved if agencies work equally and if attempts are made to maintain total clarity between all concerned about structures, lines of accountability, control of resources etc. COSLA suggest that a model of multi-agency co-ordination needs to include:

- a recognition that all agencies have a role to play;
- a balance between the interests of all agencies;
- a consensus between all members, while not compromising the underlying philosophy about supporting women in making decisions about their own lives; and
- the taking of joint responsibility for implementation of strategies and policies by the statutory and voluntary sector (COSLA, 1998: 48).

In the next section, we discuss some of the efforts of inter-agency forum to take on the issues raised by the national study, (see also the *Ways Forward* section).

Evaluation

Many multi-agency domestic violence forums monitor their work to some extent, and review it informally regularly (often annually) to check if they are achieving their objectives. Thus some assessment of effectiveness is done in many cases. In addition, well-developed projects have been able to evaluate some of their work more directly. The Leeds Inter-Agency Project, for example, has evaluated several of its projects. In 1996, inter-agency work in Surrey was evaluated, and plans for forward development recommended, in a study which included a local prevalence study and a wider analysis of domestic violence provision in the area (Dominy and Radford, 1996).

However, few inter-agency domestic violence forums systematically evaluate their work. This is partly due to the expense and time-consuming element of evaluations and the fact that, struggling as they often are, to be asked to evaluate themselves on top of everything else can be the straw to break the camel's back. Another barrier to more formal evaluation is that it is difficult to know what to evaluate in order to make the resulting evaluations useful for comparative purposes, since there is no one recognisable model of work done on which to draw, and developing specific performance indicators can be problematic and needs to avoid crudity or lack of nuance. However measures associated with improvements in safety, in take-up and developments of services, and in service user satisfaction with initiatives put in place on an inter-agency basis, are beginning to be developed, often varying depending on local circumstances.

Nevertheless, while more evaluation and monitoring work appears to be currently in development in various areas of the country than has been the case up till now, the outcomes in relation to evaluation during the national study cited throughout this chapter were unclear. In answer to research questions about whether the local inter-agency project had improved women and children's safety or the provision and delivery of services (rather, perhaps, than being a 'talking shop'), a very large number of respondents from agencies were not sure. Many made such comments as "it must have". The research study was unable to monitor these supposed improvements directly and the effects of improved service co-ordination are in any case hard to gauge.

In the national study, there was some rather tentative evidence in some of the areas studied that the actual services which women and children receive have been improved. This was especially the case where local provision has been enhanced (e.g. with additional refuges, support groups, outreach projects, housing provision, phone lines etc.) as a result of, or at least partly facilitated by, the inter-agency initiative. It was harder to gauge the effects of the implementation of good practice guidelines (e.g. in the police or the housing authority) and domestic violence training for officers, but these were thought to be positive.

Specific, observable improvements in practice brought about by the intervention of a domestic violence forum can sometimes be measured (e.g. the adoption of supportive and believing interview techniques by housing and social services staff, and their rating by women service users). Usually such improvements have only been informally evaluated, but positively so, and may or may not have been attributed to the work of the forum. As an example, in one of the study's field work areas, improvements were noted in local knowledge about domestic violence and where to turn for help, in the use of security alarms, in the arrangements for women to make benefit claims in a safe way and in the use of confidentiality. The preventative and educational work which inter-agency projects initiate (e.g. in schools) has a different long-term aim and cannot be easily measured, except in a crude short-term way, by any conventional means.

There is clearly a certain circularity in both calling for more resources for inter-agency initiatives, but also pointing to the lack of evaluated work to guide this process, as in 'no evaluation, so no resources' and 'no resources, so no evaluation'. The task is to develop specific evaluative criteria for different types of effective inter-agency work, hand-in-hand with the development of a resource base, to avoid the 'smokescreen' outcome discussed in the next section.

The smokescreen effect

From all the studies and research work on inter-agency approaches so far conducted, it is clear that, while innovative co-ordinating, preventive and educational work has been undertaken in many localities, in many others (perhaps the majority, nation-wide) very little has been done. There were suggestions in the 1996 research study, and in later consultancy work by the research team, that multi-agency initiatives could use up resources and energy, do little, waste time, and divert funds and attention away from the provision of emergency services, refuges and support for victims of domestic violence. Thus, inter-agency work could act as a way for the police and local government – and, indeed, for central government – to save face and to appear to be doing something, while in fact very little changes and few resources are invested. The research team has called this elsewhere the 'smokescreen' (or 'face saver') effect (see e.g. Hague and Malos, 1998; Hague, 1998).

While many study interviewees from agencies were enthusiastic about the potential of inter-agency work, respondents in some localities pointed out that increased co-ordination is of little use if the resources and services needed are not in place. In this analysis, 'what works' would be better provision of refuges, outreach and housing services, among others, and co-ordinated, systematic funding for these services. Without these developments, inter-agency work on its own can achieve little and can, at worst, disguise inaction and poor services.

However, importantly, inter-agency work can particularly act as a creative way forward if it is strategically situated within *a supportive, overall policy and practice framework at both local and central government level*. This wider supportive framework needs to include, at least:

- a strong justice response;
- adequate emergency, refuge and advocacy services, including provision for children who are involved;
- good, safe temporary and permanent housing provision; and,
- support throughout the criminal justice process for abused women and children; alongside the development of specific, co-ordinated multi-faceted domestic violence interventions, accountable to those experiencing the violence.

Conclusions and ways forward

During the research study, it emerged that 'the bottom line' as regards the effectiveness of multi-agency work, and informal accountability to women and children service users, was generally agreed to be *whether the activities of a domestic violence initiative have an effect on improving the safety of abused women and children*. Although the issues in question are complex and there is not necessarily any one 'right' answer, some of the factors which were recommended in order to lead to effective, rather than ineffective, local inter-agency action are:

- The active involvement of statutory agencies, at both policy-making and practitioner level with senior management support, and access to decision / policy making on behalf of their agency. These agencies to include the police, local authority housing, social services and education departments and special units; health services; probation; and legal, court and other criminal justice personnel.
- Similarly the active involvement of relevant voluntary sector agencies with management and policy-making support, both locally and nationally, and including Victim Support;

- The full participation of Women's Aid and local women's refuge and support services, and the use of concrete strategies, not only to avoid their marginalisation, but also to actively promote their central involvement (without over-burdening their already pressured and under-funded work-loads).
- Active participation of community, grassroots and women's organisations.
- The writing of inter-agency domestic violence work into relevant job specifications, so that it forms an agreed part of work programmes rather than being an 'add-on'.
- Consistent, committed and active attendance and membership, with members attending as agreed representatives of their agencies where possible.
- The adoption of *Guiding principles*, and the development of common agreements about domestic violence.
- Clear and well-developed *Aims and objectives*, *Equal opportunities policies* and other *Terms of reference*, regularly reviewed and updated;
- A workable structure, enabling clarity and lines of accountability, but avoiding layers of bureaucracy, perhaps involving an active and representative steering committee and time-limited sub-groups with achievable goals.
- Vitally, the availability of at least some resources for activities, for projects taken on, for co-ordination work, and for servicing the initiative without resource competition with women's services and emergency refuge and outreach provision.
- Where possible the employment of a co-ordinator or development worker, with administrative or secretarial support.
- The relating of all activities to meeting the needs, and increasing the safety, of abused women and children, and to decreasing domestic violence in perceivable ways.
- The development of concrete initiatives and activities which are within the capabilities of the initiative and achievable within a time-limited periods.
- The development of integrated, co-ordinated services across a locality, without compromising confidentiality and the integrity of the practice of individual agencies.
- The integration of equalities issues into all work done including all training designed and delivered.
- The involvement of, and some form of informal accountability to, women who have experienced domestic violence and their children, through consultative and participatory mechanisms.
- The use of evaluation and monitoring processes in specific relation to work done and its effectiveness against such criteria as those discussed in this chapter to ensure constructive outcomes.

- An understanding that innovation is not necessarily worthy of funding at the expense of longer-established initiatives which have been working solidly to combat domestic violence in a locality, often without any support, so that they might not qualify as cutting edge initiatives.
- Importantly, the implementation of further guidance at both national and local level, including on resource provision, to encourage relevant agencies (for example, health services) to make domestic violence a core part of their work and to encourage their participation in co-ordinated multi-agency work.

Thus, four of the major conclusions of this study are that:

- Further national and local guidance from central and local government, and from national co-ordinating agencies, is required to facilitate the involvement of all relevant agencies.
- Adequate resourcing for inter-agency domestic violence work is essential if the approach is to be successful.
- The central involvement of Women's Aid and the refuge movement and of community organisations, together with some form of accountability and involvement of women experiencing domestic violence, are vital factors.
- Inter-agency work can only work if situated within a wider, overall policy framework of support, and including adequate general service provision (e.g. of housing options, social security benefits, refuge and outreach services etc).

Overall, it was clear from the study, from the literature review and from subsequent consultancy and training work, that local policy and practice has been transformed in some areas of the UK by inter-agency domestic violence work, especially where long-established initiatives have pioneered the work, as in Leeds, Hammersmith and Fulham and Islington, and particularly where forums have been able to employ co-ordinators or development workers. New initiatives like the Crime and Disorder Act can, if used carefully, enhance these processes. There is much creativity, with the development of innovative multi-agency responses, quite new in historical terms in this country. Domestic violence is being tackled by these initiatives in previously unprecedented ways.

On the other hand, inter-agency work may become a blind alley, leading to no changes whatsoever, and tiredness and disillusion setting in. This outcome is currently common. It can be avoided with the development of overall strategies; with input of proper resourcing, funding and local energy; with some form of accountability to abused women and their children; with creative liaison between Women's Aid and women's services on one hand, and local statutory agencies on the other; and with guiding principles, action plans and concrete, observable, measurable changes in policy and practices, as discussed above. Thus, when the co-ordinating and awareness raising, preventative work done is *concrete, visible and accountable,* multi-agency initiatives can avoid becoming talking shops and potential time wasters.

At its best, inter-agency work on domestic violence can be a way of getting statutory and voluntary agencies to take on the issue in a meaningful, co-ordinated way. This can then be a creative 'next stage', after the provision of refuge and emergency services, in combating domestic violence and in moving forward to spreading the work more widely, improving policy and practice, and adopting comprehensive domestic violence strategies across a locality. The provision of services and the development of co-ordinating, campaigning, preventative and educative initiatives can thus become complementary parts of a comprehensive approach, moving towards a society in which domestic violence is no longer tolerated. The pitfalls along the way are many, however, and an uncritical adhering to the multi-agency approach can herald inaction, the loss of the centrality of the refuge movement, the exclusion of grassroots responses and the advent of 'talking shop' politics.

Assessing and managing risk

Sylvia Walby and Andrew Myhill

The prevalence of domestic violence varies along a number of dimensions. This chapter reviews the literature on this variation in risk factors associated with domestic violence. It finds firstly that the highest risk is among those who have suffered previous assaults. Secondly, those who are separating are or have been a high risk. There are further risk factors including gender, and especially marital inequality; poverty and social exclusion; and a man's criminal record. However, the data sources for the assessment of the risk of domestic violence (and sexual assault) need urgently to be improved. There is a need to develop surveys in this field so as to provide robust statistical data.

Introduction

Risk

The work reviewed in this chapter has focused on the risk factors associated with the onset of domestic violence. However, it is important also to consider the factors that are associated with desistance from domestic violence. While they are less frequently considered in the academic literature, they are of the essence when the focus is on the evaluation of interventions and programmes which aim to reduce domestic violence.

The identification of risk factors can aid both the identification of those who need special attention and long term thinking on the causes of domestic violence. The focus here is primarily on those risk factors that identify victims, but some mention will also be made of those that identify perpetrators.

It is important to distinguish between correlations and causes - not all things associated with domestic violence are actually causes of it. This is in order to ensure that programmes deal with the causes of crime, rather than with spurious or superficial correlations. While this chapter will review risk factors that are the empirically identifiable and measurable correlates of domestic violence, the causal structure linking these risk factors requires conceptual as well as empirical work (Tilley and Pawson, 1997).

Prevalence

In order to cost accurately domestic violence and the benefits of programmes to reduce it, it is necessary to have accurate estimates of its prevalence and incidence.

The methodology to estimate the extent and patterns of domestic violence is significantly less well developed than that in other areas of crime as a result of the previous lack of resources and research in this area. The further development of this methodology is a necessary early stage in the development of a capacity to evaluate programmes aimed at the reduction of domestic violence.

Sources

During the course of this review, over 300 items - articles, chapters, books - were obtained and reviewed.

Where appropriate, national random sample surveys have been given priority over small and special samples, quasi-experiments and qualitative studies. However, where these were not available, or where their reliability or validity has been questioned, then data derived from other research methods have been utilised in addition. Refuge and clinical/treatment samples are likely to address a slightly different population of the most heavily and recently abused. Meta-analyses are considered, but since these were generally of small and special samples, they are subject to limitations.

Material was initially sought of whatever national origin, but in this report priority is given to material on the UK. However, the overwhelming origin of the published material, especially that published in journals and in electronic abstracts was the US. There is some material available from other countries, in particular Canada, Australia, Finland, Iceland and the Netherlands, but it is relatively small by comparison. This US dominance creates a series of dilemmas since we do not know the extent to which these risk factors and the connections between them are similar in the US and the UK. This is particularly true because of:

- the lower rate of violent crime in the UK as compared with the US;
- differences in the criminal justice system;
- differences in the welfare system and provision of support;
- differences in the pattern of gender relations;
- differences in other social relations, such as patterns of employment, income distribution and social exclusion; and
- perhaps most crucially, the differences in the methodology between the survey which is the most important source of US risk factor analysis and that of the British Crime Survey.

If it is the only available evidence, then the US (or other overseas) material is cited, but these findings must be treated with caution before being applied to the UK.

Gathering data

In the estimation of the risk of domestic violence the nature of the methodology used is of overwhelming significance. Very considerable differences in the estimation of risk appear to result from differences in methodology. Hence it is imperative to assess these methodological issues before moving on to consider the data.

National random sample surveys are today a key data source underlying much of the current assessment of the risk of domestic violence overall, by gender, and for specific groups. They are the only way to reliably estimate the prevalence of domestic violence in the general population and the relative rates in different sub-groups. However, these surveys differ considerably in methodology and their reported rates of violence vary by factors of several times. Further, for some issues and for certain population groups findings from other research methods continue to be important. These include quasi-experimental designs and focused qualitative research.

National random sample surveys

National crime surveys were developed to measure all incidents perceived by victims as crimes, including those not reported to the police and not processed by the courts. There have been four types of survey, revealing different rates of domestic violence.

1. Generic national crime surveys

Generic crime surveys are now carried out in many countries (for example, UK British Crime Survey, the US National Crime Victimisation Survey, the Australian National Crime and Safety Survey) and reveal much crime that is not reported to the police. These surveys have been criticised for under-recording rates of violence against women. The criticisms were underpinned by findings from local surveys which found much higher rates of violence against women than that recorded in these national surveys (Mooney, 1994).

2. Revised crime surveys with special attention to domestic violence

The second generation of crime survey revised the wording of its enquiries, so as to try to ensure that more assaults would be reported to the survey, and contained more detailed questions on areas of concern.

The revision of the US National Crime Victimisation Survey led to a near doubling of the estimation of the proportion of women subject to domestic violence from 0.54% to 0.93% per annum and a larger increase in the estimation for men from 0.05% to 0.14% (Bachman and Saltzman, 1995: 8).

The UK revised its generic crime survey, both within the regular BCS, and also by carrying out in 1996 a special exercise with a specific set of questions on domestic violence (much more extensive than that in the US) which used a new computer based methodology that provided greater, though not absolute, privacy to the respondent. The 1996 special exercise also led to a near doubling of the rate of domestic violence reported against women (for detailed figures see below) (Mirrlees-Black, 1995, 1999).

However, there are still limitations to the survey design, including: a 'crime context' for recall of events which may not be conceptualised as crimes (Mirrlees-Black, 1995). These include difficulties over detail and sensitive probing as a result of the domestic violence questions being only a part of a broader survey (Mirrlees-Black, 1995), and confidentiality (32% of female BCS respondents had someone else present in the room) (Mirrlees-Black, 1999). Most important of all, some important marginalised populations are omitted from the sampling frame (Walby and Myhill, 1999).

3. *Dedicated domestic violence surveys*

A different type of survey was that which was dedicated to domestic violence. This freed the respondent from the context of a crime survey and gave time for detailed questioning and probing on domestic violence alone. There were two main examples of this type of survey in the US, the 1975 and 1985 US National Family Violence Surveys (Straus and Gelles, 1990) and also one in the Netherlands (Romkens, 1997). The US dedicated domestic violence surveys found much higher rates of domestic violence than the revised US generic survey, indeed 12 times as high. The 1985 National Family Violence Resurvey found that 16.1% of currently married or cohabiting couples reported violence during the previous year, this being violence by the husband in 11.6% of couples, and violence by the wife in 12.4% of couples. This is compared with rates of 0.93% for women and 0.14% for men in the revised US generic crime survey (Bachman and Saltzman, 1995). These US Family Violence Surveys have been subject to very extensive secondary analysis as to risk factors and many detailed assessments are derived from them.

However, these surveys have been subject to very considerable controversy over their methodology and definitions. There is dispute over whether it is the act, or the impact of the act, which is important; and whether data on acts makes sense outside of an understanding of its meaning and context. The debates have addressed:

- whether a quantitative survey, in particular, one based around the 'Conflict Tactics Scale', a pre-coded list of specific types of violence with varying degrees of severity, can adequately capture the nature, meaning and context of violence;
- whether a year recall period is adequate as compared with recall based on the life of the relationship or whole life;
- whether a lead up which focuses on conflict in the relationship is the best introduction to questions about violence; and,
- whether explicit reference to sexual assault might not be merited (Dobash et al, 1992; Smith, 1994).

It is argued that the nature of any injurious outcome is important since men are much more likely to injure women than vice versa (Schwartz, 1987). In addition, women who hit men are likely to be responding in self-defence or retaliation rather than initiating violence (Saunders, D., 1988; Nazroo, 1995). Further, sexual violence against women in the home is not included, nor are other forms of violence against women, for instance, rape and sexual assault outside the home.

4. Violence against women surveys

The last type of survey is one which has attempted to locate domestic violence in a context so as to ascertain its meaning and impact, include sexual coercion, and broaden the range of violence to include that against women outside the home. This wave of surveys was initiated by the Statistics Canada Violence Against Women Survey (Johnson, 1996; Statistics Canada, 1993), which has proved a model for surveys in several other countries. With varying degrees of modification, similar surveys have now been carried out in Australia (Australian Bureau of Statistics, 1996), Finland (Heiskanen and Piipsa, 1998), and Iceland (Gislason, 1997), and are under development in Sweden and Germany. It has often been regarded as the current state-of-the-art survey (Dobash & Dobash, 1995).

The Statistics Canada Violence Against Women survey uncovered still higher rates of life-time experience of domestic violence against women - 29% of women who had ever lived with a partner had at some point experienced violence from him. When the definition of violence was broadened beyond domestic violence to include violence outside the home and various forms of sexual violence, the Survey found that 51% of Canadian women had at some point in their lives experienced violence from someone (16% from date/boyfriend, 23% by other known man, 23% by a stranger).

The Australian Bureau of Statistics Women's Safety Survey, found more than three times as much physical assault against women as did the generic Crime and Safety Survey, 5.9% as compared with 1.8% of women reported physical violence in the previous 12 month period (Australian Bureau of Statistics, 1994, 1996: 3).

Each new generation of national survey has been an improvement on the previous one. The more recent generations have revealed higher rates of violence against women, provide richer data sources for the nature and interconnection of risk factors, and encompass a wider range of violent behaviour. A key remaining limitation is that of the sampling frame, which tends to exclude more marginalised groups, such as those living in refuges and hostels for the homeless, among whom rates of victimisation are higher (Straus, 1990; Okun, 1986). A fuller analysis of the methodology, findings and implications of these various national surveys can be found in Walby and Myhill (2001).

As these comparisons show, the regular BCS survey and the special BCS module in 1996 are likely to have underestimated the extent of domestic violence. Those surveys that are dedicated to the issue of violence within the family or against women have consistently reported significantly higher rates of violence than those which have asked the questions within the frame of a generic crime survey. Further, they are unable to address questions of detailed interest (such as comparing rates of violence before and after separation; and whether violence increases during pregnancy). However, with these caveats, the BCS findings will be reported as the best available data in the UK.

Small and special samples (e.g. from refuges and treatment populations)

While large random sample surveys might be expected to be able to address the distribution of risk across the whole population better than methods based on small scale samples drawn from special populations, there are reasons why they might not fully address the whole population. Research based on refuge samples has consistently shown more intense and more frequent abuse than those based on the sample surveys.

Unless and until such deficiencies in survey design can be remedied, it is important to utilise the information derived from small and special samples that target the most abused population. These include samples drawn from: refuges to which battered women have gone (Dobash & Dobash, 1979); and those reporting violence to the police (Kelly et al., 1999).

Quasi-experimental design

Experimental and quasi-experimental research designs are rare in this field at this stage, though see Dobash et al (2000) on men undergoing treatment. They may become more important later in assessing the impact of particular treatment regimes on the reduction of domestic violence.

Focused qualitative research

While qualitative research cannot be expected to provide estimates of risk, nonetheless it can be invaluable for investigating the validity and reliability of some of the concepts utilised in more quantitative research assessing risk, and for assessing the meaning of terms in different contexts (see for instance, Kelly, 1989). Further, it is vital for initial exploratory stages of research.

Professional records and requests for information

Most agencies keep records of their client populations. While these are typically uneven, they have potential to assist the development of professional practice, if their very specific context is borne in mind.

Sources of the best estimates in the UK

The best estimates of the risk of domestic violence in the UK are to be found in the British Crime Survey 1996 that included a special section on domestic violence. However, it is likely to underestimate the risk of domestic violence.

Overall risk of domestic violence for women and men

The British Crime Survey found that 4.2% of both men and women aged 16-59 years old who had ever been married/had a partner or a boy/girlfriend had been a victim of domestic violence in the previous year (1995). This had involved an injury for 2.2% of the women and 1.1% of the men. When threats were included, 5.9% of women and 4.9% of men reported such an event. Over their life-time 22.7% of women and 14.9% of men reported being a victim of domestic assault (Mirrlees-Black, 1999).

Mooney's (1994) local survey in North London found the higher rate of lifetime violence against women of 30% and that for the previous year was 12%, but this was not a nationally representative sample.

The extent to which women are disproportionately the victims of violence is hotly contested with disputes engaging with issues of definition, methodology and context of the violence, as noted above. There is a question as to whether the focus is properly on the act of violence, which entails greater gender symmetry, or the outcome of the act, which entails greater gender asymmetry. While the 1996 BCS finds that equal percentages of women and men have been the subject of acts of domestic assault, in many respects women were significantly more severely affected than men were. This is because:

- women are twice as likely as men to have been injured in such attacks;
- women were much more likely to have been subject to frightening threats than men, 3.9% as compared with 1.2%;
- women were more likely to have suffered multiple assaults during the course of the previous year and over a lifetime; and

- women were much more likely than men to be have been upset and frightened at the time of the incident and to be still upset at the time of the interview.

Of all violent crime experienced by women, 43% is domestic (Mirrlees-Black, 1999). As noted above, it has been shown that the acts of violence by women are largely carried out in self-defence and in retaliation (Saunders, D., 1988; Schwartz, 1987).

Homicide in Britain is much more likely to entail men killing women than women killing men. Nearly half the women who are murdered are killed by their partners, and this pattern is not gender symmetrical. Of 224 female homicide victims, 47% were killed by their partners, while of 426 male homicide victims, 8% were killed by their partner (Criminal Statistics for England and Wales, 1997).

Previous assault

One of the most robust, simple and straightforward risk factors for domestic violence is that of previous assault.

The BCS found that women who had been victims of domestic assault in the previous year reported an average of 5.2 assaults, with 2.9 resulting in injury; while for men it was 5.0 assaults, with 1.5 resulting in injury. While half the women who had been assaulted in the previous year had experienced one or two incidents, half reported three or more incidents; among men, two thirds had experienced one or two incidents and one third three or more (Mirrlees-Black, 1999).

Lloyd, et al (1994) found high rates of repeat domestic violence in a small-scale study on Merseyside. They found that 62% of all police calls to domestic incidents were from households with one or more previous such calls in a two-year period; and that 35% of households suffered a second incident within five weeks of the first.

The extent and nature of violence among these victims of domestic violence varies. There is an important question as to whether it is possible to separate those who are most at risk of serious injury and death from those who are not. There are two main perspectives here, each drawing on different empirical evidence of risk factors: the first suggests that there are two quite different populations, one with low level and infrequent violence and the other with severe and frequent violence against women (Johnson, 1995). The second perspective suggests that there is a pattern of escalation, and that any level of violence is a risk factor for escalation to severe and frequent violence (Dobash & Dobash, 1979). This acknowledges that escalation may not be inevitable and desistance is possible (Feld and Straus, 1989, Woffordt et al, 1994).

Johnson (1995) suggests that it is possible to identify two distinct populations: first, 'common couple violence', in which partners engage in mutual combat; second, 'patriarchal terrorism', in which men ferociously subordinate and batter women. He suggests that the violent population reached in the national surveys (in particular the US National Family Violence Survey) is one in which quite a lot of men and women engage in relatively low impact fighting, 'common couple violence'. The population interviewed in shelter samples, among which there was very frequent severe violence from their partners, is described as suffering from 'patriarchal terrorism' and he regards this as a distinct group.

However, this analysis implies accepting the notion that much of the violence between women and men uncovered in the US National Family Violence Survey is symmetrical, while not denying the existence of a group of severely battered women. Yet, several studies provided reasons to doubt such a view of symmetry. Saunders (1988) argues on the basis of his study that women's domestic violence is primarily that of self-defence and retaliation. In this case, it is inappropriate to consider those couples where there is two-way violence as ones in which there is 'common couple violence', since the man is the aggressor in the overwhelming number of cases. Certainly, if reports to the police have any meaning, it must be noted that the overwhelming number of cases reported to the police involve violence from a man to a woman (Kelly, 1999), and thus are not appropriately conceptualised as 'mutual combat' nor 'common couple violence'.

Dobash & Dobash (1979) in a study of a sample of battered women from Scottish refuges described a process of escalation, in which, if there was no successful intervention, low levels of violence from a man would inexorably build into more severe violence. Their current research is investigating the circumstances in which there is homicide (Dobash et al, 1999). Feld & Straus (1989) find that while desistance is possible, nonetheless, minor violence is a risk factor for an escalation to major violence. Woffordt et al, (1994) found that though half their sample showed desistance over a three year period, a prior act of violence is one of the best predictors of future violence.

While it is difficult to predict in individual cases, previous assault is a risk factor for further assault. It is probable that assaults are likely to increase in severity unless there is a change of circumstances. The robustness and simplicity of this risk factor make it especially suitable for use in many professional contexts.

Separation

Women who are separated from their partners or husbands have a significantly higher risk of domestic violence than those in other marital statuses. According to the BCS special report on domestic assault, 22% of those who are separated were assaulted in the previous year. Among men marital status is of little significance.

It is not possible to tell from this BCS data whether the separation was before or after the assault(s). However, other data suggests that post-separation is a dangerous period for women. Kelly et al (1999) found that a third of the assaults reported to the police in an Islington study were from ex-partners. Statistics Canada's Violence Against Women Survey found that among previously married women who reported violence in their relationship it occurred after separation for 19%. Among women for whom there was violence after separation, it began at separation for 8%, was a continuation of former violence for 92%, and showed an increase after separation for 35% (Statistics Canada, 1993: 26). Wilson and Daly (1994) show that in Canada the rate of husbands killing wives is elevated in the aftermath of separation. Thus, while for some women separation brings relief from violence from their partner, for others there is none, and for a significant minority it results in an escalation.

This finding of 'separation' as a very high risk factor for domestic violence is of particular relevance to those professionals who are engaged with women who are separating and/or divorcing. This includes those involved in family courts, child custody arrangements, child access, child support arrangements, and the allocation of emergency social housing.

Gender divisions and gender inequality

Patriarchal attitudes

The correlation between the holding of patriarchal attitudes and engaging in wife assault is often found. Sugarman and Frankel (1996) conducted a meta-analysis of 29 studies and showed that a majority found a correlation between a husband assaulting 'his' wife and his approving of the use of domestic violence. While some might argue that there can be some distance between holding patriarchal attitudes and actually beating a wife, this study found a clear correlation between the two phenomena.

Yllo and Straus (1990) show that there is more domestic violence against women in those US states which have strong patriarchal norms as compared with those which do not, using data from the first US National Family Violence Survey.

The significance of this risk factor is further supported by the findings from the Scottish male treatment programmes that targeted such patriarchal attitudes towards the use of violence against women. The results from this quasi-experiment showed a correlation between the reduction in such beliefs by the men on the programme and a reduction in the extent to which they used violence against their partners (Dobash et al, 2000).

Marital inequality

The two National Family Violence Surveys in the US found that inegalitarian family structures were a risk factor for violence, in that domestic violence was lowest in the most egalitarian families. Here the issue is the relative power of the partners, in which relative economic resources play a significant, but not solely determining role.

Coleman and Strauss (1986) found that when conflict occurs egalitarian households are the most resilient to the possibility of violence, that is less likely to resort to violence; that asymmetrical households were more likely to succumb to violence when conflicted than symmetrical ones. Drawing on the 1975 US National Family Violence Survey, Kalmuss and Straus (1982) found that women's dependency in marriage was a risk factor for violence, that violence was less likely where there was a more equal balance of resources between husbands and wives. Objective marital dependency was a sum of the scores of three dichotomous variables:

- whether the woman worked;
- whether she had children aged 5 or younger at home; and,
- whether her husband earned 75% or more of the couple's income.

The study found that the rate of severe violence was nearly three times higher among women in high objective dependency.

Poverty and social exclusion

Poverty is a risk factor for domestic violence. There are a number of partially separate, partially overlapping dimensions, including income, employment status and relative poverty. There are complex connections with other risk factors. There is an overlap with the issue of social isolation, in particular between non-employment and lack of social links. There is some mutual causation, with poverty partly being an outcome of domestic violence. Further, it is important to distinguish the risk factors for victims from those of perpetrators, since they entail different causal pathways, but the data is not always complete in this regard.

However, it should be remembered that domestic violence is not restricted to poor households and can be found across the economic spectrum.

Household income

People (men and women) in households that are poor are more likely to be assaulted by their partners than those that are in households which are better off. Evidence to support this can be found not only from the British Crime Survey, but also the US Family Violence Survey, and the Canadian Violence Against Women survey.

The 1996 special BCS module found that household income beneath £5,000 doubled the risk of domestic assault of the woman, but that the risk of assault of men was quite evenly spread across household income levels. Of women in households that earned less than £5,000 per year, 10% were assaulted in the previous year, while in households earning £5,000 to £20,000 3.7% were assaulted, and among households earning more than £20,000, 3.0%. However, while the risk increases significantly for poor households it does not disappear in better off households - domestic violence can be found across the income range.

Financial stress

Households in financial difficulties were two to three times more at risk of domestic violence than those that were financially secure. This was found among both sexes, with 12% of women and 10% of men being assaulted among households which were not managing (Mirrlees-Black, 1999).

Women's poverty

A low income level among women has been found to be a risk factor for domestic violence in several US studies.

Farmer and Tiefenthaler (1997) show that women's poverty is a risk factor for domestic violence. They estimate that a woman who receives an additional $100 in non-wage income per month experiences one less assault in a 6 month period; and that a woman with an additional $1,000 in monthly income has 6 fewer experiences of violence. They use data from small special samples in the US, including one from police call responses, so caution should be applied before generalising from the findings. They argue that the correlation exists because lack of income and other support decreases women's ability to threaten effectively to leave if they are subject to further domestic violence.

While the BCS does not report on women's income, it does report on related risk factors, such as access to housing, which is significantly related to household income. In the UK, housing tenure is a risk factor for women, with the BCS finding that women living as council or housing association tenants are more likely to be at risk, 8% reporting violence, as compared with owner occupiers, of whom 3% reported violence in the preceding year (Mirrlees-Black, 1999). However, it is hard to ascertain whether this is a cause or an effect of domestic violence.

Poverty and domestic violence may have mutually reinforcing impacts according to the work of the Taylor Institute in the US which is based on a series of small scale studies (Meier, 1997; Raphael, 1997; Lloyd, 1997). These studies found that the experience of domestic violence made it harder for women to hold down jobs as a result of lateness, increased ill health, and sabotage by the women's violent partners. Women receiving welfare are more likely to have been battered than other women, while poverty increases women's vulnerability to violence. Thus while women's poverty may be associated with the risk of domestic violence, it is possible that the underlying causal pathways may, to some extent, go in both directions.

As shown above (Coleman and Straus, 1986), when marriages are more egalitarian people are less at risk of domestic violence. The lesser economic resources of women as compared with men is a structural feature of gender relations in most societies, systematically increasing women's vulnerability to domestic violence.

Employment status

Employment significantly affects the risk of domestic assault for women, according to data from the 1996 BCS (Mirrlees-Black, 1999). Women who were unemployed or housewives had the highest risk of domestic violence. Among women aged 16-29, 13.1% of those who were unemployed, and 11.5% of houseworkers were assaulted, as compared with 5.0% of those in full-time work, 9.6% of those in part-time work and 7.3% of students. Among women aged 30-59, 4.4% of houseworkers and 3.2% of unemployed were assaulted as compared with 1.9% of full-time workers and 2.0% of part-time workers. Employment status does not impact on the risk of men to domestic assault to the same extent that it does for women, according to BCS data.

There are various ways in which women's employment status could link to their varying vulnerability to domestic violence: for instance, the lack of financial resources to leave, bargain or threaten to leave; and greater social isolation and thus lesser access to informal and formal support networks. Employment status is also linked to the amount of household income, so it is not unexpected to see similarities in these two risk factors. A further overlapping risk factor is that of age, since younger people are more likely to be poor, unemployed and live as tenants.

The BCS does not report on the employment status of the perpetrator of the violence, only that of the victim, thus providing no evidence to assess the impact of employment status on the propensity to commit domestic violence. However, there is a report on the social class of the 'head of household'. This is correlated with the extent of violence against women, to some extent, since households where 'the head of household' has an occupation in the two least skilled categories report the highest rates of assault against women, 6%, as compared with 3% in the professional 'households'. However, the significance of the social class of the household is not overwhelming and domestic violence exists across the class spectrum.

The Finnish national survey reports on the employment status of male perpetrators. They found that the employment status of the male partner was a risk factor in the assault of a woman. Of men who assaulted their partner in the previous 12 months, 16.1% were students, 13% unemployed or laid off, 12.6% working part-time, 9.6% working full-time, 8.8% were entrepreneurs, 5% were farming entrepreneurs, and 5% were retired (Heiskanen and Piispa, 1998).

Pregnancy

There is some correlation between pregnancy and domestic violence. However, there is a question in the literature as to whether pregnancy actually constitutes an underlying cause.

Statistics Canada found that among women who had ever been married, 21% recalled violence during pregnancy. Among this group the violence occurred for the first time in 40% of these women (1993: 27).

Mezey and Bewley (1997) have suggested that violence against women can start or intensify during pregnancy. This is the subject of ongoing research (Mezey, 1999). There are several small scale studies which appear to show a correlation between pregnancy and domestic abuse (e.g. Bohn, 1990), though at least one meta-analysis urges caution because many studies typically lack direct comparisons between pregnant and non-pregnant women (Gazmararian et al, 1996).

However, Gielen et al (1994) show that violence against women around the time of pregnancy is actually higher after the birth of the child than during the pregnancy. Their analysis is based on a longitudinal analysis of 275 women who were interviewed during pregnancy and six months after the birth.

The correlation between pregnancy and violence may exist because young women are a group at higher than average risk of domestic violence (see below) and pregnant women disproportionately fall into this group. Gelles (1988), using data from the second US National Family Violence Survey suggests that the correlation between pregnancy and domestic violence is spurious. He argues that it is not pregnancy per se which creates the higher risk, but rather age, the younger age of both the woman and the perpetrator, which is independently correlated with increased risk of domestic violence. When age is held constant the greater violence experienced by pregnant women as compared with non-pregnant women largely, but not completely, disappears.

However, violence during pregnancy can harm the foetus and ultimately have implications for the health of the new child (Bullock and McFarlane, 1989). Further, pregnancy is a time when women are subject to more regular and more intense medical scrutiny than average, so it may well be an opportune moment for intervention (Covington et al, 1997).

Ethnicity

There are no significant differences in risk of domestic violence by ethnicity reported in the BCS (Mirrlees-Black, 1999). However, Mama (1989) showed that minority ethnic women may have greater difficulties in accessing support services than white women. This is for a variety of reasons that include racism among service providers, language difficulties, and cultural differences. Specialist provision is under development in certain localities, for instance, the London Borough of Camden (Sen, 1997) as a consequence.

Ill health and disability

Various forms of physical vulnerability appear as risk markers for domestic violence. There are higher rates of victimisation by domestic and sexual violence for those who suffer from: ill health (Mirrlees-Black, 1999); bulimia (Kaner et al, 1993); and mental illness (Weinhardt et al, 1999). However, it is hard to fully disentangle cause from effect, since, while on the one hand, poor physical or mental health may be a result of physical injury or psychological harassment, on the other, physical or mental vulnerability may reduce the capacity for effective resistance to domestic violence.

Disabled women are at greater risk of victimisation from domestic and sexual violence (Chenoweth, 1997; Sobsey and Doe, 1991). The extent of the greater victimisation in the UK context would benefit from further research.

Violent family of origin

Being raised in a violent family is a risk factor associated with becoming a perpetrator that has one of the highest profiles in the literature. There is an extensive body of psychological literature that has tested this thesis and usually, but not always, found a correlation. However, a correlation is not a cause. Investigation of the causal processes which might lie behind this correlation has found that of greater importance are: beliefs in the legitimacy of beating wives and associating with other like-minded men; and an anti-social personality similar to that sometimes associated with a criminal career.

Drawing on data from the first US National Family Violence Survey, Straus, Gelles and Steinmetz (1980) found that men who as children witnessed violence between their parents as children are three times as likely to abuse their female partners in adulthood. Those who had

Witnessing abuse

Dutton, Starzomski & Ryan, 1996

Sample and Design: 140 men referred for wife assault and 45 matched controls
Findings: They found a correlation between abuse of a wife and an abusive personality. They show that paternal rejection (which included physical abuse) was the strongest predictor of abusive personality. The authors suggest that abusing men have personalities in which independence behaviours by partners could trigger extreme rage because such a loss would threaten the way their identities were constructed.

Downs, Smyth and Miller, 1996

Sample and Design: Extensive literature review on correlations between experiences of violence in childhood, partner abuse and alcohol abuse.
Findings: Although there are robust correlations between these three phenomena, mediating variables are very significant. These include both an 'anti-social personality' disorder and also 'depression'.

Simons, Wu, Johnson and Conger, 1995

Sample and Design: Analysed data from a sample of 451 white midwestern families who lived on farms or small towns.
Findings: If they controlled for anti-social behaviour trait, the relationship was eliminated between harsh treatment during childhood and adult family violence. Anti-social behaviour is here seen as the crucial mediating variable between harsh parenting and future abuse.

Silverman and Williamson, 1997

Sample and Design: A self-completion survey of a sample of 193 college men, of whom 21% admitted to abusing female partners.
Findings: There was an important mediating variable, that of associating with abusive men and holding beliefs that it was OK to beat women under certain circumstances, for instance, if they were sexually unfaithful. This latter association was more important than witnessing family violence as a child.

witnessed severe marital violence were ten times as likely to be abusive to their female partners in adulthood as those who had witnessed no such violence.

In a meta-analysis of case comparisons, Hotaling and Sugarman (1986) found an association between childhood witnessing of parental violence and husband to wife assault in 88% of the relevant empirical studies they considered.

While the correlation between violence in the family of origin and a man using violence against his partner is well established, a causal link is not. Initially it appears that there are two competing underlying models: one, a social learning perspective in which men acquire a specific form of 'normal' masculinity; the second, a perspective in which psychologically damaged men are out of control and have 'impaired' masculinity. These models were modified and made more complex by the introduction of 'mediating variables', that is, factors which intervene between the witnessing and the later abusing. Finally, some of these 'mediating variables' have been shown to be more important than the initial presenting risk factor, that is, witnessing parental assault is found to be a spurious correlation with later wife assault. There is an enormous literature in this field, albeit largely US, so only selected articles are summarised opposite.

So, while there is extensive empirical support for a correlation between witnessing violence as a child and going on to being an abusive adult, many of these studies are arguing that the 'mediating' variables are actually key to the causal analysis. The two main variables here are: anti-social personality; and, associating with other abusive men who think that it is legitimate for men to beat their wives. On the one hand some studies suggest a convergence of the factors associated with abusive men with that of typical criminal careers, especially via the factor of 'anti-social personality'. On the other hand, some studies have shown that a sub-culture of patriarchal attitudes actually constitutes the underlying causal link.

Child abuse

There is robust evidence of some degree of co-occurrence of different forms of family violence, in particular that of assault of the wife (or female co-habitee) and child abuse. In this way, child abuse may be seen as a risk marker for domestic violence (as well as vice versa). Appel and Holden (1998) found 42 studies of some co-occurrence of spouse and physical child abuse, of which they review 31, overwhelmingly of US origin. As compared with a community base of co-occurrence of 6% found in the 1985 US National Family Violence Survey, they found that clinical samples of either battered women or physically abused children found an overlap ranging from 20% to 100%, with a median rate of 40%. They suggest that the differences between the studies may be a result of variations in the definition of abuse; in the characteristics of the samples, in particular that the samples derived from refuges tap into a different and more severely victimised group; the source of the report; and the definition of the relationships at stake. The underlying models include that of the single perpetrator, usually that of a man who abuses both wife and child; a sequential model in which the man abuses the women who abuses the child; and bi- and multi-directional models in which there is reciprocal causation. They suggest that the studies they examined primarily support the identification of the man as the abuser of both spouse and child. Further reviews and studies that echo these findings include Kolbo et al (1996) and McKay (1994). Daly et al (1993) found evidence of co-occurrence of domestic violence and child abuse especially in stepfamilies where the man was not the father of the woman's child, using data from Canada, US and UK.

The UK literature on co-occurrence, though much more sparse, also provides some evidence, though less systematic, of co-occurrence of spousal assault and child abuse, and thus of child abuse as a risk marker for domestic violence. Kelly (1996), in her review primarily of the UK and Irish literature, finds that there is evidence of co-occurrence of domestic abuse of women by men and of child abuse. Browne and Hamilton (forthcoming) found that 46% of the 256 families referred for child abuse to the West Midlands police were found to experience domestic violence, making domestic violence the most common risk factor for child abuse. Further, 40% of the index children in families referred for domestic violence had previously been referred for child abuse. The figures may well be underestimates of the extent of the overlap between domestic violence and child abuse, since there appeared to be no systematic treatment of the reporting of the events between the child abuse and domestic violence units. Mullender and Morley (1994) likewise state that there is an overlap between domestic violence and child abuse in the UK.

Age

Youth is a risk factor for domestic violence. The BCS found that 10.1% of women aged 16-19 and 9.2% aged 20-24 reported that they had been assaulted in the previous year (as compared with an average of 4.2%), while 9.2% of men aged 20-24 said they had been assaulted. The risk declines steadily with age (though the survey has a cut off at age 59), with around 1% of 45-59 year olds reporting assault in the previous year.

This correlation with youth is also found in other national surveys: the Australian Women's Safety Survey (Australian Bureau of Statistics, 1996); the Statistics Finland survey (Statistics Finland, 1998); the Statistics Canada survey (Johnson, 1996), among others.

Though this is a very robust correlation, there is little attempt in the literature to explain why youth is such a highly correlated risk factor. It could be speculated that there are a number of causal pathways including:

- youth correlates with unemployment and lack of financial resources which are themselves risk factors;

- youth is related to less maturity and experience;
- youth is implicated in general theories of criminal career; or
- alternatively it may be that age has an independent correlation with criminal behaviour (Hirschi and Gottfredson, 1983).

Contexts

The literature so far considered has been comparing the risk of domestic violence between individuals within the same society. This pushes the analysis towards a consideration of individual attributes of risk. A different approach is to ask about the risk of domestic violence in different social and societal contexts. This would tend to address issues more relevant to desistance than to onset. This includes: the availability of formal and informal support services; the readiness and availability of kin and friends to provide assistance, especially sanctuary; the extent and effectiveness of sanctions, both informal and formal. The literature on many of the agencies that provide formal support and sanctions will be covered in other chapters, so the material addressed here will be limited.

Desistance is an important process in the determination of the risk of domestic violence. A far higher proportion of women have a lifetime experience of domestic violence than are currently subject to it (at least in the previous year). According to the BCS, 22.7% of women aged 16-59 who had had a partnership had experienced a domestic assault at some time in their lives, as compared with 4.2% in the previous year. Thus 18.5% of all partnered women and 81% of women who reported abuse sometime in their life had found some way of getting the violence to stop. This might involve either leaving the violent relationship or staying in the relationship and getting the man to change his behaviour.

Horton and Johnson (1993) studied women all of whom had ended abuse in order to ask what had made a difference to the outcome. They compared three groups of women: those who had left the abuser (the overwhelming majority); those who were still in a relationship with the man and were satisfied with their relationship; those who were still in a relationship with the man and were not satisfied with their relationship. The differential use of resources from outside the relationship was a major source of different outcome: those who did not use resources were more likely to have ended the relationship; those who did were more likely to have stayed. In particular, those women whose partners availed themselves of programmes, such as those treating alcoholism, were more likely to still be in a relationship. However, one of the most significant sources of different outcome was a non-treatment related variable, that of whether the man had ever forced the woman to have sex - where this was the case few women were still in a relationship. It would appear that in a few circumstances certain men are treatable and the relationship can survive if the woman is able to access outside input for both herself and her partner, but not in others. The sample was a volunteer sample and this may of course affect findings.

The importance of 'sanctions' and 'sanctuary' are the conclusion of a comparative analysis of 14 societies using ethnographies (Counts et al, 1992). Brown (1992) and Campbell (1992) in their overviews of this material conclude that sanctions against wife battering, and the availability of a sanctuary to which women can retreat are the most important factors in predicting in which societies wife battering is widespread. The sanctions were of various kinds, ranging from informal interventions and protests by neighbours and kin, to the more formal legal sanctions found in more complex societies. Sanctions from kin were more likely to be available to women who had not moved far from their families of origin. Sanctions are less available if the woman is more socially isolated. For instance, in more complex societies the greater privacy afforded the nuclear family can increase the woman's social isolation, reduce the availability of informal social sanctions, and thus increase the risk of wife battering. Sanctuary is also of great importance. To be most effective this needs to be immediate, to be available for long as well as short periods, and to involve the safety of those who offer sanctuary as well as the abused wife, and to protect the woman from the removal of her children. Economic dependency is negatively correlated with both sanctions and sanctuary, since female economic work groups or women's paid labour can reduce social isolation, thus affecting the likelihood that sanctions can be invoked and women's capacity to seek sanctuary.

Professional assessments of risk

There are many public services, support agencies, and voluntary bodies which are of enormous assistance to those who have suffered from domestic violence, and in many diverse ways make important contributions to achieving desistance and thus to reducing the risk of domestic violence. The role of some bodies, such as Women's Aid, is so obvious that they need little mention (Harwin, 1997). The sections below concentrate on those agencies and services that are currently engaged in improving the assessment and management of risk of domestic violence among the groups that they serve. There are three main issues: the ways in which assessment of risk is being integrated into policies and procedures; the extent to which this assessment is able to draw upon appropriate evidence from the research community; the relevance and practicability of targeting.

Assessing risk

Is there a single piece of information which is easy to obtain, unambiguous in form, easy to measure, the obtaining of which does not have untoward side effects, which busy professionals can use to assess robustly and consistently, the likelihood that the person in front of them is at risk of domestic violence and, in particular, is at risk of severe injury?

From some of the data in the previous section it might be thought that the risk profile of a domestic violence victim needs to be built in complex and composite terms including:

- young age;
- female;
- poor household;
- housewife or unemployed; and
- unemployed partner, whose partner witnessed his father beating his mother, associates with other men who think that wife beating is legitimate, and lives in a part of the country where support services are hard to find.

Fortunately, this is an inappropriate conclusion to draw. It is not only that this is too complex for busy professionals. More importantly it may well be counter-productive. This is because while there is some clustering of domestic violence, it is nonetheless experienced by people from all backgrounds to some extent. Any development of stereotypes of typical victims may well be extremely problematic for the effective provision of services to those who do not fit within these pictures of typical victims.

The research literature suggests a simpler answer. The simplest risk marker is that of previous assault. The best evidence of this is if the client has told the professional of this. Records of any previous incidents, or any previous pleas for help, suggest an increased risk.

A second simple risk marker is that of separation. Indeed it is at the point of separation that many women who have been subject to domestic violence go to the agencies under discussion.

While, however, the markers themselves are straightforward, many agencies might find their effective use more complicated if it entails changes to established procedures.

This risk assessment procedure is of course heavily dependent upon the victim's own assessment of her situation and her decision that she needs help to avoid further violence. Her assessment may, of course, be wrong. But she does, after all, have considerably more detailed information to hand about her case than anyone else, such as the number, frequency and severity of previous assaults. What the victim often lacks, however, is comparative information as to the likelihood of her various strategies of containment and/or resolution being successful. It is here that information and advice from agencies and meeting other women who are in or who have previously faced her predicament can be of great value (Davies, 1998). Potentially many agencies could deliver such information. Currently, the most important agency here is that of the Women's Aid refuge. Here she can reassess her own risk assessment with those who face her predicament, those who know how the system of support agencies works.

The public services

Police

The effect on crime levels of tackling repeat victimisation has led to this being set as a performance indicator for the police for 1999-2000, and domestic violence has been emphasised as a classic example of repeat victimisation. However, the information systems necessary to implement a policy prioritising repeat domestic violence victimisation by the police are often lacking. 41% of police interviewed in a Home Office study stated that their force did not even monitor the level of repeat victimisation let alone have procedures for reliably communicating this information to the responding officer (Plotnikoff and Woolfson, 1998). Recent pilot schemes may lead the way to improved practice (Hanmer and Griffiths, 1999). However, many practising officers continue to use their own risk assessments which involve criteria which are seriously at variance with policy, despite more than a decade of attempts at reform (Kelly, 1999).

Health services

In the US there is an extremely large literature about assessing the risk of domestic violence. This is focused around the extent to which health staff, especially those in front line situations such as Accident and Emergency Departments, can accurately identify those whose injuries result from domestic violence and what they should do with that information. (See for instance, Brown et al, 1993; Flitcraft et al, 1992; Furbee et al, 1998; Stark & Flitcraft, 1996). Indeed, the US Joint Commission on Accreditation of Healthcare Organisations requires written policies and procedures on domestic violence in emergency departments (Stevens, 1997). There have been important recent developments in the UK NHS about the detection and response to domestic violence, as discussed in chapter 4 of this volume. However, it should be noted that the discussion of the issue of 'screening' by academics, doctors and Women's Aid at the seminar organised by the Royal College of Obstetricians and Gynaecologists raised important practical issues. In particular, that screening would make a positive contribution only in the context of appropriately trained staff, time and resources to take appropriate action, back up support systems, and links to other agencies for specific referrals, that is, a broad range of policy innovation (Bewley et al, 1997).

Civil court agency procedures

Civil court and agency (such as the Child Support Agency) procedures around separation, divorce, child custody and child support have given cause for concern for their tendency to underestimate the frequency and impact of domestic violence among those using their services.

Additionally, a survey by the Women's Aid Federation England found that women in refuges had experienced further abuse from partners as a result of contact insisted upon by contact orders made under the 1989 Children Act (WAFE, 1993).

The trend towards mediated rather than adversarial systems of conflict resolution of separating couples, especially in relation to child custody has raised questions as to its suitability in cases of domestic violence. Hart (1990) has suggested that US evidence shows that mediation between former partners in the aftermath of domestic violence is not suitable. A history of the violence, with its power imbalances, is considered to make it impossible to achieve the fairness and balance needed to make this procedure a success. Hester & Radford (1996), on the basis of a comparison of practice in England and Denmark, reach parallel conclusions and argue that where there has been a history of domestic violence it has been rare to find child contact arrangements which are able to guarantee the safety of the women involved.

The probation service, which may be involved in these processes as part of their family court welfare work, uses a set of guidelines derived from the Home Office and Association of Chief Officers of Probation. This states that women should be free to choose separate rather than joint interviews when there has been domestic violence in order to safeguard the woman's safety (Ashworth, 1995).

However, given the extremely high recorded prevalence of domestic violence in separating couples (which itself may well be an under-reporting), and the increased dangers around enforced contact, it has been be suggested that these guidelines do not go far enough in protecting abused women and need further revision. There are ongoing localised developments in policy here that are in need of evaluation.

Housing

Women on the point of separation, need access to housing. Housing is both a safety requirement and indeed necessary to enable women to leave a violent partner. Further, since it appears that poorer women suffer higher rates of domestic violence, and are less likely to be able to afford housing in the private sector, there is an increased need to consider the allocative practices for social housing.

Improving abused women's access to housing to facilitate their escape is an issue which has been high on the agenda of those who have direct contact with women who have suffered domestic violence, as illustrated in the report of the National Inter-Agency Working Party on Domestic Violence (Victim Support, 1992). This has been recognised in the development of legislation to prioritise the needs of battered women.

There have been several examples of innovative policy development in local authorities in relation to housing. For instance, the London Borough of Camden has extensively developed innovative and comprehensive policy and procedure in relation to domestic violence over its full range of services (London Borough of Camden, 1996, 1999); while the London Borough of Newham has a proposed domestic violence strategy to co-ordinate its full range of services (Choo, 1999).

One example of an innovative policy development specifically in relation to housing which was not evaluated is that in the London Borough of Greenwich, 1993-7. This involved:

- identifying a need to improve policy in relation to domestic violence;
- arranging training courses; and
- recruiting a Housing Domestic Violence co-ordinator to oversee the new policy and procedures.

However, while the new policy remains in force, the co-ordinator's post ceased to exist in 1997, and with it systematic monitoring and consistent training (Bowstead, 1999).

Social work

Women seeing social workers appear to have a significantly higher than average rate of experience of domestic violence, for instance, one small scale study finding one in three social work client files contained reference to domestic violence (Maynard, 1985). Yet the systematic treatment of domestic violence by social work appears to be very uneven, despite its connection to other issues, in particular that a male abuser may be abusing his partner as well as the child (Mullender, 1996, 1997; Mullender and Morley, 1994). Farmer and Owen (1995) and Kelly (1996) make a strong case for the identification of domestic violence against women and support to be given to her in order to best protect children at risk of abuse, yet note that this is rarely forthcoming in child protection work.

The New Deal and leaving violent men

The combination of risk factors relating to poverty and social exclusion discussed earlier put lone parents at high risk from domestic violence. It follows therefore that clients participating in the New Deal for Lone Parents will be from a high risk group. Abused women have a worse economic position than average, being less likely to be in employment, more likely to be unemployed, and more likely to be in low income households; separating women, are a high risk group. Lone mothers are more likely to be poor. Lone mothers have lower rates of employment than married women (Walby, 1997).

Over three quarters of individuals in lone parent families are in the bottom two fifths of the income distribution. (Bradshaw et al, 1996).

Women who are leaving violent men are thus at high risk of poverty and, as a consequence of approaching the Benefits Agency for income support, and to being (voluntary) participants of the New Deal for Lone Parents. This has consequences for the training programmes for New Deal Advisers.

US policy experience suggests that some women fleeing violent men may need time and assistance before they are able to participate effectively in training and labour market placements; indeed in light of this, battered women are exempted from the new welfare benefit cut-offs in the US (Murphy, 1997).

Conclusion

The simplest and most robust risk marker for domestic violence is a previous assault. The greater the frequency of previous assaults, the more likely will be further assaults. The evidence does not support a clear separation into two populations, one of which is at serious risk of minor violence and one which is at risk of major violence. Rather, there can be escalation from minor to severe violence, although escalation is not inevitable.

Women's active attempts to achieve desistance can be successful, though it would appear that it often entails ending the relationship. The process of leaving a violent man is high risk in itself, with separation being associated with an increased risk. Agencies need to have policies and procedures that take this risk into account.

While there are significant correlations between domestic violence and poverty, these are not extreme, and domestic violence can be found throughout the class spectrum. Nevertheless, lack of economic resources (more common in women's than men's lives) makes it harder for a woman to leave a violent man.

While there is a correlation between men's experience of a violent family and subsequent abuse, there is doubt as to whether this is more than a spurious correlation. The underlying causal pathways appear to involve either an anti-social personality and the attributes traditionally linked to the concept of a criminal career; or a belief system involving the approval of wife beating and other forms of gender inequality.

Gender inequality is a risk factor in domestic violence.

Most women who successfully achieve desistance do so with the active assistance of a large number and range of outside agencies, including

Women's Aid, the criminal justice system, and welfare and support agencies.

Much of the existing research has focused on the risks associated with the onset of domestic violence, and much less on the factors behind desistance. Research on desistance would be of especial use for programmes to reduce domestic violence.

Costs and knowledge

The costs of domestic violence are enormous. However, we cannot estimate these accurately without good data on the prevalence and incidence of domestic violence.

Without an accurate estimate of the prevalence of the risk of domestic violence in the population and particular groups it is hard to develop evidence based professional practice. Many professionals have commented on the need to have better evidence as to the risk of domestic violence in order to ensure that their policies and procedures are appropriate.

A dedicated random sample national survey is the only method that can adequately provide the knowledge of the full extent of this violence. In particular, such a survey could provide information on factors associated with desistance if it included lifetime patterns of violence.

The BCS does not collect data on a range of issues pertinent to the analysis of the risk of domestic violence, partly because in a generic crime survey there is insufficient time to focus on this particular set of issues. It does not contain sufficient information to adequately address many significant issues including:

- desistance and the factors associated with this, such as use of specific agencies;
- escalation, the changing frequency and severity of assaults, and the factors associated with this;
- the impact of women's income, since there is no question on this;
- the relationship of domestic violence to other victimisation, such as stalking which might follow on from prior domestic violence, since the questions are limited to domestic violence;
- the relative prevalence of domestic violence against pregnant women; and
- the relative prevalence of domestic violence before and after separation.

The majority of the work on the assessment of the risk of domestic violence is from the US. There have been new generations of national surveys on violence against women that have been carried out in the US, Canada, Australia, Finland, Iceland and the Netherlands and are under development in Sweden and Germany. We do not know to what extent findings from other countries may be accurately applied to the UK, since there are significant differences, for instance in the nature and effect of the criminal justice system, welfare system, patterns of social exclusion and of gender relations.

Thus, there is need for a new generation survey of violence against women in the UK in order to estimate more fully the extent and nature of the risks of domestic violence. There is a need for data which can accurately assess the risks of different groups, so as to assist the public services and other agencies to tailor their policies and procedures more effectively to meet these needs. (Some, but far from all, of these additional data are being collected in the BCS2001 module on interpersonal violence.)

Many professions, services and agencies are quite rightly concerned to develop their policies and procedures in the light of new knowledge about domestic violence. There is a lot of new innovative practice, but developments are uneven. Policies need to be evaluated and the results disseminated so as to speed more widespread adoption of best practice. For many there will be costs to develop appropriate policies and protocols, which will need to be evaluated for their impact. While in many instances a type of quasi-experimental design may be an important tool in such an evaluation, it is unlikely to be sufficient in all cases, since many agencies will need an independent measure of the prevalence and incidence of domestic violence in their client populations.

The analysis of risk factors for domestic violence suggests that there are many places where new or enhanced interventions are possible to reduce domestic violence.

Monitoring costs and evaluating needs

Debbie Crisp and Betsy Stanko

Very little work has examined the financial implications of domestic violence, but the studies included in this review suggest that the costs to the public sector are substantial - particularly those borne by criminal justice agencies. There has yet to be a satisfactory assessment of the economic burden on those experiencing violence or the impact on resources of multi-agency working. We also found it hard to assess the cost-effectiveness of particular interventions as individual evaluations to date have rarely included an economic dimension. Other research into domestic violence has demonstrated a notable consistency in the patterns of abuse, and in the type and nature of services used by individuals when seeking assistance. The number of people already contacting key service providers shows that domestic violence is not 'hidden', but failure on the part of practitioners to monitor their caseloads adequately means we are unable to draw an accurate localised picture of needs or practice. We argue that agencies providing domestic violence related services should to be able to describe what they are currently doing and how they are spending existing resources. In this way baseline data can be generated against which the impact and cost-effectiveness of any future interventions can be measured.

Introduction

The Home Office Crime Reduction Programme (CRP) covers a broad range of initiatives (Dhiri and Brand, 1999). Within each area examined, the CRP aims to produce an analysis of the input, output and outcome measures used by individual project evaluations to enable evidence-based comparisons between interventions. In turn, these findings can be used to consolidate the most cost-effective strategies for crime reduction. When trying to undertake a review of this type in relation to domestic violence, however, we are presented with a number of hurdles.

Currently there is no universally accepted definition of the term 'domestic violence'. Debates continue about the nature and seriousness of the abuse to be included, the location of individual incidents and the relationship between the parties involved. The following definition is being used for the purposes of the CRP:

> violence between current or former partners in an intimate relationship, wherever and whenever the violence occurs. The violence may include physical, sexual, emotional/psychological or financial abuse. This includes violence by men on women and, by women on men and within same sex relationships but does not include other violence in a domestic setting such as child or elder abuse or between siblings or flat sharers.

Many incidents of this type do not comprise behaviours that have been criminalised, or do not fall within the existing classification of offences (Stanko et al, 1998). Definition in terms of inputs, outputs and outcomes is also problematic. Much of the knowledge we have about domestic violence has been generated by victimisation surveys such as the British Crime Survey (BCS) (Mirrlees-Black et al, 1998). These give us some insight into the nature and extent of this type of abuse, but uncover very little about the extent to which individual interventions may impact on its reduction.

These crime surveys have been supplemented by evaluations of particular projects or explorations of specific issues, as described in the specific areas covered by the other chapters in this volume. However, restricted resources have meant that the research to date has been somewhat piecemeal in nature, necessarily focusing on areas of interest to individual funders, resulting in little co-ordination between the systems of measurement used for assessment. There is an even greater paucity of material that looks explicitly at the financial implications of the work in this area. In order, therefore, to come to an understanding of the existing data on the costs and measurements of domestic violence, we have supplemented our review of the literature with an analysis of the audits commissioned under the 1998 Crime and Disorder Act. Since domestic violence was a specified part of their remit, we hoped to be able to use them to outline the empirical basis on which local strategies to reduce this type of abuse had been devised. Instead, the audits showed that non-existent or poor monitoring currently means that in general we are unable to account for the work undertaken by the key relevant agencies in a particular area. Material was also generally lacking on the nature or extent of domestic violence within individual areas. It is optimistic to attempt an assessment of costings in the absence of information on either service provision or probable demand.

We already know a good deal about domestic violence, although the studies to date may be piecemeal, there is a notable consistency in the patterns of abuse presented (see Walby, this volume). We also know about the type and nature of the services individuals are likely to approach (see Kelly and Humphreys, this volume) when seeking assistance, and that these needs will be persistent. We suggest that there is an urgent need to create systems of measurement that can be used to generate baseline data against which the impact and cost-effectiveness of any intervention can be assessed. In the last section of this chapter we offer a model aimed to facilitate the monitoring that will be required for the next phase of work to be carried out under the Crime and Disorder Act.

Agreed systems of monitoring, communication and dissemination would help to co-ordinate and apply the knowledge we do have about domestic violence in a strategic way. We must supplement this current body of research which is largely reliant on victimisation surveys: in many respects this form of data collection puts too much responsibility for data generation on the individual who has experienced the abuse. Instead, there is a great deal of information about domestic violence that could be routinely collected by service providers themselves. In the absence of stringent and adequate monitoring it is impossible to assess the extent, impact and costs of intervention on the prevalence and incidence of domestic violence. We are convinced that the introduction of such monitoring systems need not be unduly burdensome on practitioners. We are equally convinced that service providers can no longer afford not to collect, collate and share this information.

Research on costs

Studies of costs around the world have attempted to demonstrate the financial impact of inter-partner violence. Only a limited amount of research of this type currently exists, and the bulk of the work has been undertaken outside the UK. Some studies have examined how this type of abuse impacts on individuals' physical and mental well-being, and on their ability to participate in the community or in the workplace. Research so far, however, has concentrated on public, voluntary and private sector expenditure on the basis that a proportion of those experiencing domestic violence will into tap key agencies for assistance, and as a result there will be resource implications. Comparisons between the different costings studies are problematic, due to the wide range of methodologies, the units of analysis, the time period used and other variations between countries. At the same time, all of the research projects reviewed (see Table 1) - despite the disparity in their approaches - concluded that the cost implications for service providers were substantial. Figure 1 summaries the groups of individuals and organisations on which domestic violence was found to have a financial impact.

Most studies looked exclusively at the costs resulting from service provision to women experiencing domestic violence (and sometimes their children). This has usually been the focus since the majority of those who contact the key relevant agencies are women. Men's use of public services in this context is relatively low (this may be a reflection of the disparity in the impact of domestic violence by gender identified by Mirrlees-Black (1999)),

Figure 1: The impact of domestic violence

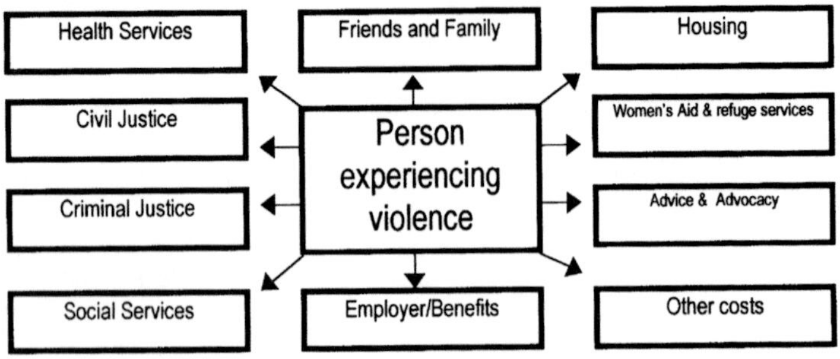

but some men do look for advice and support from statutory and voluntary agencies. There needs to be systematic monitoring of what help is asked for - and what is actually provided to those seeking assistance by sex, age, ethnicity, sexuality, disability, employment status and so forth. This can then be used to help identify whether particular groups have particular needs, and also to highlight any gaps or partial aspects of service provision.

Costs and prevalence

As noted above, debates still continue about a specific, inclusive definition of domestic violence. The definitions used for any individual study will dictate what data are collected or examined: this may explain some of the variation in the statistics used in the costings studies outlined in Table 1. The lack of consistency can also to some extent be accounted for by the variation between countries in their healthcare, welfare and legal systems. Further, often data is not available in the format required to undertake a conclusive analysis of this type, and so projects have relied on data from victimisation studies - these tend to be more to do with prevalence than they are to do with the impact of domestic violence. We can, however, take a broad overview of the types of costs that research on the financial implications of domestic violence have calculated to date. They fall within the following categories of harm or service provision:

- physical health (injury and hospitalisation, prenatal complications, stress illness such as ulcers and skin disorders, dental etc.);
- psychiatric services and other provision for people who are drug and/or alcohol dependent, are suffering from depression, have attempted suicide or have other mental health problems (including prescriptions

Table 1
Studies on costs

	UK			Holland	Switzerland		Australia		Canada		NZ
	Guildford	Stanko et al	Young	Korf et al	Godenzi & Yodanis	NSW	Northern Territories	Blumel et al	Day	Greaves	Snively
Service providers											
Criminal justice	✓	✓		✓	✓	✓	✓		✓	✓	
Civil justice	✓	✓									
Housing	✓	✓				✓	✓		✓		
Refuge services	✓	✓		✓	✓	✓	✓		✓	✓	
Counselling	✓				✓		✓				
Health		✓	✓	✓	✓	✓	✓		✓	✓	✓
Social services	✓	✓		✓						✓	
Benefits/welfare				✓	✓	✓	✓				✓
Employment				✓		✓		✓	✓	✓	✓
Child care						✓	✓				✓
Child protection		✓									
Education										✓	
Public awareness										✓	
Timescale											
Immediate/past year	✓	✓	✓	✓	✓	✓	✓		✓	✓	✓
Longer term							✓	✓	✓	✓	
Cost borne by											
Person experiencing							✓	✓			
Public/private sector	✓	✓	✓	✓	✓	✓	✓	✓	✓	✓	✓
Third party							✓				
Area covered				✓	✓	✓	✓	✓	✓	✓	✓
National/regional											
Local	✓	✓	✓								

for anti-depressants and other relevant drugs);
- civil and criminal legal remedies, from injunctions, ouster orders, divorce and child custody to policing, prosecution and criminal punishment;
- housing (including temporary and permanent, as well as refuge provision);
- criminal damage (e.g. to cars, homes, workplaces);
- advice services (such as CAB, Law Centres etc.);
- counselling (such as Relate);
- social services (these costs mainly relate to Child Protection issues);
- disruption to children's education (behavioural problems in school as well as alterations to school roll); and
- unemployment, reduced productivity at work and absenteeism from work.

Studies have attempted to produce estimates of the immediate costs of responding to individual incidents, the costs associated with long-term impact on adult life and on the costs of public sector services (such as mental health support, imprisonment, disrupted education leading to limited job prospects and so forth) stemming from the consequences of domestic violence. The majority use prevalence data to generate estimates of the unit cost of services. Some have tried to draw upon individuals' experiences of domestic violence and their helpseeking patterns to extrapolate costs. There has been a great deal of variation in the methodological approaches used, but no one project has so far produced a satisfactory blueprint for future research of this type. Only one study (Stanko et al, 1998) has tried to make a comprehensive assessment of costs in a local context (the majority of others have drawn upon national or statewide data).

The study by New South Wales (NSW) Women's Co-ordination Unit (1991) identified three 'levels' of abuse which may have attendant resource implications. The first was called 'non-disclosure' and represented domestic violence that is unacknowledged to others, either informally or formally. The second - 'acknowledgement and helpseeking' - referred to attempts to seek assistance either from an individual's social networks or from more formalised voluntary or state-funded service providers. There was a recognition that within this group there may be those who were 'heavy users' of services. The third stage was called 'building an alternative life' and speculated as to the cost implications once the abuse had come to an end. This schema of levels is helpful in that it allows us to separate the helpseeking patterns of the person experiencing violence from the nature of the abuse that is being inflicted on them. The study drew upon statewide statistics and argued that the most easily identifiable costs were those at stage two. However, the methodology contained some problematic assumptions about the prevalence of domestic violence in NSW: the estimates used for the costing calculations were informed by practice, but not grounded in data.

The New Zealand (Snively, 1994) study built upon the NSW work, and applied three different estimates of prevalence of abuse to relevant national data (including police, healthcare and welfare statistics) to calculate the amount of expenditure that was domestic violence related. The study did not, however, take into account findings from other research that people experiencing abuse may be disproportionately likely to draw upon public services. For example, the 1997 Scottish Needs Assessment Programme (SNAP) report on domestic violence found that 'women who experience [abuse] are more likely than those who do not to have poor health'.

The Canadian studies (Day, 1995; Greaves et al, 1995) took as their basis the prevalence estimates generated by the national Violence Against Women Survey (VAWS) (Johnson and Sacco, 1995), and applied these to national statistics. The research made assumptions about agency usage, which for the most part were also extrapolated from the VAWS. These costings present a homogeneous national picture, which did not give great insight into cultural or geographical diversities. On the other hand, the study shows the wide range of types of abuse women experience mean that they need to draw upon an equally wide range of services for a wide variety of reasons.

The relationship between the incidence of domestic violence and helpseeking is a complex one, but the link is important. Statistics in relation to abuse can be misleading. We may have estimates about the number of different types of incident each year, but we are unclear about how these fit together. The way that data are displayed often manages to mask any patterns (its frequency, escalation and so forth). Mirrlees-Black (1999) suggests that 2% of incidents of domestic violence result in broken bones. The 1998 BCS (Mirrlees-Black et al, 1998) estimates that there were 835,000 incidents in the previous twelve month period in England and Wales (and the survey recognises itself that this is almost certainly an underestimate). This means that there were at least 16,700 broken bones during the course of the year (equivalent to one every half an hour, 24 hours a day, 365 days a year). But these bones belong to people, a significant proportion of whom will have had the same or other bones broken in a similar way on other comparable occasions. Many of these injuries result in treatment by the National Health Service, costing tens of thousands of pounds each year. We need to inform ourselves about the nature of abuse: its realities, its regularities, its premeditation, its duration, the overlap between types of abuse, their impact on people experiencing violence and on those around them. We need to understand if there is any variation in these patterns according, for example, to an individual's culture or geography. In this way we can better comprehend when and why people turn to public services for help. There is a context to any individual incident of domestic violence and to remove that incident from that context is to impair our understanding of appropriate service provision. There is also a cumulative impact on the public purse.

The study in Hackney (Stanko et al, 1998) used information collected from case files from the police, housing department and social services to estimate the usage and costs of local service provision. Other research has shown the proportion of women experiencing abuse who are likely to have contact with these agencies (for example McGibbon et al, 1989). However, information about client usage - and the efficient and effective delivery of those services - has been virtually untapped for its insights into the scope of the problem of domestic violence, and its impact on the public and voluntary sector. Once the organisation's domestic violence-related caseload is known, it is possible to extrapolate from this an estimate of prevalence within its 'catchment' area. There was a high degree of internal consistency between the estimates derived in this way for the Hackney project (one in fifteen, one in sixteen, and one in eighteen in the previous year respectively). However, comparisons with the supplementary survey of women in a GP surgery waiting room (which found one in nine women had experienced abuse in the past twelve months) suggested that not all domestic violence-related contact was finding its way onto agencies files. It is possible that women are only getting in touch with some agencies when in acute crisis. It is probable that women are making domestic violence related contacts, but not disclosing their experiences. It is almost certain that practitioners are not recording the information even when women do choose to disclose. However, the lower estimates of service usage from the material collected from the files examined still suggest that significant resources are already being expended on servicing cases that are domestic violence related. So while we continue to state that one of the main problems with domestic violence is its hidden nature, we virtually ignore its substantial presence in the everyday workload of public and voluntary agencies.

Costs and helpseeking

The costings study carried out in Australia's Northern Territories (Office of Women's Policy, 1996) took a different approach to most other work of this sort. A number of women were interviewed about their experiences of abuse and their helpseeking behaviours. These data were used to create a number of scenarios that were then individually costed and extrapolated to give generalised costings for the state. This methodology is problematic: whilst offering useful insight into the diversity of women's contact with service providers, no sense was given as to the extent to which these scenarios were representative (for this reason the composite case studies in the Hackney study remained uncosted). The importance of this work, however, was that it attempted to link the multiple use of services with costs.

Research that does exist into helpseeking strategies has shown that where people experiencing violence choose to disclose their experiences, they often contact more than one agency for assistance (for example Dominy & Radford, 1996). The trickiest problem for any economic analysis of domestic violence - particularly when exploring ways to bring about a reduction in the prevalence and incidence of abuse - is how to estimate the intersection between the various types of costs examined. We know that people experiencing violence may approach different agencies for a variety of reasons, and that these reasons may reprioritise over time. As Kelly (1988: 131) points out, the way that people understand their situation is 'not a static process. It is changing and dynamic'. We still have very little information on the way that people experiencing violence seek help, on the barriers and triggers to contacting others to ask for help, or on the interactions with practitioners that spark different agency or individual responses. There is a contradiction here: the majority of existing data focuses on the perspective of the person experiencing abuse and allows the perpetrator to fade from the picture. Yet data in relation to helpseeking is presented in terms of agencies contacted, which means that the person seeking help disappears from view, along with their helpseeking strategies. In both situations we end up with a slightly skewed focus. This skew becomes further exaggerated when we take into account the extraordinary resource implications demonstrated by costings studies to associate with the criminal justice process. These costs would mainly attach to the perpetrators, and not the person experiencing abuse.

Costings studies have not generally attempted to come to an understanding of the extent of or reasons for the repeated nature of these contacts. For example are the women being referred on by other practitioners, or do they contact a variety of different agencies until they are able to find an organisation that is able to meet their specific needs? For the most part this is because the data used in the studies has been generated by the key agencies, and this not information that they currently record. Domestic violence is easier to ignore if potential interventions are not mapped holistically. The Northern Territories identified this as a major flaw, but sought ways to meet this obstacle head-on.

Cost-benefit analyses must be able to understand the overlap between the different services that support and assist women who approach them to escape violence and threatened or potential abuse. The timing and nature of any intervention can be crucial to prevention of future violence (Hanmer et al, 1999). Kelly et al's (1999) evaluation of Domestic Violence Matters in Islington showed that women valued the advice and support they received from the team of advocates. Further, where women were 'enabled to pursue prosecution [in this way] conviction is likely, most commonly through a guilty plea.' (p.71). This kind of service can undoubtedly result in an overall cost savings for the Treasury: the resources needed to employ a team of dedicated domestic violence workers will almost certainly require less funds than the repeated visits to health, police, housing and social services which would otherwise ensue.

In recognition of the financial implications of multiple contacts, and the need for inter-agency co-ordination, the Northern Territories (Hunter, 1996) have applied the findings of their - albeit unrepresentative - costings research and are in the process of introducing a confidential system of monitoring and tracking of domestic violence related cases. The success of such an initiative is very much dependent on whether individuals are prepared to inform practitioners of their situation. There are variations between studies in the findings of levels of disclosure to key agencies by people experiencing violence (McGibbon et al, 1989; Mooney, 1994; Dominy and Radford, 1996; Mirrlees-Black, 1999). We should also take into consideration that people experiencing violence may also not wish to disclose this fact to researchers. We are unclear as to the extent to which these variations may be geographical artefacts and the levels of disclosure affected by the local provision or perceived quality of services. For example, the need for re-housing when escaping violence may be the same in two different areas, but the amount of available housing stock may be very different. From the localised studies examined, there do appear to be regional differences in the way women seek help. A system of monitoring should therefore create a mechanism for feedback on usage of agencies as well as gaps in service.

Costs and service provision

To date, research in relation to the economic impact of domestic violence has generally been a heuristic device to raise awareness that along with the social costs of this type of abuse, there are enormous financial ramifications for society as a whole. Studies have suggested that the majority of the monetary burden is borne by the public sector (for example Godenzi and Yodanis, 1999), although this may in fact be due to the difficulty in assessing the financial impact on individuals. There has been no research that compares specific interventions and their possible cost implications. The Crime Reduction Programme aims to find the best value for public service provision, and studies found that the costs relating to criminal justice are substantial (in some it was suggested that these were the largest costs within the public sector). Interestingly, much of these resources will be directed at the arrest and prosecution of the perpetrator of the abuse. Involvement with the criminal justice process does not, however, guarantee desistance from domestic violence, neither does it even guarantee a 'successful' prosecution. Of the incidents that are reported to the police, only a relatively small proportion are recorded (just over a quarter, as opposed to nearly two thirds of burglaries, Mirrlees-Black et al, 1998), with an even fewer number resulting in arrest (Kelly, 1999). Interventions that *do* manage to put an end to a perpetrator's violent behaviour, or contribute towards the prevention of this type of abuse should be lauded. However, domestic violence service provision is - and indeed should be - primarily concerned with the person being abused. This fact should perhaps be echoed within the allocation of resources.

When examining ways in which reductions can be made in the prevalence and incidence of domestic violence, we need to cast the net wider than the criminal justice process. Somewhere between 40-60% of people reporting experiencing domestic violence will tell someone else about their situation (McGibbon, 1989; Dominy & Radford, 1996). Whether or not they also contact a service provider, almost all of these will disclose to a relative or friend (Mirrlees-Black, 1999). On a lifetime prevalence estimate, these friends and family represent in excess of 3.6 million people[1] - or one in twelve of the adult population.

In general, the relative or friend will offer the abused person information or advice. Usually they will find this support helpful (Mirrlees-Black, 1999). We are, however, unclear as to the nature of this advice and information, or about the practical backup that relatives or friends might feel that they need themselves. The relatives and friends of people experiencing violence have not been specifically targeted in campaigns that challenge domestic violence - but research has consistently shown that they are often the first port of call in an abused person's helpseeking. Due to the on-going nature of their relationship with the person experiencing domestic violence, they can offer an enhanced understanding of the abused person's needs (both shorter and longer term), and of the types of crises that may be faced. They can also give useful insight into the barriers and triggers that exist to helpseeking.

In terms of formalised helpseeking, the multi-agency approach encouraged by the revised Home Office Inter-Departmental Circular (2000) recognises that people experiencing domestic violence may prefer to look to other, non-criminal justice based agencies for help. The advice and support given by these individuals and organisations may in fact have an impact on levels of offending. Practitioners must become better informed about each other's roles and responsibilities, they must take on a more co-ordinated approach to working together, and they must be imaginative and comprehensive in the list of those they include within multi-agency initiatives. Otherwise it is too easy for domestic violence related service provision to fall between the gaps. Mullender et al (1998:13) describes services currently provided by local authorities as 'piecemeal provision'.

She suggests that this is because the work done addressing domestic violence has been 'everywhere and nowhere', that is it has cropped up everywhere across the work of an authority, yet has nowhere been recognised as anyone's particular responsibility'. Interventions need instead to be planned strategically. Such thinking within the context of a crime reduction programme may lead to the conclusion that, for example, a decrease in repeat victimisation may be achieved cost-effectively by the early intervention of a non-criminal justice based agency - say routine screening by GPs. For this reason, it is vital that the need for a multi-agency approach is also embraced at central government level.

In recent years there have been a plethora of initiatives and policies in the field of criminal justice aimed to encourage service providers to work together. For example, the Crime and Disorder Act 'gives local authorities, the police and a variety of other key partners specific responsibilities for the prevention of crime and disorder' (Hough and Tilley, 1998).

The Act obligates each Local Authority to use a multi-agency approach (working with the police, probation, health authorities and any other agency felt to be of relevance) to carry out an audit of crime and disorder within their authority boundaries. To facilitate this exchange of material, s.116 of the Act empowers 'necessary and expedient' disclosure on the part of agencies and individuals involved in the work. Data can only be exchanged with 'due regard to privacy, fairness and other relevant principles' - it is vital to acknowledge how breach of confidentiality in domestic violence cases can have direct consequences for example the safety of a person experiencing abuse. The section gave those working on the Audits an unprecedented chance to take innovative and creative approaches to data collection. The work undertaken for the Audits was then to be used to form the basis of a localised crime and disorder strategy, using the material generated to identify key priorities for future initiatives within the area surveyed. Prior to the Audit work commencing, Home Office Minister Paul Boateng wrote to each local authority area to encourage them to address the issue of domestic violence within any resulting reports.

Such a large-scale attempt to generate a picture of localised concerns in relation to criminal justice had never been previously undertaken in this country. As part of the work for this chapter, we felt it important to review the emerging Audit and Strategy documents, to see if they were able to give us some insight into the needs of those experiencing domestic violence.

Review of Crime and Disorder Audits

There are 410 local authority areas in England and Wales. We were able to look at Crime and Disorder documents for 281 - just over two-thirds (Audit only 43%, Strategy only 15%, Audit and Strategy 41%). We found that the issue of domestic violence was covered in 83% of areas examined. The contributions, however, ranged from the cursory to the considered (only Middlesbrough produced a separate report specifically on the subject). Reports from some other areas were a little confused (or at least, confusing). For example, Rutland stated that there was 'a lack of data about this topic', but proceeded to provide a definition for domestic violence (something only included by only 23% of the areas) and to analyse the subject in more detail than in a large number of other reports. To be fair, several did recognise the shortcomings of the way that information was currently collected - for example, Tandridge stated that 'the police will be revamping their crime systems and the relevant data should be available for future audits'.

The Home Office Guidance (Hough and Tilley, 1998) on how to undertake the work for the Crime and Disorder Audits tried to avoid being too prescriptive as it felt that agencies should not become too 'preoccupied with structures'. The idea was that instead, drawing upon material already available to them such as: local policing plans; probation service plans; housing investment programmes; Social Services Child Care plans; Drug Action plans; Area Child Protection Committees Annual Reviews; Community Care plans and so forth - they should find their own ways to work together.

In two out of five of the areas examined, domestic violence was felt to be sufficiently important to be allocated its own section (others included it, for example, under community safety, or a generalised heading of violence). In the overwhelming majority of the audits and strategies we looked at, we found recognition of the need for multi-agency action to help decrease the prevalence, incidence and impact of domestic violence. However, this position had generally been reached in the absence of any structured collection or analysis of localised statistics. It appears clear to us that many areas found themselves out of their depth doing this exercise in relation to domestic violence, and would in fact have welcomed a more mainstreamed approach to data collection. The data used to review the topic showed a distinct lack of imagination, and a strong over-reliance on police statistics (see Table 2 overleaf).

For all of the areas that included police data, the number of incidents that had been recorded as domestic violence related was presented. In some cases figures were included which related to the proportion of cases which involved repeat victimisation. A limited number of areas also presented information by gender and/or neighbourhood. Some gave the number of arrests, or the proportion of cases that fell into particular offence types. However, there was little parity in the way that even similar data were presented. The lack of sufficient detail on the demographics of the local population meant that it was generally impossible to estimate the level of prevalence for the local authority area.

Table 2
Data included in crime and disorder audits

Data included in audit &/or strategy	Proportion of areas examined (*n*=281)
	%
Police data	69
Women's Aid/other refuges	10
Other housing	5
Accident & Emergency	6
Social services	1
Other	6

The data for Women's Aid/other refuges, along with the other housing data and material on social services were generally presented in terms of the total number of referrals. Again, however, without the necessary detail on either the population, or - for the housing and social services material - information on total caseloads, it was not possible to gain an indication of the level of prevalence, or calculate domestic referrals as a proportion of a department's work. Data from the Accident and Emergency departments invariably comprised the proportion of assault cases that took place in the home (but again, lacked information on overall caseloads). The other agencies that supplied material were mainly Victim Support and other local advice or counselling services, including helplines (again, usually number of contacts/referrals).

In some cases, a lot of work had gone into trying to come to an understanding of the local picture, often backed up by findings from national statistics or research studies. In general, however, rather than raising specific questions and attempting to find information that might enlighten these issues, the commentary was arranged around the scant figures that a few dedicated individuals had managed to pull together. Data were rarely shown that demonstrated the differences among domestic violence victims, especially in terms of gender or ethnicity. There were only sporadic efforts to explore how domestic violence impacts on children. As a result there was no way to further interrogate the data presented about the diversity of needs.

Despite the recent recognition of domestic violence as a health issue (Radford et al, 1998), and the fact that roughly one in five women experiencing abuse will disclose this to their GP (Mirrlees-Black, 1999), hardly any of the reports included information from primary health care providers. Further, even though other government departments have undertaken similar auditing exercises, the reports did not address the possible overlap between their work and that of the Employment Action Zones, Health Action Zones or Education Action Zones. If the aim of the

Crime and Disorder Audits was to encourage strategic thinking, there were only limited examples of this in the reports in relation to domestic violence.

The audit teams were asked to identify their emerging priorities for crime and disorder within their area. The overall average number of priorities was five: these would sometimes be altered or reprioritised between the audit and strategy documents. In some cases these priorities would be set out as general mission statements; other areas drew up detailed action plans within specific targets, and input, output and outcome measures. Interestingly, four out of five areas which mentioned domestic violence in their audits and/or strategy documents also included the issue as an emerging priority. The topic was neither mentioned in the report nor included in the emerging priorities in only 4% of cases reviewed.

For the most part, domestic violence was listed as an emerging priority in its own right and/or incorporated under the priorities relating to a more generalised heading of violence. On slightly fewer occasions it was specified under a different heading - such as community safety - on a comparable number it was implicitly included - for example in priorities dealing with 'vulnerable groups'.

The Oswestry Audit was anxious to point out that domestic violence had been included within the emerging priorities not 'because of evidence of high levels existing locally. Rather, further work is required in this field because the current level of service provision, public awareness and prevention is weak'. Other areas concurred that the dearth of local data was a concern, for example in Monmouth the crime and disorder audit work 'identified wide ranging inconsistencies and gaps in statistical record keeping'. Such stances are laudable, but we are concerned that the focus of multi-disciplinary groups' energies over the next three years in drawing up policies and protocols may omit to uncover the services which people experiencing violence within their area would ideally like to access. The over-reliance on police data within the audit and strategy reports (a service which is often contacted only in times of crisis) means that the body of work generated so far from Crime and Disorder Act related work is mainly in terms of crisis provision (and very occasionally cost) as opposed to information on support and prevention. In many cases, the local agencies were keen to work together to bring about change - for example, Bromsgrove's partnership declared themselves to be 'committed to establishing a clearer picture of the domestic violence situation in the district'. Hopefully this will be taken to mean a picture of awareness and need as well as provision.

The Home Office guidance issued on how to carry out a Crime and Disorder Audit work deliberately shied away from a mainstreamed format for the reports. At the same time, it was comprehensive and clearly demonstrated how vital it was to map need. The reports generated by this first block of work should not be seen as a missed opportunity - how can they be? They provide an invaluable baseline that has not previously existed within this country. At the same time, it would seem that areas might now welcome a firmer lead - otherwise we may find ourselves still thinking in terms of 'if only' at the next point of review.

The need for monitoring

The problem lies not necessarily with how the audits were carried out (although this was a compounding factor in some cases). Even those using a far more comprehensive approach to data collection encountered difficulties in finding material with which to work. For example, Middlesbrough produced a separate multi-agency report dealing exclusively with the issue of domestic violence. They identified 28 different groups of relevant practitioners. Of the 27 groups that responded, nine (a third) reported that they did not collect statistics on domestic violence. Three others expressed an interest in generating data in the near future. Two provided estimates of how domestic violence might impact on their caseload, and a further five provided the number of cases of this type that they had dealt with recently. However, none of these seven provided sufficient information to put this material into context. In only the remaining 7 cases (i.e. just over a quarter) were data included which showed the proportion of an agency's workload relating to this type of abuse. Three agencies were also able to supply information on the extent of repeat victimisation and/or on the outcomes of domestic violence cases.

These findings represent an improvement on those of the Hackney project (Stanko et al, 1998) where only 1 in 11 of the 107 groups contacted were able to estimate the proportion of their caseload that was domestic violence related. More concerning is the continued failure of practitioners to recognise that their organisation is being used by people experiencing this type of abuse. In Hackney, one respondent from a local advice agency identified in previous research as a key service provider suggested that 'we contact the police' for information about this kind of case, as they did not see themselves as having a part to play. In Middlesbrough, despite the recent publicity about the healthcare implications of domestic violence (Radford et al, 1998), only 1 of the 60 GPs contacted responded to the survey (and that was to say that they did not have any relevant data).

Cost studies and research into helpseeking practices tell us that people experiencing domestic violence - the majority of whom are women - are contacting services and doing so in large numbers. For example, roughly one in six of the 105,640 homelessness applications each year come as a result of domestic violence (London Research Centre, 1999). This is equivalent to more than two applications, every hour, 24 hours a day, 365 days a year. Further, Women's Aid Federation of England runs a nationwide domestic violence helpline that handles 20,000 calls each year. This is equivalent to more than 11 calls for every hour that the helpline is open, and does not include the many calls that are unable to get through (WAFE, 1999b). In addition, domestic violence impacts on those beyond the person who is experiencing violence. A large number of those on the At Risk Register are included because there is violence within the household (Middlesbrough Domestic Task Group, 1999). One in three child protection cases show a history of domestic violence to the mother (Hester and Pearson, 1998). There is a statutory obligation to offer support where there are child protection issues, but we know that otherwise only limited services exist for children and young people whose parents are being abused by their partners or ex-partners (Stanko et al, 1998).

The contention has previously been that domestic violence was 'hidden': that as it took place 'behind closed doors' it was difficult to gain a detailed picture of what was deemed to be a 'private' situation (Cosgrove, 1997). It would appear instead that people experiencing this type of abuse are disclosing these experiences, but that this information is not always being recorded. Paradoxically the dearth of data from service providers may to some extent be explained by the large number of cases presenting as a result of domestic violence. Relevant practitioners are aware that this type of case comprises a substantial part of their workload (Stanko et al, 1998), but do not necessarily note it as such. For example, an application for an emergency loan from social services due to homelessness as a result of domestic violence may be classified as a call for financial aid.

We know that an abused person who chooses to disclose their situation gets in touch with - on average - roughly two service providers (McGibbon et al, 1989). We are, however, unclear about the extent agencies work together when trying to provide a service. There has been international recognition of the importance of multi-agency working (United Nations, 1993) but there is also currently a lack of information about *how* agencies work together. Plotnikoff and Woolfson (1998) suggest that only a third of police forces monitor the referrals made to other agencies in domestic violence cases. It seems unlikely that this observation would apply solely to the police.

Further, the UK is not alone in its lack of baseline data of this sort. The 1997 report evaluating the STOP formula grants in the US (a large scale, nationwide initiative funding a huge variety of projects to combat violence against women, Burt et al, 1997) uncovered a similar failure by agencies to undertake routine data collection. The report stated that this 'is as serious an obstacle [to evaluation efforts] as are issues of definition and measurement.' Australian work (Indermaur et al, 1998) looking at ways to prevent domestic violence found a similar lack of structure and a 'tendency of agencies to just 'do something', regardless of whether the efficacy of the particular program has been proven.'

Until there is an ongoing system of monitoring in place it is impossible to evaluate the impact of any government initiative, or set any individual project or piece of work in both a local and national context. To measure cost effectiveness, agencies have to be able to describe what they are doing and how they are spending existing resources. This is to do with accountability not just accounting (Weatheritt, 1993). They have a responsibility to offer a responsive service to those who are experiencing or have experienced domestic violence (Cabinet Office, 1999). To do this, they need know the proportion of their caseload that are affected by abuse and be aware of those clients' needs.

Introducing monitoring

There may well be resistance among practitioners to the idea of monitoring. There are a number of possible reasons for this:

- Fear that it is inappropriate to intervene in a private matter (Cabinet Office, 1999).
- Failure of training to show practitioners how to identify domestic violence related cases - e.g. in child protection cases where the mother is also experiencing abuse.
- Uncertainty about how to raise the issue: not asking the relevant questions because of uncertainty about how to do so appropriately (Bewley et al, 1997).
- Concern that any intervention may in fact exacerbate harm - due to lack of understanding of the issues relating to domestic violence, or how to make appropriate referrals (Bewley et al, 1997).
- Reluctance to intervene in the shorter term as to do so may add to an individual's workload - even though non-intervention may well result in repeat victimisation and therefore additional work in the longer term.
- Personal issues relating to domestic violence.
- Failure to monitor cases of this type as proportion of total workload, either because no system of monitoring exists, or because it exists but does not engage with domestic violence.
- Failure to incorporate monitoring into the dynamic of service provision - where no feedback is given from the data collected, form-filling ceases to appear important.
- Monitoring systems fall into disuse because they are provision-led rather than needs-led. This may result in input, output and outcome measures that reinforce current practice, rather than explain current practice, or help to assess whether an interaction is successful. For example, police performance indicators based on arrest rates rather than on the degree to which police action has helped to prevent repeat victimisation.

Figure 2: Monitoring and feedback

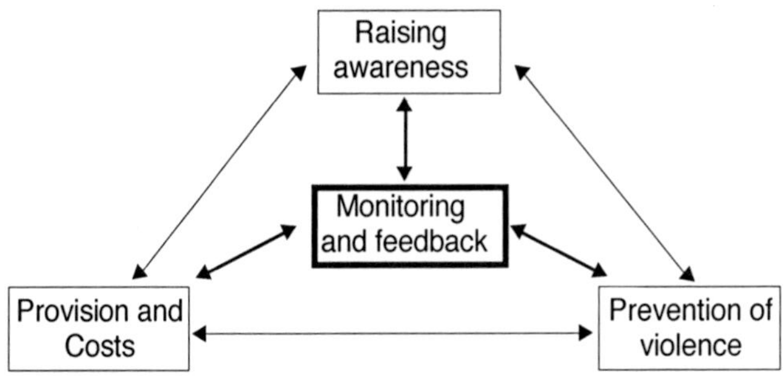

A report by the Audit Commission (1999) took an overview of issues relating to community safety (among them, domestic violence). It stressed the need for baseline data which can then be used to 'set informed targets for work and to monitor and evaluate subsequent progress'. Once common problems have been identified in this way, agencies can see 'what's in it for each of the partners'. In some areas, data are already being collected, but this is not necessarily being done appropriately. For example, Plotnikoff and Woolfson's recent study of police organisational structures in relation to domestic violence (1998) found that 'few forces used the information contained in their statistics constructively'. This criticism could be directed more widely than at just the police. Any system of monitoring must include an in-built feedback loop to create and to reinforce awareness of domestic violence issues as an ongoing dynamic of service delivery. It is hard to use statistics 'constructively' if they remain in a vacuum. Effective monitoring requires the data generated to answer what people can then be shown - by means of feedback - are relevant questions. The data impact not just on awareness but can also be used to predict needs and demand, and help to prevent further abuse (see Figure 2).

The above model centres on the work that is being carried out by individual agencies, and on how feeding back information can impact on daily work. If practitioners are told on a regular basis the proportion of their caseload that is domestic violence related, then this will highlight ways in which they may be able to address this issue. If y% of these cases requires particular types of support, then budgets can be reorganised to cater for this - where no allowances had previously been made for these needs, a strong case can be made for the allocation of any necessary additional resources. Lessons learned from this baseline data can also be used to feed into public awareness and prevention campaigns, and to inform training programmes for practitioners. It is vital that any system of monitoring be sensitive enough to register desistance from violence, or any reduction in repeat victimisation.

So what should agencies be monitoring? We suggest that the questions to be asked to generate a comparable database of material fall into two categories: the general and the specific. These are set out in Table 3.

The suggested schema of indicators set out in this table should help to give agencies a more in depth comprehension of the work they are already undertaking in relation to domestic violence - and the resources they are already investing. Cost studies have shown that there are substantial financial implications attached to the provision of services for those who are experiencing domestic violence: agencies need to do better than indulge in 'humane and well-intentioned guesses' (Maynard, 1991) when working out their budgets. In their report of an economic evaluation of policing activity, Stockdale et al (1999) draw attention to the need to make resource allocation decisions transparent. Even where there has been a blanket allocation of moneys at national level by central government - or any other organisation - in recognition of particular needs, local allocation must be done in such a way that it is sufficiently flexible to respond to local diversity. In the same way that direct application of national costing estimates to local statistics may result in data which are not sufficiently locally responsive, extrapolation of localised data to a national level may well present a skewed picture.

Paradoxically, when we review what we already know about the predictable nature of domestic violence, we should not be too unwilling to generalise to the national from the local, or to extrapolate to the local from the national. Many of the patterns appear to be consistent, and indicate that the impact of the abuse is the same: people contact the police in Port Talbot as well as Portsmouth, they visit their doctors in Dorchester as well as Doncaster, they need re-housing in Redditch as well as Richmond. Pieces of work from other regions or other countries should not be dismissed as somehow irrelevant to our area of study - as if the type of violence experienced in that locale were somehow 'different'. Instead we should look to find ways to put them into context.

We can monitor use of services. There may be tensions inherent in mainstreaming formats for data collection whilst trying to maintain local responsiveness - what may work in Southwark may not be appropriate in Shropshire. At the same time, similarities in research methodologies and units of measurement (a broken arm is a broken arm in the city as well as in the country) mean that data sets and statistics can and should be compared, contrasted and/or amalgamated. Any future work needs to operate at both a national and local level (see Figure 3 overleaf). It must also clarify in advance the purpose for which this material is being collected or

Table 3
Monitoring domestic violence

General
Aggregated data to be collected by all relevant service providers to assess costs

- ☐ What is your total annual budget?
- ☐ What is your total annual caseload?
- ☐ What proportion of your overall work does this caseload represent?
- ☐ What is your unit cost per case?
- ☐ What proportion of your cases are domestic violence related? *(dv the main feature/a factor/not dv)*
- ☐ How many cases does this represent per year?
- ☐ Do domestic violence cases require specialised services or support?
- ☐ If so, do these have financial implications for service provision?
- ☐ What proportion of your time is spent on domestic violence cases?
- ☐ What is the unit cost for a domestic violence case?

Specific
Data to be collected for each individual contact in order to record needs and track cases

- ☐ What are the client's demographic details?
- ☐ Do any of these give rise to specific needs? (for example, a translator)
- ☐ Do the parties currently live together? What is their relationship?
- ☐ Is the client the perpetrator/the person experiencing violence/other?
- ☐ What is the nature of the abuse experienced?
- ☐ What is the client's reason for contacting your service?
- ☐ Does the client have any other needs? *(emergency support/health/housing/ criminal justice/civil justice/social services/ advocacy & advice/other)*
- ☐ Has the client already been in touch with any other agencies?
- ☐ Did you make any referrals?
- ☐ Has the client been in touch with your agency before?
- ☐ If so, has there been any change in their needs since their last contact?

extrapolated to ensure that any data are generated and presented in a way that progresses the debate.

The evaluation of the US STOP Grants Initiative (Burt et al, 1997) saw communication and co-operation as pre-requisites to effective collaboration. To be truly cost-effective, work also must be done in a co-ordinated way, with local and national levels working together to produce material that is in a standardised but locally responsive format. Local Domestic Violence Forums are strategically placed to be tasked as co-ordinators for this mechanism of data generation and dissemination. This would firmly ground their role as being that of defining local needs and translating these into appropriate, supportive and cost-effective service provision.

Figure 3: National and local monitoring

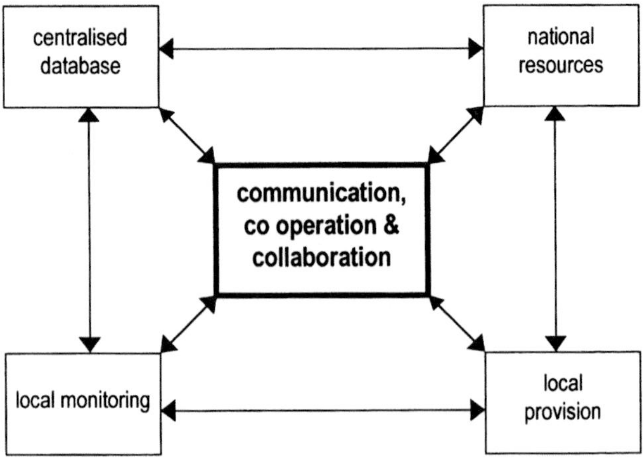

Once this baseline data source has been established (and it is an initiative that once established must be sustained and maintained), it can also be used to facilitate comparisons between research projects. Reinventing the wheel is costly, yet due to poor communication between projects in different geographical sites and, despite limited resources, there is currently a vast degree of duplication of effort. A central data source for the co-ordination of information would help to make research projects more cost effective: monitoring forms, questionnaires and methodologies could be shared adding value to each individual piece of work. Communication between studies in different areas would help to ensure that findings can be generalised or extrapolated appropriately. Recognition of existing limitations within a piece of research does not mean that that work cannot be cross-referenced to studies elsewhere. As Ferrante et al, (1996:2) point out:

> Given the shortcomings of individual data sources, a preferred approach is to identify multiple data sources, contributing their own independent perspectives on domestic violence. The methodology then proceeds on the basis that, in a situation where single data sources may possess limitations, those limitations diminish in significance as additional data sources are considered and found to be compatible.

There are ways to use such information to generate resources too. For example, following the public awareness campaign over Christmas 1998 in Scotland, by a comparison with monitoring data generated from the same period in previous years, Scottish Women's Aid were able to demonstrate an increase in the number of people getting in touch with them. As a result, they were able to secure additional funding to cope with the increase in contacts. Ultimately, the key is to find a way to respond flexibly and cost-effectively to demand.

Next steps

Firstly, service providers should make coherent, co-ordinated and consistent domestic violence monitoring a key local function. We suggest that Domestic Violence Fora are in an excellent strategic position to either generate this information themselves, or to oversee the collection of the required data by the relevant agencies. The material can be used:

- to assess the nature and extent of local needs as well as to evaluate service provision;
- to produce unit and global costings to help agencies reorganise their work most effectively and appropriately within existing budgets;
- to draw attention to the aspects of service provision which require additional resources; and
- to identify staff training needs.

It is vital that this programme of work be complemented by national research exploring the same issues. A standardised, yet flexible, methodology would enable us to draw comparisons between the local and national picture. The research findings should be fed back to practitioners in the field. This approach would serve not only to reaffirm the importance of multi-agency user-focused working, but also to help to demonstrate its impact.

Secondly, studies have already been undertaken which map service provision at both local and national level. What is urgently required is a study that attempts to chart the helpseeking strategies of people experiencing domestic violence (whilst keeping the safety of the individual as paramount). There is a large amount of regional variation in service provision. However, the needs of abused individuals are consistent wherever they live. An understanding of how individuals respond to service provision available on a local basis will also help to ensure that protocols and good practice guidance springs from the needs of user, rather than forcing them to fit within agency-defined service categories.

Thirdly, work on domestic violence should be structured within an overall schema, which encourages comparisons between findings, along with secondary and meta analysis of data. As far as possible, we should try to introduce standardised units of analysis. Baseline data generated through monitoring of local agencies can help to ensure that comparisons can then be made that are both culturally and geographically responsive. We must also explore innovative and creative ways to collect and analyse data, for example, studies that gather information from the abused's friends and family.

Note

1. The Office of National Statistics estimated the population of England and Wales to be 52.2 million in 1997, with 41.5 million people aged 16 or over. Mirrlees-Back (1999) found that 23% of women and 15% men experience violence at some point in their lives,. This is equivalent to 3.6 million people. Other research suggests that those who disclose to family and friends will in fact tell an average of 2 people (McGibbon et al, 1989).

References

Abrahams, C. (1994) *The Hidden Victims*, London: NCH

Acierno R., Resnick H.S. and Kilpatrick D. (1997) 'Health impact of inter-personal violence 1: prevalence rates, case identification and risk factors for sexual assault, physical assault and domestic violence in men and women.' *Behavioral Medicine*, 23 (2): 53-64

Advisory Board on Family Law, Children Act Subcommittee (2001) *Guidelines for Good Practice in Parental Contact in Cases where there is Domestic Violence.* London: Family Policy Division, Lord Chancellor's Department

Ali, H. (1998) 'The Experiences and Perceptions of Survivors of Domestic Violence.' Unpublished project for the MSc in Gender Relations. London: London School of Economics

ALG (1999) *Housing Benefit and Domestic Violence*, 24 September London: ALG

Allison D. (1999) 'Powers of Arrest and Orders under Part IV of the FLA 1996.' *Family Law*, September: 651-652

Ambuel B., Hamberger L.K. and Lahti J. (1996) 'Partner violence: a systematic approach to identification and intervention in outpatient health care.' *Wisconsin Medical Journal*, 95(5): 292-7

American Medical Association (1992) 'American Medical Association Diagnostic and Treatment Guidelines on Domestic Violence.' *Archives of Family Medicine*, 1:39-47

Amey, P., Hale, C. and Uglow, S. (1996) *Proactive Policing: An Evaluation of the Central Scotland Police Crime Management Model*, Crime and Criminal Justice Research Findings No. 10. Edinburgh: Scottish Office

Anderson, D., Chenery, S. and Pease, K. (1995) *Biting Back: Tackling Repeat Burglary and Car Crime*, Police Research Group, Crime Detection and Prevention Series Paper No. 58. London: Home Office

Anwen, J. (1999) *Out of Sight, Out of Mind? The Experiences of Homeless Women*, London: Crisis

Appel, A. and Holden, G.W. (1998) 'The Co-Occurrence of Spouse and Physical Child Abuse: A Review and Appraisal.' *Journal of Family Psychology*, 12 (4): 578-99

Arblaster, L., Conway, J., Foreman, A. and Hawtin, M. (1998) *Achieving the impossible: interagency collaboration to address the housing, health, and social care needs of people able to live in ordinary housing*, Bristol: The Policy Press

Ashworth, A. (1995) 'Domestic Violence, Children's Safety and Family Court Welfare Practice.' *Probation Journal*, 42: 91-94

The Audit Commission (1999) *Safety in Numbers: promoting community safety*, London: The Audit Commission

Australian Bureau of Statistics (1994) *Crime and Safety, Australia*, Canberra: Australian Bureau of Statistics

Australian Bureau of Statistics (1996) *Women's Safety, Australia*, Canberra: Australian Bureau of Statistics

Bacon N., Lawton G. and Levison D. (1996) *The provision and use of hostels by local authority housing departments*, London: Department of the Environment

Ball, M. (1990) *Children's Workers in Women's Aid Refuges: a Report on the Experience of Nine Refuges in England*, London: National Council of Voluntary Child Care Organisations

Ball, M. (1994) *Funding Refuge Services: A Study of Refuge Support Services for Women and Children Experiencing Domestic Violence*, Bristol: Women's Aid Federation of England

Barnett H. (1999) 'Child contact disputes and domestic violence.' *Family Law*, 29:104-107

Barron, J. (1990) *Not Worth the Paper..? The Effectiveness of Legal Protection for Women and Children Experiencing Domestic Violence*, Bristol: Women's Aid Federation of England

Bergman B., Brismar B. and Nordin C. (1992) 'Utilisation of medical care by abused women.' *British Medical Journal*, 305(6844): 27-28

Berenson A.B., Stiglich N.J, Wilkinson G.S. and Anderson G.D. (1991) 'Drug abuse and other risk factors for physical abuse in pregnancy among white non-Hispanic, black and Hispanic women.' *American Journal of Obstetrics and Gynecology*, 164:1491-9

Berk R., Newton P. and Fenstermaker S. (1986) 'What a difference a day makes: an empirical study of the impact of shelter for battered women.' in *Understanding partner violence: prevalence, causes, consequences and solutions*, USA: National Council on Family Relations

Bewley, S., Friend, J. and Mezey, G. (eds.) (1997) *Violence Against Women*, London: Royal College of Obstetricians and Gynaecologists Press

Bilinkoff, J. (1995) 'Empowering battered women as mothers.' In E. Peled, P. Jaffe and J.L.Edleson (eds.) *Ending the Cycle of Violence: Community Responses to Children of Battered Women*, Thousand Oaks, CA: Sage

Binney, V., Harkell, G. and Nixon, J. (1981) *Leaving Violent Men: A Study of Refuges and Housing for Abused Women*, Leeds: Womens Aid Federation of England

Birch J. (1999) 'The domestic lottery.' *Roof*, 24 (1): 14-15 London: Shelter

Birnbaum A. (1996) 'Domestic violence: Diurnal mismatch between need and availability of services.' *Academic Emergency Medicine*, 3(3): 246-251

Blackstone's Criminal Practice (1999) London: Blackstone Press

Blagg, H., Pearson, G., Smith, D. and Stubs, P. (1988) 'Inter-agency co-operation: rhetoric and reality.' In T. Hope and M. Shaw (eds.) *Communities and crime reduction*, London: HMSO

Blumel, D., Gibb, G., Innis, B., Justo, D. and Wilson, D. (1993) *Who Pays? The Economic Costs of Violence Against Women*, Queensland: Women's Policy Unit, Office of the Cabinet

Bohn, D.K. (1990) 'Domestic Violence and Pregnancy - Implications for Practice.' *Journal of Nurse-Midwifery*, 35 (2): 86-98

Bourlet, A. (1990) *Police Intervention in Marital Violence*, Milton Keynes: Open University Press

Bowstead, J. (1999) Personal communication from the Women's Equality Officer at the London Borough of Greenwich

Bradfield, J. and Nyland, J. (1998) *Evaluation of the NSW Women's Domestic Violence Court Assistance Programme: A Report to the NSW Legal Aid Commission*, Sydney: Bradfield Nyland Group

Bradshaw, J. et al (1996) *The Employment of Lone Parents: A Comparison of Policy in 20 Countries*, London: Family Policy Studies Centre

Brandon, D. with Brandon, A. and T. (1995) *Advocacy: Power to People With Disabilities*, London: Venture Press

Brannen, J. (ed.) (1992) *Mixing Methods: Qualitative and Quantitative Research*, Aldershot: Avebury

Bridgeman, C. and Hobbs, L. (2nd edition) (1998) *Preventing Repeat Victimisation: The Police Officers' Guide*, Police Research Group, London: Home Office

Brismar B., Bergman B., Larsson G. and Strandberg A. (1987) 'Battered women: A diagnostic and therapeutic dilemma.' *Acta Chirurgica Scandinavica*, 153(1): 1-5

British Medical Association (1998) *Domestic Violence: A Health Care issue?* London: BMA

Brown, J.B., Lent, B. and Sas, G. (1993) 'Identifying and Treating Wife Abuse.' *The Journal of Family Practice*, 36 (2): 185-91

Brown, J. K. (1992) 'Introduction: Definitions, assumptions, themes and issues' in D. A. J.Counts, J.K. Brown and J.C. Campbell (eds.) *Sanctions and Sanctuary - Cultural Perspectives on the Beating of Wives*, Boulder: Westview Press

Browne, K. and Hamilton, C. (forthcoming) *Making the Connection: A Comparison of Domestic Violence and Child Abuse referrals to the West Midlands Police*, Police Research Series . Research, Development and Statistics Directorate. London: Home Office

Bryman, A. (1988) *Quantity and Quality in Social Research*, London: Unwin Hyman

Buchan, I. and Edwards, S.S.M. (1991) *Adult Cautioning for Domestic Violence*, PRAS. London: Home Office Police Department

Bullock, L.F. and McFarlane, J. (1989) 'The Birthweight/Battering Connection.' *American Journal of Nursing*, September: 89(9): 1153-5

Burt, M., Newmark, L., Olson, K., Aron, L., Harrell, A. (1997) *Evaluation of the STOP Formula Grants Under the Violence Against Women Act of 1994*, Washington: The Urban Institute

Burton, S., Regan, L. and Kelly, L. (1998) *Supporting Women and Challenging Men: Lessons from the Domestic Violence Intervention Project*, Bristol: Policy Press

Burton, S. and Kitzinger, J. with Kelly, L. and Regan, L. (1998) *Young People's Attitudes towards Violence, Sex and Relationships. Executive Summary*, Research Report 002 Edinburgh: The Zero Tolerance Charitable Trust

Butler-Sloss, E. (1988) *Report of the Inquiry into Child Abuse in Cleveland* (1987),

CM 412 London: HMSO

Butt, J. and Box, L. (1998) 'Engage and provide.' *Community Care*, 9-15 July: 22-23

Buzawa, E. and Buzawa, C. (eds.) (1996) *Do arrests and restraining orders work?* Thousand Oaks, CA: Sage

Buzawa, E., Hotaling, G., Klein, A. and Byrne, J. (1999) *Response to Domestic Violence in a Pro-active Court Setting*, Grant #95-IJ-CX-0027. Washington: National Institute of Justice

Cabinet Office (1999) *Living Without Fear: An Integrated Approach to Tackling Violence against Women*, London: The Women's Unit, Cabinet Office

Cantwell B. and Roberts J. (1998) 'Presumption of Contact in Private Law – An Interdisciplinary Approach.' *Family Law* April, 29: 226-232

Campbell J.C. (1986) 'Nursing assessment for risk of homicide with battered women.' *Advances in Nursing Science*, 8(4): 36-51

Campbell, J. C. (1992) 'Wife-battering: cultural contexts versus Western social sciences.' in D.A. Counts, J.K. Brown and J.C. Campbell (eds.) *Sanctions and Sanctuary - Cultural Perspectives on the Beating of Wives*, Boulder: Westview Press

Campbell, J. (1995) 'Prediction of homicide of and by battered women.' in J. Campbell (ed.) *Assessing Dangerousness: Violence by Sexual Offenders, Batterers and Child Abusers*, Thousand Oaks, CA: Sage

Campbell, J. (ed.) (1998) *Empowering Survivors of Abuse: Health Care for Battered Women and their Children*, Thousand Oaks, CA: Sage

Caralis P.V. and Musialowski.R. (1997) 'Women's experiences with domestic violence and their attitudes and expectations regarding medical care of abuse victims.' *South Medical Journal*, 90(11): 1075-80

Chalk R. and King P. (1998) 'Assessing family violence interventions.' *American Journal of Preventive Medicine*, 14(4): 289-292

Chalk R. and King P. (eds.) (1998) *Violence in Families: Assessing Prevention and Treatment Programmes*. Washington: National Academy Press

Chen, H., Bersani, C., Myers, S. C. and Denton, R. (1989) 'Evaluating the effectiveness of a court sponsored abuser treatment program.' *Journal of Family Violence*, 4(4): 309-322

Chenoweth, L. (1997) 'Violence and Women With Disabilities - Silence and Paradox.' in S. Cook and J. Bessant (eds.) *Women's Encounters With Violence - Australian Experiences*, California: Sage

Choo, P. (1999) Personal communication about 'Proposed Newham's Domestic Violence Strategy 1999-2002'

Cleveland Area Child Protection Committee (1995) *CACPC Practice Guidance. Domestic Violence: Whose Problem Is It?* Middlesbrough: Cleveland ACPC

Clifton, J., Jacobs, J. and Tallish, J. (1996) *Helping Women Survive Domestic Violence: A Report to the Sussex Domestic Violence Multi-agency Consultative Group*, Sussex: University of Sussex

Cohen, I. and Felson, M. (1979) 'Social Change and Crime Rate Trends: A Routine Activity Approach.' *American Sociological Review*, 44:688-608

Cohen M.A. and Miller T.R. (1998) 'The cost of mental health care for victims of crime.' *Journal of Interpersonal Violence,* 13(1): 93-110

Cohen S. (1997) 'Barriers to physician identification and treatment of family violence: Lessons from five communities.' *Academic Medicine,* 72(1 SUPPL.): S19-S25

Coleman, D.H. and Straus, M.A. (1986) 'Marital power, conflict, and violence in a nationally representative sample of American couples.' *Violence and Victims,* 1 (2): 141-157

Collins K.S., Schoen C., Joseph S., Duchon L., Simantov E. and Yellowitz M. (1999) *Health Concerns Across a Woman's Lifespan: the Commonwealth Fund 1998 Survey of Women's Health,* New York: The Commonwealth Fund

Community Care (1993) 'End to battered men's refuge.' 4th February: 2

Convention of Scottish Local Authorities (1991) *Women and Violence Report,* Edinburgh: COSLA

Convention of Scottish Local Authorities (1998) *Guidance on Preparing and Implementing a Multi-agency Strategy to Tackle Violence Against Women,* Edinburgh: COSLA

Cosgrove, K. (1996) 'No man has the right.' in C. Corrin (ed.) *Women in a Violent World: Feminist Analyses and Resistance across "Europe",* Edinburgh: Edinburgh University Press

Cosgrove, K. (1997) *Private Trouble, Public Issue: an Inter-Agency strategy on domestic violence - learning from Castlemilk,* Demonstration Project on Domestic Violence, Glasgow: Greater Glasgow Health Board:

Counts, D.A., Brown, J.K. and Campbell, J.C. (eds.) (1992) *Sanctions and Sanctuary - Cultural Perspectives on the Beating of Wives,* Boulder: Westview Press

Covington, D.L., Dalton, V.K., Diehl, S.J., Wright, B.D. and Piner, M.H. (1997) 'Improving Detection of Violence Among Pregnant Adolescents...... systematic violence assessment.' *Journal of Adolescent Health,* 21(1): 18-24

Cretney A. and Davis G. (1996) 'Prosecuting "Domestic" Assault.' *Criminal Law Review* pp. 162 –174

Cretney A. and Davis G. (1997a) 'Prosecuting Domestic Assault Victims Failing Courts, or Courts Failing Victims.' *Howard Journal of Criminal Justice,* 36 (2): 146-157

Cretney A., and Davis, G. (1997b) 'The significance of compellability in the prosecution of domestic violence.' *British Journal of Criminology,* Winter 37(1): 75-89

Criminal Statistics (1998) *Supplementary Tables,* London: Home Office

Crisp, D. and Moxon, D. (1994) *Case Screening By the Crown Prosecution Service: How and Why Cases are Terminated* Home Office Research Study 137, Research and Statistics Directorate. London: Home Office,

Crisp, D. Whittaker, C. and Harris, J. (1995) *Public Interest Case Assessment Schemes.* Home Office Research Study 138. Research and Statistics Directorate. London: Home Office

Cross, M. (1999) 'Review of Domestic violence and Child Abuse: Policy and

Practice issues for Local Authorities and Other Agencies.' *Boadicea*, London: Greater London Action on Disability (GLAD)

Crown Prosecution Service (1992) *Annual Report* 1991-2 London: HMSO

Crown Prosecution Service (1993) *A Statement of Prosecution Policy: Domestic Violence*, London: CPS

Crown Prosecution Service (1994) *Annual Report*, April 1993-March 1994 London: HMSO

Crown Prosecution Service (1995) *CPS Policy for Prosecuting Cases of Domestic Violence*, August London: CPS

Crown Prosecution Service (1996) *Code for Crown Prosecutors*, London: CPS

Crown Prosecution Service (1998) *Annual Report* 1997-8. London: The Stationery Office: London

Crown Prosecution Service (1999) *Annual Report* 1998-9. London: The Stationery Office: London

Crown Prosecution Service Inspectorate (1998) *The Inspectorate's Report on cases Involving Domestic Violence*, Thematic Report 2/98 May. London: CPS

Currell, S. and Gill K. (1998) *Silenced 'n Caught: Unlocking the Barriers to Reporting Domestic Violence in an Asian Community*. PRAS, Policing and Reducing Crime Unit, Research, Development and Statistics Directorate. London: Home Office

Dalrymple, J. and Hough, J. (1995) *Having a Voice: An Exploration of Children's Rights and Advocacy*, London: Venture Press

Daly, M., Singh, L.S. and Wilson, M. (1993) 'Children Fathered by Previous Partners: A Risk Factor for Violence Against Women.' *Canadian Journal of Public Health*, 84 (3): 209-210

Davidson L.L. (1996) 'Preventing injuries from violence towards women [editorial].' *American Journal of Public Health* 86 (1): 12-4

Davies, G. Lyon, E. and Monti-Catania, E. (1998) *Safety Planning with Battered Women: Complex Lives/Difficult Choices*, Thousand Oaks, CA: Sage

Davies, J. (1998) *Safety Planning With Battered Women*. California: Sage

Day, T. (1995) *The Health-Related Costs of Violence Against Women in Canada: the tip of the iceberg*, London, Ontario: Centre for Research on Violence Against Women and Children

Dearing, A. and Forg, E. (eds.) (1999) *Police Combating Violence against Women: Documentation of the Conference of Experts*, Antwerp: Intersentia

Department of the Environment and Department of Health (1996) *Code of guidance on parts VI and VII of the Housing Act 1996: allocation of housing accommodation and homelessness*, London: DoE/DH

Department of the Environment, Transport and the Regions* (1999) *Code of guidance for local authorities on the allocation of accommodation and homelessness: parts VI and VII of the Housing Act 1996, draft consultation*. March, London: DETR

Department of Health (1995) *Child Protection: Messages from Research*, London: HMSO

* Now Department of Transport, Local Government and the Regions (DTLR)

Department of Health (1996) *Child Health in the Community*, London: Department of Health

Department of Health (1998) *Working Together to Safeguard Children: New Government Proposals for Inter-Agency Co-operation. A Consultation Paper*, London: Department of Health

Department of Health, Home Office and Department of Education and Employment (1999) *Working Together to Safeguard Children*, London: The Stationery Office

Department of Health, Welsh Office, Scottish Office Department of Health, Department of Health and Social Services NI. (1999) *Why Mothers Die. Report on Confidential Enquiries into Maternal Deaths in the United Kingdom 1994-1996*, London: The Stationery Office

Department of Health (2000) *Domestic violence: a resource manual for health care professionals*, London:Department of Health

Department of Transport, Local Government and the Regions (DTLR) *see* Department of the Environment, Transport and the Regions (DETR)

Dhiri, S. and Brand, S. (1999) *Analysis of Costs and Benefits: Guidance for Evaluators*. Crime Reduction Programme - Guidance Notes 1. Research, Development and Statistics Directorate. London: Home Office

Dobash, R. E. and Dobash, R. (1980) *Violence Against Wives: A case against the patriarchy*. Shepton Mallet: Open Books

Dobash, R. P. and Dobash, R. E. (1984) 'The nature and antecedents of violent events.' *British Journal of Criminology*, 24(3): 269-288

Dobash, R. E., Dobash, R. P. and Cavanagh, K. (1985) 'The contact between battered women and social and medical agencies', in J. Pahl (ed.) *Private Violence and Public Policy: The Needs of Battered Women and the Response of the Public Services*, London: Routledge and Kegan Paul

Dobash, R. E. and Dobash, R. P. (1992) *Women, Violence and Social Change*, London and New York: Routledge

Dobash, R.P., Dobash, R.E., Wilson, M. and Daly, M. (1992) 'The Myth of Sexual Symmetry in Marital Violence.' *Social Problems*, 39 (1): 71-91

Dobash, R.P. and Dobash, R.E. (1995) 'Reflections on findings from the Violence Against Women Survey.' *Canadian Journal of Criminology*, July: 457-84

Dobash, R., Dobash, R.E., Cavanagh, K. and Lewis, R. (1999) 'Homicide in Britain: Risk Factors, Situational Contexts and Lethal Intentions.' (http://www.brunel.ac.uk/depts/law/vrp/projects/proj006.htm)

Dobash, R., Dobash, R., Cavanagh, K. and Lewis, R. (2000) *Changing violent men*. London: Sage

Dominy, N. and Radford, L. (1996) *Domestic Violence in Surrey: Developing an Effective Inter-agency Response*, Guildford: Surrey County Council/Roehampton Institute

Downs, W.R., Smyth, N.J. and Miller, B.A. (1996) 'The Relationship Between Childhood Violence and Alcohol Problems Among Men Who Batter: An Empirical Review and Synthesis.' *Aggression and Violent Behavior*, 1 (4):327-44

Drossman D.A. (1995) 'Sexual and physical abuse and gastrointestinal illness:

Review and recommendations.' *Annals of Internal Medicine* 123(10):782-794

Drummond M.F. and Jefferson T.O. (1996) 'BMJ Economic Evaluation Working Party. Guidelines for authors and peer reviewers of economic submissions to the BMJ.' *British Medical Journal*, 313(7052):275-83

Dunning, A. (1995) *Citizen Advocacy with Older People: A Code of Good Practice* London: Centre for the Policy on Ageing

Dutton, D.G., Starzomski, A. and Ryan, L. (1996) 'Antecedents of Abuse Personality and Abusive Behavior in Wife Assaulters.' *Journal of Family Violence*, 11 (2):113-32)

Dye T.D., Tollivert N.J., Lee R.V. and Kenney C.J. (1995) 'Violence, pregnancy and birth outcome in Appalachia.' *Paediatric and Perinatal Epidemiology*, 9(1):35-47

Easteal P.W. and Easteal S. (1992) 'Attitudes and practices of doctors toward spouse assault victims: an Australian study.' *Violence Vict.* 7(3):217-28

Edleson, J. L. (1990) 'Judging the success of interventions with men who batter' in D. J. Besharov (ed.) *Family Violence: Research and Public Policy Issues*, Washington, DC: AEI Press

Edleson, J. L. and Brygger, M. P. (1986) 'Gender differences in reporting of battering incidences.' *Family Relations*, July, 35:377-382

Edleson, J. L. and Grusznski, R. J. (1988) 'Treating men who batter: four years of outcome data from the domestic abuse project.' *Journal of Social Science Research*, 12:3-22

Edleson, J. L. and Syers, M. (1991) 'The effects of group treatment for men who batter: an 18-month follow-up study.' *Research in Social Work Practice*, 1: 227-243

Edleson, J. L. and Tolman, R. M. (1992) *Intervention for Men who Batter: An Ecological Approach*, Newbury Park, CA: Sage

Edleson, J. (1999a) 'Problems associated with children's witnessing of domestic violence' . (http://www/mincava.umn.edu/arts/asp)

Edleson, J. (1999b) 'The overlap between child maltreatment and woman battering.' *Violence against Women*, 5(2):134-154

Edwards S.S.M. (1986) 'Police Attitudes and Dispositions in Domestic Disputes: The London Study.' *Police Journal*, July: 230-241

Edwards S.S.M. (1989a) *Policing Domestic Violence, Women, the Law and the State*, Sage: London

Edwards S.S.M. (1989b) 'What shall we do with a Frightened Witness?' *New Law Journal* December 22 pp: 1740,1743,1759

Edwards S.S.M. (1998) *Is change possible? An exploration of the applicability of Duluth principles of inter agency co ordination in the UK response to the crime of domestic violence*. London: Community Safety Unit and the Domestic Violence Forum, London Borough of Hammersmith and Fulham

Edwards S.S.M. and Halpern, A. (1991) 'Protection for the Victim of Domestic Violence: Time for Radical Revision.' *Journal of Social Welfare and Family Law* 2:94-109

Edwards S.S.M and Halpern, A. (1998) 'Conflicting Interests: Protecting children or protecting title to property.' *Journal of Social Welfare Law* 2:110-123

Eisikovits, Z. C. and Edleson, J. L. (1989) 'Intervening with men who batter: a critical review of the literature.' *Social Services Review*, 63(3): 384-414

Emmerson, B. (2000) 'Crime and Human Rights' *New Law Journal* 150:6921 p. 127

ESRC Violence Research Programme (1998) *Taking Stock: What Do We Know about Violence?* ESRC Violence Research Programme. Uxbridge: Brunel University

ESRC Violence Research Programme (2001) *Findings. Abused Women's Perspectives Project.* ESRC Violence Research Programme. Egham: Royal Holloway College

Fanslow J.L. (1998) 'Outcome evaluation of an emergency department protocol of care on partner abuse.' *Australia and New Zealand Journal of Public Health.* 22(5):598-603

Fantuzzo J., Boruch R., Beriama A., Atkins M. and Marcus S. (1997) 'Domestic violence and children: prevalence and risk in five major US cities.' *J. Am. Acad. Child Adolesc. Psychiatry.* 36(1):116-122

Farmer, E. and Owen, M. (1995) *Child Protection Practice: Private Risks and Public Remedies*, London: HMSO

Farmer, A. and Tiefenthaler, J. (1997) 'An Economic Analysis of Domestic Violence.' *Review of Social Economy*, LV (3): 337-58

Faragher, T. (1985) 'The Police Response to Violence Against Women in the Home.' in J. Pahl (ed.) *Private Violence And Public Police*, London: Routledge and Kegan Paul

Farrell, G., Buck, W. and Pease, K. (1993) 'The Merseyside Domestic Violence Prevention Project: Some Costs and Benefits.' *Studies on Crime and Crime Prevention Annual Review* 2: 21-33

Farrell, G. and Buckley, A. (1999) 'Evaluation of a UK Police Domestic Violence Unit using Repeat Victimisation as a Performance Indicator.' *Howard Journal*, 38 (1): 42-53

Farrell, G. and Pease, K. (1993) *Once Bitten, Twice Bitten: Repeat Victimisation and its implications for Crime Prevention.* Police Research Group, Crime Prevention Unit Series Paper No. 46, London: Home Office

Feld, S.L. and Straus, M.A. (1989) 'Escalation and Desistance of Wife Assault in Marriage', *Criminology*, 27 (1):141-161

Feldhaus K.M., Koziol-McLain J., Amsbury H.L., Norton I.M., Lowenstein S.R. and Abbott J.T. (1997) 'Accuracy of 3 brief screening questions for detecting partner violence in emergency departments'. *JAMA.* 277(17):1357-1361

Ferrante, A., Morgan, F., Indermaur, D. and Harding, R. (1996) *Measuring the Extent of Domestic Violence* Sydney: Hawkins Press

Ferris L.E. and Tudiver F. (1992) 'Family physicians' approach to wife abuse: a study of Ontario, Canada, practices'. *Fam Med.* 24(4):276-82

Flitcraft, A. et al (1992) 'American Medical Association Diagnostic and Treatment Guidelines on Domestic Violence.' *Archives of Family Medicine*, 1:39-47

Forrester, D., Chatterton, M. and Pease K. (1988) *The Kirkholt Burglary Prevention Project, Rochdale.* Crime Prevention Unit Paper No. 13. London: Home Office

Frayne B. and Muir J. (1994) *Nowhere to run: underfunding of women's refuges.*

London: London Housing Unit

Friedman L.N., Tucker S.B., Hartmann H. and Stark E. (1997) *The costs of domestic violence.* New York City: Victims Services Research

Furbee P.M., Sikora R., Williams J.M. and Derk S.J. (1998) 'Comparison of domestic violence screening methods: a pilot study'. *Annals of Emergency Medicine.* 31(4):495-501.x

Fyfe, N. and McKay, H. (1999) *Making it Safe to Speak? A study of Witness Intimidation and Protection in Strathclyde.* Scottish Office Central Research Unit, Edinburgh: Scottish Office

Gazmararian, J.A., Lazorick, S., Spitz, A.M., Ballard, T.J., Saltzman, L.E. and Marks, J.S. (1996) 'Prevalence of Violence Against Pregnant Women.' *Journal of the American Medical Association*, 275 (24): 1915-1920

Gelles, R.J. (1988) 'Violence and pregnancy: Are pregnant women at greater risk of abuse?' *Journal of Marriage and the Family*, 50 (3): 841-7

Gelsthorpe, L. (1985) *The community service volunteers / Kent initiative*, London: Whiting and Birch

Gevers, L. (1996) *Where to from here? Report on the needs of women who have experienced domestic violence*, Queensland, Australia: Department of Families, Youth and Community Care

Gielen, A.C., O'Campo, P.J., Faden, R., Kass, N.E. and Xue, X. (1994) 'Interpersonal Conflict and Physical Violence During the Childbearing Year.' *Social Science Medicine*, 39 (6): 781-787

Gill, K. and Pickles, T. (eds.) (1989) *Active collaboration: joint practice and youth strategies*, London: ITRC

Gislason, I. (1997) *Violence against women in Iceland*, Iceland: Office for Gender Equality

Goatly, R. (1999) *Domestic Violence in the London Borough of Harrow: A Research Report for Harrow Domestic Violence Forum*, Hatfield: University of Hertfordshire

Goddard, C. and Hillier, P. (1993) 'Child sexual abuse: assault in a violent context.' *Australian Journal of Social Issues*, 28:20-33

Godenzi, A. and Yodanis, C. (1999) *Report on the Economic Costs of Violence Against Women* Fribourg, Switzerland: University of Fribourg,

Goldbery W.G. and Tomlanovich M.C. (1984) 'Domestic violence victims in the emergency department: new findings'. *JAMA,* 251:3259-3264

Gondolf, E. (1988) 'The effects of batterer counselling on shelter outcome.' *Journal of Interpersonal Violence*, 3:275-289

Gondolf, E. (1995) *Discharge criteria for batterer programs.* Paper presented at the Fourth International Conference on Family Violence Research, Durham NH, July. (http://www.iup.edu/maati/publications)

Gondolf, E. (1996) *Characteristics of batterers in a multi-site evaluation of batterer intervention systems: a preliminary report.* (http://www/mincava.umn.edu/arts/asp)

Gondolf, E. (1997) 'Batterer programs: what we know and need to know.' *Journal of Interpersonal Violence*, 12(1): 83-98

Gondolf, E. (1998a) 'Do batterer programs work? A 15-month follow-up of a multi-site evaluation.' *Domestic Violence Report*, 3, June/July, pp.64-65 and 78-79

Gondolf, E. (1998b) *The impact of mandatory court review on batterer program compliance: and evaluation of the Pittsburgh Municipal Courts and Domestic Abuse Counseling Centre. Executive summary*. (http://www.iup.edu/maati/publications)

Gondolf, E. (1998c) *Multi-site evaluation of batterer intervention systems: a 30-month follow-up of court-mandated batterers in four cities*, paper presented at Program Evaluation and Family Violence Research: An International Conference, Durham, NH, July 26-29

Gondolf, E. (1998d) *Multi-site evaluation of batterer intervention systems: How batterer program participants avoid reassault*, 12/1/1998, presented at the Sixth International Conference on Family Violence, Durham NH, July 25-28. (http://www.iup.edu/maati/publications)

Grace, S. (1995) *Policing Domestic Violence in the 1990s*, Home Office Research Study 139. London: Home Office

Greaves, L., Hankivsky, O. and Kingston-Riechers, J. (1995) *Selected Estimates of the Costs of Violence Against Women* London, Ontario: Centre for Research on Violence Against Women and Children

Guildford Domestic Violence Forum (1994) *Domestic Violence: the cost*, Guildford DV Forum

Hague, G. (1998) 'Interagency work and domestic violence in the UK', *Women's Studies International Forum*, 21(4) 441-449

Hague G. and Malos E. (1993) *Domestic violence and housing: local authority responses to women and children escaping violence in the home*. Women's Aid Federation England and School of Applied Social Studies, Bristol Papers in Applied Social Studies No. 19, Bristol: University of Bristol

Hague G. and Malos E. (1994a) 'Children, Domestic Violence and Housing: The impact of homelessness' in A. Mullender and R. Morley (eds.). *Children Living with Domestic Violence*, London: Whiting and Birch

Hague, G. and Malos, E. (1994b) 'Domestic violence, social policy and housing.' *Critical Social Policy*, pp.112-25

Hague, G., Kelly, L., Malos, E. and Mullender A. with Debbonaire, T. (1996) *Children, Domestic Violence and Refuges: A Study of Needs and Responses*, Bristol: Women's Aid Federation of England

Hague, G. and Malos, E. (1998) *Domestic Violence: Action for Change*. (2nd ed.) Cheltenham: New Clarion Press

Hague, G. and Malos, E. (1996) *Tackling Domestic Violence: A Guide to Developing Multi-agency Initiatives*, Bristol: The Policy Press

Hague, G., Malos, E. and Dear, W. (1996a) *Inter-agency Approaches to Domestic Violence*, Bristol: University of Bristol, School for Policy Studies

Hague, G., Malos, E. and Dear, W. (1996b) *Multi-agency work and domestic violence: a national study of inter-agency initiatives*, Bristol: The Policy Press

Hague, G., Kelly, L., Malos, E. and Mullender, A. with Debbonaire, T. (1996) *Children, Domestic Violence and Refuges: a Study of Needs and Responses*, Bristol: Women's Aid Federation of England

Hague, G., Kelly, L. and Mullender, A. (2001) *Challenging Violence against Women: The Canadian Experience*. Bristol: Polity Press

Hague, G. Aris, R. and Mullender, A. (forthcoming) *Women Survivors of Domestic Violence: User Views, Accountability and Involvement*. London: Routledge

Hall D. and Lynch M.A. (1998) 'Violence begins at home. Domestic strife has lifelong effects on children [editorial].' *BMJ* 316(7144):1551

Hallett, C. and Prout, A. (eds.) (forthcoming) *Hearing the Voices of Children: Social Policy for a New Century*. London: Falmer

Hamberger L.K. and Saunders D.G. (1998) Physician interaction with battered women: the women's perspective. *Arch Fam Med*, 7(6):575-82

Hamberger L.K., Saunders D.G. and Hovey M. (1992) 'Prevalence of domestic violence in community practice and rate of physician inquiry.' *Family Medicine*, 24(4):283-287

Hanmer, J. and Saunders, S. (1984) *Well Founded Fear: A Community Study of Violence to Women*, London: Hutchinson

Hanmer, J. and Saunders, S. (1993) *Women, Violence and Crime Prevention*. Aldershot: Avebury

Hanmer, J. (1996) 'Women and violence: commonalities and diversities.' in Fawcett, B., Featherstone, B., Hearn, J. and Toft, C. (eds.) *Violence and Gender Relations: Theories and Interventions*, London: Sage

Hanmer, J., Griffiths, S. and Jerwood, D. (1999) *Arresting Evidence: Domestic Violence and Repeat Victimisation*, Police Research Series Paper No. 104, Policing and Reducing Crime Unit. London: Home Office

Harrell, A. V. (1991) *Evaluation of Court-Ordered Treatment for Domestic Violence Offenders. Final Report Submitted to the State Justice Institute*, Washington, DC: The Urban Institute (cited in Tolman and Edleson, 1995)

Hartmann H.I., Laurence L., Spalter-Roth R. and Zuckerman D.M. (1997) *Measuring the Costs of Domestic Violence against women and the cost-effectiveness of interventions: An initial assessment and proposals for further research*. Washington, D.C: Institute for Women's Policy Research

Harwell T.S. (1998) 'Results of a domestic violence training program offered to the staff of urban community health centers. Evaluation Committee of the Philadelphia Family Violence Working Group.' *Am. J. Prev. Med.* 15(3):235-42

Harwin, N. (1997) 'The role of Women's Aid and refuge support services for women and children' in S. Bewley, J. Friend and G. Mezey (eds.) *Violence Against Women*. London: Royal College of Obstetricians and Gynaecologists

Harwin, N. (1997) *Briefing for the Working Party from the Women's Aid Federation of England*. Bristol: Women's Aid Federation of England

Harwin, N. (1998a) *Families without Fear. Women's Aid Agenda for Action on Domestic Violence: Recommendations for a National Strategy*, Bristol: Women's Aid Federation of England

Harwin N. (1998b) *Women's Aid Briefing for WAFE Conference*. Unpublished

Harwin, N., Malos, E. and Hague, G. (eds.) (1999) *New Opportunities, Old Challenges*, London: Whiting and Birch

Hayden S.R. (1997) 'Domestic violence in the emergency department: how do women prefer to disclose and discuss the issues?' *Journal of Emergency Medicine*, 15(4):447-51

Healey, K. and Smith, C., with O'Sullivan, C. (1998) *Batterer Intervention: Program Approaches and Criminal Justice Strategies*, Washington, DC: National Institute of Justice. (http://www.ncjrs.org/txtfiles/168638.txt)

Hearn, J. (1998) *The Violences of Men: How Men Talk About and How Agencies Respond to Men's Violence to Women*, London: Sage

Heiskanen, M. and Piispa, M. (1998) *Faith, Hope, Battering - A Survey of Men's Violence against Women in Finland.* Yliopistopaino, Helsinki: Statistics Finland

Henderson, S. (1997) *Service Provision to Women Experiencing Domestic Violence in Scotland*, The Scottish Office Central Research Unit, Crime and Criminal Justice Research Findings No. 20. Edinburgh: Scottish Office

Hepburn M. and McCartney S. (1997) Domestic violence and reproductive health in Glasgow. In S. Bewley , J.R. Friend and G.C. Mezey (eds.) *Violence Against Women*. London: RCOG Press pp.233-244

Hertfordshire Constabulary (1998): *Polaroid Instant Evidence and Domestic Violence.* unpublished final report, 13th November

Hester, M. and Pearson, C. (1998) *From Periphery to Centre: Domestic Violence in Work with Abused Children*, Bristol: The Policy Press

Hester, M., Pearson, C. and Harwin, N. (1998a) *Making an Impact: Children and Domestic Violence - a Reader*, London: Jessica Kingsley,

Hester, M., Pearson, C. and Radford, L. (1997) *Domestic Violence: a National Survey of Court Welfare and Voluntary Sector Mediation Practice*, Bristol: The Policy Press

Hester, M. and Radford, L. (1996) *Domestic Violence and Child Contact Arrangements in England and Denmark*, Bristol: The Policy Press

Hirschi, T. and Gottfredson, M. (1983) 'Age and the Explanation of Crime.' *American Journal of Sociology*, 89 (3): 552-84

HMIC (1998a) *What Price Policing? A Study of Efficiency and Value for Money in the Police Service.* Her Majesty's Inspectorate of Constabulary, April, London: Home Office

HMIC (1998b) *Beating Crime*, HMIC Thematic Inspection Report, Her Majesty's Inspectorate of Constabulary, London: Home Office

Hoff, L. A. (1990) *Battered Women as Survivors*, London: Routledge

Holder R., Kelly L.and Singh T. (1994) *Suffering in Silence*? London: Domestic Violence Forum Hammersmith and Fulham

Home, A. (1991-92) Responding to domestic violence: a comparison of social workers' and police officers' interventions', *Social Work and Social Sciences Review*, 3(2): 150-62

Home Affairs Committee (1992-3) Third Report *Domestic Violence,* Vol 1 Report HL, 2 45-1 HMSO:London

Home Department, Lord Chancellor's Department and Attorney General's Department (1993) *The Government Reply to the Third Report from the Home*

Affairs Committee, Session 1992-93 HC 245, Cm 2269, London: HMSO

Home Office (1984) *Domestic Proceedings in the Magistrates Court*. Home Office Statistical Bulletin. Research and Statistics Directorate. London: Home Office

Home Office (1990) *Circular 60/1990: Domestic Violence*. London: Home Office

Home Office (1991) *Safer communities: the local delivery of crime prevention through the partnership approach*, London: Home Office

Home Office (1995) *Inter-Agency Circular: Inter-agency co-ordination to tackle domestic violence*. London: Home Office

Home Office Consultation Paper (1996) *Stalking – the Solutions*, London: Home Office

Home Office (1998) *Speaking Up for Justice, Report of the Interdepartmental Working Group on the Treatment of Vulnerable or Intimidated Witnesses in the Criminal Justice System*. June, London: Home Office

Home Office (2000) *Circular 19/2000: Domestic Violence*. London: Home Office

Homer, M., Leonard, A. and Taylor, P. (1984) *Private Violence: Public Shame: A Report on the Circumstances of Women Leaving Domestic Violence in Cleveland*, Middlesbrough: Cleveland Refuge and Aid for Women and Children

Horton, A.L. and Johnson, B.L. (1993) 'Profile and strategies of women who have ended abuse', *Families in Society: The Journal of Contemporary Human Services*, October: 481-92

Hotaling, G.T. and Sugarman, D.B. (1986) 'An Analysis of Risk Markers in Husband to Wife Violence: The Current State of Knowledge.' *Violence and Victims*, 1 (2): 101-24

House of Commons Home Affairs Committee (1992) *Domestic Violence. Volume 1. Report together with the Proceedings of the Committee*, Session 1992-93, 245-I, London: HMSO

House of Commons Home Affairs Committee (1993) *Inquiry into domestic violence*, London: HMSO

Hopayian, K., Horrocks, G., Garner, P., Levitt, A. (1983) 'Battered women presenting in general practice.' *Journal of the Royal College of General Practitioners*, 33: 506-7

Hough, M. and Tilley, N (1998) *Auditing Crime and Disorder: guidance for local partnerships* Crime and Detection Series Paper No 91, London: Home Office

Hughes, H. (1992) 'Impact of spouse abuse on children of battered women.' *Violence Update*, August, 1: 9-11

Humphreys, C. (1997) *Case Planning Issues Where Domestic Violence Occurs in the Context of Child Protection. Report to Coventry Social Services Child Protection Unit*, Coventry: Coventry City Council Social Services Department

Humphreys, C. and Kaye, M. (1997) 'Third-party applications for protection orders: opportunities, ambiguities and traps.' *Journal of Social Welfare and Family Law*, 19(4):403-21

Humphreys, C. (2000) *Social Work, Domestic Violence and Child Protection: Challenging Practice*, Bristol: The Policy Press

Humphreys, C. (2000) *Starting Over: A Consultation for Milton Keynes Women's Aid*

Outreach Project, Bristol: Women's Aid Publications

Humphreys, C., Hester, M., Hague, G., Mullender, A., with Abrahams, H. and Lowe, P. (2000) *Working with Families where there is Domestic Violence: From Good Intentions to Good Practice.* Bristol: Policy Press

Humphreys, C., Hester, M., Hague, G., Mullender, A., Abrahams, H. and Lowe, P. (2000) *From Good Intentions to Good Practice: Mapping Services Working with Families where there is Domestic Violence.* Bristol: Policy Press

Humphreys, C., Mullender, A., Lowe, P., Hague, G., Abrahams, H. and Hester, M., (2001) Domestic violence and child abuse: Developing sensitive policies and guidance, *Child Abuse Review,* 10:183-97

Humphreys, C. and Tiara, R. (forthcoming) *Routes to Safety: Protection Issues Facing Abused Women and Children and the Role of Outreach Services.* Bristol: Women's Aid Federation

Hunter, S (1996) *Data Collection Project: a report on the Northern Territory Government's Domestic Violence Strategy,* Occasional Paper No 10, Office of Women's Policy

Imam, U. F. (1994) 'Asian children and domestic violence.' in A. Mullender and R. Morley (eds.) *Children Living with Domestic Violence: Putting Men's Abuse of Women on the Child Care Agenda,* London: Whiting and Birch

Indermaur, D, Atkinson, L. and Blagg, H (1998) *Working with Adolescents to Prevent Domestic Violence: rural town model,* University of Western Australia: Crime Research Centre

Inner London Probation Service (1996) *Domestic violence policy.* ILPS: England

Island, D. and Letellier, P. (1991) *Men Who Beat the Men Who Love Them: Battered Gay Men and Domestic Violence,* Binghamton, NY: Harington Park Press (Haworth)

Jacobs, J. (1998) *The links between substance misuse and domestic violence,* London: Alcohol Concern and ISDD

Jaffee, P., Finlay J. and Wolfe D. (1984) 'Evaluating the Impact of a Specialized Civilian Family Crisis Unit within a Police Force on the Resolution of Family Conflicts', *Journal of Preventative Psychiatry,* 2 (1):63-183

Jaffee, P., Wolfe D. A., Telford, A. and Austin, G. (1986) 'The Impact of Police Charges in Incidents of Wife Abuse.' *Journal of Family Violence.* 1(1): 37-49

James-Hanman, D. (1994) *Researching the Experiences of Women in Temporary Accommodation due to Domestic Violence,* London: London Borough of Islington, Women's Equality Unit

James-Hanman, D. (1995) *The Needs and Experiences of Black and Minority Ethnic Women*

Experiencing Domestic Violence, London: London Borough of Islington, Women's Equality Unity

James-Hanman, D. (1998) *Social Exclusion and Domestic Violence,* London: Greater London Domestic Violence Project

Johnson, H., and Sacco, V. (1995) 'Researching Violence Against Women: Statistics Canada's national survey.' *Canadian Journal of Criminology,* 37(3): 284-304

Johnson, H. (1996) *Dangerous Domains - Violence Against Women in Canada*, Canada: Nelson Canada

Johnson, J. M. and Kanzler, D. J. (1990) *Treating domestic violence: evaluating the effectiveness of a domestic violence diversion program*, paper presented at the Tenth Annual Symposium on Social Work with Groups, Miami, FL, October

Johnson, M.P. (1995) 'Patriarchal Terrorism and Common Couple Violence: Two Forms of Violence Against Women.' *Journal of Marriage and the Family*, 57:283-94

Kalmuss, D. S. and Straus, M.A. (1982) 'Wife's marital dependency and wife abuse.' *Journal of Marriage and the Family*, 44 (2): 277-86

Kaner, A., Bulik, C.M. and Sullivan, P.F. (1993) 'Abuse in Adult Relationships of Bulimic Women', *Journal of Interpersonal Violence*, 8 (1): 52-63

Kaufman Kantor, G. and Straus, M. A. (1987) 'The "drunken bum" theory of wife beating', *Social Problems*, 34 (3):213-230

Kelly, L. (1989) *Surviving Sexual Violence*, Cambridge: Polity Press

Kelly, L. (1994) 'The interconnectedness of domestic violence and child abuse: challenges for research, policy and practice' in Mullender, A. and Morley, R., (eds.) *Children Living with Domestic Violence: Putting Men's Abuse of Women on the Child Care Agenda*, London: Whiting and Birch

Kelly, L. (1996) 'When Woman Protection is the Best Kind of Child Protection: Children, Domestic Violence and Child Abuse', *Administration*, 44 (2): 118-35

Kelly, L. (1998) 'How Women Define Their Experiences of Violence' in Yllo, K. and Bograd, M. (eds.) *Feminist Perspectives on Wife Abuse*, Newbury Park, California: Sage

Kelly, L. with Bindel, J., Burton, S., Butterworth, D., Cook, K. and Regan, L. (1999) *Domestic Violence Matters: An Evaluation of a Development Project*, Home Office Research Study 193. Research, Development and Statistics Directorate. London: Home Office

Kerr R. and McLean J. (1996) *Paying for Violence: the Costs of Violence Against Women in BC*, Canada: Ministry of Women's Equality, Province of British Columbia

Killeen, J. (1996) *Advocacy and Dementia*, Edinburgh: Alzheimer Scotland

Kirklees Housing (undated) *Domestic abuse advice pack*, Kirklees: Kirklees Metropolitan Council

Kirkwood, C. (1993) *Leaving Abusive Partners: From the Scars of Survival to the Wisdom for Change*, London: Sage

Kitzinger, J. and Hunt, K. (1993) *Evaluation of Edinburgh District Council's Zero Tolerance Campaign*, Glasgow: Glasgow University Media Group

Kolbo, J.R., Blakeley, E.H. and Engleman, D. (1996) 'Children Who Witness Domestic Violence: A Review of Empirical Literature.' *Journal of Interpersonal Violence*, 11 (2): 281-93

Korf, D.J., Meulenbeek, H., Mot, E and van den Brandt, T. (1997) *Economic Costs of Violence Against Women*, Netherlands

Koss M.P., Koss P.G. and Woodruff W.J. (1991) 'Deleterious effects of criminal victimization on women's health and medical utilization.' *Archives of Internal Medicine.* 151(2): 342-347

Langford D.R. (1996) 'Policy issues for improving institutional response to domestic violence.' *Journal of Nursing Administration.* 26(1): 39-45

Leeds City Council, Leeds Health Authority, Leeds Family Health Services Authority and Voluntary Action Leeds (1992) *Women Subject to Violence by a Known Man: An Overarching Theme*, Leeds: Leeds City Council

Leeds Education and Leeds Inter-Agency Project, Women and Violence (undated) *Guidance for Schools: Violence Against Women and Children by Known Men*, Leeds: Leeds City Council Department of Education

Legal Aid Board (1999) *Legal Aid Handbook,* Legal Aid Board: London

Levinson, D. (1989) *Family Violence in Cross-Cultural Perspective*, Newbury Park: Sage

Liddle, M. and Gelsthorpe, L. (1994a) *Inter-agency crime prevention: organising local delivery,* Police Research Group Crime Prevention Unit Series, paper 52, London: Home Office

Liddle, M. and Gelsthorpe, L. (1994b) *Crime Prevention and inter-agency co-operation*, Police Research Group Crime Prevention Series, paper 53, London: Home Office

Liddle, M. and Gelsthorpe, L. (1994c) *Inter-agency crime prevention: further issues*, Police Research Group Crime Prevention Series, supplementary paper to papers 52 and 53, London: Home Office

Lloyd, C. (1994) *The welfare net: how well does the net work?* Oxford: Oxford Brookes University

Lloyd, S., Farrell, G. and Pease, K. (1994) *Preventing Repeated Domestic Violence: A demonstration project on Merseyside*, Police Research Group Crime Prevention Unit Series Paper No. 49. London: Home Office

Lloyd, S. (1997) 'The Effects of Domestic Violence On Women's Employment', *Law and Policy*, 19 (2): 139-67)

Lockton D. and Ward R. (1997) *Domestic Violence,* London: Cavendish

London Borough of Camden (1996) *Domestic Violence Guidelines: A Good Practice Manual for Camden Council Officers Responding to Domestic Violence.* London: L.B. Camden

London Borough of Camden (1999) *Housing Department Procedure Note: Dealing with Harassment in Council Homes.* London: L.B. of Camden

London Borough of Hackney (1993) *The Links between Domestic Violence and Child Abuse: Developing Services*, London: L. B. of Hackney

London Borough of Hammersmith and Fulham/Metropolitan Police (1995) *Making the difference: a good practice guide in responding to domestic violence,* London: L.B. of Hammersmith and Fulham

London Borough of Hounslow (1994) *Domestic Violence: Help, Advice and Information for Disabled Women*, London: L. B. of Hounslow

London Borough of Islington (1995) *STOP: Schools Take on Preventing Domestic Violence*, London: L. B. of Islington, Women's Equality Unit

London Borough of Lewisham (undated) *Domestic Violence Alarms: Evaluation Report*, London: L. B. of Lewisham (on behalf of a partnership pilot project with the Metropolitan Police and Marks and Spencer)

London Borough of Lewisham Community Safety Team with Lewisham Domestic Violence Forum (1998) *Survey of Domestic Violence Services in Lewisham*, London: L. B. of Lewisham

London Research Centre (1991) *Length of stay in temporary accommodation: a study of homeless households in London*, London: LRC

London Research Centre (1998) *Tackling violence against women*. London: Cabinet Office and DETR

London Research Centre (1999) *Relationship Breakdown: a guide for social landlords* London: Department of the Environment, Transport and the Regions

Loosley, S., Bentley, L., Lehmann, P., Marshall, L., Rabenstein, S. and Sudermann, M. (1997) *Group Treatment for Children Who Witness Woman Abuse: A Manual for Practitioners*, London, Ontario: The Community Group Treatment Program. (Available from: The Children's Aid Society of London and Middlesex, P.O. Box 6010, Depot 1, London, Ontario, Canada N5W 5R6)

Lord Chancellor's Department (LCD) (1999a) *Information Bulletin Time Intervals for Criminal Proceedings in Magistrates Courts October 1998* Issue 2/99 June, London: LCD

Lord Chancellor's Department (LCD) (1999b). *Information Bulletin Time Intervals for Criminal Proceedings in Magistrates Courts June 1999* Issue 5/99 December, London: LCD

MacAskill, S. and Eadie, D. (1995) *An Evaluation of the Scottish Office Domestic Violence Media Campaign*, Scottish Office Central Research Unit, Edinburgh: Scottish Office

MacLeod, M., Prescott, R. and Carson, L. (1996) *Listening to the Victims of Crime: Victimisation Episodes and the Criminal Justice System in Scotland, an Examination of White and Ethnic Minority Crime Victim Experience.* Crime and Criminal Justice Research Findings No. 13. Edinburgh: Scottish Office

Malos E, (1993) *You've got no life. Homelessness and the use of bed and breakfast hotels*. Bristol: University of Bristol, School of Applied Sciences

Malos, E. and Hague, G. (1993) *Domestic Violence and Housing: Local Authority Responses to Women and Children Escaping from Violence in the Home*, Bristol: Women's Aid Federation of England, and University of Bristol, School of Applied Social Studies

Malos, E., Hague, G. and Dear, W. (1996) *Multi-agency Work and Domestic Violence: A National Study of Inter-agency Initiatives*, Bristol: The Policy Press

Mama, A. (1996) *The Hidden Struggle: Statutory and Voluntary Sector Responses to Violence against Black Women in the Home*, London: Whiting and Birch. [Reissue of a 1989 text.]

Manchester City Council (1998) *Domestic violence, policy and procedures for housing staff*, Manchester: Manchester City Council

Manchester City Council (1996) *Tenancy agreement*. February, Manchester: Manchester City Council

Marshall, L., Miller, N., Miller-Hewitt, S., Sudermann, M. and Watson, L. (1995) *Evaluation of Groups for Children who have Witnessed Violence*, London, Ontario: Centre for Research on Violence Against Women and Children

Maynard, A. (1991) 'The Relevance of Health Economics to Health Promotion' in Badira, B. and Kickbusch, I. *Health Promotion Research: towards a new social epidemiology*, World Health Organisation Regional Publication European Series No. 37

Mathews, D. J. (1995) 'Parenting groups for men who batter' in Peled, E., Jaffe, P. G. and Edleson, J. L. (1995) *Ending the Cycle of Violence: Community Responses to Children of Battered Women*, Thousand Oaks, California: Sage

Maynard, M. (1985) 'The response of social workers to domestic violence' in Pahl, J., *Private Violence and Public Policy: The Needs of Battered Women and the Response of the Public Services*, London: Routledge and Kegan Paul

McCleod, M. (1998) 'What Children Say' in *Response to Children Living With Domestic Violence*, Report No 13 Violence Between Parents: Children as Victims, London: Michael Seiff Foundation

McConville M., Sanders A., and Leng R., (1991) *The case for the Prosecution*, Routledge: London

McFarlane J., Christoffel K., Bateman L., Miller V. and Bullock L. (1991) 'Assessing for abuse: self-report versus nurse interview.' *Public Health Nursing* 8(4): 245-50

McFarlane J., Parker B. and Soeken K. (1996) 'Abuse during pregnancy: associations with maternal health and infant birth weight.' *Nursing Research* 45(1): 37-42

McFarlane J., Parker B., Soeken K. and Bullock L. (1992) 'Assessing for abuse during pregnancy. Severity and frequency of injuries and associated entry into prenatal care.' *JAMA*, 267(23): 3176-8

McFarlane J., Soeken K., Reel S., Parker B. and Silva C. (1997) 'Resource use by abused women following an intervention program: associated severity of abuse and reports of abuse ending.' *Public Health Nursing*. 14(4): 244-50

McGee, C. (1998) *Children's and Mothers' Experiences of Child Protection following Domestic Violence*, London: NSPCC

McGee, C. (2000) *Childhood Experiences of Domestic Violence*. London: Jessica Kingsley

McGibbon, A., Cooper, L and Kelly, L. (1989) *What Support? An Exploratory Study of Council Policy and Practice, and Local Support Services in the Area of Domestic Violence within Hammersmith and Fulham, Final Report*, London: Polytechnic of North London, Child Abuse Studies Unit

McGregor, H.and Hopkins, A. (1991) *Working For Change: The Movement Against Domestic Violence*. Sydney: Allen and Unwin

McKay, M. (1994) 'The Link Between Domestic Violence and Child Abuse: Assessment and Treatment Considerations.' *Child Welfare*, 73 (1):29-39

McLeer S.V. and Anwar R. (1989) 'A study of battered women presenting in an emergency department.' *American Journal of Public Health.* 79(1): 65-6

McLeer S.V., Anwar R.A., Herman S. and Maquiling K. (1989) 'Education is not enough: a systems failure in protecting battered women.' *Annals of Emergency Medicine.* 18(6): 651-3

McWilliams, M. and McKiernan, J. (1993) *Bringing It Out into the Open: Domestic Violence in Northern Ireland*, Belfast: HMSO

Meier, J. (1997) 'Domestic Violence, Character, And Social Change In The Welfare Reform Debate.' *Law and Policy*, 19 (2): 205-63

Metropolitan Police Service (1996) *Minimum standards of operational performance for police officers dealing with the allegations relating to domestic incidents.'* Internal circular. 13th December

Metropolitan Police Service (1999) *Special Notice 7/99. Minimum investigative standards for community safety units.* Internal circular 7th April

Mezey, G. C. (1997) 'Domestic violence and pregnancy.' *British Journal of Obstetrics and Gynaecology*, 104: 528-31

Mezey, G.C. and Bewley, S. (1997) 'Domestic violence and pregnancy', *British Medical Journal*, 314: 1295

Mezey, G. C., King, M. and McClintock, T. (1998) 'Victims of domestic violence and the GP'. *British Journal of General Practice*, 48: 906-8

Mezey, G.C., Bewley, S., Bacchus, A. and Haworth, A. (1999) *An Exploration of the Prevalence, Nature and Effects of Domestic Violence in Pregnancy*, (http://www.brunel.ac.uk/depts/law/vrp/projects/proj014.htm)

Middlesbrough Domestic Violence Task Group (1999) *A study of prevalence of and responses to domestic violence within Middlesbrough*, Middlesbrough: Middlesbrough Domestic Violence Forum

Milner, J. (1993) 'A disappearing act: the differing career paths of fathers and mothers in child protection investigations.' *Critical Social Policy*, 13: 48-63

Mirrlees-Black, C. (1995) *Estimating the Extent of Domestic Violence: Findings from the 1992 British Crime Survey*. Home Office Research Bulletin No. 37. Research, Development and Statistics Directorate. London: Home Office

Mirrlees-Black, C. (1999) *Domestic Violence: Findings from a New British Crime Survey Self-Completion Questionnaire*, Home Office Research Study 191. Research, Development and Statistics Directorate. London: Home Office

Mirrlees-Black, C., Budd, T., Partridge, S. and Mayhew, P. (1998) *The 1998 British Crime Survey*, Home Office Statistical Bulletin Issue 21/98. Research, Development and Statistics Directorate. London: Home Office

Mirrlees-Black, C., Mayhew, P. and Percy, A. (1996) *The 1996 British Crime Survey, England and Wales*. Home Office Statistical Bulletin 19/96.. Research, Development and Statistics Directorate. London: Home Office

Mooney, J. (1994) *The Hidden Figure: Domestic Violence in North London*, London: Islington Council, Police and Crime Prevention Unit

Morley, R. (undated) 'Public education and primary prevention', unpublished paper

Morley, R. and Mullender, A. (1993) 'Hype or Hope? The Importation of Pro-Arrest

Policies and Batterers' Programmes from North America to Britain as Key Measures for Preventing Violence against Women in the Home.' *International Journal of Law and the Family*, 6: 265-288

Morley, R. and Mullender, A. (1994a) 'Domestic violence and children: what do we know from research', in A. Mullender and R. Morley (eds.) *Children Living with Domestic Violence: Putting Men's Abuse of Women on the Child Care Agenda*, London: Whiting and Birch

Morley, R. and Mullender, A. (1994b) Preventing Domestic Violence to Women, Police Research Group Crime Prevention Unit Series Paper No. 48, London: Home Office

Morran, D. and Wilson, M. (1997) *Men Who are Violent to Women: A Groupwork Practice Manual*, Lyme Regis: Russell House Publishing

Muelleman R.L. (1996) 'Battered women: Injury locations and types.' *Annals of Emergency Medicine* 28(5):486-492

Muelleman R.L.and Feighny K.M. (1999) 'Effects of an emergency department-based advocacy program for battered women on community resource utilization.' *Ann. Emerg. Med.* 33(1):62-6

Mullender, A. (1994a) 'Groups for child witnesses of woman abuse: learning from North America', in A. Mullender and R. Morley (eds.) *Children Living with Domestic Violence: Putting Men's Abuse of Women on the Child Care Agenda*, London: Whiting and Birch

Mullender, A. (1994b) 'School-based work: education for prevention', in A. Mullender and R. Morley (eds.) *Children Living with Domestic Violence: Putting Men's Abuse of Women on the Child Care Agenda*, London: Whiting and Birch

Mullender, A. (1996) *Rethinking Domestic Violence: The Social Work and Probation Response*, London: Routledge

Mullender, A. (1997) 'Domestic Violence and Social Work', *Critical Social Policy*, 17: 53-78

Mullender, A., Debbonaire, T., Hague, G., Kelly, L. and Malos, E. (forthcoming) 'Working with children in women's refuges', *Child and Family Social Work*, 3: 87-98

Mullender, A. and Humphreys, C. (1999) *Domestic violence and child abuse: policy and practice issues for local authorities and other agencies*, London: Local Government Association

Mullender, A. and Humphreys, C. with Saunders, H. (1998) *Domestic Violence and Child Abuse: policy and practice issues for local authorities and other agencies* Local Government Association Briefing Paper from the Task Group on Domestic Violence and Child Abuse

Mullender, A., Kelly, L., Hague, G., Malos, E. and Imam, U. (2000) *Children's Needs, Coping Strategies and Understandings of Woman Abuse*, End of award report submitted to the ESRC. (Award reference no. L129251037.) Available from Department of Social Policy and Social Work, University of Warwick, Coventry, CV4 7AL

Mullender, A. and Morley, R. (1994) *Children Living with Domestic Violence: Putting Men's Abuse of Women on the Child Care Agenda*, London: Whiting and Birch

Mullender, A., Hague, G., Imam, V., Kelly, L., Malos, E. and Regan, L. (forthcoming) *Children's Perspectives on Domestic Violence.* London: Sage

Murphy, P.A. (1997) 'Recovering from the Effects of Domestic Violence: Implications for Welfare Reform Policy.' *Law and Policy*, 19 (2): 169-83

MVA Consultancy (1995) *Information Needs of Victims.* Crime and Criminal Justice Research Findings No. 5. Edinburgh: Scottish Office

National Association of Local Government Women's Committees (now Women in Local Authorities) (1989) *Responding with Authority*, Manchester: NALGWC

National Campaign Against Violence and Crime (NCAVAC) Unit (1998) *Ending Domestic Violence?: Programs for Perpetrators. Summary Volume*, Canberra, Australia: NCAVAC Unit, Attorney-General's Department

National Inter-Agency Working Party (1992) *Domestic violence*, London: Victim Support

National Practitioners' Network (1994) *Statement of Principles and Guidelines for Good Practice for Intervention Programmes Working with Men towards Ending their Violence and Abuse to Women Partners* London: DVIP, Hammersmith). Revised 1997 and 1998

Nazroo, J. (1995) 'Uncovering Gender Differences in the Use of Marital Violence: The Effect of Methodology.'*Sociology*, 29 (3): 475-94

NCH (1994) *The Hidden Victims: Children and Domestic Violence*, London: NCH

Network Directory (1999): *A Directory of Organisations and Agencies Working with Men who are Violent to Women*, May 1999 Grangemouth: CHANGE

Newman, B. (1996) *Domestic violence perpetrator groups*, (http:// www/mincava.umn.edu/arts/asp)

New South Wales Bureau of Crime Statistics and Research (1999) 'Predicting Violence Against Women: the 1996 Women's Safety Survey.' *Crime Bulletin*, New South Wales Bureau of Crime Statistics and Research

New South Wales Women's Co-ordination Unit (1991) *Costs of Domestic Violence* Haymarket, NSW: New South Wales Women's Co-ordination Unit

Norman K. (1997) *The impact of domestic violence on women and local services.* March. Wakefield: Wakefield Health Authority,

Northern Ireland Office (1995) *Tackling Domestic Violence: A policy for Northern Ireland*, Belfast: Department of Health and Social Services and Northern Ireland Office

Norton L.B., Peipert J.F., Zierler S., Lima B. and Hume L. (1995) 'Battering in pregnancy: an assessment of two screening methods.' *Obstetrics and Gynecology.* 85(3):321-5

Nosek, M. A. and Howland, C. A. (1998) 'Abuse and women with disabilities', accessed through VAWnet, a project of the National Resource Center on Domestic Violence

Office of National Statistics (1999) (http://www.statistics.gov.uk/ukinfigs/pop.htm)

Office of Women's Policy (1996) *The Financial and Economic Costs of Domestic Violence in the Northern Territory* Northern Territory: KPMG

O'Hara, M. (1994) 'Child deaths in contexts of domestic violence: implications for professional practice', in A. Mullender and R. Morley (eds.) *Children Living with Domestic Violence: Putting Men's Abuse of Women on the Child Care Agenda*, London: Whiting and Birch

Okun, L (1986) *Women Abuse: Facts Replacing Myths*, Albany: State University of New York Press

Olson L., Anctil C., Fullerton L., Brillman J., Arbuckle J. and Sklar D. (1996) 'Increasing emergency physician recognition of domestic violence.' *Ann Emerg Med.*, 27(6): 741-6

Pahl, J. (1979) 'The general practitioner and the problems of battered women', *Journal of Medical Ethics*, 5:117-23

Pahl, J. (1985) *Private Violence and Public Policy: The Needs of Battered Women and the Response of the Public Services*, London: Routledge and Kegan Paul

Parkinson, P. and Humphreys, C. (1998) 'Children who witness domestic violence: the implications for child protection.' *Child and Family Law Quarterly*, 10(2):147-160

Pease, K. (1998) *Repeat Victimisation: Taking Stock*. Crime Detection and Prevention Series Paper 90. Research and Statistics Directorate, London: Home Office

Peckover, S. (1998) *Regulation and Resistance: An Analysis of the Practices of Health Visitors and Women Experiencing Domestic Violence*. Unpublished PhD thesis, University of Warwick

Peled, E. and Edelson, J. (1992) 'Multiple perspectives on group work with children of battered women'. *Violence and Victims*, 7:327-346

Peled, E. and Edelson, J. (1994) 'Advocacy for battered women: a national survey', *Journal of Family Violence*, 9 (3): 285-296

Peled, E. and Edleson, J. (1998) 'Predicting children's domestic violence service participation and completion', *Research on Social Work Practice*, 8(6): 698-712

Pence, E. (1983) 'The Duluth Domestic Abuse Intervention Project.' *Hamline Law Review*, pp.247-280

Pence, E. (1988) 'Integrating Theory and Practice: The Challenge of the Battered Women's Movement' in K. Yllo and M. Bograd (eds.) *Feminist Perspectives on Wife Abuse*. Beverly Hills: Sage

Pence, E. and McMahon, M. (1999) 'A co-ordinated community response to domestic violence: the Duluth approach' in N. Harwin, E. Malos and G. Hague (eds.) *New Opportunities, Old Challenges*, London: Whiting and Birch

Pence, E. and Paymar, M. (1990) *Power and Control: Tactics of Men Who Batter. An Educational Curriculum* (revised edition), Duluth, Minnesota: Minnesota Program Development, Inc. (from 206 West Fourth Street, Duluth, MN 55806, USA)

Pence, E. and Shepard, M. (1999) *Co-ordinating community response to domestic violence: lessons from Duluth and beyond*, London: Sage

Phillips, C. and Brown, D. (1998) *Entry into the Criminal Justice System*, HORS 185, Research, Development and Statistics Directorate, London: Home Office

Pleace N., Ford J., Wilcox S. and Burrows R. (1998) *Lettings and sales by registered social landlords 1996/97: annual report of the CORE data*. National Housing Federation and Housing Corporation, England

Plichta S. (1992) 'The effects of woman abuse on health care utilization and health status: a literature review.' *Women's Health Issues*. 2(3):154-63

Plotnikoff, J. and Woolfson, R. (1998) *Policing Domestic Violence: Effective Organisational Structures*, Police Research Series Paper 100, Policing and Reducing Crime Unit, London: Home Office

Poynter, T. L. (1989) 'An evaluation of a group programme for male perpetrators of domestic violence.' *Australian Journal of Sex, Marriage and Family*, 10(3):133-142

Ptacek, J. (1988) 'Why do men batter their wives' in K.Yllö and M.Bograd (eds.), *Feminist Perspectives on Wife Abuse*, Newbury Park CA: Sage

Radford L., Richardson, J. and Davies, L. (1998) *Domestic Violence: A Health Care Issue?* London: British Medical Association

Rai, D. K. and Thiara, R. K. (1997) *Re-defining Spaces: The Needs of Black Women and Children in Refuge Support Services and Black Workers in Women's Aid*, Bristol: Women's Aid Federation of England

Randall T. (1990) 'Domestic violence intervention calls for more than treating injuries.' *JAMA*. 264:939-940

Raphael, J. (1997) 'Welfare Reform: Prescription for Abuse? A Report on New Research Studies Documenting the Relationship of Domestic Violence and Welfare?' *Law and Policy* 19 (2): 123-37

Reid-Howie Associates (1996) *The Zero Tolerance Campaign in Fife: Post Campaign Research, September-November 1996*, Edinburgh: Reid-Howie Associates

Renzetti, C. M. (1992) *Violent Betrayal: Partner Abuse in Lesbian Relationships*, Newbury Park CA: Sage

RESPECT (2000) 'Statement of Principles and Minimum Standards of Practice', held at DVIP, PO Box 2838, London W6 9ZE

Richardson J. and Feder G. (1997) 'How can we help? - the role of general practice?' in S. Bewley, J.R. Friend and G.C. Mezey (eds.) *Violence Against Women*. London: RCOG Press

Rights of Women (1997) *Contact between children and violent fathers in whose best interests?* London: Rights of Women

Roberts G.L., Lawrence J.M., O'Toole B.I. and Raphael B. (1997) 'Domestic violence in the Emergency Department: 2. Detection by doctors and nurses.' *Gen Hosp Psychiatry* 19(1):12-5

Roberts G.L., Raphael B., Lawrence J.M., O'Toole B. and O'Brien D. (1997) 'Impact of an education program about domestic violence on nurses and doctors in an Australian emergency department.' *Journal of Emergency Nursing* 23(3):220-7

Rodriguez M.A. (1996) 'Breaking the silence. Battered women's perspectives on medical care.' *Arch Fam Med*. 5(3):153-8

Rodriguez M.A., Bauer H.M., McLoughlin E. and Grumbach K. (1999) 'Screening and intervention for intimate partner abuse.' *JAMA*. 282:468-474

Rogers N. (1999) *Floating support: how can we know it works?* SITRA bulletin September, p20, SITRA, England

Romkens, R. (1997) 'Prevalence of Wife Abuse in the Netherlands - Combining

Quantitative and Qualitative Methods in Survey Research.' *Journal of Interpersonal Violence*, 12 (1): 99-125

Royal College of Midwives (1997) *Domestic Abuse in Pregnancy*, Position Paper No.19, London: RCM

Sachs C.J. (1998) 'Failure of the mandatory domestic violence reporting law to increase medical facility referral to police.' *Ann Emerg Med.* 31(4):488-94

Sampson, A. and Phillips, C. (1992) *Multiple Victimisation: Racial Attacks on an East London Estate.* Police Research Group, Crime Prevention Unit Series Paper No. 36. London: Home Office

Sampson, A. and Phillips, C. (1995) *Reducing Repeat Racial Victimisation on an East London Estate.* Police Research Group, Crime Detection and Prevention Series Paper No. 67, London: Home Office

Sampson, A., Stubbs, P., Smith, D., Pearson, G, and Blagg, H. (1991) 'Gender issues in inter-agency relations: police, probation and social services' in P. Abbott and C. Wallace (eds.) *Gender, power and sexuality*, London: Macmillan

Sampson, A., Stubbs, P., Smith, D., Pearson, G. and Blagg, H. (1988) 'Crime, localities and the multi-agency approach', *The British Journal of Criminology*, 28: 478-493

Sanders S. (1998) 'Personal Violence and Public Order;The Prosecution of Domestic Violence in England and Wales.' *International Journal of the Sociology of Law*, 16:478-93

Saunders A. (1994) 'Children in Women's Refuges: a Retrospective Study' in A. Mullender and R. Morley (eds.) *Children Living with Domestic Violence*, London: Whiting and Birch

Saunders, D. (1988) 'Wife abuse, husband abuse, or mutual combat?' In K.Yllo and M. Bograd, (eds.) *Feminist Perspectives on Wife Abuse.* California: Sage

Saunders, D. (1996) 'Interventions for men who batter: Do we know what works?' *Psychotherapy in Practice*, 2(3): 81-93

Saunders, D. (1998) 'Child custody and visitation decisions in domestic violence cases: legal trends, research findings, and recommendations', (http://www/mincava.umn.edu/arts/asp)

Saunders, H. (1999) 'Domestic Violence and Child Abuse' (Briefing for LGA Task Group), Bristol: Women's Aid Federation of England

Schechter, S. and Edleson, J. (1994) 'In the best interest of women and children: a call for collaboration between child welfare and domestic violence constituencies', (http://www/mincava.umn.edu/arts/asp)

Schechter, S. (1996) 'The battered women's movement in the United States: New directions for institutional reform in J. Edelson and Z. Eisikovits (eds.) *Future Interventions With Battered Women and Their Families*, London: Sage

Schei B.and Bakkesteig L.S. (1989) 'Gynaecological impact of sexual and physical abuse by spouse: a study of a random sample of Norwegian women.' *British Journal of Obstetrics and Gynaecology*. 96:1379-1383

Schwartz, M.D. (1987) 'Gender and Injury in Spousal Assault.' *Sociological Focus*, 20(1):61-75

Scottish Needs Assessment Programme (SNAP) (1997) *Domestic Violence*. Glasgow: Scottish Forum for Public Health Medicine

Scottish Office (1990) *Scottish Home and Health Department Police (Chief Constables) Circular No.3/1990: Investigation of Complaints of Domestic Assault*. Edinburgh: Scottish Office

Scottish Office (1997) *Hitting Home: A Report on the Police Response to Domestic Violence*, Edinburgh: HM Inspectorate of Constabulary

Scottish Office Central Research Unit (1995) *An Evaluation of the Scottish Office Domestic Violence Media Campaign*, Edinburgh: HMSO

Scottish Women's Aid (1998) *Young People Say*, Edinburgh: Scottish Women's Aid

Scourfield, J. B. (1994) 'Changing Men: UK Agencies Working with Men Who are Violent Towards their Women Partners', MA dissertation, Department of Social and Administrative Studies, University of Wales College of Cardiff. Unpublished

Select Committee on Violence in Marriage (1975) *Report, Minutes of Evidence, and Appendices*, session 1974-75, (HC553-II), London: HMSO

Sen, P. (1998) *Searching for routes to safety: a report on the needs of ethnic minority women dealing with domestic violence*, London: Camden Equalities Unit

Shelter Housing Aid and Research Project (1998) *Domestic Violence and Housing: A Guide for Women and Advisers in Leicestershire*, Leicester: Shelter Housing Aid and Research Project

Sherman, L. W. (1992) *Policing Domestic Violence: Experiments and Dilemmas*, New York: Free Press

Shepard, M. F. and Pence, E. (1999) *Co-ordinating Community Responses to Domestic Violence: Lessons from Duluth and Beyond*. London: Sage

Sherman, L.W and Berk, R. A. (1984) 'The Specific Deterrent Effects of Arrest for Domestic Violence.' *American Sociological Review* 49: 261-272

Short L.M., Cotton D. and Hodgson C.S. (1997) 'Evaluation of the module on domestic violence at the UCLA School of Medicine.' *Academic Medicine*. 71(Suppl 1):S75-S92

Silverman, J.G. and Williamson, G.M. (1997) 'Social Ecology and Entitlements Involved in Battering by Heterosexual College Males: Contributions of Family and Peers', *Violence and Victims*, 12 (2): 147-64

Simons, R.L., Wu, C., Johnson, C. and Conger, R.D. (1995) 'A Test of Various Perspectives on the Intergenerational Transmission of Domestic Violence', *Criminology*, 33(1):141-72

Sissons, P. (1999) *Focus on Change: Report on Consultation carried out with Women Survivors of Domestic Violence for the Lewisham Domestic Violence Forum*, London: Lewisham Domestic Violence Forum

Sixsmith D.M. (1997) 'Telephone follow-up for case finding of domestic violence in an emergency department.' *Academic Emergency Medicine*. 4(4):301-304

Skyner, D. R. and Waters, J. (1999) 'Working with perpetrators of domestic violence to protect women and children', *Child Abuse Review*, 8: 46-54

Sleutel M.R. (1998) 'Women's experiences of abuse: a review of qualitative research.' *Issues in Mental Health Nursing*. 19(6):525-39

Smith, D. and Gray, J. (1983) *Police and People in London, vols. 1-4*, London: Policy Studies Institute

Smith, J. and Stanko, E. (1999) *Femicide: the killing of women in England and Wales 1986-96* unpublished paper, Centre for Criminal Justice, Brunel University

Smith, L. (1989) *Domestic violence: an overview of the literature*, Home Office Research Studies, No 107. Research, Development and Statistics Directorate. London: Home Office

Smith, M.D. (1994) 'Enhancing the Quality of Survey Data on Violence Against Women: A Feminist Approach', *Gender and Society*, 8 (1): 109-27

Sniveley, S. (1994) *The New Zealand Economics Costs of Family Violence* Auckland: Coopers and Lybrand

Snow Jones, A. (1999) 'The cost of batterer programs: how much and who pays?' paper presented at the Sixth International Family Violence Research Conference, Durham NH, July 25-28

Spinola C. (1998) 'Developing and implementing an intervention: Evaluation of an emergency department pilot on partner abuse.' *Evaluation and the Health Professions*. 21(1): 91-119

Sobsey, D. and Doe, T. (1991) 'Patterns of Sexual Abuse and Assault', *Sexuality and Disability*, 9 (3): 243-59

Sorsby, A. and Shapland, J. (1995) *Responding to Victims of Domestic Violence*, Sheffield: Centre for Criminological and Legal Research, University of Sheffield

Southall Black Sisters (1990) *Against the Grain: A Celebration of Survival and Struggle*, London: Southall Black Sisters

Standing Together Against Domestic Violence (1999) Community Safety Unit, London Borough of Hammersmith and Fulham

Stanko, E., Crisp, D., Hale, C. and Lucraft, H. (1998) *Counting the Costs: Estimating the Impact of Domestic Violence in the London Borough of Hackney*, Swindon: Crime Concern Signal Point, Station Road, Swindon SN1 1FE

Stanko E., Marian, L., Crisp, D., Manning, R., Smith, J. and Cowan, S. (1998) *Taking Stock: what do we know about violence?* Brunel University: ESRC Violence Research Programme

Stanley, N. and Penhale, B. (1999) 'The mental health problems of mothers experiencing the child protection system: identifying needs and appropriate responses', *Child Abuse Review*, 8:34-45

Stark, E. (1993) 'Mandatory Arrest of Batterers: A Reply to its Critics', *American Behavioral Scientist*, 36(5): 651-680 May-June

Stark, E. and Flitcraft, A. (1996) *Women at Risk - Domestic Violence and Women's Health*, California: Sage

Statistics Canada (1993) *Violence Against Women - Survey Highlights and Questionnaire Package*. Canada: Statistics Canada

Stevens, K.L.H. (1997) 'The role of the accident and emergency department' in S.Bewley, J. Friend and G. Mezey (eds.) *Violence Against Women*. London: Royal College of Obstetricians and Gynaecologists

Stockdale, M.J.E., Whitehead, C.M.E. and Gresham, P.J. (1999) *Applying Economic*

Evaluation to Policing Activity. Policing and Reducing Crime Paper No. 103. Research, Development and Statistics Directorate. London: Home Office

Stonham Housing Association (1998) *Support and accommodation for women suffering from violence, discussion paper*, Stonham Housing Association: England

Straus, M.A. (1990) 'Injury and frequency of assault and the "representative fallacy" in measuring wife beating and child abuse' in M. A. Straus and R. J. Gelles (eds.) *Physical Violence In American Families*. New Brunswick, New Jersey: Transaction Publishers

Straus, M.A., Gelles, R.J. and Steinmetz, S.K. (1980) *Behind Closed Doors: Violence In American Families*, New York: Doubleday

Straus, M.A. and Gelles, R.J. (eds.) (1990) *Physical Violence In American Families*, New Brunswick, New Jersey: Transaction Publishers

Sugarman, D.B. and Frankel, S.L. (1996) 'Patriarchal Ideology and Wife Assault: A Meta-Analytic Review', *Journal of Family Violence*, 11 (1): 13-40

Sugg N.K. and Inui T. (1992) 'Primary care physicians' response to domestic violence.' *JAMA*. 267(23): 3157-3160

Sullivan C.M., Tan C., Basta J., Rumptz M. and Davidson W.S. (1992) 'An advocacy intervention program for women with abusive partners: initial evaluation.' *American Journal of Community Psychology*. 20(3):309-332

Sullivan, C. M. and Bybee, D. I. (1999) 'Reducing violence using community based advocacy for women with abusive partners', *Journal of Consulting and Clinical Psychology*, 67(1:43-53

Sullivan, C. M. and Keefe, M. (1999) *Evaluations of Advocacy Efforts to End Intimate Male Violence against Women*. (http://www.vaw.umn.edu)

Syers, M. and Edleson, J. L. (1992) 'The combined effects of co-ordinated criminal justice intervention in woman abuse.' *Journal of Interpersonal Violence*, 7:490-502

Taggart L. and Mattson S. (1996) 'Delay in prenatal care as a result of battering in pregnancy: cross-cultural implications.' *Health Care for Women International*. 17:25-34

Taylor, A.M. and Tipton, O. (1999) 'Addressing Domestic Violence'. *The British Journal of Forensic Practice* 1:2 May:3-9

Taylor-Browne. J. (forthcoming) *A Crying shame: Young people involved in prostitution* Police Research Series. Research, Development and Statistics Directorate. Home Office: London

Thelen, R. (1996) 'Advocacy in a coordinated community response: overview and highlights of three programs'. (http://www.vaw.umn.edu)

Thompson R.S. (1998) 'A training program to improve domestic violence identification and management in primary care: Preliminary results.' *Violence and Victims*. 13(4): 395-410

Thorne-Finch, R. (1992) *Ending the Silence: The Origins and Treatment of Male Violence against Women*, Toronto: University of Toronto Press

Tilden V.P., Schmidt T.A., Limandri B.J., Chiodo G.T., Garland M.J. and Loveless P.A. (1994) Factors that influence clinician's assessment and management of family violence. *Am J Public Health.* 84(4):628-633

Tilley, N. and Pawson, R. (1997) *Realistic Evaluation.* London: Routledge

Tipton D. (1999) *Evaluation Report on 'First Contact' Repeat Victimisation Pilot Scheme* Family Protection Team, Flintshire Division, North Wales Police. Internal report

Tolman, R. and Bennett, L. (1990) 'A review of quantitative research on men who batter', *Journal of Interpersonal Violence*, 5: 87-118

Tolman, R. M. and Edleson, J. L. (1989) 'Cognitive-behavioral intervention with men who batter' in B.A. Thyer (ed.) *Behavioral Family Therapy*, Springfield IL: Charles E. Thomas

Tolman, R. M. and Edleson, J. L. (1995) 'Intervention for men who batter: a review of research', in S.R. Stith and M.A. Straus (eds.) *Understanding Partner Violence: Prevalence, Causes, Consequences and Solutions*, Minneapolis, MN: National Council on Family Relations

Tutty, L. M., Bidgood, B. A. and Rothery, M. A. (1993) 'Support groups for battered women: research on their efficacy', *Journal of Family Violence*, 8: 325-43. (Cited in M. Shepard (1999) *Evaluating coordinated community responses to domestic violence.* (http://www.vaw.umn.edu)

United Nations (1993) *Strategies for Confronting Domestic Violence: a resource manual,* New York: United Nations

Ursel, E. (1997) 'The Possibilities of Criminal Justice Intervention in Domestic Violence: a Canadian Case Study', *Current Issues in Criminal Justice*, 8(3): 263-274

Van Cleemput, P., Storey, M. and Traveller Women Living in Sheffield (undated) 'Supporting Gypsy and Traveller Women and Children Living with Domestic Violence', Sheffield: Community Health Sheffield. (Leaflet)

Victim Support (1992) *Domestic Violence: Report of a national inter-agency working party*, London: Victim Support

Violence Against Lesbians in the Home: Lesbians' Own Accounts (1998) JJ Publications. (Place of publication not cited)

Violence Research Programme Homepage. Accessed September 17, 1999. Web Page. (http://www1.rhbnc.ac.uk/sociopolitical-science/vrp/REALHOME.htm)

WAFE (1989) *Breaking Through: Women Surviving Male Violence* Bristol: Women's Aid Federation of England

WAFE (1993) *Information Material on the Children Act.* Bristol: Women's Aid Federation England

WAFE (1997) *Briefing paper on Child Contact and Domestic Violence.* Bristol: Women's Aid Federation England

WAFE (1998a) *Annual Report 1997-1998.*, Bristol: Women's Aid Federation of England

WAFE (1998b) *Families without Fear. Women's Aid Agenda for Action on Domestic Violence: Recommendations for a National Strategy*, Bristol: Women's Aid Federation of England

WAFE (1998b) *Annual Report 1997-1998*, Bristol: Women's Aid Federation of

England
WAFE (1999b) Personal Communication
WAFE (1999b) *Annual Report 1998-9*, Bristol: Women's Aid Federation of England
WAFE (2001) *Annual Report 2000-01*, Bristol: Women's Aid Federation of England
Walby, S. (1997) *Gender Transformations*, London: Routledge
Walby, S. and Myhill, A. (1999) 'Methodological issues in the new national surveys of violence against women: Findings from a Nuffield Foundation research project'. Mimeo. (Leeds: University of Leeds, Department of Sociology and Social Policy)
Walby, S. and Myhill, A. (2001) 'New survey methodologies in violence against women'. *British Journal of Criminology 41: 502-522*
Walker, J. (1999) *Information Meetings and Associated Provisions Within the Family Law Act 1996: Summary of Research in Progress, June 1999*, London: Lord Chancellor's Department
Waller A.E., Hohenhaus S.M., Shah P.J. and Stern E.A. (1996) 'Development and validation of an emergency department screening and referral protocol for victims of domestic violence.' *Ann Emerg Med.* 27(6):754-60
Warshaw, C. (1994) 'Domestic Violence: Challenges to medical practice' in A.J. Dan (ed.) *Reframing Women's Health*, London: Sage
Watts S. (1998) *What Are Effective Health Care Interventions in Response to the Needs of Victims of Domestic Violence.* Policy Report Prepared for MSc in Public Health at the London School of Hygiene and Tropical Medicine. London: LSHTM
Weatheritt, M. (1993) 'Measuring Police Performance: accounting or accountability?' in R. Reiner and S. Spencer (eds.) *Accountable Policing: effectiveness, empowerment and equity* London: Policy Studies Institute
Webster J., Chandler J. and Battistutta D. (1996) 'Pregnancy outcomes and health care use: effects of abuse.' *American Journal of Obstetrics and Gynecology* 174(2):760-7
Weinhardt, L.S., Bickman, N.L. and Carey, M.P. (1999) 'Sexual Coercion Among Women Living With a Severe and Persistent Mental Illness: Review of the Literature and Recommendations For Mental Health Providers.' *Aggression and Violent Behavior*, 4 (3): 307-17
Wells C. (1997) 'Stalking: The Criminal Law Response' *Criminal Law Review* pp: 463-471
Weyland I. (1995) 'Judicial attitudes to contact and shared residence' *Journal of Social Welfare and Family Law* 17(4): 445- 450
White, C. (1999) 'Farewell to fear.' *Community Care*, 12-18 August, p.22
Williams, O. (1994) 'Group work with African American men who batter: toward more ethnically sensitive practice.' *Journal of Comparative Family Studies*, 25: 91-103
Williams, O. (1994) 'Healing and confronting the African American man who batters' in R. Carrillo and J. Tello (eds.) *Healing the Male Spirit: Men of Color and Domestic Violence*, New York: Springer Publishing
Williams, O. (1999) 'African American men who batter: treatment consideration

and community action', in J. Staples (ed.) *Black Family: Essays and Studies*, Boston: Wadsworth Press

Wilson, M. and Daly, M. (1992) *Homicide*, New York: Aldine de Gruyter

Wilson, M. and Daly, M. (1994) *Spousal Homicide*. Canada: Statistics Canada, Juristat, 14: 8, March

Wilson, M. and Daly, M. (1996) 'Spousal homicide: risk and estrangement.' *Violence and Victims* 8(1): 3-16

Wist W.H.and McFarlane J. (1999) 'The effectiveness of an abuse assessment protocol in public health prenatal clinics.' *American Journal of Public Health* 89:1217-1221

Woffordt, S., Mihalic, D.E. and Menard, S. (1994) 'Continuities in Marital Violence', *Journal of Family Violence*, 9 (3): 195-225

Wolfe, D. A., Zak., L., Wilson, S. and Jaffe, P. (1986) 'Child witnesses to violence between parents: critical issues in behavioural and social adjustment.' *Journal of Abnormal Child Psychology*, 14(1): 95-104

Women and Children in Refuges (undated) *You Can't Beat a Woman*, Bristol: Women's Aid Federation of England

Women's Aid *see* WAFE

Women's Equality Unit (1995) *The needs and experiences of black and minority ethnic women experiencing domestic violence*, London Borough of Islington, England

Wood, G. G. and Middleman, R. (1990) 'Re-casting the die: a small group approach to giving batterers a chance to change', paper presented at the Tenth Annual Symposium on Social Work with Groups, Miami, FL, October

Wright J. and Kasiya A. (1997) 'Characteristics of female victims of assault attending a Scottish accident and emergency department.' *Journal of Accident and Emergency Medicine* 14(6): 375-378

Yllo, K.A. and Straus, M.A. (1990) 'Patriarchy and violence against wives: the impact of structural and normative features', in M.A.Straus and R.J. Gelles (eds.) *Physical Violence In American Families*. New Brunswick, New Jersey: Transaction Publishers

Young, D. (1994/5) *The Economic Implications of Domestic Violence in Greater Glasgow* Unpublished MSc thesis in Health Economics, University of York

Young, M.E., Nosek, M.A., Howland, C.A., Chanpong, G., and Rintala, D.H. (1997) 'Prevalence of abuse of women with physical disabilities.' *Archives of Physical Medicine and Rehabilitation Special Issue* 78 (12, Suppl. 5) S34-S38

Zebedee J and Ward M (1999) *Guide to Housing Benefit and Council Tax Benefit 1999-2000*. Chartered Institute of Housing/Shelter, England

Zero Tolerance Trust (1995) *Zero Tolerance Guiding Principles*, Edinburgh: Zero Tolerance Trust

Zorza, J. (1995) 'Mandatory Arrest for Domestic Violence', *Criminal Justice*, Fall, pp. 2-54

About the contributors

Sheila Burton, at the time of writing the chapter included in this book had been working for over ten years at the Child and Woman Abuse Studies Unit, University of North London, which has a national and international reputation for its research, training and consultancy work. The Unit exists to develop feminist research methodologies, theory and practice, especially in relation to connections between forms of sexualised violence. Their work involves a creative combination of large and small-scale research projects, training, policy development and networking, which requires bridging the worlds of academia, policy, practice and activism. Three recently completed projects were: an evaluation of a programme for violent men; a review of the literature and experience of sex offender registration and community notification and with colleagues from Warwick, Durham and Bristol universities, a research project investigating children's understandings and experiences of domestic violence. The Unit is currently undertaking a European Commission funded project on the sexual exploitation of children in the context of children's rights and child protection in Europe and a project looking at what is currently known about trafficking of women in the UK.

Debbie Crisp worked for six years in the Home Office Research and Planning Unit, before becoming a contract researcher. She has been working with Professor E. Stanko on domestic violence related projects for the past four years, including the 'Counting the Costs' study in Hackney. She is currently based at Royal Holloway, University of London, where she is the researcher on the Domestic Violence Data Source project.

Leslie Davidson is a paediatrician and a public health doctor. After medical school and paediatric training she studied Epidemiology. After two years of research in London, she worked in child health and public health in New York for eight years, returning to England in 1992 to work in the NHS first as Paediatric Epidemiologist to a regional health authority and then in a health authority in South East London before becoming Director of the National Perinatal Epidemiology Unit and Reader in Public Health Medicine at the University of Oxford. Her main research interests have been disability in children, international child health, screening, and in the epidemiology and prevention of accidents and violence.

Susan Edwards has degrees in both social science and in law. She is currently Reader in Law at the University of Buckingham where she teaches Family Law, Criminal Law and the Law of Evidence. She was a Visiting Fellow at the Law School Australian National University in 1999. She has conducted numerous research projects in the area of domestic violence since 1983 and written widely on justice issues around homicide and violence against women including pornography and child pornography. She is Director of Research for the Pornography and Violence Research Trust. Her latest book is *Sex and Gender in the Legal Process* (Blackstone, 1996).

Jo Garcia: graduated in Psychology and Philosophy at Oxford University in 1971 and then studied Medical Demography at the London School of Hygiene and Tropical Medicine. Jo joined the National Perinatal Epidemiology Unit as its Social Scientist in October 1979. Her research interests have included methods for assessing the views of service users, outcomes in randomised controlled trials, women's postnatal health, midwifery policies and organisation, methods for evaluating patterns of services and the experience of participation in trials.

Sue Griffiths is a Senior Research Fellow at Leeds Metropolitan University. Her areas of research are domestic violence, domestic homicide, policing and violence against women, law, women in prison, child abuse and sex offenders. Sue was a principal researcher on the domestic violence repeat victimisation project in Killingbeck. This project has been rolled out across the West Yorkshire Police Force and extended to include racist and homophobic incidents. Sue will be one of the principal researchers evaluating this new 2-year project.

Gill Hague has worked on violence against women issues as both an activist and, more latterly, as an academic, for 25 years. She is the joint co-ordinator, with her colleague Ellen Malos, of the Domestic Violence Research Group in the School for Policy Studies at the University of Bristol. The group conducts national and international studies of domestic violence and offers wide-ranging consultancy, teaching and training on the issue, working broadly alongside the Women's Aid movement. Gill works closely with other activists and researchers in the UK and internationally, and has very many publications on domestic violence including, with Ellen Malos, the very popular book, *Domestic Violence: Action for Change*, Hague, G., Malos, E. and Dear, W. *Multi-agency Work and Domestic Violence* (The Policy Press 1996) and, with Nicola Harwin and Ellen Malos, *The Multi-Agency Approach to Domestic Violence: New opportunities, old challenges?* (Whiting & Birch).

Jalna Hanmer is Professor of Women's Studies at University of Sunderland where she is a member of the International Centre for the Study of Violence and Abuse. Current research activities include an evaluation of a policing project on domestic violence, racially motivated and homphobic crime in West Yorkshire; a study of attrition in domestic violence cases entering the criminal justice system in Northumbria; and she is a partner in a European consortium researching the impact of women's studies on women's employment in Europe. She is active in CROP, the coalition for the removal of pimping, and in the development of a re-education programme for kerb crawlers. Her most recent publications include *Arresting Evidence: Domestic Violence and Repeat Victimisation*); and *Home Truths about Domestic Violence: Feminist Influences on Policy and Practice. A Reader (co-editor, Routledge, 2000).*

Nicola Harwin is currently Director of the Women's Aid Federation of England, the leading national charity working to end domestic violence with a national network of over 250 local services. With over 20 years experience of providing local and national services, Nicola has played a key role in monitoring and responding to legislation and policy affecting abused women and children, including giving evidence to the 1992 Home Affairs Select Committee Inquiry into Domestic Violence, responding to numerous government consultations, working as an expert advisor with a wide range of statutory and voluntary bodies, and acting as a consultant to several research projects into domestic violence. She also provides training on domestic violence and is the author of numerous publications: advice leaflets for survivors, training resources and handbooks for service providers, briefing papers for government and the public, and contributions to recent and forthcoming books. From January 2000, she has been a member of the Steering Committee of the Women's National Commission, the UK Government's Advisory Body on Women.

Catherine Humphreys is a senior lecturer in the School of Health and Social Studies at the University of Warwick. Her primary research interests lie in the area of violence against women and children, focusing on domestic violence, child protection and child sexual abuse. She has worked in a voluntary capacity for Women's Aid for 6 years and worked particularly with outreach services in her local area.

Liz Kelly is a feminist researcher and activist from the UK, who has worked in the field of violence against women and children for 25 years. She is the author of *Surviving Sexual Violence* and over 50 book chapters and journal articles. The Child and Woman Abuse Studies Unit (CWASU), University of North London, of which she is Director, has a national and international reputation for its research, training and consultancy work. The has completed 25 research projects, primarily in the areas of child sexual abuse, rape and sexual assault, and domestic violence. CWASU are known for their work on making connections – between forms of gender violence, and between violence against women and child protection – and are special advisors to the British Council on violence against women. Liz drafted the Council of Europe Plan of Action on violence against women published in 1997. Her latest publications are *Stopping Traffic*, the first study of trafficking in women within the UK and *Rhetorics and Realities*, a study of sexual exploitation of children in Europe. In 2000 she was appointed Professor of Sexualised Violence.

Valerie King studied Medicine at the University of North Carolina at Chapel Hill. She trained in Family Medicine and has been Clinical Instructor in Family Medicine at UNC since 1994. Valerie was awarded an Atlantic Fellowship to study maternity care policy and practice in the UK for the 1998 academic year. She conducted systematic reviews of a woman's decision-making regarding mode of delivery and vaginal birth after previous caesarean delivery.

Debra Levison is a Senior Policy Officer in the Greater London Authority's (GLA's) Housing and Homelessness Team. She worked as a Housing Researcher for the London Research Centre (LRC) for twelve years and for the National Housing Federation (NHF) for two years and has undertaken many studies involving the evaluation of policies and practices and the production of good practice guidance. She has also designed, executed, analysed and written up numerous surveys on a range of housing and related issues. She has written reports covering a diverse range of housing policy, including homelessness and temporary accommodation, lettings and allocations, Housing Benefit and the housing needs of black and minority ethnic households. Her work includes a number of major research projects for the DTLR, including one looking at accommodation and support for households experiencing domestic violence.

Sally Marchant: Following her midwifery training in Perth, Scotland, Sally worked as a clinical midwife for nine years, mainly in the areas of postnatal and neonatal care. Sally joined the National Perinatal Epidemiology Unit in February 1990 as Research Midwife to the Postnatal Care Project. Women's health postpartum and survey research remain the focus for the majority of her work.

Audrey Mullender is Professor of Social Work at the University of Warwick. She is the immediate past Editor of the British Journal of Social Work and has herself produced over a hundred publications in the social work field, including 12 books. Amongst these are: *Children Living with Domestic*

Violence: Putting Men's Abuse of Women on the Child Care Agenda (edited jointly with Rebecca Morley and published in 1994 by Whiting and Birch) and *Rethinking Domestic Violence: The Social Work and Probation Response* (Routledge, 1996). She is currently jointly disseminating research on children's perspectives on domestic violence and also the ways in which services can be more accountable to women.

Andrew Myhill was a research assistant at Leeds University when he worked on this project with Sylvia Walby. He was also employed on a Nuffield Foundation funded project on the new national surveys on violence against women. He has a MA in Social Research and a BA in Political Studies from Leeds University. He currently works in the Crime Survey Section at the Home Office. This work was completed before he was employed at the Home Office.

Betsy Stanko is the Director of the ESRC's Violence Research Programme. Over the past two plus decades, she has written a number of articles and books examining violence and its impact on women's and men's lives. Most notable among these are *Intimate Intrusions* (1985) and *Everyday Violence* (1990). Her research interests include exploring the nature and impact of public and private violence, and at the same time challenging the invisibility of the impact of unsafety on people's lives. Her recent publications include *Counting the Costs: Estimating the impact of domestic violence in the London Borough of Hackney* (1998), and a number of contributions to edited collections throughout the world on violence and social policy. She is currently working on two books, and editing a number of volumes arising from the Violence Research Programme. She continues to take a keen interest in the development of innovative strategies to challenge domestic violence. She is currently Professor of Criminology in the Department of Social and Political Science, Royal Holloway, University of London.

Julie Taylor-Browne was formerly a Principal Research Officer at the Policing and Reducing Crime Unit at the Home Office and was responsible for the Violence against Women Initiative. She was responsible for much of the research carried out on sexual violence and child abuse during her four years at the Home Office. Prior to this she worked at Lancaster University as a research officer, and gained her PhD in the Department of Applied Social Science. She is currently an Honorary Research Fellow at Lancaster University, and now works as an independent consultant and researcher in sexual violence and child abuse.

Sylvia Walby is Professor of Sociology at the University of Leeds. She is joint author of *Sex Crime in the News* (Routledge 1991) and articles on violence against women in *Journal of Law and Society; Theory Culture and Society; British*

Journal of Criminology; and *New Society*. She has held a grant from the Nuffield Foundation on the methodology of the new national surveys of violence against women. She is a consultant on the Home Office British Crime Survey 2001 section on inter-personal violence and directing the analysis. She is author of *Gender Transformations* (Routledge, 1997), *Theorizing Patriarchy* (Blackwell, 1990), *Patriarchy at Work* (Polity 1986); joint author of *Localities, Class and Gender* (Pion 1985), *Contemporary British Society* (Polity, 1988, 1994), *Restructuring Place Class and Gender* (Sage 1990), and *Medicine and Nursing: Professions in a Changing Health Service* (Sage 1994); editor of *Gender Segregation at Work* (Open University Press 1988) and *New Agendas for Women* (Macmillan 1999); and co-editor of *Out of the Margins: Women's Studies in the Nineties* (Falmer 1991), and *European Societies: Fission or Fusion* (Routledge 1999). She has previously been the Professor and Head of Department of Sociology at Bristol University; Reader in Sociology and Director of the Gender Institute at the LSE; Lecturer in Sociology and Director of the Women's Studies Research Centre at Lancaster University. She was the first President of the European Sociological Association and has been Chair of the Women's Studies Network UK.

Printed in the United Kingdom
by Lightning Source UK Ltd.
126320UK00001B/49/A